D0078116

MORE ADVANCE PRAISE FOR *CRITICAL THINKING FOR STRATEGIC INTELLIGENCE*

In *Critical Thinking for Strategic Intelligence*, the Phersons have provided an invaluable road map for anyone seeking to improve the ability to conceptualize, research, and write compelling analysis. It stands apart from other literature in making a persuasive case for critical thinking up front to pave the way for clarity of message and rigor in argumentation. It is simply a must-read for any serious student of intelligence analysis.

—Fran Moore, former Director of Intelligence, US Central Intelligence Agency

Critical thinking is essential for solid business decision making. The good news is that it can be learned. In the challenging post-pandemic business environment, only companies taking the best thought-through decisions will flourish. Kathy and Randy Pherson provide their Ivy League business school quality of thinking to support you to do just that. This book illuminates how to find and weigh the data you need, validate your data sources, structure your decision logic, and report your conclusions in a persuasive way. One of my best business decisions was to embed in my own work the logic and checklists featured in their book.

—Erik Elgersma, Director, Strategic Analysis Services BV, The Netherlands; author, *Strategic Analysis Cycle Handbook*

No one has given more thought to the improvement and the teaching of analytic techniques than Kathy and Randy Pherson. The third edition of *Critical Thinking for Strategic Intelligence* is a welcome update of their now–must-have book. Dealing with an increasing flow of incoming information and creating from that well-written, thoughtful analysis is a daunting challenge. This book is well organized, extremely accessible, and profusely illustrated with useful figures. It will continue to benefit analysts—in all fields, not just intelligence—as well as managers of analysts and those who teach courses on analysis.

—Mark M. Lowenthal, former US Assistant Director of Central Intelligence for Analysis and Production

The third edition of *Critical Thinking for Strategic Intelligence* is an outstanding contribution to one of the most important aspects of intelligence practice globally and often one of the most overlooked and least understood. The focus of the book encapsulates the very essence of critical thinking in strategic intelligence. It will resonate with intelligence professionals tasked with producing quality strategic intelligence product both in their analysis of the data collected and in writing the final product. The book builds successfully on earlier editions; it amplifies important principles and complements other research into critical thinking and strategic intelligence. The book makes a significant contribution to the body of knowledge on this essential feature of intelligence analysis and practice. As a retired senior intelligence manager and now president of the Australian Institute of Professional Intelligence Officers, I appreciate the value of this book and congratulate Kathy and Randy Pherson for their dedication to the craft.

—Philip Kowalick, President, Australian Institute of Professional
Intelligence Officers

Kathy and Randy Pherson artfully weave together scholarship and experience in this update to their foundational work. The book reveals—not answers—something much more important: how to ask questions. It provides readers the skills they need to navigate the ocean of the often-conflicting, irrelevant, and incorrect information in which we all live today.

—Alan Wade, former Chief Information Officer, US Intelligence Community

In an era where reliance on large volumes of information and associated data analytics will grow exponentially to provide indications and warning, the application of critical thinking to provide decision advantage for all decision makers will grow proportionally. The wide array of national security threats continues to expand, as we are reminded by the most recent pandemic that has affected the lives of tens of millions of people. Objective, data-driven analysis will remain the bedrock of what any national or tactical decision maker will require from intelligence professionals, and we can all benefit from this book to provide the tradecraft for achieving sound analysis.

—David Shedd, former Acting Director, US Defense Intelligence Agency

Critical thinking is a fundamental part of any learning process, and when uncertainties in information are present, humans are prone to making misjudgments and errors. The knowledge in this book, drawn from both practical examples and well-researched methods, gives you the basic tools you need to provide your peers and stakeholders with nuanced views. Whether you are a seasoned professional or just getting started, working as a government analyst or as a high school teacher, these are tools you should know as part of the craft.

—Tommy Skaug, Norwegian National Cyber Security Centre

The range of possible answers to a seemingly simple question can expand in many directions. *Critical Thinking for Strategic Intelligence* provides a fundamental guide for both novice and experienced analysts in determining how to best approach the question, wade through an ever-expanding universe of information, avoid cognitive traps and biases, and effectively convey their analysis and conclusions to inform and support critical decisions. The Phersons' latest update adds strategic context and a broader set of examples to what is already a foundational volume, a timeless desk reference on the concepts and conduct of critical thinking.

—Charles Phalen, former Acting Director, US Defense Counterintelligence and
Security Agency, and former Director of Security, US Central Intelligence Agency

Critical Thinking for Strategic Intelligence

3rd Edition

To our students and our children, Richie and Amanda. We learn from you. We hope our experience helps you make your lives easier and your analysis more compelling.

Sara Miller McCune founded SAGE Publishing in 1965 to support the dissemination of usable knowledge and educate a global community. SAGE publishes more than 1000 journals and over 800 new books each year, spanning a wide range of subject areas. Our growing selection of library products includes archives, data, case studies and video. SAGE remains majority owned by our founder and after her lifetime will become owned by a charitable trust that secures the company's continued independence.

Los Angeles | London | New Delhi | Singapore | Washington DC | Melbourne

Critical Thinking for Strategic Intelligence

3rd Edition

Katherine Hibbs Pherson

Randolph H. Pherson

FOR INFORMATION:

CQ Press

An imprint of SAGE Publications, Inc.

2455 Teller Road

Thousand Oaks, California 91320

E-mail: order@sagepub.com

SAGE Publications Ltd.

1 Oliver's Yard

55 City Road

London, EC1Y 1SP

United Kingdom

SAGE Publications India Pvt. Ltd.

B 1/I 1 Mohan Cooperative Industrial Area

Mathura Road, New Delhi 110 044

India

SAGE Publications Asia-Pacific Pte. Ltd.

18 Cross Street #10-10/11/12

China Square Central

Singapore 048423

Acquisitions Editor: Anna Villarruel

Editorial Assistant: Lauren Younker

Production Editor: Tracy Buyan

Copy Editor: Taryn Bigelow

Typesetter: Hurix Digital

Indexer: Integra

Cover Designer: Adriana Gonzalez

Marketing Manager: Jennifer Jones

Copyright © 2021 by CQ Press, an Imprint of SAGE Publications, Inc. CQ Press is a registered trademark of Congressional Quarterly Inc.

All rights reserved. Except as permitted by U.S. copyright law, no part of this work may be reproduced or distributed in any form or by any means, or stored in a database or retrieval system, without permission in writing from the publisher.

All third party trademarks referenced or depicted herein are included solely for the purpose of illustration and are the property of their respective owners. Reference to these trademarks in no way indicates any relationship with, or endorsement by, the trademark owner.

Printed in Canada

Library of Congress Cataloging-in-Publication Data

Names: Pherson, Katherine Hibbs, author. | Pherson, Randolph H., author.

Title: Critical thinking for strategic intelligence / Katherine Hibbs Pherson, Randolph H. Pherson.

Description: Third edition. | Thousand Oaks, California : CQ Press, [2021] | Revised edition of: Critical thinking for strategic intelligence, c2017. | Includes bibliographical references (p.) and index.

Identifiers: LCCN 2020017430 | ISBN 9781544374260 (paperback) | ISBN 9781544374284 (epub) | ISBN 9781544374277 (epub) | ISBN 9781544374291 (ebook)

Subjects: LCSH: Business analysts. | Business planning. | Strategic planning. | Critical thinking.

Classification: LCC HD69.B87 P53 2021 | DDC 658.4/012—dc23

LC record available at https://lccn.loc.gov/2020017430

This book is printed on acid-free paper.

20 21 22 23 24 10 9 8 7 6 5 4 3 2 1

CONTENTS

LIST OF FIGURES

FOREWORD

Whether you are a practicing intelligence professional or a decision maker who depends on intelligence, *Critical Thinking for Strategic Intelligence* is required reading. Critical thinking skills are foundational and thus essential not only for the analysts themselves, but for collectors, managers, and consumers as well. When I was a senior intelligence official and asked that a paper be prepared for me, everyone knew the draft had to be crisp, tightly reasoned, and deftly organized. What I did not need was a memory dump—a mindless recitation of everything known or imagined. I needed the factual bases and their relevance; I eschewed fluff. Kathy and Randy Pherson have produced a book that tells you exactly what is needed to do this well.

I have long felt the need for a book that helps intelligence practitioners apply critical thinking skills to their profession. Given the growing complexity of our intelligence milieu, that need is increasingly desperate. The book approaches this challenge in a comprehensive and satisfying way, focusing on those twenty most important questions all analysts should ask of themselves on a regular basis. One of the most important admonitions is to "stop and reflect" before "plunging into" any newly assigned task. Time spent properly framing and refining the question and scoping what is needed saves endless hours of unnecessary toil down the road.

The authors provide helpful advice on where to look for the most useful information. More important, I think, are their valuable checklists to help determine if the sources can be trusted, if deception may be present, or if some caveat for the reader is appropriate. They not only tell you what makes up a good analytic product, but how to fashion the message in an appropriately compelling manner. Although the authors spent their careers as intelligence analysts working for the US government, the book is enriched with insights from colleagues in Canada, the United Kingdom, Norway, and Australia which adds useful perspective and offers models US analysts would be smart to incorporate as their own. *Critical Thinking for Strategic Intelligence* can also help inoculate producers of intelligence against the growing tendency to require sources for virtually every sentence or paragraph analysts write. In this era of time dominant, tactical reporting, it is vital that analysts be allowed to think independently, make seasoned judgments, and issue warnings based on their mastery of analytic tradecraft.

As the need for ever-better intelligence has grown, formal analytic training in government and academia has become more fashionable. This book should be front and center on the reading lists for students as well as practitioners of the intelligence arts. The inclusion of six case studies should make it a winner in the classroom. The case studies focus on a diverse set of topics ranging from Digital Disinformation to defense budgeting to food safety, each case vividly illustrating the utility of applying these skills across a broad range of issues.

This book complements eight previous works by Pherson et al. that have been well received within the profession both in the United States and abroad: *Analytic Writing Guide, Analytic Briefing Guide, Analytic Production Guide, Analyst's Guide to Indicators, Handbook of Analytic Tools and Techniques, Structured Analytic Techniques for Intelligence Analysis, Cases in Intelligence Analysis: Structured Analytic Techniques in Action,* and *Intelligence Communication in the Digital Era: Transforming Security, Defence and Business.* When you add this *Critical Thinking* volume to your shelf, you have what it takes to establish the analytic arm of any intelligence service.

In *Critical Thinking for Strategic Intelligence,* Kathy and Randy Pherson provide the best guide I have seen on how to satisfy the analytic needs of busy executives both in business and government. In essence, the authors frame how analysis should be done in a direct and practical way. When it comes to critical thinking skills, this book is meant for all of us whether we are intelligence collectors, analysts, or consumers. From personal experience inside US intelligence and Homeland Security, I know this book will be an invaluable guide and will advance analytic excellence. My only regret on reading it is that it was not available sooner.

UPDATE TO THIRD EDITION

In reviewing this third edition of *Critical Thinking for Strategic Intelligence,* I recall well my impressions when I read the first edition nearly a decade ago. In 2011, the surprise of Arab Spring, the impact of the death of Osama bin Laden, and the implications of the end of the Iraq War kept our intelligence analytic focus on counterterrorism and warfighter support. Now the world is even more complex with political and economic polarization, shifting alliances, sociological and environmental disruptions, and disinformation. The need for insightful warning and solid, dispassionate analysis has never been greater.

Kathy and Randy Pherson's book stands the test of time. It tackles change head on, incorporating timely issues and sources to help analysts deal with evolution in the ways they work as well as the issues they study. *Critical Thinking for Strategic Intelligence* focuses on the fundamentals of effective intelligence analysis no matter what the problem or client. This one-of-a-kind guide should be used by all practitioners from the front lines to the C-suite.

Charles E. Allen

Principal, The Chertoff Group

Former Under Secretary for Intelligence and Analysis,
Department of Homeland Security

Former Assistant Director of Central Intelligence for Collection,
Central Intelligence Agency

January 2020

PREFACE

When we first contemplated writing this book in 2009, one of the authors was invited to speak to a class at a prestigious graduate school of management about the value of using Structured Analytic Techniques in business analysis. He decided to begin the class by discussing how outlines can save time while enhancing the quality of a paper. Writing an outline or making a sketch or flowchart helps analysts organize available information, develop their lines of argument, and identify gaps in knowledge. It only takes minutes, but over the long run it can save hours or days of effort compared to just plunging in. The author thought this simple example would be a good metaphor for showing the value of using Structured Analytic Techniques, such as a Key Assumptions Check, to avoid common cognitive pitfalls—as well as major intelligence failures.

To his astonishment, only one-third of the students said they had ever prepared an outline before writing. Was this an anomaly? Apparently not. When we subsequently asked the same question of new analysts entering government service, usually half said they do not prepare outlines or otherwise sketch out how they plan to organize their paper.

With the advent of powerful search engines on the internet, the process of writing a paper appears to have changed. A common practice is for students to use the search capability to find documents and other sources of information on their topic, select the best sources, extract the most relevant information, copy and paste the various blocks of information, and then edit the compilation of inputs to create the final paper.

What is not apparent is whether any critical thinking occurred throughout this process (see the Critical Thinker's Checklist on the inside front cover and the Analyst's Roadmap on the inside back cover). Did the student develop an actual line of argument in preparing the paper? Validate the key questions being asked? Test any assumptions or consider alternative hypotheses? Identify contrary evidence or notice gaps in information or logic?

We believe all these steps, which are often ignored by Google-generation drafters, are essential to producing high-quality analytic products. This book intends to provide students as well as government and private sector analysts with a practical guide for instilling more rigor in their analytic process and generating more compelling final products.

AUDIENCE

We wrote this book for anyone who wants to think smarter and write better and who seeks guidance on how best to achieve these goals. Its organization is drawn from our past experiences as intelligence analysts, managers of analytic products, instructors, and commercial consultants. We fervently believe the book has value to audiences far beyond our "home base," the US Intelligence Community.

Producing good analysis is both an art and a science. Seasoned analysts in the government and the private sector can use this book to perfect the art of writing, refine their conceptual skills, and learn new techniques. A more important audience, in our view, consists of the up-and-coming analysts in colleges and universities—and even teachers in high schools and lower grades. Teachers should be inculcating the basic principles of critical thinking in students of all ages, both to enrich their daily lives and to enhance their professional opportunities.

CONTENT AND DESIGN

The book is organized around twenty key questions that all analysts should ask as they prepare to conduct research, draft papers, and present their analysis. We divided the twenty questions into four groups, focusing on the four stages of generating an analytic product:

1. How do I get started?

2. Where is the information I need?

3. What is my argument?

4. How do I convey my message effectively?

We have long contended that the best way to learn is by doing. In writing this book, we practice what we preach by including a set of case studies that the reader can use to reinforce understanding of key points. The case studies focus on a wide range of topics, covering political, economic, military, cyber, disinformation, and health-related issues. At the end of each chapter, we provide a set of questions instructors and students can use to test whether the key teaching points have been absorbed. The answers to the questions found at the end of each chapter are available as a free downloadable PDF to all who purchase the book. To learn more, contact your SAGE representative at **sagepub.com/findmyrep** or by e-mailing publications@pherson.org.

Throughout the book, a series of figures will alert you to stop and reflect and to identify which Structured Analytic Techniques best support the activities discussed in that chapter. We also include some of our favorite quotations and a robust set of figures and graphics. The Critical Thinker's Checklist is displayed on the inside front cover to make it easy to access. The inside back cover includes a graphic, the Analyst's Roadmap, that captures on one page the key points made in the book.

ACKNOWLEDGMENTS

For this third edition, the authors are pleased to acknowledge the thoughtful comments and suggestions they received from practitioners and managers of intelligence analysis in the United Kingdom, Australia, Canada, Norway, Spain, and Romania. We wish in particular to thank Abby DiOrio for updating the food poisoning, aircraft carrier, and Arctic case studies, Sally Maxwell for helping research and write the cyber case study, Deanna Labriny for refreshing the Iraq case study, Abby and Deanna for researching and co-drafting the Russian MH17 Digital Disinformation case study, and Casey Cannon for helping us refresh and expand the MH17 and Arctic case studies. We are also grateful for the insights Vincent Bonner provided in reviewing several chapters and the assistance we received from Richard Pherson and Linda Budinski as our proofreaders and Adriana Gonzalez as our graphics designer.

For the first edition, we thank Gordon Barrass, Douglas Beck, Anthony Campbell, Ray Converse, Jack Davis, Averill Farrelly, Edward Farrelly, Rick Gill, Nick Hare, Georgia Holmer, Matt Jolly, Lou Kaiser, Laura Lenz, Joe Markowitz, Frank Marsh, Gary Oleson, Mary O'Sullivan, John Pyrik, Todd Sears, Kevin Sherman, Cynthia Storer, David Terry, and Gudmund Thompson for their substantive contributions. We would also thank Alysa Gander, who co-drafted the case study, "The End of the Era of Aircraft Carriers."

We are indebted to Richards J. Heuer Jr., Ellen Kane, and Marilyn Scott, who reviewed the first edition manuscript and made several excellent suggestions for substantive and editorial revisions. In addition, both authors are grateful to the many others who helped create the graphics, reviewed parts of the book, critiqued and tested the case studies, and assisted in editing and proofreading, including Nigah Ajaj, Richard E. Hayes, William Johnson, Amanda Pherson, Richard Pherson, Paul Pillar, David Ramer, Joshua Rovner, Karen Saunders, Kevin Sherman, and Michael Scott. We also thank students at the London School of Economics, the University of Mississippi, and James Madison University; and the many helpful commentators on chapters of the book presented at the International Association for Intelligence Education (IAFIE) and International Studies Association (ISA) conferences.

For the second edition, we thank Stacey Kaminski for significantly revising Chapter 10, and Ryan Larson who contributed valuable feedback from his and his classmates' use of the first edition in Professor Steve Marrin's class at James Madison University. We again are grateful to our children for their assistance on this labor of love: to Amanda Pherson for creating the new graphics appearing in Chapters 13 and 18 and to Richard Pherson for again serving as our main proofreader.

For the third edition, we would like to thank the following reviewers:

Mary Manjikian, Regent University

Professor William O. Waddell, Liberty University Helms School of Government

Rev. Christopher Dreisbach, Ph.D., Johns Hopkins University

John Hodgson, Penn State

Gregory Moore, Ph.D., Notre Dame College

DISCLAIMER

All statements of fact, opinion, or analysis expressed in this book are those of the authors and do not reflect the official positions of the Central Intelligence Agency or any other US government agency. Nothing in the contents should be construed as asserting or implying the authentication of information or endorsement of the authors' views by the US, UK, or Canadian governments. This material has been reviewed by the Central Intelligence Agency only to prevent the disclosure of classified material.

Pherson's suite of collaborative tools (Te@mACH®, Indicators Validator®, Multiple Hypotheses Generator®) are patents of Pherson Associates, LLC and are referenced with its permission. Circleboarding™, Inconsistencies Finder™, Quadrant Crunching™, and the Opportunities Incubator™) are trademarks of Globalytica, LLC, and are used with its permission.

ABOUT THE AUTHORS

 **Katherine Hibbs Pherson** is chief executive officer (CEO) of Pherson Associates, LLC, President of Globalytica, LLC, and a founding director of the nonprofit Forum Foundation for Analytic Excellence. She consults with government and private industry on building strong analytic communities, the use of Structured Analytic Techniques, and security issues. She teaches certificate courses and workshops on structured thinking and presentation for a variety of audiences in government, private industry, and academia, both in the US and internationally. As vice chair of the Intelligence and National Security Association (INSA) Security Policy Reform Council, she has been a thought leader, and drafter and editor of its publications, which have generated a decade of productive exchanges among government and industry. She is a founding director of the Intelligence and National Security Foundation (INSF) and a member of AFCEA International's Intelligence Committee.

Ms. Pherson retired from the Central Intelligence Agency in 2000 after a twenty-seven-year career in intelligence and security analysis and resource management. Her leadership in the security arena led to the adoption of a risk management methodology, the strengthening of overseas security countermeasures, and improvements in dealing with unsolicited contacts. As head of the Director of Central Intelligence's Center for Security Evaluation, she managed the US Intelligence Community's involvement in rebuilding the penetrated US Embassy in Moscow. She is a recipient of the CIA's Distinguished Career Intelligence Medal and the Intelligence Community's National Distinguished Service Medal. She received her AB from Vassar College, an MA in Spanish linguistics and Latin American studies from the University of Illinois, and an MA in communications from the University of Oklahoma.

 **Randolph H. Pherson** is president of Pherson Associates, LLC; CEO of Globalytica, LLC; and a founding director of the nonprofit Forum Foundation for Analytic Excellence. He teaches advanced analytic techniques and critical thinking skills to analysts in the government and private sector. Mr. Pherson coauthored *Structured Analytic Techniques for Intelligence Analysis* with Richards J. Heuer Jr. and collaborated with him in developing and launching use of Analysis of Competing Hypotheses. He has developed several analytic techniques, many of which were incorporated in his *Handbook of Analytic Tools and Techniques*. He coauthored *Cases in Intelligence Analysis: Structured Analytic Techniques in Action* with

Sarah Miller Beebe, and several other guides for analysts on writing, briefing, indicators, communicating analysis in the digital age, and managing the analytic production process. He has taught courses on critical thinking skills and structured techniques in Australia, Canada, Denmark, Dubai, Germany, Hong Kong, Ireland, the Netherlands, Norway, Portugal, Romania, Saudi Arabia, Spain, the United Kingdom, and the United States.

Mr. Pherson completed a twenty-eight-year career in the US Intelligence Community in 2000, last serving as national intelligence officer (NIO) for Latin America. Previously at the CIA, Mr. Pherson managed the production of intelligence analysis on topics ranging from global instability to Latin America, served on the Inspector General's staff, and was chief of the CIA's Strategic Planning and Management Staff. He is the recipient of the Distinguished Intelligence Medal for his service as NIO and the Distinguished Career Intelligence Medal. Mr. Pherson received his BA from Dartmouth College and an MA in international relations from Yale University.

INTRODUCTION TO THE THIRD EDITION

As we begin to write the third edition of *Critical Thinking for Strategic Intelligence*, we reflect on our experience over the previous three months of teaching and working with intelligence professionals in Europe, the Pacific, and Latin America as well as government, law enforcement, industry, and academic groups in the United States. Most of them are current consumers of our books, therefore our most important source of feedback and guides for the future. They encourage us by validating that the basics of good analysis apply to the range of intellectual practices—most recently including legal, financial, security, and cyber—and remind us to keep our focus on the practical "how" rather than the theoretical "what."

We are struck by how radically different the world is now from when we wrote the first edition in 2011. Our mentor and friend Charlie Allen in the Foreword notes that today's divisions, disruptions, pandemics, and Digital Disinformation present new challenges to analysts trying to make sense of the present and prepare decision makers for the future. We underscore the differences in the analytic work environment generated by the availability of *data*, the capability brought by *technology*, and the *speed* with which they can be accessed and manipulated.

In response, this third edition not only updates references and examples but also includes significant new material to help analysts address these challenges. We have done the following:

- Supplemented the second edition's discussion of Big Data by adding new source categories for cyber issues and suggesting best practices to deal with Digital Disinformation and Deepfakes. We stress the importance of evolving sources in imagery, video, and social media and the importance of recognizing how they can hamper as well as enhance analytic conclusions.

- Addressed how humans and machines can best work together—with humans using the strengths of machines without being cowed by them or immune to understanding that programming might be susceptible to error or bias.

- Buttressed the contention that analysts must be prepared to produce and tailor products quickly and succinctly, becoming adept at written, visual, oral, and virtual presentation. We advocate for increased use of online training to build skills and expertise.

- Added material on politicization in a polarized world as well as thinking about the future, where, by definition, data for deductively accurate point predictions do not exist.

- Kept our eyes on our primary theme of clarifying what is meant by "critical thinking" by discussing how it relates to other kinds of "thinking," including "creative thinking," "design thinking," "computational thinking," and "visual thinking." In response to a reader's suggestion, we have incorporated how concepts like "mindfulness" and "self-awareness" fit into the critical thinking process. Our goal is to help analysts save time and effort by focusing on the commonalities rather than the differences.

In the end, we are pleased with how the structure and content of the book have held up over time and with practical use. We applaud one university that took student recommendations some years ago that the book be introduced in freshman classes rather than holding it for the senior year. We treasure a review of the second edition written by a Spaniard who began using the first edition living and working in a tent in a dangerous area in Africa in support of the United Nations. We will never forget a long-ago email from a law student in Angola who thanked us for writing in a style that was understandable to non-native English speakers.

To deal critically and analytically with the changes in the world today, we offer the following Key Takeaways:

- **Data:** Be skeptical if your issue hinges on one or two key pieces of data and maintain alternative "bins" in case critical information is false.

- **Technology:** Frame your issues consciously so that you can act effectively and efficiently with machines, and not be cowed by them.

- **Speed:** Master the art of simple argumentation, visualization, and online communication to get your message across quickly and effectively.

Make no mistake, the fundamentals of analysis are as relevant today as at any time in the past. Good analysts will use them to anticipate and adapt to breathtaking changes in the context, information, and tools that are reshaping a world that needs critical thinking more than ever.

As always, we welcome feedback and comments on our approach, gaps, and improvements needed. Feel free to contact us by email at pherson@pherson.org.

Kathy and Randy Pherson

INTRODUCTION

WHY THIS BOOK, AND WHY NOW?

As we were writing this book, dear colleagues gave us a bumper sticker that sums up the need for a book on critical thinking. It says, "Critical Thinking: The Other National Deficit." Our goal is to make a dent in reducing that deficit.

Internet searches and library catalogs point to hundreds of erudite books that detail how to structure arguments, differentiate between intuition and structured reasoning, and explore how the brain works so that we learn from our experiences and apply them to the challenges we face every day. Academics, logicians, and researchers carry out exquisitely designed experiments, conduct research, and publish detailed accounts of their results. Others apply these tenets to the world of analysis, diagnosing why an analyst's mental crystal ball fails to predict unexpected events, dissecting these events to distill lessons learned. All these activities make important contributions to the understanding of critical and analytic thinking. In and of themselves, however, they do not produce better analytic thinkers or lead to more refined analytic products.

The problem is fairly straightforward: Too much information is out there, and analysts simply do not have the time to absorb all of it. Even with automated search and extraction assistance, analysts still need to think their way through an issue, recognizing the most salient data and rejecting that which is wrong, misleading, or unhelpful. How can analysts identify the best critical thinking practices and, more important, learn the most effective ways to incorporate them into their daily work processes?

The solution lies in seeking help in four different ways. Most analysts should be able to benefit from all four pathways:

1. On-the-job training by experienced managers and other mentors

2. Training courses and workshops that attempt to develop basic, intermediate, and advanced skills

3. Improved analytic techniques

4. Self-initiated study, practice, and experience

On-the-Job Training

Some analysts come naturally to a way of thinking that leads to success in the world of analysis, easily incorporating disparate sources of information into insightful narratives and conclusions that their readers can use in making decisions about difficult issues. Most analysts, however, need to be schooled and mentored to think more rigorously and reduce the chances of being led astray by mental mindsets that help us simplify data and deal with complexity.

Unfortunately, not all managers and mentors were created equal. We came to the US Intelligence Community in the mid-1970s from exceptional university programs, but we still needed on-the-job experience writing and rewriting our work to become good analysts. We had to justify our thought processes and data interpretation, and we were edited at multiple levels on a daily basis. We were held accountable by our supervisors for having clear mental frameworks for our areas of responsibility, being on top of all the information relating to our frameworks, and writing quickly and succinctly about events and their implications. If we got stuck or overreached our data, our supervisors guided us to a better path.

Training Courses

Training underscored what we learned on the job and provided additional perspective on our craft, but its value paled in comparison to what we learned by doing our job under the watchful eyes of managers and editors who were experienced analysts.

The same is true today. In an increasingly challenging and globalized world, we look to analysts to make sense of incomplete and ambiguous information. In the wake of 9/11, over seventy fusion centers have been created across the United States to promote information sharing and analysis among state, local, tribal, and territorial entities and with the federal government. Many global corporations also have established special analytic units to deal with challenges ranging from cyber and supply chain threats to money laundering. Their clients sometimes view analysts as a sort of panacea, expecting them to find the critical information in avalanches of data, develop expertise on complicated topics in weeks, and generate with little guidance products that will head off catastrophic mistakes and prevent surprise. Much like the Sidney Harris cartoon in which the difficult part of a mathematical proof is accounted for by the words "and then a miracle occurs," analysts become the critical node in which the human brain is expected to take advantage of the systems that have been built, the processes that have been developed, and the information that has been shared. Although they work under the job title "analyst," many lack the critical thinking skills and knowledge to meet these high expectations as well as the training programs to get them to this standard.

The analysts we teach and mentor across the intelligence, homeland security, law enforcement, defense, and corporate communities appreciate the training they get but characterize much of the coursework as descriptive or too theoretical. They learn some "interesting stuff" but are not coached in how actually to do analysis or how to know when they are doing it well. As one student wrote on an evaluation form, "I don't just need to know that the 'So What' is critical, I need to be told how to find it and to recognize it when I have found it." In short, students are asking to be taught the "How" of intelligence analysis and not just the "What." They know they are at risk, and they do not want to be wrong.

Analytic Techniques

When we look back on past responses to intelligence surprises or analytic shortcomings, recommendations for improvements are uncannily similar. Almost every postmortem of past intelligence failures concludes that analysts were working from outdated or flawed mental mindsets and had failed to consider alternative explanations. The Iraq Weapons of Mass Destruction (WMD) Commission's indictment of "poor tradecraft" and the 9/11 Commission's judgment that analysis suffered from a "failure of imagination" signaled the need to incorporate more rigor and creativity into the analytic process. Much the same criticism has been levied on segments of the corporate world.

Governments have responded by commissioning major research and development (R&D) efforts to create new models, new algorithms, and new computer tools to address analytic weaknesses. Unfortunately, most of this investment has gone to collection, data mining, and other IT infrastructure improvements and precious little to supporting the analytic process. Major corporations are beginning to confront the challenge, often investing in software that is more likely to inhibit rather than to enhance analytic productivity.

These R&D efforts and investments often fail to produce analytic tools that analysts have integrated into their daily routines. Many programs aspire to develop tools that will do the analysts' work for them, crunching reams of data and extracting answers with the application of sophisticated algorithms. Far more preferable would be the development of simpler tools that can structure analysts' thinking, help them engage peers in problem solving, and, most important, save them time.

One successful example dates back to well before the Iraq WMD intelligence failure. As a result of the Nosenko double agent controversy in the 1960s, Richards J. Heuer Jr. studied cognitive psychology and suggested the application of a form of the scientific method to intelligence analysis called Analysis of Competing Hypotheses (ACH). The method received traction as a result of the CIA's publication of *Psychology of Intelligence Analysis* in 1999, and it is now a standard technique taught across the Intelligence Community.[1] The technique is well received by analysts as a diagnostic tool and an effective way to track the relevance of key data. Even those whose work is heavily focused on quick assessments and current intelligence reporting have learned the value of constantly scanning incoming reports for data that are inconsistent with their lead hypotheses. We are always alert for ways to simplify techniques and have developed a simpler version of ACH, the Inconsistencies Finder™.[2]

Self-Study

Many analysts have tried to overcome the lack of experienced managers, well-focused training courses, and useful analytic techniques by engaging in self-study programs. The key frustration they encounter in this realm is a lack of good case studies and tailored on-the-shelf—and preferably online—instructional materials.

Most analysts are under serious time pressure and have access to limited resources. They need simple but elegant solutions to these challenges. This book is intended to help overcome these obstacles by providing practical advice and easily digestible answers to what we consider are the twenty most important critical thinking questions. We seek to help you traverse the four pathways in the following manner:

1. Turn to this book for guidance if you lack an experienced supervisor or mentor who can look over your shoulder as you conceptualize and write your product.

2. Use the book as a framework to reinforce what is taught in the classroom and to direct your attention to which sections of the course deserve the most attention.

3. Learn more about the simple analytic techniques referenced in the various chapters to ensure that you pick the right technique for the problem that confronts you.

4. Read the case studies and do the exercises to test what you have learned and make sure you did not miss any key learning points.

We also in the past few years have become staunch advocates for online mechanisms for learning and refreshing concepts and best practices for analysts. This has become critically important in the wake of fundamental changes brought by COVID-19. Students of varying ages, cultures, and disciplines have responded favorably to our Fundamentals of Critical Thinking course, which combines descriptions and exercises relating to key concepts from this book with an instructor-led discussion board to relate the concepts to students' lives and work. We are supplementing it with Quick Looks, which provide short, focused exposure to concepts like the Analytic Spectrum (see Chapter 5).[3] These opportunities for self-study and reinforcement will increasingly enable analysts to improve their understanding and skills totally on their own initiative.

We learn how to do good analysis by practice. When good analysts are asked how they can remember so much or juggle so many themes or details simultaneously, the answer often is "fear." Analysts can avoid making major mistakes by embracing the rigors of science within the time constraints and practical limitations of the analytic process. The best way to mitigate the fear of failure is to internalize core critical thinking skills and persist in always identifying a client's true needs, developing a persuasive line of argument, checking key assumptions, looking for disconfirming data, and entertaining multiple explanations as long as possible.

Definitions of critical thinking abound—from the philosophical to the biological—but the authors subscribe to the definition proffered by long-time intelligence methodologist and practitioner Jack Davis:

> *"Critical Thinking is the adaptation of the processes and values of scientific inquiry to the special circumstances of strategic intelligence."*[4]

WHY THESE TWENTY QUESTIONS?

The organization of this book is based on what we have learned from our students, what has resonated from in-class discussions, what our students have identified each day as their greatest takeaway, or "Aha!" and what students tell us later when they get back to their jobs. One student confided that she always remembers what she should be doing after sitting through a training session, but old habits rapidly take over when she returns to her desk. Her focus quickly shifts to what has to be done as quickly as possible and to the "satisficing" strategies that answer the immediate question but could be analytically flawed. We believe she—and all of us—need to constantly remind ourselves that by instilling more rigor into the analytic process we will actually make our jobs easier.

Recognizing that time is an increasingly precious commodity, we have sought to convey our message as concisely as possible, providing what you need to know while avoiding longer theoretical discussions of why it matters. For such information, we direct you to the endnotes, the glossary of terms, and the list of recommended readings at the back of the book. We have also provided a list of names of people mentioned in the twenty chapters and where they were cited. Particularly important is the series of repeating figures that appears in most chapters identifying the Structured Analytic Techniques that apply to the concepts being discussed; this book is a companion that provides the context within which the various techniques are most useful.

We understand that the provision of questions, steps, and checklists is not the entire answer. They are a means to get started—what one of our colleagues calls the "training wheels." The devil, as always, is in the details. The burden is on you to apply what is contained in these twenty chapters with sufficient care and precision, internalizing the processes and using them as a baseline for more sophisticated and complex analytic efforts.

In writing this book, we tried to take into account individual differences in learning traits and reasoning styles, such as curiosity, and the different levels of effort with which people approach intellectual tasks. We are gratified when students with diagnosed learning disabilities tell us they usually have trouble getting all they should out of most training classes but learn easily from us. While we attribute this mostly to the sound application of adult learning principles, we believe analysis should be viewed as a multifaceted activity that is done well only if we use all our brain power—both the logical left brain and the creative right brain. We encourage you to use the book as a reference guide, constantly practice what you are learning, and use the case studies to assess how well you have learned.

NOTES

1. The book is available at no charge online at https://www.cia.gov/library/center-for-the-study-of-intelligence/csi-publications/books-and-monographs/psychology-of-intelligence-analysis/PsychofIntelNew.pdf. It has also been republished by Pherson Associates, LLC, and can be purchased in book format by going to https://shop.globalytica.com.

2. A description of both ACH and the Inconsistencies Finder™ can be found in Randolph H. Pherson and Richards J. Heuer Jr., *Structured Analytic Techniques for Intelligence Analysis*, 3rd ed. (Washington, DC: CQ Press/SAGE, 2021).

3. Information on this course, which is part of Globalytica's Intelligence Analyst Professional certification program, is available on the Globalytica website at https://shop.globalytica.com/collections/iap/products/critical-thinking-skills.

4. Jack Davis, personal communication, February 24, 2011.

HOW DO I GET STARTED?

Most courses and books on critical thinking are about logic, types of arguments, and demonstrations of perceptual foibles. Analysts in the classes we teach just want to know how to do their jobs. And the hardest part of performing their task is to get started.

The tendency is to do a quick search for what has already been written on a topic, select the best material in our computer databases, and just plunge in. We muddle about in the data until we become sufficiently familiar with what is out there or desperate enough that our brains focus on the categories that make the most sense and the information that appears most salient. Then we fashion some judgments that rise above the mire, organize what we have in hand, and write it down crisply. Fortunately, we get better at this as we absorb the details, learn the history, and build models that can help us look to the future.

That strategy will work over time, but this book gives you a better way. Part I lays out an array of tasks that should be undertaken before selecting sources or beginning to write the paper. The secret to successful analysis is targeting the analytic product to specific clients and answering the questions they are, or should be, asking. Make sure you understand the broader perspective by considering the full analytic landscape (see the description of Issue Redefinition in Chapter 3) before narrowing the focus to conceptualize a specific product. The last chapters in this section explore the range of approaches that can be employed to produce the analysis and the benefits of including others in the process.

Many analysts say they do not have time to do all this under the pressure of deadlines. They are wrong. This is the preparatory foundation that enables you to turn out consistent and insightful analysis no matter how tight the time limitations. You need only a few minutes to orient yourself in the production process using the Analyst's Roadmap for guidance (see the inside back cover). Diagram the environment in which you are working and try to use both the right (creative) and the left (logical) sides of your brain to speed the integration of the data and sensemaking.

Over the long run, the tips offered in this section will save you considerable time while sharpening your analysis. This analytic infrastructure is the essence of good critical thinking. Stop and reflect when you are at your desk but also when you are exercising or getting up in the morning. How do you know you are generating a high-quality product? You can measure your success by tracking what your clients do, how often they seek your input, and the extent to which what they do is based on what you have said or written.

1 WHO ARE YOUR CLIENTS?

SETTING THE STAGE

The importance of pausing at the start of a job or a project to identify explicitly the primary recipient of your analysis cannot be overstated. When preparing a briefing, the answer to the question, "Who are your clients?" is usually obvious, although you may need to target your presentation to a larger group with several subsets of clients, interests, and desired outcomes.[1] When writing a product, however, this step is often overlooked—and the cost to analysts and their organizations can be substantial.[2]

The raison d'être for analysts and analytic organizations is to bring a broad range of information to bear on difficult questions, select that which is most significant, then tailor and package it for decision makers. These functions are similar for analysts whether they work in national security, homeland security, law enforcement, or private industry.

Most clients, however, have much more on their minds than absorbing the details and historic data in which analysts are immersed. Successful analysts translate their expertise into forms that "sing" to busy clients and respond to their needs and interests without them having to ask. The first step is to understand the clients' responsibilities, problems, pressures, and preferences as receivers of information. This is often best accomplished by establishing a working relationship with the client that allows for more informal interaction and feedback.

LOOKING MORE DEEPLY

As you begin a new job and read to familiarize yourself with the subject matter, make a list or draw a diagram of those who are interested in or will be counting on your analysis to help them carry out their responsibilities. This client base will guide the questions you formulate, the information you seek and monitor, and the products you generate. Most of your analyses should be targeted at a specific client, but you may prepare reports intended for large audiences interested in your organization's authoritative judgment. The more specific you can be in defining the individuals or positions you support, the better. Be sure to include those in your chain of command as well as those outside your organization who receive your products.

As a working-level analyst, you probably know something about your clients from the media, have learned about them from colleagues, or have met or briefed some of them in person. Ideally, you have established a process that allows you to engage with them in person or electronically to identify their most pressing needs, better scope their requirements, and obtain feedback on the value of the analysis you have provided.

When beginning a project, make every effort to visualize those for whom you are preparing your briefing or paper and what they will be doing as a result of your analytic conclusions. The one thing they most likely have in common is insufficient time for processing and absorbing all the data they need to make effective decisions. They are counting on you to do some of the thinking and anticipating for them, giving them insights so they can "grab it and go."

Understanding Busy Clients

The more senior your clients, the broader their scope of responsibilities and the less time they will have to read your analysis. Senior clients share several characteristics that you should take into consideration in your products and other support.

- *Their time is limited and precious.* Senior clients might be given a hundred pages of information to read each morning. You should expect them to move quickly through volumes, keying off words that catch their attention and interest. Your products should be focused and easily digestible with a prominent "So What" that points the clients to the implications and options for decisions they will make.

- *They depend on you to prioritize what is important.* Your selection of topics helps clients manage their time and focus their intellectual energies on what is most critical. The human brain, however, can follow only a limited number of topics at any given time. Do not assume your clients read or remember previous products. A good strategy is to insert simple graphics or provide supporting or explanatory data in a separate text box.

- *They expect transparency in your facts and your analysis.* Source Summaries and the rationale behind why you know what you know and how you came to your conclusions create the backdrop for your clients' acceptance or rejection of your work. The need for such transparency is even more important if you expect your clients will disagree with your analysis. Some clients will simply disregard your hard work, but others may stop to rethink the issue. If you do not present clear argumentation, however, you may never know if you missed the opportunity to change their thinking or inform their knowledge base.

- *They "use" information from "trusted" analysts and organizations.* Your organization's "brand name" can determine the weight your clients give to your products. Just like we develop preferences for credible service providers, information sources, and commercial products, clients pay more attention to the producers they believe are more thoughtful, reliable, and accurate.

- *You are only one source of their information flow.* Busy executives—from generals to cabinet officials to chief executive officers—have multiple sources of information, many of whom may be closer to the issue than you are. Never assume you are the only or even the most knowledgeable source; know what you have that is different from the others.

Preparing Yourself to Serve Busy Clients

Whether you are an intelligence analyst at the Defense Intelligence Agency, the Chicago Police Department, Citibank, or Walmart, you have prepared yourself for an analytic position by at least earning academic credentials and probably building perspective through developmental experiences, such as military service, government or industry internships, or foreign study. These are the essential foundations to help you get the opportunity to demonstrate and develop your analytic "chops," but you also need to be aware of the internal, cognitive characteristics that will help you successfully serve your organization and your clients.

Mindfulness. In recent years the practice of mindfulness has become a growing movement in institutions ranging from universities to prisons, but self-awareness and the ability to distinguish one's personal experience from observation of the external world has long been a hallmark of the best analysts. This awareness—attention and acceptance—of our thoughts and feelings, without placing a value of rightness or wrongness on them, is fundamental to freeing our minds both to observe what is actually happening in the situation we are analyzing and to weigh the alternatives and possibilities that can explain the past, present, and future.

The popularity of this integration of Zen Buddhist teaching with scientific findings stems from University of Massachusetts medical professor Jon Kabat-Zinn's design of programs to reduce stress, anxiety, and pain, but has strong application in professional as well as personal life. As one of our academic colleagues writes, "we must be aware of ourselves just as much as we need to be aware of our subject matter, our audience, and the purpose of our analysis."[3]

Kabat-Zinn in a recent presentation[4] noted that "moment-to-moment nonjudgmental awareness is hard to attain but is key to being open." He explained that this entails "holding judgment at bay while envisioning the problem and possibilities, before fitting known information into the frame" (see Chapter 3 for Gary Klein's data/frame concept of "sensemaking"). The practice of mindfulness brings a discipline to the starting point in much the same way as the practice of Structured Analytic Techniques does throughout the critical thinking process. In mindfulness terminology, this "beginner's mind" helps overcome "minds that are so full of expertise" that they leave "little room for novelty or freshness" (see Chapter 12 for Rob Johnston's model for building analytic expertise).

This means that we will cultivate discernment, the capacity to see what is unfolding, to understand it with clarity, wisdom, understanding the interconnections between things, noticing the tendency to recognize judgment and recognize that it creates a veil or filter in front of our eyes . . . that is practically blinding to us.

—Jon Kabat-Zinn
"The Dharma Foundations of Mindfulness in the Mainstream:
The Art and the Science of MBSR and Other Mindfulness-Based
Programs"[5]

The goal of "not judging the judging" is to balance our thinking and the brain's natural tendency to come to Premature Closure, forming opinions that are often bipolar—"this" or "that," "good" or "bad." Kabat-Zinn advocates developing the mindfulness disciplines through guided meditation and practice of seven foundational attitudes, several of which you will see reflected in the discussions of analytic skills development throughout this book:

1. *Non-judging.* Recognizing judgments so you can assess them more clearly.

2. *Patience.* Appreciating the present moment, understanding that things unfold in their own time.

3. *Beginner's mind.* Seeing the world through fresh eyes, opening the door to creativity and clarity.

4. *Trust.* Consciously assessing the degree to which we can trust what we see, think, and perceive.

5. *Non-striving.* Recognizing that goals can be achieved by backing off and focusing on the present.

6. *Acceptance.* Willingly seeing and coming to terms with things the way they really are.

7. *Letting go.* Letting things be the way they really are.[6]

Trust. Mindfulness refers to the idea of "trust" in terms of how you trust yourself and your thinking, but trust also refers to whether and how much your clients trust and therefore depend on and use your analysis. Stephen Covey[7] lays out a mental model with five "waves" of trust ranging through self, relationships, organization, market, and society that he likens to concentric ripples in water because "trust always flows from the inside-out."

All the waves provide context for the role and impact of analytic products, but analysts need to focus primarily on the first two. The extensive literature on trust provides a variety of ways to categorize the components of trust; for our purposes, the simplest way is to think of trust as a function of capability and credibility.

- *Capability* means that you have developed the knowledge, skills, and abilities (see Chapter 3 for a discussion of analytic competencies) to add value in your assessment of the issues for which you are responsible. It is measured based on your track record of products, judgments, and assessments and their utility to your clients.

- *Credibility* is built based on that track record, but also by your clients' perception of your honesty, integrity, and intent. Do you do what you say you will do in serving your clients? Do you or your products have a bias or hidden agenda that diminishes their overall value and utility?

Covey identifies thirteen behaviors associated with "high-trust leaders" that apply equally to professional analysts and rest on the foundation of consistent action.

In today's polarized environment (see Chapter 14 on politicization), where analysts can be attacked as they try to do their jobs, these behaviors may be challenging to exhibit but are the only way to bridge differences and attempt to establish a common focus on the potential meanings of observable data.

- Talk straight
- Show respect
- Be transparent
- Right wrongs
- Show loyalty
- Deliver results
- Get better

- Confront reality
- State expectations
- Be accountable
- Listen first
- Meet commitments
- Extend trust[8]

The good news is that research on trust indicates that humans are physically hard-wired to trust others. Malcolm Gladwell in his most recent book, *Talking to Strangers*,[9] writes that we naturally default to believing another person is telling the truth because the benefits of trust usually outweigh the risks of being burned. To avoid negative consequences, he advocates exercising mindfulness and several of the traits that should be commonplace in analysts—careful listening, not reading too much into words or gestures of those who might be deceptive, and never rushing to judgment (see Chapter 9 for a further discussion of Gladwell's writing on how this bias impacts our ability to detect deception).

The bad news for analysts, however, is that other research[10] suggests that the more status, power, and wealth individuals have, the less they trust others and the less trustworthy they are. Analysts should strive to build trust with clients, but they should expect that their efforts will not always meet with success. This is why analysts need to be particularly adept at assessing client needs and priorities that will at least demonstrate credibility through their professional tradecraft.

A Growth Mindset. Previous discussions make clear that our analytic workspace is not set in stone—it changes and we must develop the skills and mindset to grow with it. While one of our colleagues famously said that "good analysts are born and not made," we believe that each of us can improve the analytic skills and predilections with which we were born. Psychologist Carol Dweck[11] helps us understand that our mindset makes a critical difference in whether or not we believe we can change our abilities and grow. People with a *growth mindset* believe they can develop expertise in anything if they just work hard enough as opposed to those with a *fixed mindset*, who are convinced that their natural abilities are all they have (see Figure 1.1). At the extremes of these mindsets, the former pass through life learning new skills, evolving relationships, and continually developing, while the latter are continually trying to prove themselves and get stuck when they fail, avoiding accountability and blaming others. These mindsets

FIGURE 1.1 ■ Comparing Fixed and Growth Mindsets	
Fixed Mindset	**Growth Mindset**
Seeks validation	Seeks development
Sees failures as disasters	Sees failures as opportuniites
Avoids challenges	Relishes challenges

appear as soon as children begin to evaluate themselves—one of Dweck's experiments was with four-year-olds—with those demonstrating fixed mindsets being reluctant to take on challenges and afraid of not looking smart.

Analysis demands mental stretching to keep pace with the clients you are serving, the world you are interpreting, and the tools with which you are working. According to Dweck, if you believe you can develop yourself, you are more likely to seek accurate information because you are looking for ways to improve and impact your performance and environment. She notes that you can learn to adopt a growth mindset.

Influence. Analysis without impact wastes both analyst effort and organizational resources so it is natural and expected that analysts should seek to understand what they can do to maximize the influence or effect that their analysis has on their clients' thinking and actions. Babson professor Allan Cohen and Stanford business professor David Bradford's model for "influence without authority"[12] was devised for the business world but has strong applicability to building the analyst–client relationship. They contend that influence is based on exchange—in this case, technically competent analysts provide intelligence assessments that help their clients succeed at their jobs. In return, analysts receive feedback—whether directly or indirectly from clients or their chain of command—that informs and enhances their ability to succeed at their analytic tasks.

Cohen and Bradford's six-step model for gaining influence underscores the critical importance not only of knowing your client but understanding the value of what you provide and how you can maximize your impact.

1. Consider everyone as a potential friend and ally.

2. Clearly identify and define your objectives and priorities.

3. See the world through the eyes of those you seek to influence.

4. Find out what other people value, and what you can offer in exchange. Know also precisely what you value and will accept.

5. Understand your relationship with those you want to influence, and understand what kind of relationship they want.

6. Exercise influence through a process of mutual exchange and mutual benefit.[13]

Cohen and Bradford encourage developing strategies to respond to clients' needs, but warn of several pitfalls, including the following:

- Failure to plan ahead, accurately gauging what the client really needs, or accounting for changes in situations or priorities

- Attachment to your own assessments, even in the face of change

- Overplaying what you can deliver or the significance of your information

- Diffidence in offering information or services that might be of value for fear they will not be accepted[14]

Empathy. The most valuable analysts are able to view issues from their clients' perspectives, empathetically "seeing the world through others' eyes." Excellent salespeople or managers are empathetic because they recognize and respond to the needs of clients, or subordinates. They are easy to approach and probably approach you first with interest in your wants and needs. They "get it right," making you feel they understand you even if they do not have the color shirt you want or are unable to accommodate a request to shift time schedules. Empathy is at the core of successful social interactions, facilitating communication, trust, and cooperation.

How do you know if you are empathetic? Psychologists have entire workshops on assessing and developing capacities for empathy, but here is the shorthand answer: empathetic people may more accurately sense how they are perceived by others because they intuit another's perception of them and adjust their behaviors so they are seen in ways they want to be seen. The interconnection of this concept with mindfulness, trust, growth mindset, and influence provides analysts with more food for thought on consciously planning how they can develop their capacity to understand their client.

Empathy has both cognitive and emotional components, the latter of which Yale psychologist Paul Bloom[15] notes limits its usefulness and can lend to the dangerous reinforcement of biases. "Cognitive empathy" allows for the understanding of another's circumstances without having to actually emotionally "feel their pain." For instance, doctors should rationally care about their patients, but should not become emotionally empathetic. Bloom advocates a "rational compassion" that brings an aware, reflective attitude of affiliation that holds out for skeptical consideration of knee-jerk or biased reactions (see Figure 1.2).

A growing amount of research over the past few years indicates that empathy might even create boundaries by hardening our ability to see all sides of an issue or situation. Scholars hypothesize that the strength of empathizing with one side—which may be attractive or similar to the empathizer—may actually create antipathy toward the "out side." The fear is that empathy could be "tearing us apart."[16] One recently published study[17] showed that those who scored high on an empathy scale also had higher levels of "affective polarization"—the difference between the rating they gave their political party as opposed to the opposing party—and were more prone to schadenfreude, or taking pleasure at the other side's misfortune.

FIGURE 1.2 ■ **"Rational Compassion": Empathizing With Your Clients and Coworkers**

Here are some steps you can take to build empathy with your work colleagues and clients:

- **Listen actively.** If we focus on clarifying what we see or believe is needed rather than judging, then we can move more quickly toward broadly applicable solutions. Active listening implies we are paying attention to others and can repeat, paraphrase using similar words, or reflect on what we have heard using our own words to express key messages.

- **Take personal responsibility for improvement.** Those who are "stress hardy" exhibit three characteristics:

  1. Commitment (rather than alienation) that gives passion and purpose to their lives

  2. Perception of challenges as opportunities

  3. Willingness to devote time and energy to situations over which they have some control or influence

- **Ask clear, forward-looking questions about things that matter.** Try to define the problem or issue with the following questions:

  1. Address a specific need, containing the actionable "So What." What will someone do with your solution and what is the impact?

  2. Include the specifics of the issue: Who, What, How, When, Where, and Why. Think about the difference between process and substance in your solutions: Will things be better by doing them in a different way, by looking at the problem differently based on the data, or both?

  3. Fit into one sentence. Can you capture the bottom line in a simple, crisp sentence?

  4. Have an answer, at least theoretically, or options. The best questions are puzzles and not mysteries. For example, what I had for breakfast this morning is a puzzle that someone else can figure out. It happened; there are clues. What I will have for breakfast a week from now is a mystery because even I don't know. Do you need to consider or present alternative explanations?

- **Track and collect accurate data.** Ensure that you have good sources for your data. Read the speeches or statements from leaders within your organization or that relate to your problems; be familiar with the laws, regulations, and policies that underlie your organization's operations; and pay attention to the surveys, assessments, and reports that provide the data that can strengthen your arguments.

Source: Suzanne Kobasa, Salvatore R. Maddi, and Stephen Kahn, "Hardiness and Health: A Prospective Study," *Journal of Personality and Social Psychology* 42 (January 1982): 168–177.

Assessing Client Needs

The best technique for gauging your clients' needs is to put yourself in their shoes through Red Hat Analysis,[18] focusing on their responsibilities and interests. The more you internalize their priorities, burdens, and goals, the better you can discern the questions they need addressed and target your analytic responses. The following questions can help guide your assessment:

1. *What is their role?* Your clients' responsibilities are the most important input to determining the analytic products that will help them do their jobs. Do they deal with specific issues or geographic areas? What kind of analysis are they looking for—a compendium of facts, an evaluation of developments, or a projection of future trends? Who do they report to, what decisions must they make, and who do they serve? In Washington, for example, senior government officials respond to their cabinet secretary, the White House, Congress, and the media. In corporations, executives may have to respond to stockholders or product consumers as well as to their own chain of command.

2. *What are their interests?* Be alert for hints about client interests in all your interactions, meetings, and readings. Are they seeking specific data that support their current policies or asking you to help frame the problem for them? If you are fortunate to have firsthand contact with your clients, they may tell you about their interests. More likely, you will have to figure it out by reaching out to their staff, briefers, or your chain of command. You can learn a lot by reading press reports, congressional testimony, websites, and other source and analytic reports. Once you know the decision-maker's interest, you can determine why the issue is important; whether the issue is an opportunity, threat, or decision point; and how best to shape your response.

> "Twenty-first century analysts will need to become less independent and neutral in favor of greater tailoring to customer needs."
>
> —Carmen Medina
> "What to Do When Traditional Models Fail: The Coming
> Revolution in Intelligence Analysis"[19]

Calendars are an excellent source of information about what is driving clients' immediate concerns. Are they preparing for a meeting or trip or for negotiations rather than just following an issue? How does your analysis affect those preparations?

Your analysis should focus on clients' core interests while addressing other concerns in the broader context. Some argue that analysts' focus should be on the specific, hard questions of their primary clients rather than on simply tracking developments on their account. This means analysts would start their days by reviewing feedback and tasking from clients rather than first reading the morning traffic.[20]

3. *What is their expertise?* Understanding the depth of clients' knowledge of the topic is critical in crafting analytic responses. This level of knowledge

will determine whether terms need definition, how much evidence is needed to support claims and judgments, whether historical details should be included, and how much context is necessary. For example, clients who are already experts in their fields require only quick turnaround information about a new development. In these instances, analysts need to focus on how they can best add value in an era of information abundance. Other clients are generalists who will need more context and often a full introduction to an unfamiliar topic.

In some cases, your clients may have firsthand knowledge of a situation or a personality that varies from what you portray in your analysis. You should expect probing questions and disagreements from your most knowledgeable clients. Prepare for this by ensuring that your sources and judgments are carefully selected and accurately portrayed (see Chapter 6 for dealing with analytic disagreements).

In both situations, informing the policymaker or decision maker about unknowns, uncertainties, and contradictory information is essential to meeting the client's needs. As Carmen Medina, a former deputy director for intelligence at the Central Intelligence Agency (CIA), noted, "The analysts' real value increasingly will lie in identifying discontinuities that shatter precedents and trends."[21] Moreover, client needs and preferences change rapidly, as does the environment in which analysis operates, requiring analysts to constantly reassess how best they can respond to clients' needs.

4. *How do they absorb information?* The President's Daily Brief, produced by the Director of National Intelligence, for example, changes with each president to reflect the chief executive's information-processing preferences, tolerance for detail, and interest in intelligence. Does the client prefer to receive information written or orally? Should the product be short or long, in paragraphs or bullets, with few or many graphics, delivered in hard copy, on a tablet, or as an infographic?

5. *What is the interaction with your organization?* Did the client ask a question? Are you trying to educate, convince, or alert? Is there an action to be taken or options to be considered? Intelligence analysts in national security do not formulate or recommend policy but should be aware of circumstances in which they can alert their clients to opportunities for beneficial action or avoidance of danger.

Analysts should always seek to know the circumstance for a request, even if they do not get a clear response in return. It helps to know if the client is responding to a crisis, a strategic challenge, or an ongoing issue. Are requesters seeking to learn more about a new situation, or are they already well informed and just checking to ensure they have full command of the most recent facts and analysis before making a decision?

If you are concerned that the question you have been given is poorly formulated or just plain wrong, seek clarification before drafting your response. Often a question will be reinterpreted or revised multiple times as it moves down the chain of command. Try to reach back to the initial source—preferably directly or through institutional channels if necessary—to seek clarification. Answering the wrong question is a waste of everyone's time.

6. *What other sources of information do they consult?* Do the clients read specific publications or watch certain news channels? To which blogs or news feeds do they subscribe? Do they have experts in your field on their staff who filter or explain your analysis for them? This is a particular challenge for analysts who write on technical topics; your clients may rely on others to interpret your material rather than reading it themselves.

Do you have concerns about the sensitivity of your information and how it might be used? Could that have an impact on your analysis or use of sources?

7. *What will your client do with your information and insights?* The actions that will be taken based on your work help determine the questions you will answer, the level of detail you will include, and the frequency or turnaround for your products. Imagine what reactions you would have if you were in the client's job receiving your analysis and consider what actions you might take. You can categorize these projected actions along a set of dimensions, such as *inaction* to *action, indirect* to *direct,* or *positive* to *negative,* to develop a second sense for the potential impact your analysis might have. Your understanding of the broader context within which you perform your analysis (see Chapter 3) will improve your ability to empathize with your clients and craft products that respond to their needs.

Do not get swept away in the quest for the perfect prediction; we are convinced this is an exercise in futility. The principal goal of analysis is to properly frame the problem, accept that multiple outcomes are possible, and help the decision maker better understand the underlying forces, factors, or key drivers that are most likely to shape the final outcome. Only if policymakers and decision makers are armed with that knowledge can they perform their roles effectively.

Figure 1.3 provides a simple client checklist analysts can use to ensure that they have considered all aspects of a client's needs. The checklist also helps focus attention on what matters most and to generate a rigorous response to the task at hand.

8. *Can you bound the problem to tell clients what they do not need to worry about?* Analysts often ignore the strategy of focusing clients on what is most important by telling them what is *not* important. Busy people value being told what issues will not require their attention. Some of the most positive feedback the authors received from senior policymakers at the cabinet and subcabinet levels came when we provided analysis on why a government was unlikely to fall or a particular situation was unlikely to devolve into a crisis.

FIGURE 1.3 ■ Knowing Your Client Checklist

The following questions will help you explore how best to serve your ultimate client:

1. Who is the key person for whom the product is being developed?

2. Will this product answer the question the client asked? Did the client ask the right question or is it more important to place your answer in a broader context?

3. What is the most important message to give this client? What value-added contribution can you make?

4. How is the client expected to use this information?

5. How much time does the client have to digest your product?

6. What format would convey the information most effectively?

7. Is it possible to capture the essence of your message in one or a few key graphics?

8. What is the client's level of tolerance for technical language and detail? Can you provide details in backup materials, graphics, or an annex?

9. Does distribution of this document need to be restricted? What classification or handling caveats are most appropriate? Should you prepare different products at different levels of restriction?

10. Would the client expect you to reach out to other experts for assistance in answering this question? If so, how would you flag their contribution in presenting your product?

11. To whom might the client turn for other views on this topic? What data or analysis might others provide that could influence how the client will react to what you are preparing?

12. What perspectives do other interested parties have on this issue? What are the responsibilities of the other parties?

Source: Copyright 2020 Globalytica, LLC. All Rights Reserved.

Identifying Key Clients

When starting to work on a specific project, list your principal client and what he or she might do as a result of reading your analysis. This will start you on the right foot by establishing a clear focus up front and enabling detailed discussions about your analytic plan of attack with your supervisors, reviewers, and mentors.

In some cases, your analysis will be geared toward serving a variety of clients. At the Department of Homeland Security, for example, analysts usually have to address the needs of several very different clients—the secretary of Homeland Security, state and local law enforcement officials, private industry, and their Intelligence Community counterparts. A single document sent to a senior decision maker who is looking for strategic perspective but also to a local law enforcement body that requires tactical information to perform its mission would end up frustrating both clients as each would receive substantial information of little value to them (see Figure 1.4). In these circumstances, analysts should consider drafting two or more distinct products tailored to the specific needs of each client or customer set.

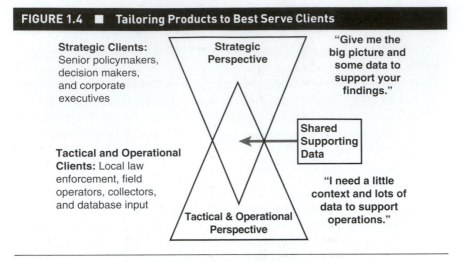

FIGURE 1.4 ■ Tailoring Products to Best Serve Clients

Strategic Clients: Senior policymakers, decision makers, and corporate executives

Strategic Perspective

"Give me the big picture and some data to support your findings."

Shared Supporting Data

Tactical and Operational Clients: Local law enforcement, field operators, collectors, and database input

Tactical & Operational Perspective

"I need a little context and lots of data to support operations."

Source: Copyright 2020 Globalytica, LLC. All Rights Reserved.

In general, researching, drafting, and sourcing different products for each client or customer set can be accomplished most efficiently as a parallel process. Simultaneous production of tailored products helps the author address the specific—and sometimes unique—needs of each client and helps ensure that each client receives the information that is of greatest value to him or her.

Expectations for Feedback

Busy clients are consumed with responding to multiple demands on their time and are focused on their problems rather than on providing feedback to their analytic support. Many analytic organizations structure themselves to solicit and receive feedback from readers of assessments and periodic publications. But analysts rarely get as much feedback as they would like, particularly from their most senior clients. Formal surveys that seek periodic, written feedback have rarely proved to be effective and reliance on an interviewing process can be overly time-consuming. Two mechanisms that offer more promise are for the analyst to attend regularly scheduled staff meetings hosted by the client or to arrange for periodic briefings of the client. In some circumstances, an informal dialogue can be pursued over email, but in-person contact almost always ensures more effective communication while building trust.

We urge analysts to keep in mind that our brains are wired to overestimate the impact of our analysis on others and for decision makers to underestimate the value of analytic support of their decision processes. Be thrilled when you get a compliment and pleased when you have evidence your analyses have been read. If you put yourselves in your busy clients' shoes, you will understand why their feedback can be sporadic and sparse. Your objective should be to provide analysis of sufficient value that your clients keep coming back asking for more.

KEY TAKEAWAYS

- When starting work on a new issue or account, analysts should take a moment to identify the client base and how the various users will apply and benefit from the analysis.

- These few minutes of reflection will result in a more focused product that will move more quickly through the editing and coordination processes.

- Busy clients have limited time to read analysis, are dependent on analytic products to help focus their attention on what is important, and expect transparency in facts and sourcing.

- Analysts can build empathy by understanding their clients' roles, interests, expertise, information processing, and predilection for action.

- The goal of analysis is to properly frame the problem, accept that multiple outcomes are possible, and help the decision maker better understand the underlying forces, factors, or key drivers that are most likely to shape the final outcome.

- Analysts should look for ways to tell clients what is not important and what they do not need to worry about.

- Specific projects should be directed to a principal client. If analysts need to support a varied client set on the same issue, they should consider simultaneous researching, drafting, and sourcing of parallel products tailored to each client or customer set.

- Analysts should explore ways to establish periodic contact with key clients to obtain effective informal feedback.

CONSIDERING THE CASE STUDY

Review Case Study I, "Uncharted Territory: Conflict, Competition, or Collaboration in the Arctic?"

- Do anticipated developments in the Arctic pose a serious threat—or offer significant opportunities—to the international community? To the organization that you work for?

- Who would you consider the principal client or clients in preparing a report on the future of the Arctic?

1. What would be the most important issues for senior policymakers to consider?

2. What would be the most important issues for senior defense planners to consider?

- Should the issue be posed as a threat, an opportunity, a key decision point, or some combination of these?

- Are there critical unknowns, uncertainties, or contradictory information that should be highlighted?

NOTES

1. Throughout this chapter—and this book—we have opted for the term *client* as opposed to *customer*. *Client* infers an established relationship and some degree of interaction between the producer and consumer of the analysis. *Customer* commonly describes those who simply receive products and have

little interaction with the producer. *Client* is a more appropriate term for a service-based industry and *customer* for a manufacturing-based culture. We firmly believe that analytic support entities are most successful when they are client centered and service oriented.

2. The information used in this chapter is adapted from Pherson Associates training materials (www.pherson.org).

3. Email exchange with Jorhena Thomas, May 3, 2019.

4. Jon Kabat-Zinn, "The Dharma Foundations of Mindfulness in the Mainstream: The Art and the Science of MBSR and Other Mindfulness-Based Programs" (presentation at Mahachulalongkornrajavidyalaya University, Bangkok, Thailand, May 14, 2019), https://www.youtube.com/watch?v=NH1K2BSQw9o.

5. Kabat-Zinn, "The Dharma Foundations of Mindfulness."

6. Jon Kabat-Zinn, *Full Catastrophe Living: Using the Wisdom of Your Body and Mind to Face Stress, Pain, and Illness*, rev. ed. (New York: Bantam Books, 2013).

7. Stephen Covey, *The Speed of Trust: The One Thing That Changes Everything* (New York: Simon & Shuster, 2006).

8. Covey, *The Speed of Trust.*

9. Malcolm Gladwell, *Talking to Strangers* (New York: Little, Brown, 2019).

10. David DeSteno, *The Truth About Trust: How It Determines Success in Life, Love, Learning, and More* (New York: Penguin, 2014).

11. Carol S. Dweck, *Mindset: The New Psychology of Success* (New York: Random House Digital, 2008).

12. Allan R. Cohen and David L. Bradford, *Influence Without Authority*, 3rd ed., (Hoboken, NJ: John Wiley, 2017).

13. Cohen and Bradford, *Influence Without Authority.*

14. Cohen and Bradford.

15. Paul Bloom, *Against Empathy: The Case for Rational Compassion* (New York: HarperCollins, 2016).

16. Robert Wright, "Empathy Is Tearing Us Apart," *Wired*, November 9, 2019, https://www.wired.com/story/empathy-is-tearing-us-apart/.

17. Elizabeth N. Simas, Scott Clifford, and Justin H. Kirkland, "How Empathic Concern Fuels Political Polarization," *American Political Science Review* 114, no. 1 (February 2020): 258–269, https://doi.org/10.1017/S0003055419000534.

18. A description of the Red Hat reframing technique can be found in Randolph H. Pherson and Richards J. Heuer Jr., *Structured Analytic Techniques for Intelligence Analysis*, 3rd ed. (Washington, DC: CQ Press/SAGE, 2021), 198–202.

19. Carmen A. Medina, "What to Do When Traditional Models Fail: The Coming Revolution in Intelligence Analysis," *Studies in Intelligence* 46, no. 3 (2002), https://www.cia.gov/library/center-for-the-study-of-intelligence/csi-publications/csi-studies/studies/vol46no3/article03.html.

20. Medina, "When Traditional Models Fail."

21. Medina.

2 WHAT ARE THE KEY QUESTIONS?

SETTING THE STAGE

Most poorly written analysis lacks focus. The reader is left wondering, "What is the point of the product? Where are we going with this story? What is the thesis or the key argument?" A well-crafted analysis is tightly focused on a single primary message. The best way to formulate that message is to ensure that it responds to your clients' needs, answering thought-provoking questions that they are—or should be—asking. Questions stimulate and guide the analytic process, engaging and enabling interaction among analysts, reviewers, and clients to develop a message that will hit the target. Quite simply, questions beg for answers.

Articles on fast-breaking events should be directed to answering a single key intelligence or policy question. More extensive and less time-sensitive articles should be designed to answer a key question and several closely related subsidiary questions. In the government, Key Intelligence Questions (KIQs) guide analysts in their research, monitoring, and analytic production. These questions usually are more general and overarching than the ones you will generate to focus your products because they are used for a variety of purposes, including resource allocation and collection priorities. Nonetheless, they provide a good starting point for developing the questions and issues that you will address in your products. In business, analytic products should focus on a specific, well-defined issue.

> "In order for answers to become clear, the questions have to be clear."
>
> —Abdulkarim Soroush, Islamic Philosopher[1]

LOOKING MORE DEEPLY

Often the key intelligence or policy question is provided by the client or your boss. In this case, you must understand exactly what is needed. Do not be shy about seeking clarification if the question appears overly broad or poorly formulated. For example, a question that asks for "everything you know" about a particular subject is a disservice to both the analyst and the requester. These questions usually mask much more specific needs, but the requester has not had the time or does not have the knowledge to research, think, or articulate these needs.

You can save yourself, the requester, and all the editors substantial time over the long term by going back to determine exactly what these needs may be. Formulating a choice of questions that you believe might be applicable can spur requesters' thinking; yes-or-no answers are much easier to elicit than waiting for clients to have time to work their way through the problem themselves.

In some circumstances, you will find the question is specific, but the assumptions driving the question are unsupported. This places the analyst in a more difficult position. For example, prior to the US invasion of Iraq in 2003, intelligence analysts were frequently asked, "Where are the weapons of mass destruction (WMD) hidden in Iraq?" This question assumed that the weapons did exist—an assumption that later proved to be false. If, in this instance, the analyst was uncertain the weapons existed, the best strategy would have been to place the original question in a broader context by rephrasing the question to read, "What is the status of the WMD program in Iraq?" In this way, the analyst still responds to the question posed by the requester but does so in a way that offers additional perspective on the issue.

If direct clarification from the requester is not possible, then the analyst's duty is to rephrase the question in a more meaningful way. Just as when you identified your client base (see Chapter 1), this is best accomplished by conducting your own Red Hat Analysis exercise[2] by putting yourself in the shoes of the requester and asking, "What exactly do I want to find out? What is my primary concern or interest?"

To do this well, particularly if you are new to the area of interest, you will have prepared for the Red Hat Analysis by

- *Asking essential and foundational questions to understand your account.*[3]

  o **Essential questions** capture the core purposes for your analytic responsibilities. Are certain nations planning or carrying out disinformation campaigns against the United States? Are newly developed weapons systems able to harm targeted adversaries? Is the risk acceptable for your company to build a new facility or complete an agreement to work in countries undergoing political change?

  o **Foundational questions** are the building blocks that must be probed to enable you to answer the essential questions. These questions tend to be open-ended or if closed-ended, then the "yes/no" or factual answer suggests the need for elaboration. Foundational questions provide the basis for research, information collection, and monitoring: Which nations are suspected of carrying out disinformation campaigns? What tactics are they using? What are the targets? What do these elements tell us about the nations' intentions and objectives?

- *Scanning the environment to find out what others think about the subject.* What issues surface repeatedly in the media or government publications? What can you learn from agendas or notes from decision maker meetings? On what issues are other intelligence and policy organizations focusing?

- *Identifying trends.* What can you learn from available data sets like economic indicators, crime statistics, episodes of civil unrest, health statistics, or environmental indicators?

- *Engaging in Outside-In Thinking.*[4] How will developments outside an organization or not directly related to an issue affect it? Consider, for example, how the invention of cell phones and the internet have impacted our personal and professional lives—from making contact to accessing knowledge to shopping and elections. By the same token, developments such as in artificial intelligence and machine learning merit the attention of all analysts who seek to understand the impact of "outside" drivers on "inside" issues.

- *Considering the "white space."* White space in publication design is empty or negative space that focuses visual attention on what is there. In so doing, it can help aim your attention toward what is known and what is important that is missing, poorly articulated, or not yet defined. White space provides the opportunity to reflect on what is missing or could be reframed to be more relevant and valuable to your client. Analysts then can help bridge differences or advance understanding by addressing questions in new or different ways.

- *Brainstorming key questions.* MIT Leadership Center executive director Hal Gregersen advocates brainstorming with colleagues for questions instead of for answers[5] to energize thinking and yield unexpected insights. For intelligence organizations, this is a common technique for rethinking the KIQs that guide their research programs. The brainstorming can help identify better ways to frame issues, identify new or evolving drivers, and get beyond biases or established ways of approaching the issues.

Five Characteristics of a Good Question

A good intelligence or policy question should require deeper levels of thinking that go beyond merely summarizing surface-level facts (see the discussion of the Analytic Spectrum in Chapter 4 that defines four levels of thinking).[6] The question should be[7]

1. *Relevant.* The question should focus on that aspect of an emerging issue, problem, or challenge that is of greatest interest to the client. Has recent reporting signaled the possibility of a new challenge or opportunity emerging? For example, are recent technological developments likely to drastically alter the market for your product? Does social media contain indications of looming political instability and social unrest that could undercut (or support) the client's key policy objectives?

2. *Timely.* Is there an action-forcing event that warrants alerting the client to this issue at this time? For example, does the client need to know something before meeting with someone in the coming days? Or before attending a meeting to set

policy on this issue? Have we gained critical new insights about the negotiating position of an adversary or a competitor? Will the new development require that action be taken to preempt an undesirable condition before it is too late? Is there a critical time frame outside of which the issue loses relevance?

3. *Precisely worded.* Is the issue framed precisely, in context, and with syntax the client will understand? Is the question stated clearly with sufficient focus to enable the client to take action?

4. *Actionable.* What are the implications of this issue for the client? What is the "So What"? Will this issue require action by the client? Are there obvious implications if the client acts or does not act? Will the client or his or her organization be harmed? Does attention need to be focused on what actions should be taken to prevent or mitigate risk? Does the client have the power to influence the outcome significantly? Is the response posed in such a way that it offers several possible courses of action and identifies opportunities but does not prescribe policy or suggest which option is preferable?

5. *Answerable in more than one way.* Is the question posed in such a way that the answer has more than one credible alternative or course of action? Can the question be answered by a range of possible hypotheses and not simply by a yes-or-no response? Is the question devoid of any hidden assumptions that might lead the client to take an ill-advised action not supported by the facts? Are there key uncertainties that could greatly affect the outcome?

Refining the Question

Helping clients frame their question to inform their decision making is a key analytic task.[8] If the analyst does not understand exactly what information is being sought by the client and interprets the question too broadly, then substantial resources will be wasted and the client will be disappointed with the response. Analysts should consider the following questions when framing a question prior to writing their paper:

- Is it clear what would constitute an answer to the question?

- Is it obvious what information is needed to answer the question? If not, try to clarify exactly what information or analytic judgment the client seeks.

- Is the client really interested in something else but has cast the question too broadly or narrowly, assuming the analyst knows what is being sought?

- Are there any hidden assumptions underlying the question?

- Does the client's decision depend on whether the answer meets a threshold or a set of thresholds rather than a precise answer? If so, frame your response appropriately.

For open-ended questions, some of the best techniques to use in preparing a response are Multiple Hypothesis Generation, Quadrant Crunching™, What If? Analysis, and

Foresight analysis. For yes-or-no questions, techniques to consider include the Key Assumptions Check, Structured Analogies, and Analysis of Competing Hypotheses.

The Five Ws and an H

A highly effective strategy for identifying the key intelligence or policy question is to ask the six questions often used by journalists: Who, What, When, Where, Why, and How. Practical experience in using this strategy has shown that a better order for asking these questions is Who, What, How, When, Where, and Why. We recommend changing the order for two reasons: (1) The new order best follows the structure of a standard English sentence, and (2) the "What" and the "How" often overlap or are used to describe similar aspects of the issue.

Techniques that use the so-called Five-Ws-and-an-H strategy include Circleboarding™, Starbursting, and Mind Mapping.[9] Each technique enables you to explore all aspects of a problem or an issue. Jot down two or three responses to each of the questions and then go back and assess which set of responses is most deserving of attention. Prioritize the six sets of responses and reframe the original question to address the set of responses that was given the highest priority.

The Circleboarding™ technique adds a seventh question: "So What?" (see Figure 2.1). The inclusion of this question stimulates discussion beyond just consolidating what is known by spurring the analyst to identify weak points in the group's knowledge and encouraging discussion of what assumptions are being made.

These processes are particularly helpful when the question asked by your client appears too broad or too encompassing. In conducting this simple exercise, note what types of information are available to answer each question. Also consider whether any major information gaps exist that would require more research or the tasking of others to collect more information.

FIGURE 2.1 ■ The Circleboarding™ Technique

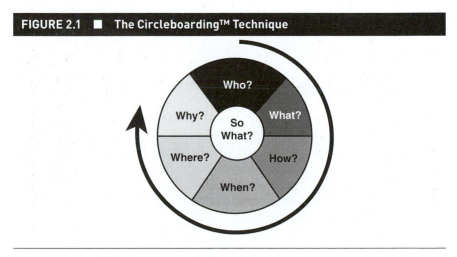

Source: Copyright 2020 Globalytica, LLC. All Rights Reserved.

The Question Method

The Question Method (see Figure 2.2) is another simple technique analysts can use to organize a long-term research project or a short-fused memo.[10] It helps analysts structure a paper by focusing first on the question of greatest interest to the client or customer set and then on subsequent questions in descending order of priority.

One of the greatest strengths of the Question Method is that it eliminates inclusion of any information that is not deemed to be of direct interest to the client. By organizing the paper around a small number of key questions, the time needed to edit and review the paper is significantly reduced. We will build on the Question Method as a component of the AIMS (**A**udience, **I**ssue or intelligence question, **M**essage, and **S**toryline) approach to conceptualizing a product discussed in Chapter 4.

FIGURE 2.2 ■ Using Key Questions to Organize Your Product

1. Identify the key issue or problem your principal client or client set is currently wrestling with or likely to confront in the near future.

   • Remember that clients at different levels are likely to be dealing with different types of decisions on the issue.

2. Brainstorm a list of focused key questions relating to that topic that the client is likely to ask or that the client anticipates will be asked of her or him.

   • Answering a focused question that clients are currently asking increases the chances your product will be useful. It will have immediate appeal.

   • Answering a set of focused questions is easier than generating an overall assessment on a topic from scratch.

3. Add any questions to the list that the client may not be asking but probably should be.

   • Draw on your expertise and analytic tools to add any questions that the client—because of more limited time and knowledge of the topic—has not thought about yet.

4. Select the questions on the list that you can answer or to which you can contribute a useful perspective.

   • If you cannot answer an essential question, consider starting work to get the answer.

   • If you have received a direct question from a client, be sure to include this question near the top of your list.

5. Prioritize and organize the list of questions to guide your collection, collaboration, and research—and the outline of the finished product.

   • Organize (order) the questions into a story line that will most effectively present the information and analysis, starting with the issues of greatest concern or interest to the client.

   • Your organized set of questions now becomes the outline to begin researching and drafting the finished product.

   • Remember that the questions may change as your research and drafting progresses.

KEY TAKEAWAYS

- A well-crafted analytic product contains a single, primary message that answers a key intelligence or policy question.

- Analysts can help clients by using questions as a means of engagement to determine if they have correctly determined their needs. A Red Hat Analysis is one technique that enables analysts to put themselves "in the client's shoes."

- Analysts can best prepare for an effective Red Hat Analysis by asking "essential" and "foundational" questions to frame the analytic need; scanning the environment to understand what others think about the issue; identifying trends from available data; engaging in Outside-In Thinking; considering the "white space" of what is missing,

poorly articulated, or not yet defined; and brainstorming key questions with colleagues.

- A good intelligence or policy question is relevant, timely, precisely worded, actionable, and answerable in more than one way.

- The journalists' list of Who, What, How, When, Where, Why, and our addition of the question "So What?" provides an efficient schema for exploring the key intelligence or policy questions on which to focus an analytic product.

- The Question Method is a fast and effective technique for organizing a paper that addresses a client's key concerns in priority order.

CONSIDERING THE CASE STUDY

Review Case Study III, "Blackout on the Eastern Seaboard!"

- What are the key questions a senior policymaker is likely to ask of energy infrastructure and national security officials when fashioning his or her initial public response to the blackout? Formulate "essential" and "foundational" questions and ensure that the responses satisfy the five characteristics of a good question.

- What are the key questions those responsible for restoring power are

likely to ask about the event? Formulate "essential" and "foundational" questions and ensure that the responses satisfy the five characteristics of a good question.

- How would you use the Five-Ws-and-an-H strategy to identify the key question for a senior decision maker?

- How would you organize a paper on the implications of the blackout using the Question Method?

NOTES

1. Ali Asghar Seyyedabadi, "The Muddled Dream of Returning to Tradition: An Interview With Abdulkarim Soroush," *E'temad-e Mellli*, November 19, 2006, translated

from Persian by Nilou Mobasser, www.drsoroush.com.

2. For more information about the Red Hat Analysis technique, see

Randolph H. Pherson and Richards J. Heuer Jr., *Structured Analytic Techniques for Intelligence Analysis*, 3rd ed. (Washington, DC: CQ Press/SAGE, 2021), 198–203.

3. Development of essential and foundational questions is adapted from Pherson Associates training materials (www.pherson.org).

4. For more information about the Outside-In Thinking technique, see Pherson and Heuer, *Structured Analytic Techniques*, 191–194.

5. Hal Gregersen, *Questions Are the Answer: A Breakthrough Approach to Your Most Vexing Questions at Work and in Life* (New York: HarperCollins, 2018).

6. Many books on critical thinking, particularly in the educational domain, use Bloom's Taxonomy to describe levels of cognitive processes. These abilities include Knowledge (recalling facts, opinions, and concepts), Comprehension (interpreting information in one's own words), Application (applying learning to a new situation), Analysis (determining internal relationships), Evaluation (making judgments using criteria and standards), and Creation/Synthesis (linking facts into a coherent whole or new understanding). Anderson's revised taxonomy (Remembering, Understanding, Applying, Analyzing, Evaluating, Creating) renames the categories as gerunds and identifies Creating as a category of its own, dropping the concept of Synthesis. See Lorin W. Anderson and David R. Krathwohl, eds., *A Taxonomy for Learning, Teaching, and Assessing: A Revision of Bloom's Taxonomy of Educational Objectives* (New York: Addison Wesley Longman, 2001).

7. This checklist is adapted from Pherson Associates training materials (www.pherson.org).

8. Much of the information for this section was taken from "Selecting an Analytic Technique or Approach, Step One: Refining the Question," distributed by the United Kingdom's Professional Head of Defence Intelligence Analysis, UK Ministry of Defence. The material is used with their permission.

9. The Circleboarding™ technique is discussed in Pherson and Heuer, *Structured Analytic Techniques*, 101–103. Starbursting is discussed on 104–106. Mind Mapping is discussed on 106–112.

10. This technique was first developed by David Terry; it was revised by Randolph H. Pherson in 2010 and was incorporated in Pherson Associates and Globalytica course materials used to train analysts in the United States and overseas.

3 WHAT IS THE BROADER CONTEXT FOR THE ANALYSIS?

SETTING THE STAGE

Context is shorthand for saying you have taken into account the operational environment in which you are working. If, for instance, you write about thefts of railroad track keys as a potential terrorist act that presents vulnerabilities for homeland security and you do not mention that these keys—which secure track switching connections—have been popular with collectors of train memorabilia for decades, you have taken your data out of context. At best, you can mislead your readers or focus their attention on the wrong topics. At worst, you are "cherry picking" data to reach conclusions that are incorrect or will later prove to be wrong.

Intelligence analysis—indeed, analysis in any domain—is a service. Your job is to help your clients make the leap from reviewing available data to understanding what it means in the context of their area of responsibility. Clients then can best decide what to do to anticipate or deal with problems. Your analysis helps them prioritize how to spend their time and resources to deal with or head off problems. You must not waste their time by telling them what they already know or present them with only what they want to hear. If you are alert to the broader context, you will adapt your work to the varied interests of a wide array of clients and customer sets.

LOOKING MORE DEEPLY

Richards J. Heuer Jr. in the classic *Psychology of Intelligence Analysis*[1] describes the constraints analysts face as a result of limitations in their working memories, suggesting the best way to cope with complexity and reduce errors is to create explicitly defined representations of the problem. These structures clarify and frame your thinking to bring consistency and replicability to observations, insights, and judgments. They also make your thinking visible and transparent so that others can review and assess it. Two of the most common ways to do this are to (1) decompose the issue so its component parts can be considered separately and (2) visualize the parts on paper or a computer screen.

The most basic critical thinking skill is to resist plunging into your project without taking time to scope out a preliminary structure that organizes the knowledge you have and will be accumulating (see Figure 3.1). Cognitive psychologists, ranging from Frederic Bartlett in the 1930s to Gary Klein and Daniel Kahneman today, have written extensively about the explanatory structures we naturally create to account for the data, beliefs, and other "environmental abstractions" in our daily lives. We try to find or generate a story, script, map, or other mechanism that makes sense of disparate and

FIGURE 3.1 ■ Stop! Frames, Actors, Forces

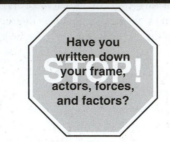

sometimes conflicting data. People primarily rely on "just-in-time" mental models that can change over time, but this is a dangerous practice for professional analysts who are subject to standards of accountability, consistency over time, and accuracy. Klein et al. explain, "The data/frame concept is that a frame is needed to efficiently and effectively understand data; attempting to review data without introducing frames is unrealistic and unproductive."[2]

> The purpose of a frame is to define the elements of the situation, describe the significance of these elements, describe their relationship to each other, filter out irrelevant messages, and highlight relevant messages.
>
> —Gary Klein et al.
> "A Data/Frame Theory of Sensemaking"[3]

Be Aware of Your Mental Model

Sensemaking is the simultaneous automatic process by which our brains fit data into a frame or mental model and fit a frame around the data.[4] When the results match, we have made sense of the situation and move on, using the frame and its routines to guide us in interpreting and taking action until incompatible data again challenges our frame. Several key precepts underlie how we take advantage of frames and sensemaking in our analysis:[5]

- *Unconscious thinking.* Even deliberate thinking is influenced by unconscious processes. Klein et al. describe the relationship between conscious and unconscious thinking as a continuum with pattern matching at the conscious end and frame comparison at the unconscious extreme.

- *Initial frame formation.* In new or surprising situations, we form initial frames based on a few key pieces of data. If not created externally, researchers speculate that most people rely on at most three or four anchors or key pieces of data from which to create a frame. Flawed analysis results when one of the early anchors is not accurate.

- *Early articulation.* Early commitment to a hypothesis or recognition of a frame is "inevitable and advantageous" because it focuses information gathering and sets expectations that can be challenged by incongruous data. The challenge is to have the mental agility to adjust the initial frame if the new data no longer support it.

- *Frame adjustment.* People can fixate on a frame or go to the opposite extreme and passively receive data without a conscious frame. In the latter case, researchers discovered that those with markedly "open minds" were likely to miss significant problems as they developed.

- *Role of data.* More data does not always lead to better analysis. In fact, the opposite can be the case. Researchers note that trouble arises when the data have too many meanings rather than too few, supporting Richards Heuer's contention that analysts need help in evaluating and interpreting data, not acquiring more.[6]

- *Individual perspectives.* Everyone's frames are different depending on the information available, the quality and variety of frames typically employed, and each individual's condition—including motivation and health.

- *Expertise.* Experts and neophytes use the same reasoning processes, but experts have greater experience and can articulate multiple ways of getting things done; this gives them a richer set of frames from which to select. They also have tested and rejected enough information that their frames are usually more sophisticated but still subject to error since no set of mental models is entirely accurate or complete.

In short, sensemaking sets largely unconscious parameters for the personal mental models on which we base our analysis. Understanding the precepts leads us to strategies for strengthening our frames by adding rigor, both in terms of the explicit outlining of the frame and alertness to the potential for adjustment to account for changing circumstances. This structured agility takes advantage of and develops our deliberative and intuitive thinking. It enables us to make best use of a full range of structured decision-making and problem-solving techniques without fencing ourselves into rigid models or encouraging us to forge deeper mental ruts. Concrete models play important roles in framing tactical, short-term tasks, particularly in crisis situations, but may not serve analysts well in ambiguous, rapidly changing situations over the longer term.

"Models are used so extensively in intelligence that analysts seldom give them much thought, even as they use them."

—Robert Clark
Intelligence Analysis: A Target-Centric Approach[7]

Another way of distinguishing mental models dates back to the ancient Greek poet Archilochus, who wrote, "A fox knows many important things but a hedgehog one important thing."[8] When applied to how we *think* as opposed to what we *know*, the implication is that hedgehogs see the world through one lens and may be prone to fit varying or anomalous data into their fixed conception of it. Foxes in knowing many things might be more agile in assessing data in multiple contexts but less likely to have clear overarching theories or concepts of how those things and concepts fit together.

Analysts can benefit from the efforts of several authors[9] who have catalogued from a range of disciplines some of what they find are the most useful mental models to sort, organize, and understand the world. Several were inspired by Berkshire Hathaway vice president and psychology buff Charlie Munger's reference in a 1995 speech[10] to the need for a "latticework of theory" to make "isolated facts" useful. Structured Analytic Techniques (SATs) give us steps to follow in increasing the rigor of our thinking. Much in the same way, mental models provide a type of map that helps us make sense of and navigate in a confusing and ambiguous world.

A key criterion for mental models is that they be useful. Sometimes this may require organizing data in more creative ways. For example, subway maps distort geographic reality to enable us to navigate the network of stations. Intelligence analysts need to be able both to try out different models to test that might be useful in a given situation and to build models that are accurate. If the information has to be "massaged" to illustrate a complex point or to spur more imaginative thinking, then it is incumbent on analysts to note that some data are incorrect.

Conceptual models are the tools analysts use to collaborate, communicate, and make sense of what is going on in their area of responsibility; they are the means by which analysts agree the system works. During the revision of this book, one of the authors participated in sessions where subject matter experts, information systems specialists, and analysts collaborated to create a conceptual model to reform personnel security processing. This required each to adapt their mental models to create a single one that could work for all stakeholders being granted access to US government assets. Robert Clark details several types of models most used in intelligence analysis,[11] such as targeting models, anticipatory models, systems performance and process models, network and link models, and geospatial models (see Chapter 7 for a discussion of conceptual models for intelligence analysis).

The interaction between mental models and conceptual models also helps explain how analysts work with automated tools. The conceptual model design for the system is based on the developer's mental model of how he or she believes the user will interact with it. If the designer gets it right, the system in theory will be intuitive and coherent enough for the users to adapt their mental models to the new way of doing business.[12] Failure can result in systems that are suboptimal, not used, or trashed.

As Artificial Intelligence (AI) capabilities transform the way we work, analysts must be ever more cognizant of the mental models they are bringing both to the issue being studied and to their understanding of how the AI system functions. Much of the attention of the human–machine partnership is focusing on the latter—how the human will know how to control the system, assessing whether the machine has erred, and whether to accept or override the system's recommendation.[13] We believe that

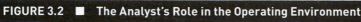

FIGURE 3.2 ■ The Analyst's Role in the Operating Environment

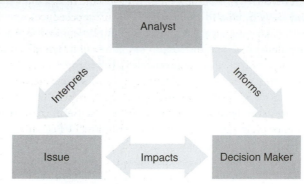

much more study and resources should be focused on training and developing analysts' mental models to preclude their being intimidated by the machine's prowess in handling vast amounts of data (see Chapter 7 for further discussion of analyst–machine interaction).

To begin to rise above analysts' limited perspectives, frames should focus on three key components that comprise the operating environment (see Figure 3.2):[14]

1. What is the issue?

2. What is the role of the analyst?

3. Who is the decision maker or the audience?

Scope Your Issue

Becoming oriented and reading up on a topic are optimal opportunities to create an explicit framework to structure your analytic research, thought, and production. All too often we surf and sample, thinking we are building expertise. In reality, we are wasting time by leaving the hard work up to our unconscious thought processes rather than giving our brain hints or guidelines about where we should be headed or where we need to end up. A key trap is to focus on a few anchors that may or may not be accurate.

Your goal should be to ground—or familiarize—yourself with the forces and personalities driving the situation, honing your ability to recognize what is known, unknown, and uncertain. This will keep you focused on the questions about which your audience wants clarity, thought, data, and foresight rather than being sidetracked into what is easily collected and answered. Prepare yourself to be able to diagnose problems and changes by paying attention to context, background, and characteristics that are important or distinguishing.

Structure your efforts using the questions listed below. Be sure to record your structure on paper or the computer so you can expand, adjust, and refine your frame as your knowledge base becomes more detailed and sophisticated. Visualizing your structure helps you clarify your anchors, think consciously about the quality of your thinking, and exercise your creativity through diagramming. Mind Maps and Concept Maps[15] can quickly and easily be created and retained for future reference. Consider starting out drawing by hand so you engage both sides of your brain in the design and text for the map. Your product can be transferred to an automated format using a variety of software packages, several of which are available as freeware.[16]

1.   *What or who are the key components or actors?*

An easy way to start is by doing what the dictionary definition of analysis tells us to do: Break a complex topic down into its component parts. We can brainstorm a list of key sectors or categories and then branch down into layers of subcategories. Whether the issue is defense, diplomacy, law enforcement, or technology, most decision makers focus on the key players: the organizations, groups, and individuals who run or influence the situation. What are their goals, capabilities, vital interests, and identity? Are there conflicts between individuals in groups or among groups in categories? The components can also be processes and functions that have to be mapped and understood.

Make sure your organizing framework covers the entire issue to protect against overlooking significant components or actors. A matrix or spreadsheet is an effective way to decompose and record critical information about your key components and actors. It provides a mechanism for organizing, collating, and comparing information from a variety of sources and holds the background data you need to characterize and understand the strengths, weaknesses, relationships, and influences of the sources.

2.   *What are the factors at play?*

The most prominent factors are likely to be found in the surrounding political, economic, military, security, cultural, demographic, and ideological aspects of an issue. Analysts in various fields have created mnemonics to guide their analyses of various environments. One of the most common is PEST, which signifies political, economic, social, or technological variables. Other analysts have combined PEST with legal, military, environmental, psychological, or demographic factors to form abbreviations such as STEEP, STEEP+2, STEEPLE, or PESTLE.[17] We recommend using STEMPLES+ (social, technological, economic, military, political, legal, environmental, and security plus possible additional factors such as demographic, psychological, cultural, or religious; see Figure 3.3).

You may find that you gravitate to those factors with which you are most familiar, but this could be a trap. Economists, for example, need to take the time to understand the impact of technology. Criminal justice majors need to become familiar with demographics and political change. Reaching outside your specific area of academic or practical expertise through internet research, outside reading, or active questioning of peers and experts should be part of your continuing development as an analyst.

These factors or driving forces are critical to understanding the dynamics that spur disruptive change and form the basis for Structured Analytic Techniques, such as Multiple Scenarios Generation.[18] Because the factors interact differently as a situation evolves—sometimes working together and at other times competing—analysts must recognize which ones are most influential at any particular moment.

FIGURE 3.3 ■ STEMPLES+		
	Social	Social cohesion, diversity, cohabitation
	Technological	Role of digitalization, internet of things, industry 4.0
	Economic	Macro-economic performance, jobs, education and training
	Military	External threats, power projection
	Political	Political culture, political climate, political debate, mainstreaming
	Legal	Legislation, constitutional issues (i.e., asylum, citizenship)
	Environmental	Global commons, natural resources, sustainability
	Security	Internal stability, securitization of migration debate
	Plus Other	Psychological (xenophobia, perceptions, stereotypes) Cultural (values, religion, habits, traditions) Demographic (population growth, youth bulge)

Source: Copyright 2020 Globalytica, LLC. All Rights Reserved.

Asking yourself "why" for several iterations will help you get to the root causes behind the drivers. For example, when conducting a Foresight analysis of the future of the Black Sea, participants listed Russia as a key driver. The facilitator asked them what made Russia a factor, and they responded, "It's their ability to project power and influence in the region." When next asked what most determined their capability to project influence, the answer was the strength of their economy. Then when asked what drives the economy, the response was Russia's oil and gas industry. This simple exercise derived a more meaningful key driver that is likely to influence future developments in the Black Sea region: Russia's continuing ability to leverage its fossil fuel industry to gain substantial export revenue for its economy.

As with the actors, decomposing the key components allows you to record basic, relevant data—the low-hanging fruit—in an organized format so it is readily available for further manipulation. This will reveal patterns, relationships, and other novel insights that only become obvious when potentially related data are combined or compared. Analysis (breaking an entity into its component parts) and synthesis (form-ing something new by bringing together separate entities) are the yin and yang of the analytic thinking process, complementary and necessary for a successful outcome.

3. *What relationships and patterns exist among the actors and factors? Which are most dynamic and changing?*

    To help your data take on meaning, you can sort, graph, or diagram your data to depict or discover patterns and relationships (see Chapter 7 on models and Chapter 18 on visualization). Many books cover a myriad of techniques for sorting, visualizing, and understanding data relationships and patterns.[19] The following categories will give you an idea of the range of techniques that are most commonly used:

- Categories and dimensions

  o   Affinity diagrams organize data into logical groups.

  o   Venn diagrams show differences and similarities.

- Patterns over time and space

  o   Chronologies and Timelines show event sequences and gaps.

  o   Mind Maps show location and can be overlaid with other data to show presence, frequency, and intensity.

- Relationships that are connective or influencing

  o   Network Analysis or Link Charts map connections among people, groups, or information-processing entities.

  o   Influence Diagrams identify hierarchical or other power relationships among individuals or organizations.

- Process flows

  o   Process Maps diagram each step in a complex process, including event flow, activity flow, and commodity flow.

  o   Gantt Charts use a matrix to track the progress of component processes over a specified period of time.

- Comparisons across factors

  o   Graphs depict data as functions of usually two factors, such as time and frequency or time and intensity, to show the relative significance of each.

  o   Cross-Impact Matrices and Complexity Matrices show the strength and direction of relationships between key variables.

No matter which sorting or visualization technique you decide is best suited to your issue and your data, keep in mind the different time frames at play: current, past, evolving, and potential (see Figure 3.4).

FIGURE 3.4   ■   SATs for Context

WHAT STRUCTURED ANALYTIC TECHNIQUES APPLY?

Techniques that improve the rigor of the analysis at the start of a paper or project include the following:

Getting Started Techniques

- Sorting

- Ranking, Scoring, and Prioritizing

- Matrices

- Mind Maps and Concept Maps

- Process Maps and Gantt Charts

Exploration Techniques

- Brainstorming

- Circleboarding™

- Starbursting

- Venn Analysis

- Network Analysis

Diagnostic Techniques

- Chronologies and Timelines

- Cross-Impact Matrix

- Multiple Hypothesis Generation

- Analysis of Competing Hypotheses

- Argument Mapping

- Red Hat Analysis

4. *Are there historical analogies? What are the similarities and differences?*

Identical situations rarely occur, but analogous situations can help analysts respond to their clients' interests. You are rarely starting from scratch on any issue and can complete your work faster with less effort if you build on similar work. But it must be your own, demonstrating your best understanding of what makes today different from yesterday and what is likely to influence what will be tomorrow.

Beware of the temptation to "copy and paste" from previous work or to assume that what has happened before will happen that way again. Conveying the trajectories that dynamic forces and factors are most likely to project will help your clients avoid errors or be taken by surprise.

Recognizing and characterizing similarities and differences from previous situations can help frame issues for your clients and clarify your analytic line. For example, in considering the likely impact of imposing economic sanctions on a country, an analyst could consult with others about how effective economic sanctions have been when imposed on other states, how successful these states were in finding ways to circumvent the sanctions, and whether similar work-arounds could be arranged by the country about to be sanctioned. Highlighting the differences is probably even more important; the goal is to focus your client on alternative ways the situation can evolve, particularly if high-impact scenarios are among the possibilities.

5. *How can your issue be redefined?*

Experimenting with different ways and techniques to reframe and focus your issue, such as Issue Redefinition, is one of the best ways to keep your research and production on track. When new information is introduced, when the difficulty of the core question leads you into easier areas of inquiry, or when your thinking is mired down, you can do any of the following to force yourself to think of your issue in different ways:

- Write down what you know and what you do not know.

- Rephrase or paraphrase the issue.

- Ask a series of "Why" or "How" questions to get to the root cause.

- Look at the issue from different perspectives, including

   o   macro or overarching views across several components

   o   micro views or breaking the components down even further

   o   Outside-In Thinking or exploring the impact of external forces

   o   views that are opposite or diametrically opposed to what you think you know.

Figure 3.5 provides an example of the power of Issue Redefinition by exploring the question "Is China Selling Missiles to Iran?"

Understand Your Role

Analysis is portrayed as a conceptual, reflective, and intellectual exercise, but its success is gauged by how well the judgments are communicated as well as the degree to which the actions and impacts are accomplished as a result. The analyst is responsible for executing critical thinking skills both as an individual and as a team member. The professional context determines the course of the analyst's career and the ability to accomplish personal interests and goals.

Each agency or company has its own set of written and unwritten rules and operating cultures. This suggests that you should always try to put on the hat of an anthropologist to understand the system within which you work. In this way, you can better understand the organizational context and how to optimize your role in it if you ask the following questions.

1. *How does your portfolio fit within the broader organization of your agency or company? How does that affect the scope of your analysis and production?*

FIGURE 3.5 ■ Issue Redefinition: Is China Selling Missiles to Iran?	
Initial question	**Is China selling ballistic missiles to Iran?**
Rephrase	**Is Iran buying ballistic missiles from China?**
Ask "Why?"	**Why would China sell ballistic missiles to Iran?**
	Because China seeks influence with Iran.
	Why does China want influence with Iran?
	Because China wants to reduce US influence in the Persian Gulf region.
	Why does China want to reduce US influence in the Persian Gulf region?
	Because China wants to reduce US influence throughout the world.
	Final Question: Is China's sale of military equipment to the Middle East part of a worldwide strategy to reduce US influence?
Broaden the focus	**Is there a partnership between China and Iran?**
Narrow the focus	**What kinds of ballistic missiles would China sell to Iran?**
Redirect the focus	**Why would Iran want Chinese missiles? How is Iran going to pay for any purchased missiles?**
Turn 180 degrees	**Is China buying ballistic missiles from Iran?**

Source: Copyright 2020 Pherson Associates, LLC. All Rights Reserved.

How has your issue been covered before your tenure? What has your organization produced previously? You may bring a different set of knowledge, skills, and experience to your issue, but you should maintain the integrity of your organization's analytic line.

- Review previous production with a critical eye, assessing how earlier frames and factors fit with the ones you are developing.

- Ask predecessors and managers for perspective and feedback on how your work fits into previous production.

- Seek training and other learning opportunities to expand and develop your cognitive frame.

- Become familiar with peers, managers, mentors, editors, collection managers, and colleagues in related components, agencies, companies, and partners.

2. *What are the analytic competencies you are expected to exhibit in your work?*

Competencies reflect the skills, abilities, behaviors, and other characteristics that intelligence professionals need to meet the challenges in their current and future

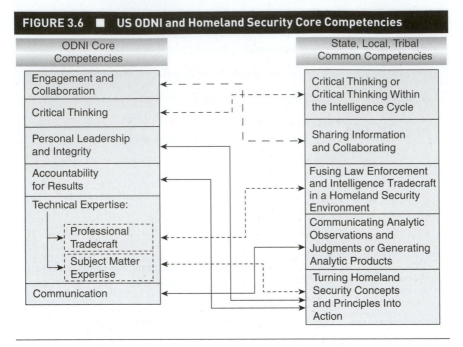

FIGURE 3.6 ■ US ODNI and Homeland Security Core Competencies

Source: Copyright 2020 Pherson Associates, LLC. All Rights Reserved.

work. To be useful in a learning environment and for performance evaluation, these competencies—like any kind of indicator—must be observable and measurable. Within the US intelligence analytic community, for example, at least two sets of competencies relate to homeland security analysts. Both detail behaviors that exemplify competency in critical thinking.

- Intelligence Community Directive (ICD) 610 defines core competencies as applying to all IC employees (see Figure 3.6). Annex G in the ICD specifies competencies for analysis and production.[20]

- A working group established by the Office of the Director of National Intelligence (ODNI) consolidated common analytic competencies from existing training and tradecraft documents to create a nationally recognized set of competencies for analysts working in homeland security.[21]

In the United Kingdom (UK), the Professional Head of Intelligence Assessment (PHIA) published in 2019 its *Professional Development Framework*, which describes the skills required of analysts to conduct all-source intelligence assessments (see Figure 3.7). The framework will be used to develop career pathways for all-source analysts and an overarching Talent Strategy for the profession. It identifies the skills analysts are expected to demonstrate across four ability levels: Foundation, Proficient, Highly Proficient, and Advanced.

FIGURE 3.7 ■ UK Professional Development Framework Skills

Informing Decision-Making

You understand the customer's requirements, the decisions that customer needs to make, and why the assessment is required in order to ensure the end product can assist and inform the decision-making process.

Gathering, Organising, and Evaluating Intelligence & Information

You plan and gather sufficient intelligence and information required to answer the customer's question. You organize and evaluate your sources, recoding them clearly, to facilitate effective audit.

Analysis, Tradecraft and Assessment

You use creative and critical thinking skills to ensure assessments are robust, applying appropriate structured methods, techniques and approaches that are relevant to the intelligence requirement.

Written and Visual Communication of Intelligence Assessment

You articulate complex matters clearly and concisely. You present information in a way that aids comprehension as well as using visualization effectively in your products.

Verbal Communication of Intelligence Assessment

You verbally articulate complex matters in a manner appropriate to the audience.

Co-operation, Co-ordination and Challenge

You build a range of effective working relationships with the most relevant individuals and organizations, both inside and outside of government. You enable and encourage effective challenge from across the community, to ensure the production of the best assessments possible.

Source: Professional Development Framework for All-Source Intelligence Assessment (2019), reproduced with permission of the UK government.

Analysts can use the framework to evaluate their own skill levels and identify development needs. Managers can use the framework to define the skills required in their assessment teams, guide recruitment, and ensure that expectations of skill levels are applied consistently across all departments.

The skill levels were designed to be cumulative as analysts advance through their careers. Most of the workforce will fall within the first three levels with only a small number of analysts functioning at the advanced level. The *Professional Development Framework* describes six technical skills required of those undertaking intelligence assessments:

1. Informing Decision-Making

2. Gathering, Organising and Evaluating Intelligence & Information

3.   Analysis, Tradecraft and Assessment

4.   Written and Visual Communication of Intelligence Assessment

5.   Verbal Communication of Intelligence Assessment

6.   Co-operation, Co-ordination and Challenge

Strong parallels can be found when comparing the UK and the US lists of core skills and competencies. Both emphasize the need for collaboration and effective engagement with decision makers, the need to develop critical thinking skills, and the ability to present information clearly in written products and briefings. The UK framework goes a step further, noting the growing importance of visual and digital communication and placing a higher priority on information gathering and evaluation.

3.   *What are the standards and other guidelines by which the quality of your work will be judged?*
     Whether in academia, private industry, or government, standards for content, integrity, accountability, and style have been established to guide the quality and

---

FIGURE 3.8 ■ US Intelligence Community Analytic Standards

Intelligence Community Directive 203
Analytic Standards

1. Objectivity

2. Independent of political considerations

3. Timeliness

4. Based on all available sources of intelligence information

5. Implements and exhibits analytic tradecraft standards, specifically

   • Properly describes quality and credibility of underlying sources, data, and methodologies

   • Properly expresses and explains uncertainties associated with major analytic judgments

   • Properly distinguishes between underlying intelligence and analysts' assumptions and judgments

   • Incorporates analysis of alternatives

   • Demonstrates customer relevance and addresses implications

   • Uses clear and logical argumentation

   • Explains change to or consistency of analytic judgments

   • Makes accurate judgments and assessments

   • Incorporates effective visual information where appropriate

---

Source: Office of the Director of National Intelligence, *Intelligence Community Directive 203: Analytic Standards*, January 2, 2015, https://www.dni.gov/files/documents/ICD/ICD%20203%20Analytic%20 Standards.pdf.

consistency of analytic production. These standards provide the context within which the analysts' analytic competency will be assessed. They are critical to the organization's assessment of itself, its products, and its employees.

Within the US Intelligence Community, for example, standards define the components of good analysis (see Figure 3.8). Other guidance and regulatory documents set intelligence priorities, establish substantive and functional authorities and product lines, and protect citizens' privacy.[22]

The Common Analytic Standards published by the UK in 2019 parallel most of the standards on the ODNI's list (see Figure 3.9).

- Independent

- Clear

- Comprehensive

FIGURE 3.9 ■ UK Common Analytic Standards

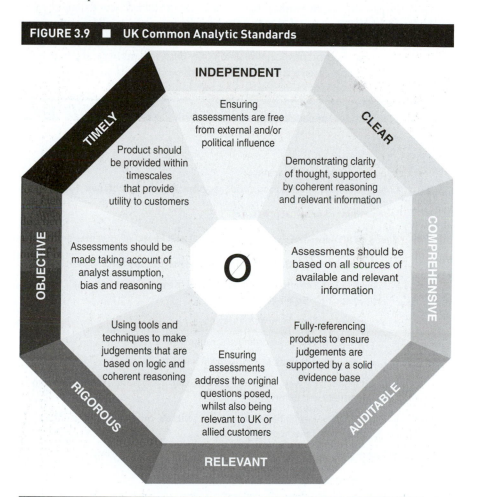

Source: Professional Development Framework for All-Source Intelligence Assessment (2019), reproduced with permission of the UK government.

- Auditable
- Relevant
- Rigorous
- Objective
- Timely

The UK standards basically replicate the ODNI's four primary standards (independent, objective, timely, and comprehensive) but compress the ODNI's nine analytic tradecraft standards into four (clear, relevant, rigorous, and auditable). The auditable standard focuses on more than just the quality of the evidentiary base; it flags the value of including any contradictory information that affects a judgment and documenting the use of analytic methods or structured techniques.

Over the past decade, the authors have learned that this basic set of analytic standards stands up well in organizations that extend well beyond the intelligence community. When teaching critical thinking skills to analytic units outside the government (for example, in the legal and medical professions as well as in banking and commercial enterprises), the authors often ask their students if these standards are relevant to the

FIGURE 3.10 ■ Generic Analytic Standards

1.	Timely
2.	Actionable
3.	Cognizant of the need to minimize analytic mindsets and biases
4.	Independent of political pressures
5.	Based on all accessible sources of internal and external information
6.	Consistent with analytic production requirements, specifically it • Focuses on the **client's needs**, addresses the **right question**, and articulates the "**So What**" • Uses clear and logical **argumentation** • Explains **changes** to major analytic judgments • Considers **alternatives** and incorporates structured analytic techniques • Distinguishes between data and evidence (or information) and underlying **assumptions** and judgments • Describes the credibility of underlying **sources**, the quality of the data, and the rigor of methodologies • Incorporates effective **visual information** where appropriate

Source: Copyright 2020 Globalytica, LLC. All Rights Reserved.

work they perform. Invariably, the response is a resounding "Yes." One or two standards may be deemed too esoteric for non-intelligence work and a few may need to be tweaked, but the basic framework appears sound.

In recent years, the authors have sought to capture this feedback and develop a more generic list of standards that apply to any analytic organization (see Figure 3.10). One interesting "lesson learned" from this project led to the inclusion of a new standard, that analysts should be cognizant of the need to minimize as much as possible the impact of mental mindsets and cognitive biases. Also receiving more emphasis is the importance of focusing attention on the "So What" and incorporating structured techniques to enhance the rigor and transparency of the analysis.

Know Your Audience

Your audience is not just the decision makers who act on your work but also analysts in other organizations who have different missions, functions, and views and who provide analytic support to the same clients, their colleagues, or their competitors. We have already discussed the importance of identifying your primary clients (see Chapter 1), but you should be aware of what your broader audience is thinking and doing about your topic.

1. *Who else is writing on your topic and why? Do your clients read their work?*
    Clients are generally well served by receiving analytic assessments from more than one source. Because mental models are influenced by organizational roles, available information, and personal factors, analysts weigh factors differently and often make different assumptions about gaps or uncertainties in information.

    If the views of other analysts differ from yours, explore the reasons for the differences in your mental models about how events are transpiring in the situation and the factors at play. Differences often stem from organizational roles, as popularized by former Bureau of the Budget manager Rufus E. Miles, Jr., who coined the phrase known as Miles' Law: "Where You Stand Depends on Where You Sit."[23] Analysts in one organization found that differences in their analytic perspectives on the development of a terrorist group were based on the function of their branch of the organization. The branch with responsibility for external threats saw the group as hierarchical and a serious threat, while the branch responsible for tracking internal threats viewed the group's organization as diffuse and the threat as minimal. In separating the facts from the assumptions, these differences can be explained by the lack of information on real-time pressure and priorities for action that would clarify the imminence of the threat.

    Always pay attention to media, social media, and other open-source assessments on your topic. They most likely will be the first to report public statements, disasters, and precipitous changes, but their priority is to get the news disseminated quickly rather than to provide a critically argued assessment. Any analyst or reporter working within a sophisticated mental frame, however, can use these sources to produce thoughtful, cogent, insightful analysis in a short time.

2. *Are there other stakeholders who impact your analysis? Will they have access to your analysis or take action based on your information and insights?*

Stakeholders are individuals or organizations that can affect or be affected by your analysis. They can be primary stakeholders who are directly affected, secondary stakeholders who are less involved or indirectly affected, or key stakeholders who influence the effects. Identifying those who are impacted by or who impact your analysis can help you think through how you present controversial topics or how you prepare your organization should sensitive analytic products be leaked or disclosed without authorization.

For instance, national security intelligence is usually written for federal executive branch consumers but shared with legislative stakeholders who approve federal budgets and appointments. Homeland security intelligence analysis is produced and shared with state, local, and tribal organizations that serve as links between national intelligence analysts and first responders.

Stakeholders can be categorized and ranked in a variety of ways, reflecting their influence, requirements, support, or role. The important point is to make them a part of your production planning.

3. *Has this question or a similar question been answered before? How is it the same or different?*

Past products from other organizations can help analysts judge the strengths and weaknesses of their own production history (see Figure 3.11). They may find useful information not in their files or derive insights on what sorts of information were critical to previous judgments or consumer decisions. Comparing production can confirm the existence of information gaps that can be translated into collection requirements. Even more important, awareness of historical context can head off the tendency to make simplistic analytic conclusions out of ignorance of what has come before.

If a poorly reasoned analogy or inaccurate historical metaphor is being trumpeted in the popular media, analysts need to bring this to the attention of the client and detail why it is fallacious or problematic. For example, several administration commentators

FIGURE 3.11 ■ **Stop! Previously Written?**

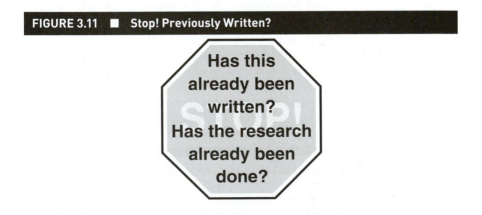

cited the Marshall Plan for the reconstruction of Western Europe after World War II as the model for rebuilding Iraq after the Americans removed Saddam Hussein.[24] Perceptive analysts noted at the time that the situations were highly dissimilar, suggesting that the British experience in Iraq in the 1920s was far more illuminating.

Lessons can be learned from previously published documents even if the issues are not analogous. Analysts can use them to get ideas for how to structure projects, use background material, and design maps or graphics.

4. *Is your issue part of a larger one or at a different level?*

Your analysis differs according to its function and purpose. If your specialty is Indian economic analysis, you will want to stay on top of political and military events to gauge their impact even though they will play a secondary role in your products.

Much of the homeland security analysis performed at the state and local level is tactical, developing cases for response or prosecution. Some of the early attempts at strategic analysis tackled threats to a geographic area or detailed sets of extremist groups but resembled research papers rather than high-level assessments.

You should be aware of which category your analysis fits into—tactical, operational, or strategic—and use the tools and techniques best suited to that level (see Figure 3.12). Tactical and operational analysis relies heavily on organizing and sharing

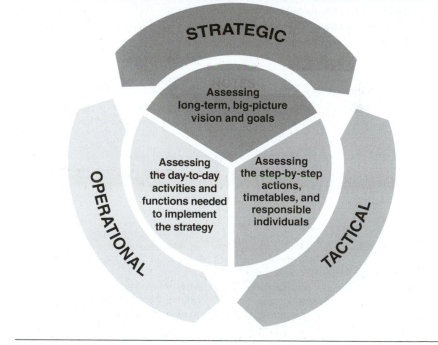

FIGURE 3.12 ■ Strategic, Operational, and Tactical Analysis

STRATEGIC

Assessing long-term, big-picture vision and goals

OPERATIONAL

Assessing the day-to-day activities and functions needed to implement the strategy

Assessing the step-by-step actions, timetables, and responsible individuals

TACTICAL

Source: Copyright 2020 Pherson Associates, LLC. All Rights Reserved.

critical data. Strategic analysis should look to the future, using techniques such as Multiple Scenarios Generation and High Impact/Low Probability Analysis.

"A new idea comes suddenly and in a rather intuitive way. But intuition is nothing but the outcome of earlier intellectual experience."

—Albert Einstein[25]

KEY TAKEAWAYS

- Analysts must be alert to the broader contexts that can impact them, their issue, and their audience; this makes the analysis more relevant and less susceptible to error.

- Early identification of a cognitive framework for an issue can guide effective data collection and facilitate adjusting frames to changing circumstances.

- Analysts should become familiar with a variety of mental models that can help them consciously formulate their own, particularly as they partner with artificial intelligence systems.

- Conceptual models are tools that enable individuals to fuse their internal mental models into a single construct to guide coherent and consistent analytic production and systems development.

- External visualizations of an analytic framework, including key components and factors influencing change, will make the analysis more consistent and easier to share with colleagues and clients.

- Historical analogies help the analyst understand the background for an issue.

- Frameworks help analysts focus on both similarities and differences because events rarely happen the same way twice.

- Analysts should always first check to see what their organization and others have written on the issue, particularly if this research is available to the client.

CONSIDERING THE CASE STUDY

Review Case Study I, "Uncharted Territory: Conflict, Competition, or Collaboration in the Arctic?"

- Describe the broader political and economic context within which this case study is taking place. How does this historical and theoretical background apply to what is happening now in the Arctic?

- In the international discussions and debate surrounding the development of the Arctic, what is the context, and how is this portrayed?

- What are the key components of this story? Construct a matrix of the key components and how they interact.

- List the key issues your client (a well-informed general reader) would like you to address in this article.

- How well did the author answer the "So What" question in the article?

NOTES

1. Richards J. Heuer Jr., *Psychology of Intelligence Analysis* (Reston, VA: Pherson Associates, 2007), 85–94.

2. Gary Klein et al., "A Data/Frame Theory of Sensemaking," in *Expertise Out of Context: Proceedings of the 6th International Conference on Naturalistic Decision Making*, ed. R. R. Hoffman (New York: Taylor & Francis, 2007), 130.

3. Klein, "A Data/Frame Theory of Sensemaking," 119.

4. The authors' sensitivity to the concept of sensemaking was formed when one was employed as Director of International Programs for Evidence Based Research, Inc., during its groundbreaking work with the Command and Control Research Program of the Office of the Assistant Secretary of Defense for Command, Control, Communications, and Intelligence in 2001. See Dennis K. Leedom, "Final Report" (Sensemaking Symposium, October 23–25 2001), http://www.dodccrp.org/files /sensemaking_final_report.pdf, for one of the earliest applications of developing cognitive theories to intelligence and intelligence analysis. A growing body of research and application literature covers these topics, particularly since the increased focus on improving analytic shortfalls in the wake of 9/11. Our intent is not to review the literature but to highlight some of the salient observations that analysts may not think of as they go about their daily work.

5. Klein et al., "A Data/Frame Theory of Sensemaking," 113–155.

6. Heuer, *Psychology of Intelligence Analysis*, 51.

7. Robert M. Clark, *Intelligence Analysis: A Target-Centric Approach*, 6th ed.

(Washington, DC: CQ Press/SAGE, 2019), 137.

8. Archilochus' quote was made famous in Isaiah Berlin's *The Hedgehog and the Fox: An Essay on Tolstoy's View of History*, which was first published in 1953 and in subsequent versions (New York: Simon & Schuster, 1986). The analogy also has been adopted by University of Pennsylvania professor Phil Tetlock in several works, including *Expert Political Judgment: How Good Is It? How Can We Know?* (Princeton, NJ: Princeton University Press, 2006) and *Superforecasting: The Art and Science of Prediction* (New York: Penguin Random House, 2015).

9. See, for instance, James Clear, "Mental Models: Learn to Think Better and Gain a Mental Edge," https:// jamesclear.com/mental-models; Gabriel Weinberg and Lauren McCann, *Super Thinking: The Big Book of Mental Models* (New York: Penguin Random House, 2019), and works of Shane Parrish, founder of the Farnam Street website, https://fs.blog/.

10. The text of Munger's 1994 speech to the University of Southern California Business School, "A Lesson on Elementary, Worldly Wisdom as It Relates to Investment Management & Business," can be found in Charlie Munger, *Poor Charlie's Almanack: The Wit and Wisdom of Charles T. Munger*, expanded 3rd ed. (Marceline, MO: Walsworth, 2005).

11. Clark, *Intelligence Analysis*, 137.

12. Don Norman, *The Design of Everyday Things: Revised and Expanded Version* (New York: Basic Books, 2013).

13. See, for example, Gagan Bansal et al., "Beyond Accuracy: The Role of Mental Models in Human-AI Team Performance," 2019, https://www

.semanticscholar.org/paper/Beyond
-Accuracy-%3A-The-Role-of-Mental
-Models-in-Team-Bansal-Nushi/568
8b8077117b3aafd54c2e71d959284f
4d5c8b9 and Stuart Russell, *Human
Compatible: Artificial Intelligence and
the Problem of Control* (New York:
Viking, 2019).

14. Jerry Ratcliffe has produced a similar
model that better explains the specific
components of the law enforcement
model for intelligence-led policing.
While the terms and focus of this
version are slightly different, the concept
of the analyst interpreting data to aid in
decisions and actions is the same.

15. These visualization techniques are
discussed in Randolph H. Pherson
and Richards J. Heuer Jr., *Structured
Analytic Techniques for Intelligence
Analysis*, 3rd ed. (Washington, DC:
CQ Press/SAGE, 2021), Chapter 5
on Getting Organized Techniques,
67–86; Chapter 6 on Exploration
Techniques, 87–131; the Cross-Impact
Matrix, 141–146; and the Complexity
Manager, 339–346.

16. The Institute for Human and
Machine Cognition offers software
for constructing concept maps that is
free to US government and educational
organizations and for beta testing for
commercial entities (http://cmap.ihmc
.us/). Two websites offer free trials of
their mind mapping software: http://
www.mindgenius.com and http://
www.smartdraw.com/downloads/.
SmartDraw also offers freeware for
flow charts and other visualization
tools.

17. STEEP stands for social, technological,
economic, environmental, and
political; STEEP+2 adds psychological
and military; STEEPLE appends
legal and ethical to the original
STEEP list; STEEPLED further
adds demographics; and PESTLE

signifies political, economic,
social, technological, legal, and
environmental.

18. For more information on Multiple
Scenarios Generation, see Pherson and
Heuer, *Structured Analytic Techniques*,
272–276.

19. Some of our favorites include matrices,
Mind Maps, and Link Charts.

20. Office of the Director of National
Intelligence, *Intelligence Community
Directive 610: Competency Directories
for the Intelligence Community
Workforce*, October 4, 2010, http://
www.dni.gov/files/documents/ICD
/ICD_610.pdf.

21. United States Department of Justice,
*Common Competencies for State, Local,
and Tribal Intelligence Analysts*, June
2010, https://it.ojp.gov/documents
/d/common%20competencies
%20state%20local%20and%20Tribal
%20intelligence%20analysts.pdf. The
skills-based competency charts were
developed by one of the authors in
support of the working group.

22. Office of the Director of National
Intelligence, *Intelligence Community
Directive 203: Analytic Standards*,
January 2, 2015, http://www.dni.gov
/files/documents/ICD/ICD%20203
%20Analytic%20Standards.pdf.

23. Rufus E. Miles, Jr., "The Origin
and Meaning of Miles' Law," *Public
Administration Review* 38, no. 5 (1978):
399–403.

24. Ian Vasquez, "A Marshall Plan
for Iraq?" *Investor's Business Daily*,
May 9, 2003, https://www.cato.org
/publications/commentary/marshall
-plan-iraq.

25. Walter Isaacson, *Einstein: His Life
and Universe* (New York: Simon &
Schuster, 2007), 113. Einstein was
addressing Dr. H. L. Gordon.

4 HOW SHOULD I CONCEPTUALIZE MY PRODUCT?

SETTING THE STAGE

In previous chapters, we discussed the importance of focusing on a principal client, identifying the key question, and understanding the operating environment for our issue and our analytic production. Now we are ready to move forward with planning our product. The Analyst's Roadmap (see the inside back cover) reminds us to stop and reflect on the most effective—and efficient—way to proceed. This habit of reflection usually needs to be learned and consciously reinforced because most analysts are highly task oriented and want to plunge in immediately to begin working a problem.

Analysts can take time to conceptualize a product whether working alone or, preferably, in a small group.[1] Holding a conceptualization or whiteboarding session prior to beginning an analytic project can save substantial time later in the production process and help assure that the most compelling argument is presented.

LOOKING MORE DEEPLY

The conceptualization process can vary from a quick five-minute "huddle" or phone call for a short turnaround product drafted in less than a day to a day-long whiteboarding session for a major assessment or national estimate that will take months to produce. The time lost up front to do this initial conceptualizing invariably will be repaid many times over in the editing, coordination, and review process.

Focusing on What Is Important

The first question to ask is whether a *threshold* has been crossed to justify the decision to generate a product. Threshold is a judgment call about whether an issue or event is new, different, significant, useful, or of sufficient personal interest that your clients would like or need to know. Here are some questions you can ask yourself to determine if your project "meets threshold" for a good use of analyst time and resources.

- What is new or different about your issue or event?

- Is it an indicator of significant change?

- Do you need to warn of an imminent or potential threat?

- Does the issue or event relate to your clients' interests or schedule?

- What can you add that will support your clients in meetings or policy discussions?

- Does the event or issue present opportunities or pitfalls for your clients' programs, actions, or policies?

- Is the issue or event important to your organization or a broader audience?

Scoping the Product

If it is decided to generate a written product, the next question is what type of paper should be written. If the requester or supervisor does not predetermine the product type, the conceptualization session is the best place to do that. All analytic organizations have established product lines—some more sophisticated and adaptable than others—but they generally fall into three categories. These categories largely mirror the progression portrayed in the Analytic Spectrum (descriptive to explanatory to evaluative to estimative analysis), which is described in the next chapter.

1. Short, current pieces that introduce new information on front-burner or developing topics. These generally convey information about an event or reporting from a unique source. They may also update or augment existing databases. They are intended to keep customers as well-informed on breaking issues as their colleagues, even if the issue or event does not come under their job responsibilities.

2. Medium-term analyses that frame issues, interpret new data, or highlight new trends. These can serve as the basis for building a storyline and as foundations for future assessments based on longer-term research and the application of analytic techniques and methodologies.

3. Longer-term assessments that look back over a period of time at events or issues or forward-looking estimates of trends, changes, and what happens next.

Analysts often work on multiple projects at the same time, balancing current and longer-term responsibilities. They should maintain personal files of their drafts and final productions so they can be sure to pick up the storyline at exactly the same point they left it in the last product. We discuss analytic approaches further in Chapter 5.

The product of a conceptualization session will differ depending on the category of analysis.

- For quick turnaround papers, the conceptualization session might consist of simply engaging the author and his or her supervisor in a brief discussion focusing on a few critical questions. It could also be an informal list of key decisions recorded on the whiteboard.

- Concept Papers are good vehicles for conceptualizing medium-term assessments. Their primary purpose is to lay out a work plan that captures the expectations of both the analyst and supervisor.

- A more formal Terms of Reference document is often used when a complex assessment or national estimate is being prepared.

For medium- and longer-term assessments, conceptualization or whiteboarding sessions should include the author or authors, the product's primary reviewer or reviewers, and the author's first- and sometimes second-line supervisors. Including those who will play significant roles in coordinating the paper—including both substantive and nonsubstantive stakeholders—always pays dividends down the road. Inviting one or more outsiders who have strong conceptualization skills or who can bring fresh perspectives to the topic also adds value to the exercise. Usually the more complex or sophisticated the project, the more participants should become engaged in the conceptualization stage.

When possible, convene the group in a small room with plenty of whiteboards. If whiteboards are not available, find an easel to visually track the conversation and record the key decisions. In our experience, critical gaps will remain undiscovered and the participants' recollection of what was said will often differ later on if you fail to record the conversation for all to see.

Getting Started Checklist

The Getting Started Checklist (see Figure 4.1) is a tool analysts should use to launch any new paper or project.[2] By getting the fundamentals right at the start, analysts can ensure that their research and analysis is focused on what matters the most to their client or key customers.

For short papers, taking a few minutes to review some basic questions will make the process more efficient by focusing participants on exactly what needs to be done and how quickly. Sample questions to address up front include the following:

- What is the deadline?

- Who is the primary consumer?

- Do we need to seek any additional information or insight before drafting?

- Is there a need to alert someone or issue an immediate warning?

A longer checklist will help analysts develop a strategy for crafting medium- and longer-term papers. It will spur them to think about how to obtain the best information, tap the best expertise, and incorporate the right techniques in the most efficient way possible. For example, by asking if a paper has already been written on the topic, the analyst can avoid spending hours or days doing unnecessary research and drafting.

FIGURE 4.1 ■ Getting Started Checklist

1. What has prompted the need for the analysis? For example, was it a news report, a new development, a new intelligence report, a perception of change, or a client request?

2. What is the key intelligence, policy, or business question that needs to be addressed? Are we answering the right question?

3. Why is this issue important, and how can you make a unique and meaningful contribution?

4. Has this question or a similar question already been answered by you or someone else, and what was said? To whom was that analysis delivered, and what has changed since then?

5. Who are the principal clients or customer sets? Are their needs well understood?

6. Are there any other stakeholders who would have an interest in the answer? Would any of them prefer that a different question be answered?

7. How soon is an answer needed to the question? How much time do we have to conduct the research, draft the paper, review it, and deliver our response?

8. What are all the possible answers to the question? What alternative explanations or outcomes should be considered before making an analytic judgment on the issue?

9. What Structured Analytic Techniques would help us the most in generating our analysis?

10. What potential sources or streams of information would be most useful—and efficient—to exploit to learn more about this topic or question?

11. Where should we reach out for expertise, information, or assistance within our organization or outside our unit?

12. Should we convene an initial brainstorming session to identify and challenge key assumptions, examine key information, identify key drivers and important players, explore alternative explanations, and generate alternative hypotheses?

Source: Copyright 2020 Pherson Associates, LLC. All Rights Reserved.

Determining the AIMS of Your Product

An easy way to structure a conceptualization session is to start by working through the product's AIMS—specifically, the *Audience, Issue* or *intelligence question, Message,* and *Storyline*.[3] Beginning the conceptualization session with a discussion of AIMS provides the opportunity to validate your perception of the key client, define the issue precisely, and solicit perspectives and vet your progress with others in the context of the specific product on which you are beginning to work.

- *Audience.* Who is the primary audience for the article? Is it a short, focused article for a senior client or a longer piece with more detail that will serve a less strategic and a more tactical or operational customer set? Is there more than one primary client? If so, then a conscious decision can be made whether two different papers should be conceptualized and drafted in parallel.

- *Issue or intelligence question.* What intelligence or policy issues is your client struggling with now or will have to deal with in the future? What is the client's greatest concern or greatest need at the moment? Is the key question tightly focused, actionable, and answerable in more than one way?

- *Message.* What is the bottom line that you want to convey to your client in one sentence? What is your "elevator speech" or key point you would express to the client if you had a minute together between floors on an elevator? This message should be formulated as the title to the product or a short, clear, and direct statement before drafting the article. Do the title and the answer provide unique, significant insights and go beyond what was said in the last item read by the client on the subject?

- *Storyline.* With the clear bottom-line message in mind, can you create an overall package with a succinct line of argumentation that flows easily and logically from paragraph to paragraph and tells a compelling story? How does this message fit with your previous products and others that you should have in the planning stages? If the line of analysis has changed or is changing, be clear about what is different and why. Can you illustrate this storyline with equally compelling pictures, videos, or other graphics?

If the AIMS of the article or assessment are not considered before drafting, your product will be less effective in meeting the needs of your clients. In fact, chances are it will take more time to reach publication and could languish in the editing and coordination process. This impacts its timeliness and relevance to your client, who may decide not to read it even if it eventually reaches his or her desk.

Writing a Concept Paper

A Concept Paper helps you tighten your focus before you start researching and writing an article or assessment. It can serve as a research design contract between you, your boss, and your collaborators on how the paper will be produced. Concept Papers do not contain your judgments (see Figure 4.2). (See Chapter 5 for developing research strategies and plans for your Concept Paper.)

A good Concept Paper should, at a minimum, accomplish all of the following tasks:

- Identify the client or customer set and their requirements

- Identify the key questions

- Lay out a research plan

- Identify key sources and methods

- Outline the line of argument

- Indicate planned graphics, matrices, and appendices

- Identify any needed resources

- Propose a timeline for completion

FIGURE 4.2 ■ Concept Paper Outline

1. **Working title**

2. **Author(s)**

3. **Type of product**

4. **Scope:** Brief statement of the thrust of the paper, why it is being written, what it is intended to accomplish, key questions it will answer.

5. **Audience:** Key clients and key issues they want addressed.

6. **Data gathering:** Best sources of information, potential gaps, collection requirements, data analysis methods.

7. **Outline:** Preliminary ordering of topics to be covered.

8. **Deadlines:** Timeline for producing draft and publishing paper.

9. **Contributions:** Need for input from other offices or experts and tasks they will perform.

10. **Resource requirements:** Estimated overall level of effort for principal drafter and contributors.

11. **Methodological support:** List of analytic techniques that could enhance the analysis and work plan for employing them.

12. **Graphics:** Preliminary list of figures, including text boxes, that could help tell the story.

13. **Collaboration:** Potential sources of expertise both within and outside of the organization.

14. **Coordination:** Who must coordinate the draft before publication?

Make sure everyone involved in the project signs off on the Concept Paper before you start work. You now have something to refer to when others adopt different views on the subject, you change your analysis or run into resource problems, managers or clients change their minds about what they want or when they want it, or some other issue takes priority.

Establishing Terms of Reference

Terms of Reference (TOR) are often generated when writing more complex papers or forward-looking estimates. The purpose of a TOR is to establish expectations with your reviewers, coordinators, and perhaps your clients on the substantive scope of the draft and when they will receive it. The TOR document is based on an established template and is used frequently for US Intelligence Community products that capture the scope and timelines for the paper and establish the responsibilities of all the key players. Often it is signed by the authors, supervisors, and other key stakeholders.

In addition to establishing the AIMS of the paper, the TOR should do the following:[4]

- Establish the time frame for the analysis, including the period of the estimate or how far into the future it will look, if appropriate

- Provide a research plan with deadlines for completing various stages of research

- Expose any gaps in the existing information or analysis and identify corresponding strategies to fill the gaps

- Identify the roles of any contributors and assign drafting responsibilities

- Include the views of outside experts to either provide unique input or to review the draft

- Identify what analytic techniques should be used to help structure the analysis (see Figure 4.3)

- Establish deadlines for delivering sections of the paper to the primary drafter and delivering the draft itself to the editors

- Set a target date for delivering the final paper to the client

One of the primary benefits of crafting a TOR is that it provides a contract between the authors, the managers, and the stakeholders—who are usually from different analytic organizations—regarding what the paper will address, what resources will be committed, and what deadlines must be met. The process helps prevent surprises later in the editing, coordination, and production processes.

TOR sessions are also useful as a means to underscore that the final paper is a joint product generated as part of a collaborative team process. It will smooth the coordination process because the key equities of the major stakeholders have been articulated early in the drafting process and appropriately factored into the author's analysis. By inviting junior officers to the session, senior managers and analysts can also use the session to impart corporate values and teach key analytic tradecraft skills.

FIGURE 4.3 ■ SATs for Getting Started

WHAT STRUCTURED ANALYTIC TECHNIQUES APPLY?
Techniques that can be used to improve the rigor of the analysis at the start of a project or paper include the following:

- Cluster Brainstorming

- Chronologies and Timelines

- Sorting

- Ranking, Scoring, and Prioritizing

- Matrices

- Circleboarding™ and Starbursting

- Mind Maps and Concept Maps

- Venn Analysis

- Argument Mapping

- Analysis of Competing Hypotheses

KEY TAKEAWAYS

- A little planning at the start of a paper or project will almost always save considerable time for analysts in the coordination, editing, and review process.

- Threshold is a judgment call about whether an event or issue is new, different, significant, useful, or of sufficient personal interest that clients would like or need to know.

- A conceptualization session is an essential first step in producing a well-organized, tightly focused, and rigorous analysis. It provides an opportunity for analysts to vet perspectives on clients, questions, and products with supervisors, colleagues, and reviewers.

- The AIMS of the product identify the **A**udience, **I**ssue or intelligence question, **M**essage, and **S**toryline.

- Concept Papers provide a research design contract between the author, the supervisor, and other analysts that establishes the scope and timeline for the product. They focus attention on predefined stages and keep analysts from veering off into unproductive or time-consuming areas of research.

- For longer papers, a Terms of Reference (TOR) session can prove invaluable in avoiding surprises later in the process and committing analysts and managers to reasonable deadlines.

- Analysts should always be looking to work on two or three projects at a time that expand their understanding of short-, medium-, and long-term prospects of their topic or area.

CONSIDERING THE CASE STUDY

Review Case Study III, "Blackout on the Eastern Seaboard!"

Assume that you are a cyber analyst working in the US Department of Homeland Security. Your account is the electric infrastructure. You have been asked to prepare a paper assessing what could have caused the blackout. Draw from the case study to perform the following tasks:

- Describe the AIMS of the paper.

- Review the Getting Started Checklist (Figure 4.1) and identify five things you need to focus on before beginning to draft the assessment.

- Draft a two-page Concept Paper.

NOTES

1. The information used in this chapter was taken from Pherson Associates training materials (www.pherson.org).

2. This checklist was first published in Richards J. Heuer Jr. and Randolph H. Pherson, *Structured Analytic Techniques for Intelligence Analysis*, 2nd ed. (Washington, DC: CQ Press/SAGE, 2015), 47–48.

3. The AIMS process was first conceived by David Terry and later refined and incorporated into Pherson Associates training materials (www.pherson.org).

4. The TOR process has been a recommended—and at times a mandated—process for producing US National Intelligence Estimates for several decades in the US National Intelligence Council. Several other intelligence organizations employ a similar process when committing analytic resources to draft major assessments; each tailors the specific requirements to its unique organizational needs.

5 WHAT IS MY ANALYTIC APPROACH?

SETTING THE STAGE

To turn your conceptual framework into an organizing structure, such as a Concept Paper, for your product, you will need to consider and select from a variety of analytic approaches or strategies. All of these are based on an underlying discipline of logic, which is the meat of analytic argumentation. By explicitly defining an approach, good critical thinkers create a consistent baseline from which they can track their work and show their progress to their boss or colleagues. Having an established plan also makes it easier to adjust the scope of the paper or reset timelines to meet changing needs and deadlines. If you know where you are in the analytic process and can communicate your plan of action, you build credibility and confidence among your peers as well as with your supervisors. A plan or written strategy is a tether to keep you on point and on pace while you explore new sources of data, implications, and possibilities.

Much of the literature on critical thinking processes and models focuses on the logic and argumentation thinkers use to make their points. But successful analysis is part of the larger process of inquiry, research, reasoning, and communication that we cover in this book. Good critical thinkers consider the broader picture. They seek the common elements among all the good advice they have received, apply them to specific frames, and tailor them to a strategy that works for the author, the client, and the context of the problem.

Your strategy and how much time you allocate to each step will depend on the type of analysis you are producing. Many of us are expected to produce shorter-term, tactical, or current intelligence products on a regular basis; these need to meet a threshold for interest and novelty. Periodically, analysts are asked to take operational views that explore rationales and implications. Senior decision makers and policymakers also rely on analysts to provide strategic analysis to help them frame their issues and estimative papers to help them anticipate future challenges and opportunities.

"If you don't know where you're going, you might not get there."

—Yogi Berra
*When You Come to a Fork in the Road, Take It! Inspiration and
Wisdom From One of Baseball's Greatest Heroes*[1]

LOOKING MORE DEEPLY

In all analytic endeavors, a good plan begins with defining the client, purpose, and question and then continues with a plan to guide you in collecting, organizing, and evaluating the information needed to answer the question. One of our colleagues thinks of this process in anthropological terms.[2] Primitive humans first gathered food and materials they knew existed, then hunted for what else they needed, and finally grew or raised food they could not obtain in other ways. Applied to analysis, this translates as follows:

- Gathering—surveying current knowledge relating to the question

- Hunting—figuring out what is needed to answer the question

- Farming—creating knowledge relevant to answering the question

Whether you are writing on gangs, international money laundering, cyber threats, or nuclear terrorism, success in defining strategies to produce analytic products relies on having a defined context (see Chapter 3). This context or baseline includes both knowledge of what has already been written or collected on the topic to avoid "re-creating the wheel" and a plan of action that helps you consciously and systematically with the following:

- Sorting the wheat from the chaff by assessing information needs, identifying gaps, and weeding out irrelevant, incorrect, or misleading information

- Setting the parameters for knowledge you need to acquire to formulate good hypotheses and make judgments

The intellectual journey from formulating the question to presenting the conclusion can be circuitous depending on the following:

- The clarity of the question to be answered or product generated

- The complexity of the problem or issue

- The ambiguity and availability of the information needed

- The amount of time available to the analyst

Analysts benefit from understanding the cognitive steps needed to amalgamate discrete bits of information into knowledge on which judgments and understanding can be based. The way our brains handle this task is often more intuitive and integrated than linear and scientific. In our definition of critical thinking (see p. xxviii), we highlight the importance of both intuition and intellectual rigor to make sense of issues in the real world, which does not allow the control and time for scientific experiments.

For this reason, constantly incorporating critical thinking strategies and structured thinking techniques into the analytic process is fundamental to producing insightful analysis. It is a core theme illustrated and repeated throughout this book (see Figure 5.1).

FIGURE 5.1 ■ Critical Thinking Strategies: The Eight Steps

Critical Thinking Steps	Associated Chapters in This Book
1. Ask the right questions.	2
2. Identify one's assumptions.	11
3. Reach out to other sources.	8
4. Evaluate the data for accuracy, relevance, and completeness.	9, 10
5. Assess the data and form hypotheses.	12, 13
6. Evaluate the hypotheses; look for conflicting data.	15
7. Draw conclusions.	16
8. Present your findings.	19

Variations on a Theme

These processes of planning, collecting information, assessing, communicating, and reviewing are central to the completion of any task. Organizations and authors portray the intelligence cycle in many different ways. The components—whether depicted in six or seven steps or as a cycle or process—are similar to most problem-solving methods (see Figure 5.2). Some now pointedly refer to the *intelligence cycle* as the *intelligence process* to minimize any implication that the steps occur sequentially or exclusively.

Different terms are used to fit particular circumstances or environments, such as the OODA (*Observe, Orient, Decide, Act*) decision-making processes designed by former US Air Force Colonel Charles G. Boyd for military actions and often cited as a model for security risk management.[3] Scientific problem-solving, business problem-solving, and mathematical problem-solving methods parallel the critical thinking approach but employ different sets of data and timing. The steps may have slightly different names or be combined in slightly different ways. Figure 5.2 shows the similarities by giving similar actions the same degree of shading.

It's never enough to tell people about some new insight. Instead of pouring knowledge into people's heads, you need to help them grind a new set of eyeglasses so they can see the world in a new way.

—John Seely Brown
Seeing Differently, Insights on Innovation

FIGURE 5.2 ■ Comparison of Problem-Solving Methods

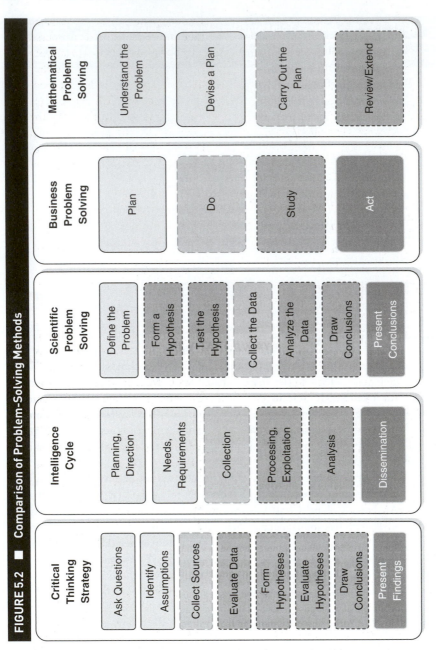

We encourage analysts to look for the commonalities in various methodologies and techniques to view their issue and way forward through different lenses. For instance, try comparing the steps of critical thinking to other popular "thinking" methods to gain an understanding of their strengths in addressing particular problems and how they might be useful in your analytic process.

- *Design Thinking*[4] focuses on understanding the end users and what they will do with your analytic products. Like the critical thinking process, this iterative problem-solving methodology challenges assumptions, asks questions to redefine problems, and seeks alternative solutions before testing the "best available" option to meet the need. It is fundamentally human centered, which its practitioners say distinguishes it from scientific approaches that keep the users' needs and emotions at a distance. IDEO, the company best known for popularizing Design Thinking, focuses on three essential pillars of empathy, ideation, and experimentation. IDEO founder David Kelley also started Stanford's Hasso Plattner Institute of Design, which teaches a five-step iterative process:

  1. *Empathize* to understand the clients

  2. *Define* the clients' problems and needs

  3. *Ideate* to challenge assumptions and create ideas for innovative ways to meet the clients' needs

  4. *Prototype* to turn the ideas into realizable solutions

  5. *Test* the solutions

- *Computational Thinking*[5] in contrast expresses problems and solutions in ways that computers can execute. While its recent popularity has been focused on integrating computational skills in schools to further STEM (**S**cience, **T**echnology, **E**ngineering, and **M**athematics) education in our increasingly automated world, one intelligence agency considered it important enough to have a training course for all its employees. Stephen Noonoo, K–12 editor at the education technology company EdSurge, recently wrote that "Computational Thinking is critical thinking. And it works in any subject."[6] Computational Thinking approaches problem-solving through three iterative processes:

  1. *Abstraction.* Decompose the problem, identifying data patterns that enable best representation of the variables.

  2. *Automation.* Create algorithms that result in a generic solution.

  3. *Analysis.* Execute and evaluate the solutions.

- *Geospatial Thinking* encompasses the unique domain of geospatial problem solving in which analysts also use spatial reasoning to match data to frames that involve the "location, extent, distribution, pattern, association, interaction, or change of data within a geospatial sphere or space." One of the authors collaborated in 2018 on an essay for the US Geospatial Intelligence Foundation's *2018 State and Future of GEOINT Report* that detailed the need for geospatial, computational, and critical thinking, concluding that "the community needs exquisite collection, adept data handlers, automated assistance to manipulate and visualize, and the ability to put all this together into insights that lead to effective actions. The common thread needed to weave all these things together is rigorous thought."[7]

For any of these methodologies, the devil is in the details of the intellectual power brought to the process; it is the "Wow" and not just the "How." Analytic strategies should reflect the process appropriate for your organization or discipline, but analysts should focus on how to best employ their thinking skills to create products that make a difference and enable the reader to take action.

Another of our colleagues, for example, advocates an analytic problem-solving method that emphasizes ways to deeply understand the problem by posing questions (see Figure 5.3).[8] Forcing analysts to think through all aspects of a problem using a questioning approach can prove a powerful tool in helping them sort out the fundamental structure of a product—and their analysis. In contrast to using the Question Method to organize your product's argument (see Chapter 2), this version uses questions to guide analysts through different stages of the analytic process, which he

Habit 2: Begin With the End in Mind.

—Stephen R. Covey
Seven Habits of Highly Effective People[9]

FIGURE 5.3 ■ Problem Solving With the Question Method

One Problem-Solving Method

- Identify the problem.
  - Asking questions
- Divide the problem.
  - Asking questions
- Question and define the problem.
  - Asking questions
- Group the problem.
  - Asking questions
- Eliminate the obvious and focus on the pertinent.
  - Asking questions
- Answer the questions in a systematic manner.
  - Stating, defining, supporting, clarifying
  - Connecting ideas, words, and themes through transitions or linguistic chain links

defines as *analysis* (dividing the problem), *synthesis* (grouping the problem), *informa-tion selection* (identifying the "So What"), and *argumentation* (forging the line of analysis).

Categories of Analytic Arguments

The specific analytic strategy and how much time is allocated to each step will depend on the type of analysis you are producing and what level of sophistication is required to answer the question. In the years the authors have been teaching, mentor-ing, and managing analysts, we find this is one of the hardest concepts to commu-nicate. The authors created the Analytic Spectrum to depict how the various types of analytic arguments relate to one another (see Figure 5.4). It is based on an amal-gamation of hierarchies and conceptual categories from knowledge management, intelligence, cognitive psychology, and rhetoric and argumentation.[10] In making the transition from novice to journeyman and from journeyman to expert, analysts must understand where each type of analytic product fits in the spectrum.

Many in the law enforcement and homeland security analytic communities seek to move beyond traditional data-, fact-, and case-based research and display to stra-tegic and future-oriented frames. The Analytic Spectrum graphically displays this range of analytic endeavor by arraying the categories and required thinking skills on scales depicting value (reactive to proactive) and complexity (data-driven or simpler to

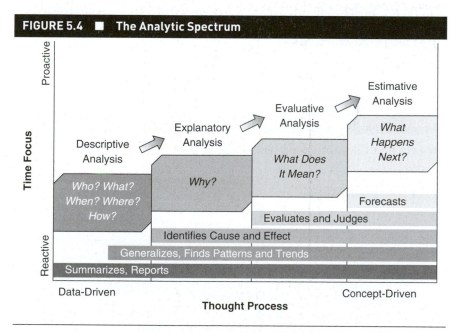

FIGURE 5.4 ■ The Analytic Spectrum

Source: Copyright 2020 Pherson Associates, LLC. All Rights Reserved.

concept-driven or more complex).[11] The skills are directly related to lines of analytic argumentation (see Chapter 12).

- *Descriptive Analysis* reports or summarizes what is known about situations, people, places, or objects (see Figure 5.5). It identifies what is valid or worth noting about the Who, What, How, When, and Where and organizes the data in a way that is easy to comprehend and recall. Sherman Kent, the Yale professor whose foundational work on intelligence analysis in the 1950s earned him the title of the "Father of Intelligence Analysis," identified basic intelligence (background information on nations and issues) and current intelligence (reporting on events and items of immediate interest) as examples of Descriptive Analysis. In law enforcement, bulletins, spot reports, BOLOs (**Be On the LookOut**), and analyst case support also are examples of Descriptive Analysis.

Research papers or assessments that clump data and reports without a useful judgment or "So What" and without providing the client an analytic line of argument are descriptive analyses masquerading as higher-order products. If an annual assessment consolidates reports or incidents relating to crimes committed with guns or activities of foreign intelligence services, it is basic intelligence. If it discusses differences over time, highlights changes, or addresses the significance of the events in a broader context, then it becomes explanatory or evaluative.

Most analysts learn the craft of analytic presentation by writing descriptive products that allow them to become familiar with their issues and data sources while they learn the substantive and professional operating environments. All levels of analysis require careful attention to identify and overcome mindsets, challenge thinking, and make good use of colleagues for collaboration. The analytic techniques used at this

---

FIGURE 5.5 ■ SATs That Describe

WHAT STRUCTURED ANALYTIC TECHNIQUES APPLY?

Techniques that summarize include the following:

- Chronologies and Timelines
- Matrices
- Sorting
- Starbursting
- Venn Analysis

Techniques that generalize include the following:

- Resorting, Scoring, and Prioritizing
- Minds Maps
- Link Charts

level involve source selection and assessment and organization at the low end, mostly involving sorting, organizing, and prioritizing data.[12] Current intelligence has much in common with journalism, which also ascribes to the goals of timeliness, accuracy, and relevance.[13]

- *Explanatory Analysis* probes the reason for or cause of a situation, getting at Why it has developed or is transpiring in the way portrayed by valid sources. At this level, analysts do not just organize and report interesting information but must use argumentation to give context for the facts, judgments, and observations about patterns or changes in behavior. Target analysis, a subset of intelligence analysis that focuses on discovering the identities and vulnerabilities of key intelligence objectives, usually falls into this category.

Explanatory Analysis of complex events may be the basis for intelligence assessments that aim to make sense of complex but ambiguous information and situations, such as economic disruptions or changes in crime patterns. Explanatory Analysis is also often included in current intelligence products to provide a rationale for a recent trend, such as increasing violence in a locale or potential test preparations around a missile site.

Explanatory Analysis is buttressed by techniques for manipulating and displaying information, then drawing logical conclusions that add value to the evidence and create knowledge through the derivation of novel explanations. The analytic techniques used in Explanatory Analysis mostly involve hypothesis generation and testing and other Diagnostic Techniques (see Figure 5.6).[14] The quality and accuracy of the conclusions depend on analysts' ability to apply expertise (their own and others) to the data, generate and test a variety of hypotheses, and identify diagnostic data to determine the most likely explanations.

- *Evaluative Analysis* examines the significance of a problem or topic as it relates to clients' interests, using logic to interpret and make judgments about various values or meanings behind the data. All of the previously mentioned analytic skills and techniques are used in evaluative analysis, but the distinction is primarily in the structure, data selected, and argumentation of the product. This may entail evaluating the nature of a situation (Is it a military exercise or

FIGURE 5.6 ■ SATs That Explain

WHAT STRUCTURED ANALYTIC TECHNIQUES APPLY?

Explanatory techniques include the following:

- Multiple Hypothesis Generation
- Analysis of Competing Hypotheses
- Structured Analogies
- Delphi Method
- Argument Mapping

an attack?), the quality of a course of action (Will the immigration policy have a positive or negative effect on the border?), extent of a problem (Will falling economic indicators precipitate a crisis?), or significance of a situation (Do decision makers need to pay attention now rather than next year?).

Most Evaluative Analysis will be written in the form of an assessment. Product success depends not only on the quality of your argumentation and judgments but on how well you have defined the question and whether it holds current or pressing interest for your clients. The Structured Analytic Techniques most often used in Evaluative Analysis come from the families of Diagnostic and Reframing Techniques and mostly involve hypothesis generation and testing, assessment of cause and effect, and challenge analysis (see Figure 5.7).[15]

- *Estimative Analysis* looks to the future, asking what might happen next and proactively anticipating courses of action that decision makers may take in response to potential stimuli. Estimative Analysis by definition is carried by its underlying framework of drivers, influences, and assumptions in the absence of hard data. Forecasts are based on analysts' experience, knowledge, and strategies for modeling evidence that include scenarios and the full range of Structured Analytic Techniques to instill rigor, spur imagination, and challenge mindsets.

The authors have a strong preference for the terms *estimative, anticipatory,* and *forecast* or *Foresight analysis* rather than formulations using the word *predict,* which imply point solutions that may be appropriate for scientific experimentation but are fraught with danger in assessing developments in the real world. Analysts are not handed a crystal ball at the start of their careers and should not be forced to promise what they cannot realistically deliver consistently and reliably. The job of an analyst is to provide accurate depictions of the range of potential events so that no matter what happens, clients are not surprised. The key to success for an estimative, anticipatory, or strategic foresight analyst is to imagine and portray the range of realistic scenarios, what decision makers might observe as the future is unveiled, and the implications of

---

FIGURE 5.7 ■ SATs That Evaluate

WHAT STRUCTURED ANALYTIC TECHNIQUES APPLY?

Evaluative techniques include the following:

- Cross-Impact Matrix

- Key Assumptions Check

- Indicators

- Premortem Analysis

- Structured Self-Critique

- Deception Detection

FIGURE 5.8 ■ **SATs That Estimate**

WHAT STRUCTURED ANALYTIC TECHNIQUES APPLY?

Estimative techniques include the following:

- Foresight Techniques
- Quadrant Crunching™
- What If? Analysis
- High Impact/Low Probability Analysis
- Red Hat Analysis

---

alternatives and choices available to deal with those futures. Structured Analytic Techniques employed for Estimative Analysis include Foresight Techniques, and variants of Challenge Analysis and Decision Support Techniques (see Figure 5.8).[16]

The Director of National Intelligence's *National Intelligence Strategy of the United States of America 2019*[17] distinguishes in its mission objectives *Strategic Intelligence*, which enables "deep understanding" of issues that have "enduring national security interest" from *Anticipatory Intelligence*,[18] which seeks to identify "new, emerging trends, changing conditions, and undervalued developments."

Both Strategic Intelligence and Anticipatory Intelligence incorporate critical elements of warning analysis and opportunities for action. Anticipatory Intelligence incorporates both Foresight analysis ("identifying emerging issues") and forecasting ("developing potential scenarios"). The primary challenge for analysts seeking to warn, identify opportunities, foresee, or forecast is to break free of established analytic mindsets and identify key assumptions that have ceased being valid. Analysts rarely succeed at this task unless they employ structured techniques like Quadrant Crunching™ or Cluster Brainstorming that help them reframe an issue or think about it more creatively. Anticipating clients' potential for action using decision support tools like the Opportunities Incubator™ can enhance analysts' ability to think freshly about an issue from the clients' perspective.

Hindsight Bias makes analysts prone to overestimate the accuracy and significance of their products about the future and clients prone to underestimate the value of those products on their perspectives and decisions. Analysts can mitigate this through strong analytic strategies and active client service; this provides a rich and consistent line of analytic products that support the ongoing decision-making processes.

"The future is plural."

—Peter Schwartz
The Art of the Long View

System 1 and System 2 Thinking

Intelligence analysts employ a wide array of approaches for describing the various ways they think about problems. Researchers and others who study intelligence analysis write about the relative benefits of qualitative versus quantitative techniques or the use of intuitive versus scientific or empirical methods. They debate passionately and periodically whether intelligence analysis is an art or a science. The National Academies of Science/National Research Council Committee on Behavioral and Social Science Research to Improve Intelligence Analysis for National Security has recommended testing analytic techniques to ensure they are more scientific.[19]

We are among the first to support testing and research to improve analytic methods, but we have worked long enough in the glare of crisis and with time and resource constraints to understand that intelligence analysis will never be synonymous with scientific research. We need to embrace the art as well as the science of doing good analysis, using the entire range of human cognitive abilities to illuminate difficult issues. When the US Institute of Peace tackled the question of whether quantitative models based on algorithms developed with historical data should replace qualitative models based on analysts' knowledge and experience, the report concluded that "the best results for early warning are most likely obtained by the judicious combination of quantitative analysis based on forecasting models with qualitative analysis that rests on explicit causal relationships and precise forecasts of its own" and warns decision makers to "insist" on getting the results from multiple methods.[20]

Over the past two decades, substantial research has been done on the cognitive processes involved in human judgment. One result has been the emergence of Dual Process theory, which posits two systems of thinking: System 1, which is intuitive, fast, efficient, and often unconscious, and System 2, which is analytic, slow, deliberate, and conscious.[21] This distinction is best described in Daniel Kahneman's book, *Thinking Fast and Slow*.[22] Analysts traditionally have relied mostly on System 1 thinking—intuitive judgment—when constructing their lines of analysis, drawing on evidentiary reasoning, historical case studies, and reasoning by analogy.

System 2 thinking posits four distinct methodological approaches, which are defined by giving different weights to two key drivers that are arrayed in a 2x2 matrix. The key drivers are determined by whether[23]

- the data to be manipulated are available for use in the analysis or partially or entirely unknown, and

- the analytic techniques to be used are qualitative or quantitative.

Each approach requires distinct expertise, some of which analysts will have learned in undergraduate studies, but some of which is pursued in specialized and advanced programs. Analysts should strive to become familiar with all types of analytic methods and proficient with several (see Figure 5.9).[24]

- *Critical thinking* helps the analyst apply expert judgment to structure mostly known data and generate qualitative evaluations. Analysts should learn many

FIGURE 5.9 ■ Matching Problem-Solving Techniques to Types of Thinking

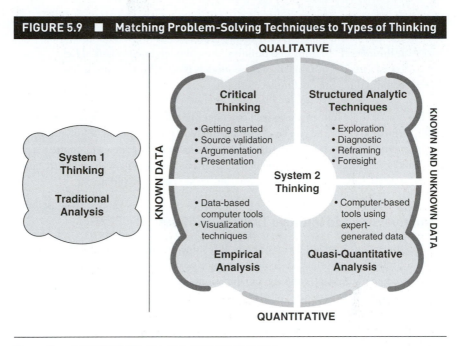

Source: Copyright 2020 Globalytica, LLC. All Rights Reserved.

of these critical thinking skills in liberal arts and social science academic programs, often in conjunction with geographic area or language expertise.

- *Empirical analysis*, statistics, and data-based computer models apply quantitative techniques to known data. Analysts should have sufficient grounding in mathematics and basic statistics to organize and aggregate quantitative data.

- *Structured Analytic Techniques* provide a means to instill more of the rigor of scientific inquiry into qualitative processes involving ambiguous situations where all the facts are not and may never be known. By externalizing the analyst's thinking step by step, it can be examined, questioned, and compared in collaboration with others to overcome mindsets, creatively anticipate the potential for disruptive change, and focus on information that helps distinguish one hypothesis or developing scenario from another. Over the past two decades, these techniques have become broadly taught and used by intelligence communities across the globe and increasingly in academia, business consulting, and private industry. Pherson and Heuer have grouped the techniques into six families: Getting Organized, Exploration, Diagnostic, Reframing, Foresight, and Decision Support.[25]

- *Quasi-quantitative analysis* is performed by computer-based models that attempt to deal with the unknown or unknowable by incorporating expert estimates into their algorithms. Special procedures designed to do this consistently and logically include Bayesian networks and simulation techniques. Designing and building these models is a specialized field; translating the insights from these models is often best accomplished in conjunction with qualitative methods.

No one of these four methods is better or more effective than another. The use of multiple methods over the course of a single analytic project should be the norm, not the exception. Of these four methods, structured analysis is the "new kid on the block." It is usually employed by a group, which helps protect against gaps in expertise, faulty mental models, incorrect key assumptions, and other cognitive pitfalls.

Cognitive Bias and Intuitive Traps in Analysis

As good as intuitive judgment often is, it is subject to many different types of cognitive limitations. Potential causes of bias include professional experience leading to an ingrained mental mindset, training, or education; the nature of one's upbringing; type of personality; past experiences; or personal equity in a given situation.

Cognitive biases are mental errors caused by the brain's simplified information-processing strategies. Some heuristics or experience-based techniques that generate a quick solution can save analysts time but may inject bias into the analysis. Hundreds of biases have been described in the academic literature using a wide variety of terms. The authors have identified a set of thirteen heuristics and cognitive biases that intelligence analysts are most likely to experience (see Figure 5.10).

These cognitive biases are well documented in the professional literature but do not cover all of the mental mistakes that analysts make. Additional research on the topic by the authors has generated a second list of eighteen intuitive traps that are common, everyday errors analysts make when evaluating evidence, describing cause and effect, estimating probabilities, and evaluating intelligence reporting (see Figure 5.11). Some of the classic intuitive traps analysts encounter are their tendencies to do the following:

- Ignore information when they lack a category for that bit of information

- Discount facts that do not support the analysis

- Overstate conclusions when only a few data points are consistent

- Fail to change the analysis when confronted with mounting contradictions

- Assume the present (or the future) is like the past

The role of System 2 thinking, and specifically Structured Analytic Techniques, is to help analysts overcome, avoid, or at least mitigate the impact of these cognitive biases and intuitive traps. Structured techniques spur analysts to question their intuitive judgments and think more rigorously about difficult problems. The process by which an analytic conclusion is developed is more transparent and therefore easier for a client to accept than one based solely on traditional intuitive analysis. The use of structured

---

FIGURE 5.10 ■ Glossary of Heuristics and Cognitive Biases

Selected heuristics that—when misapplied—can impede analytic thinking:

- **Anchoring effect:** Accepting a given value of something unknown as a proper starting point for generating an assessment.

- **Associative memory:** Predicting rare events based on weak evidence or evidence that easily comes to mind.

- **Availability heuristic:** Judging the frequency of an event or category by the ease with which instances of this comes to mind.

- **Desire for coherence and uncertainty reduction:** Seeing patterns in random events as systematic and part of a coherent world.

- **Groupthink:** Choosing the option that the majority of the group agrees with or ignoring conflicts within the group due to a desire for consensus.

- **Mental shotgun:** Lacking precision and control while making assessments continuously; providing quick and easy answers to difficult questions.

- **Premature closure:** Stopping the search for a cause when a seemingly satisfactory answer is found before sufficient information can be collected and proper analysis can be performed.

- **Satisficing:** Selecting the first answer that appears "good enough."

Selected cognitive biases that can impede analytic thinking:

- **Confirmation bias:** Seeking only that information that is consistent with the lead hypothesis, judgment, or conclusion.

- **Evidence acceptance bias:** Accepting data as true unless it was immediately rejected when first reviewed. Focusing more on the coherence of the story than the reliability of the underlying data.

- **Hindsight bias:** Claiming the key items of information, events, drivers, forces, or factors that actually shaped a future outcome could have been easily identified.

- **Mirror imaging:** Assuming that others will act the same as we would, given similar circumstances.

- **Vividness bias:** Focusing attention on one vivid scenario while other possibilities or potential alternative hypotheses are ignored.

Source: Copyright 2020 Globalytica, LLC. All Rights Reserved.

techniques and other critical thinking skills also saves time by expediting review and thereby compressing the production process.

For each of the six families of Structured Analytic Techniques, in Figure 5.12 we list two cognitive biases or misapplied heuristics as well as two intuitive traps that the techniques in that family are most effective in countering. The matches we selected are only illustrative of what we think works best. Additional research is needed to empirically validate the matches we have identified from our experience teaching the techniques over the past decade and exploring their relationship to key cognitive limitations.

FIGURE 5.11 ■ Glossary of Intuitive Traps

- **Assuming inevitability:** Assuming that an event was more certain to occur than actually was the case. Also referred to as the *illusion of inevitability*.

- **Assuming a single solution:** Thinking in terms of only one likely (and predictable) outcome instead of acknowledging that "the future is plural" and several possible outcomes should be considered.

- **Confusing causality and correlation:** Inferring causality inappropriately; assuming that correlation implies causation. Also referred to as *perceiving cause and effect*.

- **Expecting marginal change:** Focusing on a narrow range of alternatives representing marginal, not radical, change.

- **Favoring firsthand information:** Allowing information we receive directly to have more impact that what we learn or are told secondhand.

- **Ignoring the absence of information:** Not addressing the impact of the absence of information on analytic conclusions.

- **Ignoring base rate probabilities:** Failing to accurately assess the likelihood of an event when faced with statistical facts and ignoring prior probabilities or base rates.

- **Ignoring inconsistent evidence:** Discarding or ignoring information that is inconsistent with what the analyst expects to see.

- **Judging by emotion:** Accepting or rejecting what another group member says because the analyst likes or dislikes everything about that person. Also referred to as the *halo effect*.

- **Lacking sufficient bins:** Failing to remember or factor something into the analysis because the analyst lacks an appropriate category or "bin" for that item of information.

- **Misstating probabilities:** Miscommunicating or misperceiving estimates of subjective probability (most likely, could, probable).

- **Overestimating probability:** Overestimating the probability of multiple independent events occurring in order for an event or attack to take place.

- **Overinterpreting small samples:** Overdrawing conclusions from a small sample of data that is consistent.

- **Overrating behavioral factors:** Overrating the role of internal determinants of behavior (personality, attitudes, beliefs) and underestimating the importance of external or situational factors (constraints, forces, incentives). Often referred to as *fundamental attribution error*.

- **Presuming patterns:** Believing that actions are the result of centralized planning or direction and finding patterns where they do not exist.

- **Projecting past experiences:** Assuming the same dynamic is in play when something seems to accord with an analyst's past experiences.

- **Rejecting evidence:** Continuing to hold to an analytic judgment when confronted with a mounting list of evidence that contradicts the initial conclusion.

- **Relying on first impressions:** Giving too much weight to first impressions or initial data, especially if they attract our attention and seem important at the time.

Source: Copyright 2020 Globalytica, LLC. All Rights Reserved.

FIGURE 5.12 ■ **Matching Cognitive Limitations to Structured Techniques**

Cognitive Bias or Misapplied Heuristic	Family of Structured Analytic Techniques	Intuitive Trap
Vividness Bias Associative Memory	Getting Organized	Ignoring the Absence of Information Overinterpreting Small Samples
Mental Shotgun Satisficing	Exploration	Projecting Past Experiences Lacking Sufficient Bins
Confirmation Bias Evidence Acceptance Bias	Diagnostic	Relying on First Impressions Ignoring Inconsistent Evidence
Anchoring Effect Mirror Imaging	Reframing	Expecting Marginal Change Rejecting Evidence
Hindsight Bias Availability Heuristic	Foresight	Assuming Inevitability Assuming a Single Solution
Groupthink Premature Closure	Decision Support	Overrating Behavioral Factors Overestimating Probability

Source: Copyright 2020 Globalytica, LLC. All Rights Reserved.

Planning Your Analytic Project

Whether you are preparing to write about current events, interpret a newly collected set of data, explore emerging trends, or look into the future, your plan for research and production showcases what you are learning and the quality of your analytic skills and tradecraft. Here are some important things to keep in mind:

- Write down your plan and change it as needed rather than researching without a strategy, plan, or structure. Your plan and your products are the yardstick by which your analysis will be measured. An explicit strategy becomes particularly critical when you are engaged in a lengthy, high-profile, or multi-organization project.

- Plan for multiple products to highlight your progress. Research aids can provide valuable way stations as part of the process for producing a longer analytic product. Short pieces on new developments help you develop the expertise needed to produce longer papers on difficult, evolving, or more complex issues.

- Keep a list of your key assumptions, intelligence questions, and multiple hypotheses to be explored. Keep in mind that you are looking for evidence to disprove or eliminate a hypothesis. Review these lists as you complete the final draft of your paper or presentation.

- Search for the best information in the time you have available. Keep the ratio of time spent in research and production in balance. This is particularly useful if you can contact experts in government, academia, or private industry, or levy requirements on field collectors or external partners rather than being a prisoner of your inbox.

- Beware of the most common analytic pitfalls:

  o Not defining the problem or issue correctly

  o Jumping to a solution before analyzing the problem

  o Not involving people who know the most about the problem

  o Not having an open mind

  o Using the wrong criteria

  o Mirror imaging or assuming others think or act as you would

  o Assuming actors have more control or power than they do

Considering Research Methods

Research Purpose

The research phase involves both searching for the information and processing it to determine what it means with regard to the questions you are seeking to answer. Research methods are the ways—tools, techniques, and processes—you use to collect your data. Some use the terms *methods* and *methodologies* interchangeably, but they are at different levels of abstraction. You select appropriate methods—the "how to"—from the range of research methodologies—the "why to choose this method"—to discover insights and gain knowledge. Quantitative research methodologies, for instance, include statistical methods. Qualitative methodologies include methods such as interviewing and focus groups.

The methodology, of course, is based on the reason for the analysis and the type of argument you anticipate making in your product (see Figure 5.4). Depending upon your discipline and issue, your research might have one or more of these purposes:

- *Exploratory research* seeks to define and understand the key components or variables and how they relate to one another. It might involve a literature search, internet research, or expert interviews to build the conceptual framework on which your work on this issue will be based. It is the first step in attacking any new issue or project, whether in management, science, or social disciplines, but analysts need to be disciplined in their searches and not allow exploratory research to eat up valuable time needed for the rest of the analytic process.

Exploratory research establishes the intellectual footing that will help you fine-tune your questions, suggest methods or areas for investigation as part of this study or a following one, propose products for the near term or longer term, or start to pinpoint the criteria or drivers for conceptual types of analysis for which data do not readily exist (see Figure 5.2).

- *Descriptive research* aims to provide an accurate description of the issue and its key components; it fills in the features—the Who, What, How, When, and Where that comprise Descriptive Analysis on the Analytic Spectrum. What demographic or economic data will help us understand population movements in and out of urban areas? Who is managing and providing expert advice to political candidates and how does that play out in the candidates' platforms and communications strategies?

- *Explanatory research* probes the cause/effect relationships of the components, seeking the data that enable testing of hypotheses to understand how strongly variables are correlated and whether some are causes of others. Empirical research refers to experiments carried out to test hypotheses based on observations using physical senses or other sensing mechanisms.

- *Evaluative research* enables the construction of analytic arguments by providing evidence to support judgments and assessments about fast-moving events or recommendations for policy changes. Are risks increasing to US travelers to France and how can those risks be mitigated? What are the best strategies for improving the quality of analysis in our organization? Researchers must be careful to explore the full set of variables and find the best descriptive data, challenging the relationships among the variables to make solid arguments and not solutions with cherry-picked reasons to support it.

Quantitative Versus Qualitative

Researchers commonly distinguish between quantitative and qualitative methods, but many use a combination of both in their studies. The easiest way to distinguish between the two is that quantitative methods deal with numerical data and qualitative methods with words or images. Many projects use both methods—for instance, immigration data combined with interviews or case studies give a richer picture of the scope and detail of challenges on the southwestern US border.

- *Quantitative.* If the data you are collecting involves entities (people, places, things, events), then you can count and measure them using statistical methods to collate, interpret, compare, and verify your numbers. Mechanisms for collecting quantitative data include document reviews for numeric information, surveys, structured interviews and observations, and statistical applications.

  o *Benefits:* Data can be gathered from large numbers of participants, compared across groups, and generalized to broader populations.

Numerical information gives the impression of concreteness and is easy to use with statistical techniques to determine relations between variables.

- o *Cautions:* Quantitative methods provide an evidence-based perspective that appears objective and factual, but statistics and graphical representations can be misleading (see Chapter 18). They can also be just plain wrong and have difficulty recognizing and accounting for new phenomena. Quantitative data intended to measure opinions, beliefs, or preferences should be collected following established best practices They are by definition estimates provided by humans in response to questions posed by humans and, as a result, more subjective than the numbers might appear on the surface.

FIGURE 5.13 ■ Comparing Quantitative and Qualitative Research Methods	
Quantitative	**Qualitative**
Objective is to test hypotheses that the researcher generates.	Objective is to discover and encapsulate meanings once the researcher becomes immersed in the data.
Concepts are in the form of distinct variables.	Concepts tend to be in the form of themes, motifs, generalizations, and taxonomies. However, the objective is still to generate concepts.
Measures are systematically created before data collection and are standardized as far as possible; e.g., measures of job satisfaction.	Measures are more specific and may be specific to the individual setting or researcher; e.g., a specific scheme of values.
Data are in the form of numbers from precise measurement.	Data are in the form of words from documents, observations, and transcripts. However, quantification is still used in qualitative research.
Theory is largely causal and is deductive.	Theory can be causal or noncausal and is often inductive.
Procedures are standard, and replication is assumed.	Research procedures are particular, and replication is difficult.
Analysis proceeds by using statistics, tables, or charts and discussing how they relate to hypotheses.	Analysis proceeds by extracting themes or generalizations from evidence and organizing data to present a coherent, consistent picture. These generalizations can then be used to generate hypotheses.

- *Qualitative.* Qualitative methods seek to get at meanings, focusing on and describing subjects' experiences, perspectives, attitudes, beliefs, and values that might explain their behaviors and doing so in ways that cannot be conveyed in numbers. Mechanisms for collecting qualitative data include document exploitation for themes; observation of participant activity; interviews, surveys, or questionnaires that are unstructured or semi-structured using open-ended questions; focus groups; and case studies.

  o *Benefits:* Qualitative methods do not have response limitations so can provide richer content, relate anecdotal information, uncover new phenomena, and aid in deeper, more nuanced understanding. Verbal information can be captured in digital form to take advantage of the strengths of quantitative techniques.

  o *Cautions:* Verbal input can be difficult to generalize and to use to assess relationships between variables. It cannot be directly assessed by statistical methods.

W. L. Neuman in one of the most highly regarded textbooks on research methods offers detailed explanations on how to undertake specific methods and provides a useful table regarding the differences between qualitative and quantitative research methods (see Figure 5.13).[26]

Choosing Your Methods

What is the best means to get information that will help you answer the questions you have posed? For each question, you can brainstorm the possible sources of information and means of collecting it (see Figure 5.14). Work on the assumption that you have multiple ways of accessing information, some of which will be more feasible

FIGURE 5.14 ■ Research Method Planning Matrix					
Research Questions	Evidence Needed to Answer Questions		Methods to Gather Evidence	Difficulty	Priority
	Quantitative	Qualitative			

Source: Copyright 2020 Globalytica, LLC. All Rights Reserved.

within your time and resource limitations and some of which will be more essential to ensuring the quality of your study. Your ultimate plan will be a series of trade-offs to maximize your available time and capabilities.

As you make your trade-offs for collection activity, you will understand in which order you should do the following:

- Identify and check your assumptions

- Outline the Who, Where, What, and When of the collection method

- Identify specific collection procedures or statistical tests to be followed

- Specify requirements for materials and other logistical and personnel support

Standards for Research Methods Quality

Research standards have been recommended or defined for some disciplines or specialized areas of research, but not generalized. In our opinion, the most important rule is to design your research methods to withstand the scrutiny of your peers, supervisors, and reviewers who might support or criticize your work.

- Ensure your research methods clearly address the questions you are answering.

- Justify your scope and methods based on solid exploratory research of the context and existing literature or data sets.

- Make your methods and processes transparent to facilitate external review.

- Identify clearly how you conceptualized representative samples and implemented quantitative measurements.

- Evaluate the quality of all sources and the currency and accuracy of all data.

- Avoid asking leading questions in surveys, interviews, or focus groups.

- Test any research instruments before using them in a live research setting.

- Obtain appropriate permissions of any human subjects or interviewees, protecting their personal information and ensuring they are fully informed of the research purpose and how their input will be used.

- Check your key assumptions and potential impact of cognitive or political bias.

- Buttress findings or conclusions when possible with multiple sources of information.

- Consider alternative explanations for findings or conclusions.

- Keep careful and accurate notes, adhering to production standards for research reports.

Understanding the Limits of Research

The next chapter will go into more detail on types and evaluation of information sources. We cannot mention frequently enough, however, that all the sources, research, and hypothesis testing in the world will not yield answers to today's most difficult and relevant questions. Good research and good data are necessary but not sufficient to stay on top of the most pressing issues in our changing world or to find solutions to our most serious problems. Analysts must learn the critical thinking skills, modeling, and Structured Analytic Techniques to reason through problems for which they do not have—nor will ever have—all the data they need to come up with certain solutions.

KEY TAKEAWAYS

- An explicitly defined strategy builds credibility for the product by providing a baseline the analyst can use to communicate progress and make adjustments to deal with changing needs and deadlines. It guides the analysts' research and analysis by sorting the wheat from the chaff and identifying information gaps and other areas in which to create knowledge.

- Critical thinking involves asking the right questions, identifying analysts' own assumptions, reaching out for sources, assessing the data for quality and pertinence to answering the question, forming and evaluating hypotheses, and drawing conclusions. The process of planning, collecting, assessing, and concluding is similar to most problem-solving processes.

- Analysts should seek out and understand the commonalities among various problem-solving methodologies—such as Design Thinking, Computational Thinking, and Geospatial Thinking—that can enable them to view their problem through a different lens.

- The strategy will depend upon whether the analyst's analytic argument will be descriptive, explanatory, evaluative, or estimative; what kind of data—if any—exist regarding the question; and whether to use qualitative or quantitative methods to exploit these data.

- Analysts should make a plan; write down their plan, assumptions, questions, and hypotheses; and monitor whether any of these change while drafting the paper.

- Before starting work, analysts should always check that the product meets the threshold for being new, different, or of particular or pressing interest to the client.

- Research methods can be for the purposes of exploring the issue, describing the components and dynamics, explaining relationships, and evaluating evidence to support analytic arguments.

- Quantitative methods allow numerical manipulation of data; qualitative methods focus more on verbal nuances.

- Research plans should be transparent, address the questions, follow best methodological practices, check for the impact of bias, consider multiple sources of information and alternative conclusions, and be well documented.

- Critical thinking skills and Structured Analytic Techniques help analysts reason their way through problems for which they do not have—nor will ever have—all the data they need for deductive conclusions.

CONSIDERING THE CASE STUDY

Review Case Study IV, "The End of the Era of Aircraft Carriers," and briefly answer the following questions:

- How would you define the issue for a global strategist, naval commander, weapons designer, or a senior policy official?

- What problem-solving methodologies might be useful in guiding your collection and analysis planning?

- What information is each client likely to request?

- Where would you look for information on the new technologies and evolving naval strategies and how would you structure a research plan?

- Name three cognitive biases and intuitive traps to which analysts working on this issue might fall victim.

- Is your analytic argument descriptive, explanatory, evaluative, or estimative? Do sufficient data exist to address this issue?

- How could a conference of experts help to answer the key questions?

NOTES

1. Yogi Berra, *When You Come to a Fork in the Road, Take It! Inspiration and Wisdom From One of Baseball's Greatest Heroes* (New York: Hyperion, 2002), 53.

2. We are indebted to Cynthia Storer for sharing this metaphor with us and have incorporated it into our teaching materials.

3. Robert Coram Boyd, *The Fighter Pilot Who Changed the Art of War* (New York: Back Bay Books, 2002).

4. For more on Design Thinking, check out IDEO's website, https:// designthinking.ideo.com/, and Stanford's Hasso Plattner Institute of Design, which includes online offerings such as a "Virtual Crash Course in Design Thinking," https://dschool .stanford.edu/resources/a-virtual-crash -course-in-design-thinking. IDEO chair Tim Brown's 2009 classic has recently been updated. See *Change by Design: How Design Thinking Transforms Organizations and Inspires Innovation*, rev. ed. (New York: Harper Business, 2019).

5. For more on Computational Thinking, see Peter J. Denning and Matti Tedre, *Computational Thinking* (Boston: MIT Press, 2019).

6. Stephen Noonoo, "Computational Thinking Is Critical Thinking. And It Works in Any Subject," EdSurge.com, May 21, 2019, https://www.edsurge .com/news/2019-05-21-computational -thinking-is-critical-thinking-and-it -works-in-any-subject.

7. See Katherine Hibbs Pherson et al., "Geospatial Thinking Is Critical Thinking," in US Geospatial Intelligence Foundation, *2018 State and Future of GEOINT Report*, February 1, 2018, http:// trajectorymagazine.com/wp-content /uploads/2018/02/SFoG_2018.pdf.

8. We thank Frank Marsh for sharing this analytic problem-solving method with us in his comments on the outline for this book.

9. Stephen R. Covey, *Seven Habits of Highly Effective People* (New York: Simon & Schuster, 2013), 102.

10. This categorization of types of analytic arguments is based on a wide range of academic and career experience but is specifically informed by Aristotle's *Rhetoric*; contributions of Sherman Kent as cited in Rob Johnston, "Foundations for Meta-Analysis: Developing a Taxonomy of Intelligence Analysis Variables," *Studies in Intelligence* 47, no. 3 (2003); Russell Ackoff as cited in Gene Bellinger, Durval Castrol, and Anthony Mills, "Data, Information, Knowledge, and Wisdom," 2004, www.systems-thinking.org/dikw/dikw.htm; and David T. Moore, *Species of Competencies for Intelligence Analysis* (Washington, DC: Advanced Analysis Lab, National Security Agency, 2003).

11. In the late 1970s, a study conducted for the US Army studying signals intelligence and imagery intelligence task processes concluded that "intelligence analysis is conceptually driven as opposed to data driven. What is critical is not just the data collected, but also what is added to those data interpreting them via conceptual models in the analyst's store of knowledge." Robert V. Katter, Christine A. Montgomery, and John R. Thompson, "Human Processes in Intelligence Analysis: Phase I Overview," *Research Report* 1237 (Woodland Hills, CA: Operating Systems, December 1979).

12. See Randolph H. Pherson and Richards J. Heuer Jr., *Structured Analytic Techniques for Intelligence Analysis*, 3rd ed. (Washington, DC: CQ Press/SAGE, 2021), Chapter 5 on Getting Organized Techniques, 69–87, and Chapter 6 on Exploration Techniques, 87–126.

13. Office of the Director of National Intelligence, "Intelligence Community Directive 203: Analytic Standards," January 2, 2015.

14. See Pherson and Heuer, *Structured Analytic Techniques*, Chapter 7 on Diagnostic Techniques, 127–179.

15. See Pherson and Heuer, Chapter 7 on Diagnostic Techniques, 127–179, and Chapter 8 on Cause and Effect and Challenge Analysis Techniques, 190–224.

16. See Pherson and Heuer, Chapter 9 on Foresight Techniques, 249–304; Chapter 8 on Conflict Analysis Techniques, 203–234; and Chapter 10 on Decision Support Techniques, 305–346.

17. Director of National Intelligence, *National Intelligence Strategy of the United States of America 2019* (January 22, 2019), https://www.dni.gov/files/ODNI/documents/National_Intelligence_Strategy_2019.pdf?utm_source=Press%20Release&utm_medium=Email&utm_campaign=NIS_2019.

18. The Intelligence Advanced Research Projects Activity (IARPA), the research arm of the DNI, defines Anticipatory Intelligence as focusing on "characterizing and reducing uncertainty by providing decision makers with timely and accurate forecasts of significant global events," https://www.iarpa.gov/index.php/about-iarpa/anticipatory-intelligence.

19. Committee on Behavioral and Social Science Research to Improve Intelligence Analysis for National Security/National Research Council, *Intelligence Analysis for Tomorrow: Advances From the Behavioral and Social Sciences* (Washington, DC: National Academies Press, 2011), 84.

20. Jack A. Goldstone, "Using Quantitative and Qualitative Models to Forecast Instability," *US Institute of Peace Special Report*, no. 204 (March 2008): 1.

21. For further information on Dual Process theory, see the research by Jonathan Evans and Keith Frankish in *Two Minds: Dual Processes and Beyond* (Oxford: Oxford University Press, 2009) and Pat Croskerry in "A Universal Model of Diagnostic Reasoning," *Academic Medicine* 84, no. 8 (2009).

22. Daniel Kahneman, *Thinking Fast and Slow* (New York: Farrar, Straus and Giroux, 2011).

23. A more detailed description of System 1 and System 2 thinking and the four types of System 2 thinking can be found in Pherson and Heuer, *Structured Analytic Techniques*, 15–18.

24. Examples of models that have been used in the US Intelligence Community to support empirical, quasi-quantitative, and structured forms of analysis are provided in Chapters 7 and 18.

25. Pherson and Heuer, *Structured Analytic Techniques*, 35.

26. W. L. Neuman, *Social Research Methods: Qualitative and Quantitative Approaches*, 7th ed. (Boston: Allyn & Bacon, 2014).

6 CAN COLLABORATION CONTRIBUTE TO A BETTER ANSWER?

SETTING THE STAGE

As our world grows ever more complex and interconnected, analysts are increasingly taking on risk if they choose to produce stand-alone analytic products. The blurring of boundaries between analyst, operator, and decision maker means that expertise is increasingly distributed. As a result, reaching outside our immediate organization for information, insight, and assistance becomes more necessary every day. The Canadian government has underscored the value of analytic collaboration by highlighting the building of collaborative networks as one of eight best practices all analysts should emulate (see Figure 6.1).[1] The Canadian list provides a succinct catalog of critical thinking skills and the fundamental relationship between good analysis and collaborative teamwork.

We are all encouraged to collaborate, but the reality often proves far more difficult to achieve. Why is this so? Collaboration has become a buzzword that makes sense in principle but is hard to make work in practice. In 2008 and 2009, one of the authors led an interagency study for the Office of the Director of National Intelligence (ODNI) that focused on how best to achieve a robust collaborative environment in the US Intelligence Community. The first major finding was that the community had far more examples of collaboration failures than successes. As a result, the study focused on discovering what makes collaboration work. After establishing several collaborative networks and examining how they functioned, the study team identified six imperatives,

---

FIGURE 6.1 ■ Analytic Best Practices for Canadian Analysts

1. Reflect on the problem, determining possible approaches.
2. Be resourceful and systematic in collecting information, documenting sources, and noting caveats.
3. Critically evaluate the quality of all information.
4. Develop multiple hypotheses and explanations and show tolerance for uncertainties.
5. Challenge mindsets, assumptions, and biases.
6. Build collaborative networks.
7. Use Structured Analytic Techniques (SATs).
8. Write clear, concise, well-documented, and client-focused reports.

Source: Reproduced with permission of the Canadian government.

some associated doctrine, and four critical enablers that are necessary for collaboration to succeed.[2]

LOOKING MORE DEEPLY

Collaboration is known to work effectively when all participants are located in a task force or other interagency or interoffice grouping that has been specially created to deal with a pressing problem of mutual concern. It has proved far more difficult, however, to build robust collaborative networks in the virtual work environment.

The authors' extensive involvement in the interagency process has led them to conclude that the key to establishing a robust collaborative environment lies in focusing attention primarily on human factors. Collaboration is fundamentally about behaviors and interactions among individuals working toward common objectives enabled by information technology, organizational policies, and underlying cultural norms. Key factors to consider when engaged in building or sustaining a collaborative network include the following:

- The correct nexus for virtual collaboration is the human interface with other minds, not the human interface with information systems.

- Robust social networks serve as an essential underpinning of collaboration; they ensure that communities can come together to bring more expertise to bear on the topic, promote analytic excellence, and facilitate informed decision making.

- Achieving a robust collaborative environment requires sustained leadership commitment on the part of all senior leaders.

Inviting colleagues from sister units or other organizations to engage in a Key Assumptions Check or a brainstorming session is a good method for facilitating the establishment of collaborative networks (see Figure 6.2).[3] Bringing in outside expertise also guarantees a richer and more productive discussion. Similarly, participating in a Delphi Method or Outside-In Thinking, or conducting an informal workshop to fill out a Cross-Impact Matrix, are useful ways to elicit information at the initial stages of a collaborative process.

We often tell our students that the choice of technique is secondary; the primary objective is to create a structured environment that people can use to work together on a project. The message is simple: We need your help and expertise on this issue to apply this technique successfully, so please join our session. Invariably, once the initial contact is made, the chances are greatly improved that the participants will begin collaborating more effectively.

One hypothesis that remains to be tested is that collaboration is most effective when relatively small groups of eight or fewer individuals are involved. When the group gets larger, maintaining trust among all the participants becomes more difficult. Another hypothesis is that collaboration is hard to achieve if group members have not met one

FIGURE 6.2   ■   SATs for Promoting Collaboration

WHAT STRUCTURED ANALYTIC TECHNIQUES APPLY?

Techniques for promoting collaboration include the following:

- Cluster Brainstorming
- Key Assumptions Check
- Cross-Impact Analysis
- Delphi Method
- Outside-In Thinking
- Impact Matrix
- Opportunities Incubator™

another in person. Some argue that this is less critical with younger analysts who are more practiced with virtual social networking. The ODNI study also concluded that the difficulty of collaborating in virtual environments is often underestimated. When we cannot read others' body language in a virtual world, knowing if someone is making assumptions or using definitions that are different from our own is much harder.

Six Imperatives

The ODNI study determined that successful, sustained collaboration is most likely to occur when members foster a collaborative environment that promotes positive, even enthusiastic, participation. The following characteristics, which we have dubbed the six imperatives, are key to creating and sustaining such an environment, particularly when participants need to rely on virtual collaboration to sustain their interactions (see Figure 6.3):

1. *Mission criticality.* Members of a collaborative community must see their participation as essential to their core activities and not as a "nice-to-have" activity or as a resource to exploit when they have extra time. For virtual collaboration, users should feel a personal need to tap the network, engage their colleagues, and work in the shared environment as part of their daily routine. If several organizations decide to collaborate in creating a joint database, the data should only reside in the shared space; no one should be required to enter data into their home system and then enter it again into a shared database.

2. *Mutual benefit.* Participants must derive benefits from each other's knowledge and expertise in ways that help them perform their missions. They must recognize that they will not succeed—or their product will be inferior—if they work alone. Participants should possess a shared sense of mission and articulate a common set of goals and objectives for the collective good.

FIGURE 6.3 ■ Achieving a Robust Collaborative Environment

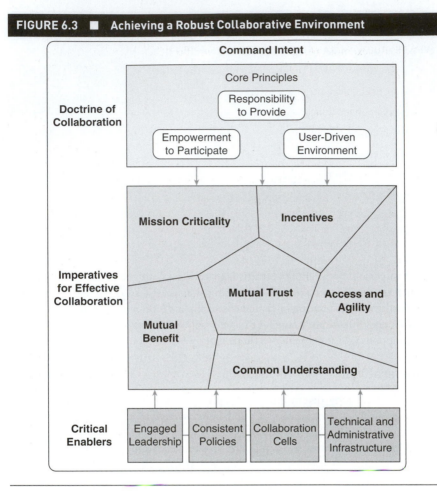

Source: Copyright 2020 Pherson Associates, LLC. All Rights Reserved.

3. *Mutual trust.* True collaboration is a personal process that requires the willingness to share partly formed opinions and insights, risk being wrong, expose one's vulnerabilities, and adopt new business practices. For these reasons, people feel the need to trust those with whom they collaborate. A good way to develop such trust is to organize face-to-face meetings. Such sessions lay the groundwork for future interactions in the virtual environment. As trust develops, participants become more willing to engage in collaborative behavior.

4. *Incentives.* Collaborative work practices must save participants time over the long run and increase the impact of their analysis. The most important and often overlooked incentive for collaborating is the psychic reward that comes from solving a hard problem, making a unique contribution, or contributing a profound

insight. Effective collaboration at the start of a project almost always leads to faster coordination at the end. Managers need to reinforce these messages by setting an example, recognizing the benefits of collaboration, and giving credit for collaboration and teamwork when evaluating their personnel.

5. *Access and agility.* Collaboration requires that users can quickly connect with each other and, given the pace of world events, coalesce into virtual work groups or add new members to their group within hours, if not minutes. Policies and collaboration tools must enable innovation, "public" thinking, broad dissemination, and the tracking of information sources but also permit compartmented and confidential small-group collaborations.

Achieving the necessary degree of agility requires business processes that foster the organic shaping and reshaping of collaborative communities. One innovative approach is to establish "trust bubbles" made up of interlocking cells of six to eight colleagues. A high level of trust is easier to maintain in such small cells. Individuals who belong to two or three cells are much more efficient human sharers of information. They know exactly how much information their colleagues can absorb when transferring data or insights from one trust bubble to the other. They also know what is most appropriate to share given that group's culture and work style.

6. *Common understanding.* A concerted effort to understand cultural differences across multiple organizations and to develop a common lexicon and transparent rules of engagement can reduce misunderstanding (see Figure 6.4). Given the wide variety of organizational cultures, the chances for miscommunication abound. The authors have derived anecdotal evidence from decades of working with interagency teams and task forces that suggests the amount of miscommunication that occurs in such settings is consistently underestimated. For example, perceptions of how much time one has to respond to a new discovery or tasking can vary greatly across national and organizational cultures. Similarly, the need for lists of common terms, acronyms, and definitions cannot be understated. The development of mutually agreed-upon rules of engagement for a collaboration initiative or environment can promote a common understanding and build mutual trust.

Core Principles

Overcoming the many obstacles to collaboration will require that senior leaders—and the entire workforce—understand and embrace a new doctrine composed of three core principles:

1. *Responsibility to provide.* Analysts should not be at the mercy of information "owners" who must give them permission before they will be allowed to share information with others who need it to do their jobs. In the US Intelligence Community, this means that the culture and mindset of "need to know" must

FIGURE 6.4 ■ **Stop! Define Your Rules**

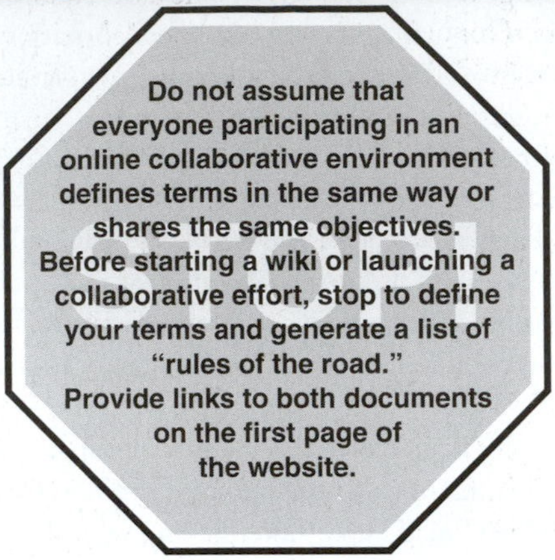

Do not assume that everyone participating in an online collaborative environment defines terms in the same way or shares the same objectives. Before starting a wiki or launching a collaborative effort, stop to define your terms and generate a list of "rules of the road." Provide links to both documents on the first page of the website.

be replaced with a culture in which everyone accepts responsibility to share information with those who need it to perform their mission. While responsibility to protect sources and methods or proprietary information remains, the expectation is that analysts must act to ensure that the right people get the right information in a timely manner. As the workforce takes more responsibility to share knowledge, management must also take responsibility to provide clear guidelines and training on the characteristics of a good sharing environment that enables the mission while safeguarding sensitive information.

2. *Empowerment to participate.* People should be empowered to engage with others and share their insights, information, and work in progress (within preestablished and clearly communicated guidelines) without having to first seek the permission of their superiors. Empowerment also carries responsibility. Guidelines are essential to establish what can be shared, how, and with whom. Explicit "rules of the road" govern how people engage with others within and outside their organizations. The function of management is to audit—not restrict—these exchanges. Risk-averse managers may prefer the alternative—to require preapproval for every interaction—but this will ensure that little or no collaboration takes place.

The key is to foster an open, sharing environment and accept the risk that on occasion someone might cross the line. From an information-sharing standpoint, reeling someone in who starts to cross the line is far better than setting inflexible boundaries and enforcing penalties whenever those boundaries are crossed. A philosophy of risk management should replace the all-too-frequent bureaucratic norm of risk aversion that discourages sharing in order to diminish or eliminate risk. Some mistakes may be made, but the overarching value is that a culture has been created in which true collaboration may take place.

3. *User-driven environment.* Collaborative communities should be self-defining, self-creating, agile, and adaptive. The users should effectively own their work environments. This principle simply acknowledges the complexity and fluidity of the world in which we now must function. In the intelligence and law enforcement communities, the adversary is increasingly likely to be a network, not a state or a well-defined, hierarchical organization. It usually takes a network to confront a network, underscoring the need to instill a high degree of agility in our collaborative work environments if we are to succeed.

Critical Enablers

Successful implementation of a robust culture of collaboration requires proactive engagement by all participants to ensure that the leadership is committed, the technical and human support infrastructure is in place, and organizational policies are aligned. These four critical enablers are as follows:

1. *Engaged leadership.* Virtually every study of successful transformation of a business culture includes a key finding that change must be led from the top. If chief executive officers do not practice what they preach, then their employees will view pronouncements about the need to collaborate as empty rhetoric or just another fad. More important, engaged leaders send powerful messages to the workforce when they integrate collaborative practices into their daily work practices and those of their staff.

2. *Collaboration cells.* Collaborative systems are almost certain to fail in large bureaucracies if the participants do not have access to "human enablers" or facilitators who can advise on how best to collaborate and assist in tailoring a set of collaborative tools to specific work objectives.[4] Collaboration cells or analytic tradecraft support units provide this essential ingredient in the process, addressing key human factors that have traditionally been overlooked.

3. *Consistent policies.* Policies must support collaboration and be consistent across all participating organizations and adjusted when they are not. Managers should be particularly alert to situations where oft-cited, restrictive "policies" turn out to be better described as deeply encrusted traditions. In many cases, when collaboration collides with bureaucracy, closer scrutiny will reveal that what was asserted as dogma is no more than common practice that managers who value collaboration can change fairly easily.

4. *Technical and administrative infrastructure.* One of the quickest ways to discourage an analyst's desire to collaborate is to make collaboration software difficult to obtain, too challenging to use, or much-needed technical support too hard to access when problems arise. Analysts are much more inclined to use collaborative software when the software is intuitive, access is easy, and technical support is readily available.

Coordination: Avoiding Battles and Encouraging Dialogue

Disagreements generally arise from one of three root causes.[5] Think about your disagreements in the office or at home and you will find that they generally fall into one of three categories:

1. Having different facts or perceptions

2. Interpreting those facts differently

3. Having different goals or objectives for the desired outcome

If we can learn to diagnose which of these three root causes is leading to a coordination problem, we have a much better chance of finding a way to resolve our differences.

Different Facts

Differing data, views of what happened, or information about any topic is the most obvious and basic cause of disagreements. Exercises show that when faced with a new problem, most people usually start with the de facto assumption that others around them are working with the same information. Obviously, that is often not the case; by nature we each draw on different historical knowledge and observation skills. When you assess that others' information differs from yours, uncovering the discrepancy and communicating the "missing" facts is much easier said than done.

In a situation where you and a subordinate or a colleague have reached an impasse that you think is caused by disparate facts, consider the following ABCs of sharing information.

- *Ask* the other person for more information. Note that proactive attitudes will be key to making this—and every subsequent step in the process—work. If the discussion appears to have stalled, begin by first asking the other person for the facts or data that lead them to their views or assessments. Telling others your facts before asking for theirs can be viewed as lecturing or trying to correct the other person's facts. You also put yourself at risk of being misinformed or just plain wrong if the other person's facts are more complete than yours.

Always ask open-ended questions that will encourage others to share their information, such as, "Where did you look for your data?" Resist the temptation to counter each fact others present. It may take several data points for them to fully lay out their argument. Focusing on your response to each will keep you from seeing their broader point and appear to be unduly confrontational. When in doubt, ask for clarification.

- *Brief* the other person on your facts. Fill in the gaps, provide additional facts, or gently correct information they have that you assess is incorrect. Try to use as much context as you can with your facts, showing similarities, historical parallels, or other ways to help them make sense of your facts and eventually accept them. If they do not initially accept your whole set of facts, remember that—just as opinions can take time to change—some people need time to process.

FIGURE 6.5 ■ SATs for Managing Conflict

WHAT STRUCTURED ANALYTIC TECHNIQUES APPLY?

Techniques for managing conflict in the coordination process include the following:

- Key Assumptions Check
- Analysis of Competing Hypotheses
- Argument Mapping
- Mutual Understanding
- Joint Escalation
- The Nosenko Approach

Techniques for identifying and resolving differences include:

- Analysis of Competing Hypotheses

Techniques to support the decision-making process include the following:

- Pros-Cons-Faults-and-Fixes
- Force Field Analysis
- Impact Matrix

● *Continue* cooperative communication. If you sense that others are reluctantly accepting your facts, continued communication is always needed to maintain trust. If their facts were correct, your continuing engagement shows you are not a sore loser. If you were right, you should show you have not discounted them and their opinions.

● *Document* the facts. If you are confident your facts are correct, and the ABC process has been unsuccessful, consider different ways to portray your facts to others. Illustrating data in a matrix, chart, graphic, or any other tangible, visual form can prompt others to see it differently and help both of you "visualize" the correct information (see Figure 6.5, Chapter 16 on argumentation, and Chapter 18 on graphics).

Different Interpretations

You and your colleagues may interpret information differently because:

- You hold different assumptions about the facts
- You weigh or value the same data differently
- You have different experiences working with similar facts or situations
- You bring varying skills to processing and interpreting information

Resolving differences depends on identifying why you view or value information differently. These variations are not unnatural or "bad"—they are opportunities for strengthening your products and team relationships. They provide you with insights into how others' experiences influence their analysis and reveal different worldviews that can benefit yours. Structured Analytic Techniques can be used to identify which data are driving the analytic conclusion or what assumptions are being made about the data or lack of data.[6] Once "all the cards are laid on the table," disputants can more effectively focus on the key differences, how these differences can best be resolved, and what strategies would be most effective in bringing the issue to closure.

If your colleague is not open to discussing your differences, then a structured debate or arbitration by an objective third party—usually a senior analyst or manager—is likely to be the most productive option. Six approaches to adversarial collaboration are described in *Structured Analytic Techniques for Intelligence Analysis*.[7] These approaches have proved effective for solving interpersonal analytic disagreements—as long as both players are open to a meeting of the minds. Two techniques that work particularly well in reducing conflict in coordination situations are Mutual Understanding and Joint Escalation:

- *Mutual Understanding.* In a meeting with a facilitator, the first side explains to the second its understanding of the other's position. The first must do so in a way that satisfies the second that its position is fully understood. Then the roles are reversed, and the second must explain the first's position to its satisfaction. This mutual exchange is difficult to do without listening closely to each other's position and trying to understand both the logic and facts that provide the foundation for the other side's position. Once both sides understand each other's positions, they can more effectively resolve differences and agree how best to disagree.

- *Joint Escalation.* The most successful way to refer disputes to higher authorities is to have both sides collaborate on a single document laying out both positions that will be provided to both superiors. This requires each analyst to understand—and address—the other analyst's position. It also ensures that the managers have access to all aspects of the problem before weighing in on the issue.

Different Goals or Objectives

The most difficult situation occurs when parties have the same facts and have evaluated them the same way, but each party wants a different outcome because of personal values or beliefs, personal defensiveness, or bureaucratic defensiveness. Uncovering those psychological differences is hard and, even when they can be identified, the parties may not be able to overcome or circumvent them. While this is the norm with political discourse, every effort should be made to avoid it in professional analytic organizations (see Chapter 14 on politicization).

KEY TAKEAWAYS

- The key to successful collaboration is trust. This usually means that the number of people involved in the collaborative effort must be kept small.

- If the six imperatives for effective collaboration—(1) mission criticality, (2) mutual benefit, (3) mutual trust, (4) incentives, (5) access and agility, and (6) a common understanding—are not met, the experiment will almost always fail.

- The biggest incentives to collaborate are that it will save the analyst time over the long run and will make the analysis more compelling.

- The best antidote to coordination battles is empathy—being a good listener and striving to understand what motivates others (facts, varying interpretations of the facts, or different value systems) to challenge the analysis.

CONSIDERING THE CASE STUDY

Review Case Study IV, "The End of the Era of Aircraft Carriers."

- The article involves analysis of military, political, economic, and technological topics. The author is an expert in only one of these areas. What would be a good strategy to get the author's peers in the other disciplines to collaborate in producing the article?

- When considering the six imperatives, which would you expect to offer the

greatest opportunities and which the greatest challenges?

- If the analyst had access to a collaboration cell, how might the cell have assisted with this case?

- If conflict arises in coordinating this article within the author's organization, would you expect the arguments to center on different facts, different interpretations, or different goals and objectives?

NOTES

1. This list was compiled by the Office of the Privy Council, Government of Canada, and is distributed to all intelligence analysts in Canada. It is used with their permission.

2. Randolph H. Pherson and Joan McIntyre, "The Essence of Collaboration: The IC Experience," in *Collaboration in the National Security Arena: Myths and Reality—What Science and Experience Can Contribute to Its Success* (June 2009), https:// nsiteam.com/social/wp-content /uploads/2016/01/Collaboration -in-the-National-Security-Arena -Myths-and-Reality.pdf. The article is part of a collection published by

the Topical Strategic Multilayer Assessment (SMA), Multi-Agency/ Multi-Disciplinary White Papers in Support of Counter-Terrorism and Counter-WMD in the Office of the Secretary of Defense/DDR&E/RTTO. Other articles in the collection that have direct relevance to collaboration in the intelligence arena include "Analytic Teams, Social Networks, and Collaborative Behavior"; "Small Groups, Collaborative Pitfalls, and Remedies"; "Blueprints for Designing Effective Collaborative Workspace"; "Breaking the Mold in Developing Training Courses on Collaboration"; and "Transformation Cells: An

Innovative Way to Institutionalize Collaboration."

3. See Randolph H. Pherson and Richards J. Heuer Jr., *Structured Analytic Techniques for Intelligence Analysis*, 3rd ed. (Washington, DC: CQ Press/SAGE, 2021), Chapter 6 on Exploration Techniques, 87–126; Key Assumptions Check, 132–137; Cross-Impact Matrix, 142–145; Delphi Method, 230–234; and Conflict Management Techniques, 235–248 for descriptions of these techniques and several others that could be used to stimulate more collaborative behavior.

4. For more information on this concept, see Randolph H. Pherson, "Transformation Cells: An Innovative Way to Institutionalize Collaboration," in *Collaboration in the National Security Arena*, 207. See note 2 above.

5. The information used in this section was adapted from Pherson Associates training materials (www.pherson.org).

6. See Pherson and Heuer, *Structured Analytic Techniques,* 345–346, which discusses four techniques analysts can use to evaluate where they have differences and develop action plans to resolve them, including the Decision Matrix, Pro-Cons-Faults-and-Fixes, Force Field Analysis, and the Impact Matrix.

7. See Pherson and Heuer, *Structured Analytic Techniques,* 237–242, which discusses six Conflict Management Techniques: Key Assumptions Check, Analysis of Competing Hypotheses, Argument Mapping, Mutual Understanding, Joint Escalation, and the Nosenko Approach.

WHERE IS THE INFORMATION I NEED?

Equipped with questions, context, and a plan to keep you on track, you can make sense of the information you already have and consciously set out to get what you need—or the best you think you can get—to provide answers, perspectives, or options. Will it be from direct observation or will you find that reports from secondary sources are satisfactory? How do you evaluate the validity of sources whose mindsets and biases may have influence on what they remember and how they report it? Can you trust the internet to provide credible information?

Part II provides more detail on building models to help organize your data search as well as tips on finding information that is relevant and credible. There is no lack of resources to tap, including substantive websites, publications, expert opinions from many sources, blogs and news feeds, forensic data, videos, overhead imagery, and many other forms. The goal of this section is to provide context for thinking about the information you seek and how you evaluate its applicability and validity.

We often ask our students what kinds and sources of information they typically use. Depending on their organization and their function, answers usually include internal databases, open-source data, intelligence or police investigative reports, and information volunteered by sensitive sources or informants. When we ask them where else they turn for additional information if their usual sources do not satisfy the need, they usually mention other analysts, outside experts, and social media.

When we brainstorm about what additional knowledge might be "created" or how they can combine bits of information in ways that will give them new insights into the problem, our students cite surveys, maps, polling data, matrices, link diagrams, and grey literature that usually is not available on the internet. The key is to gather the data readily available on established databases and then conduct research or send out collection requirements for others in your organization to fill important gaps. As you conduct your search for more data, you might even encounter pointers to data in places you never knew could be exploited.

The explosion of digital information, computing power, and processing methods is changing the landscape of what we know as data. Big Data is everywhere, opening extraordinary possibilities for understanding our environment on a continuous, real-time basis. But in the end, Big Data to an analyst is just more data; it fits into the same substantive categories and is subject to the same strengths and weaknesses in its interpretation and use as other types of data. Critical thinking skills are fundamental to both the data scientists who set up and extract insights from large data sets and the teams of analysts from other disciplines who will use those insights as data in their own work.

7 HOW DO MODELS HELP MY ANALYSIS?

SETTING THE STAGE

Models help analysts focus on the critical elements of an issue, viewing it holistically and in all its dimensions. Mathematical models strip away nonessential material so that analysts can see the key operational elements of a situation or the main structural elements of an argument. Visual models reduce a problem or a process to its essential elements and portray graphically exactly how these elements interrelate.

Analysts have long used models, including diagrams, charts, maps, tabletop terrain displays, and videos to analyze and visualize an issue. Political analysts create models to help project the outcome of elections. Economists create complex models to forecast economic trends and trade activity. Law enforcement agencies create fake "downtowns" comprising many city blocks to train officers in realistic urban settings. Military special operations units build life-size replicas of targeted facilities to give their soldiers an opportunity to practice operations such as hostage rescue.

Models help analysts organize their search for information in many ways. Well-built models should capture both the overarching dynamic of a situation as well as the critical internal parts. They will assist the analyst in doing the following:

- Identifying all the known parts of a problem and presenting them in a meaningful way that is both comprehensive and mutually exclusive

- Determining if any key information gaps exist and organizing research strategies to fill those gaps

- Generating collection or research requirements that are tightly focused on the underlying fundamentals

We are rapidly moving into a world where analysts are assisted by **A**rtificial **I**ntelligence (AI) and **M**achine **L**earning (ML) capabilities to process and draw meaning from complex sets of Big Data. Models are key to how analysts can prepare and harness the power of automated partners to take their analysis to new levels.

LOOKING MORE DEEPLY

Consciously identifying their internal mental models helps analysts organize their thinking. Turning the mental models into conceptual models enables them to communicate and interact with clients, colleagues, and machines enabled by AI/ML capabilities.

By working through a model of a system, process, set of relationships, anticipated situation, or even a geospatial/meteorological simulation, analysts can create systematic and coherent views of how to understand a problem or unravel a seeming puzzle or mystery. They can walk clients through the model step-by-step or—even better yet—have them interact with a dynamic model or simulation to test their own perceptions, predilections, or alternatives.

Models create opportunities for analysts to rethink their analysis by conducting sensitivity analysis on key variables by adjusting their weights. Once a quantitative or quasi-quantitative model has been developed and loaded with data, analysts can easily explore multiple outcomes by varying the weight or influence of key factors in the analysis. This allows analysts to isolate what really matters—to identify the factors that exert the most influence over what will be the final outcome. Once identified, this information can be extremely valuable to policymakers and decision makers whose job it is to manipulate the variables in ways that most benefit national or corporate interests.

Remember that the model is a tool to enable analytic thinking and judgments, not the analysis itself. Creating models to explain a phenomenon or situation provides an ideal platform for representing a line of analysis. If the model is used to create the outline for the paper, the analyst should be more confident that the paper will capture all the key elements, illuminate key links and relationships, and present a coherent overall picture of the phenomenon being studied. The model can also lay the framework for a graphic that illustrates the primary line of argument in a paper. It is often said that a picture is worth a thousand words; having a simple but elegant model can make your analysis compelling.

Models can be used to support each of the four types of qualitative and quantitative analytic techniques introduced in Chapter 5.

Critical Thinking Skills

A simple model that is prevalent in most texts about intelligence analysis is the depiction of the intelligence cycle (see Figure 7.1).[1] Most intelligence agencies have their own version of the cycle, but all versions depict a process of generating requirements, tasking collection, collecting the information, processing it, analyzing it, and disseminating the analysis to the client or policymaker. The Canadian example of the intelligence cycle (see Figure 7.2) expands the model to show how the intelligence cycle interacts with law enforcement to support intelligence-led policing.

The models shown in Figures 7.1 and 7.2 capture all the key functions of intelligence analysis, but most intelligence professionals will say that it is never that simple. All of these processes do occur, but almost never in a serial fashion. Seasoned analysts will explain that the arrows should be circles, and every element should have its own feedback loop. If presented in all its complexity, the actual intelligence cycle would look more like a bowl of spaghetti. If crafted with the appropriate precision, it would present a powerful—and highly complex—graphical display of how the community actually functions.

FIGURE 7.1 ■ Depictions of the Intelligence Cycle

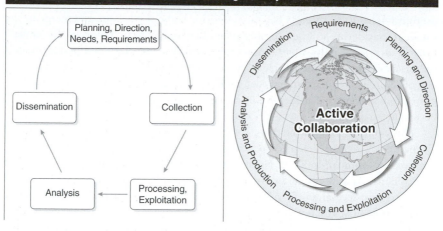

Source: Reproduced with permission of the Canadian government.

FIGURE 7.2 ■ Intersection of the Intelligence and Law Enforcement Cycles in Canada

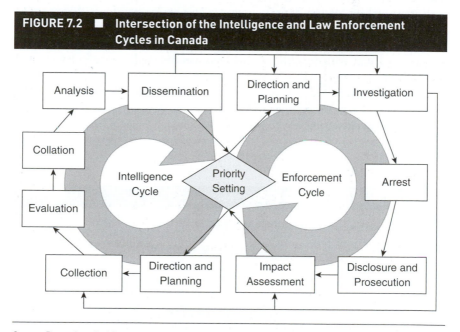

Source: Reproduced with permission of the Canadian government.

Structured Analysis

Several Structured Analytic Techniques, such as the Cross-Impact Matrix, Network Analysis, Multiple Scenarios Generation, Quadrant Crunching™, and the Complexity Manager,[2] can generate useful models for the profession of analysis (see Figure 7.3). One of the strengths of Multiple Scenarios Generation and Quadrant Crunching™ is that they fabricate multiple models that can be used in Foresight analysis to help analysts think about what might emerge in the future. Considering a large number of models reduces the potential for embarrassing surprise. Analysis by Contrasting Narratives develops competing models for describing a phenomenon from the perspective of the policymaker, adversary, and other interested parties and then melds them into an overarching picture. The more models that are considered, the more confident the warning message and the better the analysis!

This concept is illustrated in Figure 7.4, which is taken from a Quadrant Crunching™ exercise designed to help analysts anticipate the kind of attack that occurred in Mumbai, India, in November 2008.[3] In this exercise, analysts are asked to consider alternatives to the lead hypothesis that insurgents will launch simultaneous attacks against several tourist sites in Mumbai using grenades and AK-47s. Analysts generate alternatives for both the "How" and the "What" in this case, positing that the attack could be either a single large attack or an extended attack that involves taking hostages (the "How") and that it could involve either preplaced or portable bombs or suicide bomb attacks (the "What"). The Quadrant Crunching™ model tasks analysts with arraying these contrary dimensions in a 2×2 matrix to create four different stories about how an attack might be launched. The 2×2 matrix forces the analyst or team of analysts to reframe the problem in four different ways. As a result, four distinct stories are generated, each with very different consequences and implications for law enforcement officials.

The example provided in Figure 7.4 illustrates only one of several matrices that would be produced by this technique. For example, if the lead hypothesis contains five distinct elements involving two contrary dimensions for Who, What, How, Where, and Why, then at least ten matrices would be created, generating at least forty mutually

---

FIGURE 7.3 ■ SATs for Generating Models

WHAT STRUCTURED ANALYTIC TECHNIQUES APPLY?

Techniques that can generate useful models include the following:

- Cross-Impact Matrix

- Network Analysis

- Venn Analysis

- Multiple Scenarios Generation

- Morphological Analysis

- Analysis by Contrasting Narratives

- Counterfactual Reasoning

FIGURE 7.4 ■ Mumbai Quadrant Crunching™ Exercise: Sample Matrix

Lead Hypothesis	Contrary Dimension 1	Contrary Dimension 2
How: Simultaneous Attacks	Single Large Attack	Extended Attack With Hostages
What: Grenades and AK-47s	Preplaced and Portable Bombs	Suicide Bomb(s)

How
Single Large Attack

+

Label: **Wreaking Havoc**

Key Characteristics

- Insurgents attack a major tourist hotel placing bombs at entrances and in all major public spaces.

Endpoint of Scenario
- Large numbers of civilian casualties, including many foreigners; attackers escape.

Label: **Making a Statement**

Key Characteristics

- Insurgents drive a huge truck bomb into the front entrance of a well-known tourist hotel at dinnertime causing major structural damage.

Endpoint of Scenario
- Truck bomb explodes, substantial civilian casualties and attackers die.

WHAT
Preplaced and Portable Bombs

-

+

WHAT
Suicide Bomb(s)

Label: **Maximum Chaos**

Key Characteristics

- Attackers overrun several major tourist sites taking hostages and exploding small bombs periodically to sow terror.

Endpoint of Scenario
- Extended sieges, a few lasting over a week resulting in many hostages and all attackers killed.

Label: **Deadly Deception**

Key Characteristics

- Attackers take over three trains, take hostages, enter into prolonged negotiations for publicity but eventually detonate suicide bombs.

Endpoint of Scenario
- Period of terror lasts over a week and all hostages and attackers die.

-

How
Extended Attack With Hostages

Source: Copyright 2020 Globalytica, LLC. All Rights Reserved.

exclusive stories. By creating multiple models and stories with this reframing technique, analysts can greatly increase their confidence that they have considered all the possible ways a situation could develop.

Empirical Analysis

Most models do more than just summarize the available information; they explain how each of the parts relates to others and what the sum of the parts will produce. A perfect example of this is the Political Instability Risk Assessment Model, depicted in Figure 7.5,[4] which captures all the critical dimensions of the political instability process. The model is built by first documenting the root causes or sources of discontent and conflict and then assessing the opposition's ability to articulate and mobilize them. The likely impact of these forces is weighed against the government and society's capacity to respond effectively. Is the government perceived as legitimate? Are adequate resources available to respond and counteract? Are the institutions strong? Does the government hold a monopoly over the use of coercive force? Once these factors are taken into consideration, the analyst can assess the potential for political instability and whether it is most likely to be manifested as a form of civil unrest, conspiracy, insurgency, turmoil, or peaceful political change.

The task of the social scientist is to find empirical data that can be used to represent each critical dimension of the model and then apply various algorithms to generate an assessment of a government's vulnerability to each form of instability. For example, specific drivers of instability can be posited, such as the level of corruption of senior officials, lack of health care, and the presence of refugee populations. Inhibitors of instability can include foreign direct investment, regional integration, and deflationary economic policies.

The elegance of the model is that traditional analysts can use it to gain a deeper understanding of the process of instability and credentialed social scientists can use it to create highly sophisticated empirical predictive models of a government's vulnerability to several forms of political instability.

The value of a model is that it simplifies highly complex systems by capturing the underlying dynamics in a systemic fashion. Models can also mislead, however, if key elements are missing, linkages are incorrect, or the evidentiary base for building the model is flawed. This latter point was vividly illustrated by Alan Greenspan in congressional testimony on October 23, 2008, when he described what precipitated the US financial crisis in late 2007 and 2008:[5]

> In recent decades, a vast risk management and pricing system has evolved, combining the best insights of mathematicians and finance experts supported by major advances in computer and communications technology. A Nobel Prize was awarded for the discovery of the pricing model that underpins much of the advance in derivatives markets. This modern risk management paradigm held sway for decades. The whole intellectual edifice, however, collapsed in the summer of last year [2007] because the data inputted into the risk management models generally covered only the past two decades, a period of euphoria.

FIGURE 7.5 ■ **Political Instability Risk Assessment Model**

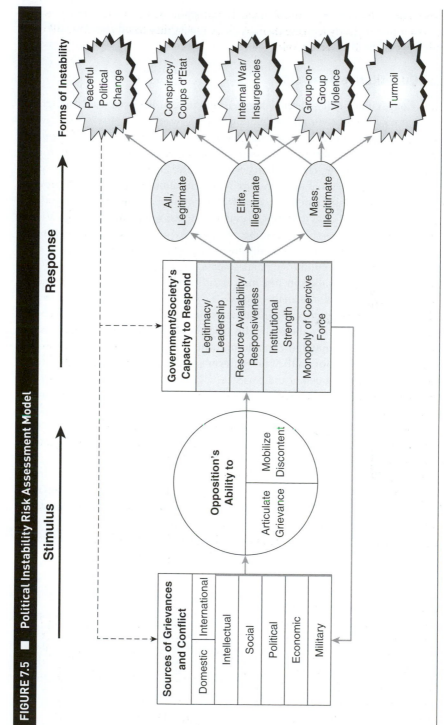

Source: Reproduced with the permission of Evidence Based Research, Inc.

Had instead the models been fitted more appropriately to historic periods of stress, capital requirements would have been much higher and the financial world would be in far better shape today, in my judgment.

Quasi-Quantitative Analysis

The Coup Vulnerability Methodology (see Figure 7.6) has been used with great success to track levels of civil-military tensions.[6] When a country is assessed to have a high level of vulnerability to civil–military tensions, a military coup is a distinct possibility. The model organizes fifty-four distinct factors that have been known in the past to contribute to rising civil–military tensions into a four-stage process analysts can use to monitor the level of such tensions in a given country. The model has proven most effective when analysts are confronted with reports that a coup is likely, but they lack the expertise or sufficient reporting to evaluate the seriousness of the threat. When run on a periodic basis for a large number of countries of interest, this model is an invaluable tool for anticipating potentially disturbing new developments.

Analysts must rate a country on a high–medium–low scale for each factor. If the ratings of the long-term indicators (the most significant factors in forecasting a coup) meet a predesignated level, the analyst proceeds to the next stage to rate short-term indicators that assess a country's vulnerability in the next six months. If sufficient short-term motives exist, then the analyst investigates both the triggering mechanisms necessary to spark a coup and any inhibiting factors. The model then generates an assessment of a country's overall level of vulnerability for serious civil–military tensions that often result in a coup.

The model was originally developed over the course of a three-day conference involving both academic specialists and government analysts. It was later refined to include data from both successful and unsuccessful coup attempts. It forces analysts to assess all the factors that might instigate or inhibit a coup attempt and helps them rate countries to determine which are the most important to monitor.

A key benefit of the coup vulnerability tool—and most models—is that it allows analysts to go back and change debatable ratings to see if a different rating has a major impact on the overall prediction—in this case, a vulnerability rating. It also helps analysts identify areas for future research or intelligence collection. Often this process will uncover key variables that a decision maker or policymaker can influence to decrease the potential of a coup or mitigate its impact.

Models and Artificial Intelligence

AI is founded on the promise of automated modeling—that "every aspect of learning or any other feature of intelligence can in principle be so precisely described that a machine can be made to simulate it."[7] As AI capabilities become part of our daily lives and work flow, analysts must understand what those capabilities are, how they are developed, and how they operate to be able to take advantage of the computing, storage, and data power being brought to the analytic workspace (see Figure 7.7 for definitions of key concepts).

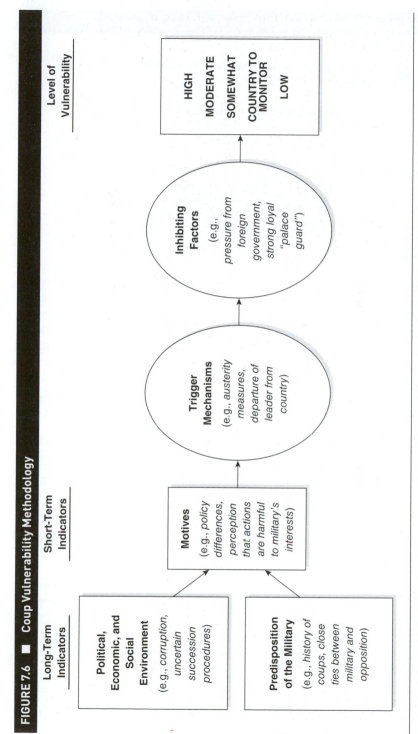

FIGURE 7.6 ■ Coup Vulnerability Methodology

Long-Term Indicators

Short-Term Indicators

Level of Vulnerability

Political, Economic, and Social Environment

(e.g., corruption, uncertain succession procedures)

Predisposition of the Military

(e.g., history of coups, close ties between military and opposition)

Motives

(e.g., policy differences, perception that actions are harmful to military's interests)

Trigger Mechanisms

(e.g., austerity measures, departure of leader from country)

Inhibiting Factors

(e.g., pressure from foreign government, strong loyal "palace guard")

HIGH

MODERATE

SOMEWHAT

COUNTRY TO MONITOR

LOW

Source: Reproduced with the permission of Evidence Based Research, Inc., and Pherson Associates, LLC.

FIGURE 7.7 ■ Definitions of AI/ML Concepts

Artificial Intelligence: Machines performing functions we associate with human minds.

Machine Learning: Algorithms detect patterns in very large data sets and are trained to make predictions and recommendations, improving over time with new data.

Deep Learning: Statistical models based on biological neural networks train the computer to learn on its own by recognizing patterns and using many layers of processing.

"Big Data"—which leverages today's computing power to harness and exploit burgeoning masses of digital information—is portrayed by some as the grand solution to analytic dilemmas. It holds incredible potential for improving and expanding the data sets and potential meanings that underpin our analyses, but to an analyst Big Data is just more nifty data to frame or build out their analytic arguments. It includes sources that are tangible or intangible, credible or questionable, entered correctly or entered incorrectly (see Chapters 8 and 9 for discussion of categories of data and how to assess them). Just because a data set is big and seemingly inclusive does not mean it is accurate. The same standards and criteria for judging its value apply to it and to its components as to any other data set.

Whether we are talking about IBM's Watson or interacting with the latest visualization or search tool, analysts must still employ the basic skills of critical thinking and analytic framing to use the data appropriately and come up with assessments that can be used by decision makers.

Thinking About AI and the Future of Analysis. At a 2019 conference in Australia, the authors framed a discussion about AI and analysis by tasking attendees to make two lists, one detailing what machines do best and the other what humans do best (see Figure 7.8 for a portion of the input).

This simple exercise made it clear that that the AI-enabled machine should be considered as what one of the authors calls "another smart colleague on the analytic team." Its contributions include the following:

- Rapid ingesting, processing, and triaging of data that frees analysts to do higher-level tradecraft practice

- Pattern recognition across data sets that identifies new and emerging threats

- Hypothesis and scenario generation that create new ways to think about and anticipate evolving threats

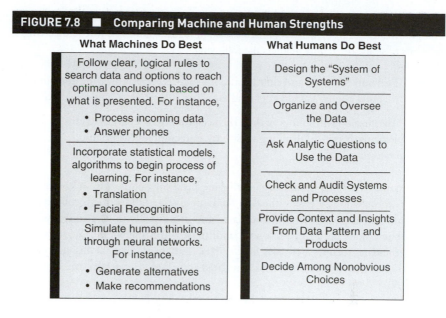

FIGURE 7.8 ■ Comparing Machine and Human Strengths

What Machines Do Best	What Humans Do Best
Follow clear, logical rules to search data and options to reach optimal conclusions based on what is presented. For instance, • Process incoming data • Answer phones	Design the "System of Systems"
	Organize and Oversee the Data
Incorporate statistical models, algorithms to begin process of learning. For instance, • Translation • Facial Recognition	Ask Analytic Questions to Use the Data
	Check and Audit Systems and Processes
Simulate human thinking through neural networks. For instance, • Generate alternatives • Make recommendations	Provide Context and Insights From Data Pattern and Products
	Decide Among Nonobvious Choices

Production is enhanced, not replaced. Human abilities and skills are improved, not supplanted. Deputy Associate Director of CIA for Learning Joe Gartin envisions an analytic environment in 2030 where

> ever-smarter algorithms mean analysts are focused on work that is consistently higher on the value chain. Artificial intelligence sifts data, spots discontinuities, and synthesizes results; analysts provide theory and structure. . . . But beyond just data, the information technology ecosystem our analyst is experiencing knows *much* more: her past analytic lines, sources of information, competing hypotheses, and alternative views. It also knows how good she is at her job.[8]

Gartner Group[9] captures this expansion of AI influence in its 2019 "Hype Cycle for Analytics and Business Intelligence." Beyond the data preparation/AI work that it calls "*augmented analytics*," the Gartner Group foresees an accelerating trend in building *digital cultures* with added emphasis on digital literacy for all and ethics to combat Digital Disinformation. Other growth areas include using AI to deepen our ability to understand connections through *relationship analytics*, behaviors through *decision analytics*, and implementation through *operationalizing and scaling* for "analytics everywhere."

Much Promise, Much Challenge. The McKinsey Global Institute, which has been tracking AI developments for many years, assessed in 2018 that AI's "time may have finally come after periods of hype followed by several 'AI winters' over the past 60 years."[10] It attributes the progress to algorithm development based on Machine Learning and Deep Learning, increases in computing capacity, and the gigantic amounts of data available to train the algorithms. Challenges remain that require advances in technology, broader adoption across companies and industries, and workforce skill changes. In terms of skills, the report predicts the following:

- "Demand for social and emotional skills such as communication and empathy will grow almost as fast as demand for many advanced technological skills."

- "Automation will spur growth in the need for higher cognitive skills, particularly critical thinking, creativity, and complex information processing."

We could not agree more about the future need for people with a combination of skills—those who can ensure the data fields are distinctly identified, collected, and cleansed as well as possible and then collated and processed with well-conceived algorithms. These skills need to be balanced with those of people who look for the weak spots in the data, identify new uses for the data, and ensure that the insights gleaned are communicated compellingly and translated into logical and effective action (see Figure 7.9).

In short, solid analytic practices can ensure that Big Data and AI enhancements do not become bad data or flawed analysis. University of California, Davis professor Duncan Temple Lang, in a National Institutes of Science report on training students to extract value from Big Data, noted that "with large data sets, it is easy to get mired in detail, and it becomes even more important to reason through how to solve

---

FIGURE 7.9 ■ Questions to Ask When Considering AI

- **What's the problem or purpose?**

  Is it clearly suited to AI technology?

- **What data are needed to fulfill the purpose or solve the problem?**

  Are data sources reliably identified and acquired?
  Can the data be validated?
  Are there standards for how the data will be consistently labeled and organized?

- **How are the AI processes and algorithms checked and audited?**

  Are they checked for accuracy, bias, and expected performance?

- **Does the implementation address ethical or financial trade-offs?**

  Are privacy and other human concerns identified and mitigated?
  Are the benefits worth the cost?
  Are potential negative implications anticipated and addressed?

Source: Copyright 2020 Pherson Associates, LLC. All Rights Reserved.

a problem."[11] Babson University professor Tom Davenport reminds us that "whether you're talking about Big Data or conventional analytics, intuition has an important role to play. One might say that developing the right mix of intuition and data-driven analysis is the ultimate key to success with this movement. Neither an all-intuition nor an all-analytics approach will get you to the promised land."[12]

Techniques for Harnessing the Power of AI and Big Data

1. Prepare to get value from the AI capability and data sources available to you.

    - Use the Getting Started Checklist (see Figure 4.1).

        ○ Focus on asking good questions.

        ○ Identify what data are needed.

    - Organize your mental framework based on your knowledge of the client's needs.

        ○ Understand how the AI conceptual model corresponds to your mental model and what adjustments might need to be made in either of them.

        ○ When identifying driving forces, be sure to define the end points of the axes to aid you in thinking of them not as a single phenomenon but as continua with a collection or progression of multiple possibilities.

        ○ Know the strengths and weaknesses of the data sources included in the big data set to take advantage of the automated strength in pattern recognition and visualization.

    - Try Cluster Brainstorming to identify the big picture and gaps.

    - Check your key assumptions about your issue.

2. Begin using the data sets in your analysis.

    - Generate multiple hypotheses.

    - Recognize disconfirming data.

    - Detect misinformation or disinformation.

    - Establish a clear context.

3. Build a compelling case.

    - Identify indicators for your key drivers.

    - Validate your sources.

    - Map your argument.

    - Look to the future with Foresight Techniques

- Ask how you might be wrong by conducting Premortem Analysis and Structured Self-Critique.

4. Present your conclusions.

- Take full advantage of visualization tools and capabilities.

Analysts can use Structured Analytic Techniques to help them identify what data are needed, analyze the data, and portray the data in a compelling way. Figure 7.10 summarizes how well fifteen structured techniques perform these three functions.

FIGURE 7.10 ■ Assessing the Value of SATs to Extract, Analyze, and Present Data			
	Value[a] of Using the Technique to		
Structured Analytic Technique	**Identify What Data Are Needed**	**Analyze the Data**	**Publish the Data Visually**
Key Assumptions Check	H	L	L
Mind Maps	H	L	L
Circleboarding™	H	L	L
Cluster Brainstorming	H	M	L
Chronologies	H	M	L
Timelines	H	M	M
Matrix	H	M	M
Argument Maps	H	H	M
Starbursting	M	H	L
Analysis of Competing Hypotheses	M	H	L
Inconsistency Finder™	L	H	M
Link Charts	M	H	H
Venn Diagrams	M	M	H
Gantt Charts	M	M	H
Flow Charts	L	M	H

H = high, M = medium, L = low.

Source: Copyright 2020 Globalytica, LLC. All Rights Reserved.

Argument Maps and Link Charts, for example, perform all three functions well but most others are stronger in some areas and weaker in others.

Cautionary Notes

Our biggest concern about AI/ML is that human analysts will come to accept the machine as knowing more or being infallible, perhaps out of lack of expertise, lack of transparency, or just plain laziness. Each of the studies we have cited underscores the need for analysts to be alert to the strengths and weaknesses of the technologies and the data sources and to develop thinking skills that enable them to keep pace with their automated partners. Key cautions include the following:

- Machine algorithms, like human judgment, are subject to biases and design errors.

- AI can be fooled. Deepfakes—videos that have been digitally altered through AI techniques—are inherently hard to detect. Deep Neural Networks (DNNs) will classify something with near certainty as a familiar object when the image produced is totally unrecognizable to human eyes.

- The data and its quality are key drivers.

Beware of the following traps:

- *Correlation/causation.* Big Data is great for rapidly discovering correlations that humans would miss, particularly if dealing with smaller data sets, but it does not infer causation. Tyler Vigen, a former Harvard Law student, in *Spurious Correlations*[13] demonstrates that "causation does not equal correlation" through a series of absurd line graphs, such as the almost identical curves of data comparing "per capita cheese consumption" with "deaths from entanglement in bedsheets." On his website (www.tylervigen.com), you can compare data sets to come up with your own ridiculously incorrect conclusions.

- *Intentionality/predictive accuracy.* Big Data connections and correlations do not in and of themselves infer intentionality or predictive certainty. This is one of the concerns of privacy advocates and others about using Big Data for highlighting potential security and insider threats. Even if the algorithms are good enough to be right more than 90 percent of the time, those taking action based on the data still need to leave open the possibility that the conclusion will not be correct in that single case.

- *Data fallibility.* Data, whether big, midsized, or small, is subject to the same weaknesses—it can be mischaracterized, miscopied, left out, or intentionally altered. New technologies can limit some of the unintentional errors and perhaps even the impact of some insertion of erroneous data, but important decisions and actions should be based on more than data crunching alone. The hacking of US government security clearance databases at the Office of Personnel Management (OPM) in 2015 and the potential that more could be corrupted remind us how easily trusted sources can become suspect. The authors once heard a senior government official say "data don't lie," but indeed they can, and they certainly can lead you and your analysis astray.

● *Data quality.* Experian's 2018 data quality study reported 89 percent of C-level executives believe inaccurate data hampers their ability to provide excellent customer service. They report the major sources were human error, which had increased significantly over the previous year; lack of communication between departments; and inadequate data strategies.

● *Web-based data.* Big Data analyses based on web-based data that appear initially useful can lose impact over time as source mechanisms morph. They can even become circular, reinforcing citations of themselves. Gary Marcus and Ernest Davis[14] point out that Google Flu Trends was once the "poster child for big data," but its predictive success has faltered in part because the Google search engine itself changes so that patterns in data collected at one time do not necessarily apply to data collected at another time. They also note it is particularly risky to draw conclusions from web hits that collect data in different ways with different purposes or that reinforce themselves by hitting on circular sources.

Cautions aside, this remains one of the most exhilarating times in history to be an analyst. Former secretary of state Henry Kissinger, former Alphabet CEO Eric Schmidt, and MIT dean Daniel Huttenlocher put it all in perspective in a 2019 article in *The Atlantic*:[15]

AI is neither malicious nor kind; it does not have independently developed intent or goals; it does not engage in self-reflection. What AI can do is to perform well-specified tasks to help discover associations between data and actions, providing solutions for quandaries people find difficult and perhaps impossible. This process creates new forms of automation and in time might yield entirely new ways of thinking.

Yet AI systems today, and perhaps inherently, struggle to teach or to explain how they arrive at their solutions or why those solutions are superior. It is up to human beings to decipher the significance of what AI systems are doing and to develop interpretations. In some ways, AI is comparable to the classical oracle of Delphi, which left to human beings the interpretation of its cryptic messages about human destiny.

If AI improves constantly—and there is no reason to think it will not—the changes it will impose on human life will be transformative.

KEY TAKEAWAYS

- Models improve critical thinking skills because they

  o are powerful tools for organizing the analysis and refining the line of argument;

  o help analysts discover key information gaps and develop research strategies;

  o aid the organization of an analyst's thinking as well as the visualization of key linkages and relationships; and

  o provide visually robust and effective presentations of lines of analysis and depict complex dynamics in readily digestible ways.

- Artificial Intelligence is based on "knowledge" models that combine with real-world observed data to derive conclusions. Analysts must understand how those models are developed and how they correspond to the analysts'

  mental model and other available conceptual models.

- AI, fueled by Machine Learning and Big Data, is a tool—or perhaps another "smart colleague down the hall"—that can help us

  o detect even obscure patterns so we can more quickly and accurately identify problems and anomalies;

  o generate alternative explanations and potential solutions; and

  o plan more effectively for the future, telling us in increasingly greater fidelity what *is* known so we can deal with what is *not* known.

- Analysts must continue to use solid analytic tradecraft and Structured Analytic Techniques to make the best use of AI capabilities and detect weaknesses in data, algorithms, or design.

CONSIDERING THE CASE STUDY

Review Case Study II, "Russian Disinformation: Lessons Learned From the MH17 Shootdown."

- What models were the Russians employing in trying to manage perceptions following the shooting down of Malaysian Airlines Flight 17?

- To what extent were these models utilized, refined, or augmented with the use of social media in the 2016 elections in the United States and the Brexit vote in the UK?

- Would you say these models were drawn from traditional analysis (critical thinking skills), structured analysis, empirical analysis, or quasi-quantitative analysis?

- How does an understanding of the models facilitate your understanding of the issue?

- What can you learn on the internet and through Foresight analysis about how AI technology and Big Data might impact Russia's disinformation programs?

NOTES

1. In Figure 7.1, the model on the left was taken from the report of "The Commission on the Intelligence Capabilities of the United States Regarding Weapons of Mass Destruction," March 31, 2005, https://fas.org/irp/offdocs/wmd_report.pdf. The model on the right is used by the FBI. The Canadian model in Figure 7.2 is taken from Gudmund Thompson, "Aide Memoire on Intelligence Analysis Tradecraft" (Ottawa, ON, Canada: Chief of Defence Intelligence, 2009), 8.

2. See Randolph H. Pherson and Richards J. Heuer Jr., *Structured Analytic Techniques for Intelligence Analysis*, 3rd ed. (Washington, DC: CQ Press/SAGE, 2021), for a description of the Cross-Impact Matrix, 142–145; Network Analysis, 118–125; Multiple Scenarios Generation, 272–276; Quadrant Crunching™, 204–211; and the Complexity Manager, 339–346.

3. A detailed description of the Mumbai attack and the Quadrant Crunching™ technique is provided in Sarah Miller Beebe and Randolph H. Pherson, *Cases in Intelligence Analysis: Structured Analytic Techniques in Action*, 2nd ed. (Washington, DC: CQ Press/SAGE, 2015), 259.

4. The Political Instability Risk Assessment Model was developed by Richard E. Hayes, president of Evidence Based Research, Inc. (www.ebrinc.com), and further refined by Randolph Pherson. It is one of the premier models for assessing political instability in the US Intelligence Community—and the political science community *writ large*—and has often been applied successfully by US government analysts.

5. Testimony of Alan Greenspan, US Congress, House, Committee on Oversight and Government Reform, *The Financial Crisis and the Role of Federal Regulators*, 110th Congr., 2nd sess., 2008, https://www.gpo.gov/fdsys/pkg/CHRG-110hhrg55764/html/CHRG-110hhrg55764.htm.

6. The Coup Vulnerability Methodology was first developed in the late 1980s by Randolph Pherson when he was managing analysis of political instability. It is based on an exhaustive literature review that identified key indicators and vulnerabilities based on a survey of 120 military coups between 1950 and 1985. Weights were developed for each indicator to reflect the relative historical impact of the factor on a country's level of vulnerability. US government analysts conducted the initial research and created a preliminary coup vulnerability model, adding additional indicators to reduce false positives. Grace I. Scarborough and Richard E. Hayes of Evidence Based Research, Inc. (www.ebrinc.com), validated the methodology, extended the historical research to 1989, researched and added 120 attempted—but failed—coups to the database, recalibrated the weights, and created a computer-based model that was used with notable predictive success by US government analysts for several years.

7. John McCarthy et al., "A Proposal for the Dartmouth Summer Research Project on Artificial Intelligence," August 31, 1955, http://jmc.stanford.edu/articles/dartmouth/dartmouth.pdf.

8. Joseph W. Gartin, "The Future of Analysis," *Studies in Intelligence* 63, no. 2 (July 2019).

9. Gartner Group, "Gartner Reveals Five Major Trends Shaping the Evolution of

Analytics and Business Intelligence," press release, October 2, 2019, https://www.gartner.com/en/newsroom/press-releases/2019-10-02-gartner-reveals-five-major-trends-shaping-the-evoluti

10. McKinsey Global Institute, "The Promise and Challenge of the Age of Artificial Intelligence," briefing note, October 2018, https://www.mckinsey.com/~/media/McKinsey/Featured%20Insights/Artificial%20Intelligence/The%20promise%20and%20challenge%20of%20the%20age%20of%20artificial%20intelligence/MGI-The-promise-and-challenge-of-the-age-of-artificial-intelligence-in-brief-Oct-2018.ashx.

11. National Research Council, *Training Students to Extract Value From Big Data: Summary of a Workshop*

(Washington, DC: National Academies Press, 2014).

12. Thomas H. Davenport, "Big Data and the Role of Intuition," *Harvard Business Review*, December 24, 2013, https://hbr.org/2013/12/big-data-and-the-role-of-intuition.

13. Tyler Vigen, *Spurious Correlations* (New York: Hachette Books, 2015).

14. Gary Marcus and Ernest Davis, "Eight (No, Nine!) Problems With Big Data," *New York Times*, April 7, 2014, https://www.nytimes.com/2014/04/07/opinion/eight-no-nine-problems-with-big-data.html.

15. Henry A. Kissinger, Eric Schmidt, and Daniel Huttenlocher, "The Metamorphosis," *The Atlantic*, August 2019.

WHAT TYPES OF INFORMATION ARE AVAILABLE?

SETTING THE STAGE

Developing solid practices for finding the right information will not only save time but also help ensure that the paper or briefing is tightly focused on the primary message. Analysts should first determine what type of information is needed to answer the question and to support the argument. The next step is to focus on what is knowable and how to get needed information that is comprehensive, detailed, up-to-date, and free of bias. Even if the information is known to exist, it may be private or proprietary and not readily accessible. If it is not knowable, then analysts need to turn to other techniques to anticipate what decisions might be made or how events may unfold in the future.

If the information is knowable and can be obtained, then the challenge is to identify credible sources that can provide it. Ideally, multiple independent sources can be found, particularly to corroborate new or controversial material. The best strategies are to seek direct observable evidence, to tap the knowledge bases of established experts, and/or to find well-placed and credible sources in positions to know the answers to the questions being asked.

LOOKING MORE DEEPLY

The goal is to locate or develop comprehensive, detailed, and up-to-date information that does not appear to be biased or to reflect an agenda. More often than not, particularly in intelligence, analysts must deal with data gaps, inadequate sources, fragments of information, and lots of ambiguity. Other authors have done a superb job of describing specific intelligence sources, collection techniques, and collection strategies, but that is outside the scope of this book.[1] Our concern is more generic. We believe all analysts need to understand the functions of the informational building blocks on which their analytic judgments will be based and know how to determine if the information supporting their judgments is based on weak reeds or strong foundations.

Generating an information-gathering strategy is a key task in drafting a Concept Paper or research design contract. In the Concept Paper, the analyst should lay out what data are needed and identify the mechanisms, time frames, resources, and anticipated obstacles in getting them. The information-gathering process, however, is not always straightforward. As your expertise on your issue grows, your analytic framework will grow in sophistication, as will your awareness of the available resources and the need to develop additional sources of information. Your source library will be made up of the following:

- Primary sources or the original, firsthand material and data that will underpin your analysis (i.e., transcripts, speeches, interviews, surveys, data from sensors, or other empirical data)

- Secondary sources or materials that use or interpret the primary data or sources (i.e., analyses, commentaries, reviews, or critiques)

- Tertiary sources or overviews or syntheses that are useful for establishing the scope of your issue (i.e., bibliographies, Wikipedia, encyclopedias, almanacs)

The Joy of the Data Hunt

For many analysts, seeking sources and researching relevant information is the most enjoyable part of an analytic project. It can become an end in itself, however, so analysts benefit from having guidelines and discipline to keep them on track when generating analytic products. Some key rules of the road that have guided the work of good analysts for decades include the following:

- *Check your framework for what you know and what you do not know.* Analysts first need to determine what information they already have before searching for additional data to fill known information gaps. Are they looking for facts, opinions, reasoned arguments, statistics, descriptions, or narratives? If census data or other authoritative records are needed to fill the gap, analysts are well served to search for the information on government websites or in other government publications. If, however, the questions concern a crisis—such as an earthquake, a major flood, or a sudden outbreak of violence—cell phones or a microblogging site such as Twitter or Instagram might be best placed to provide on-the-ground data about and images of moment-by-moment developments.

The easiest way for analysts to relate the knowns to the unknowns is with a matrix. Consider it to be a work in progress because you will likely not think of all the items the first time through. You can add a column to record the information you later learn is important, aptly dubbed by former defense secretary Donald Rumsfeld, "What you don't know you

> "The message is that there are
>
> - Things that we know that we know.
>
> - Known unknowns, that is to say, there are things that we now know we don't know.
>
> - And unknown unknowns—things we do not know that we don't know.
>
> Usually we pull together the known knowns and the known unknowns and each year we discover a few more of those unknown unknowns."
>
> —Donald Rumsfeld
> Department of Defense Press
> Briefing, February 12, 2002[2]

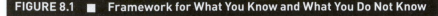

FIGURE 8.1 ■ Framework for What You Know and What You Do Not Know

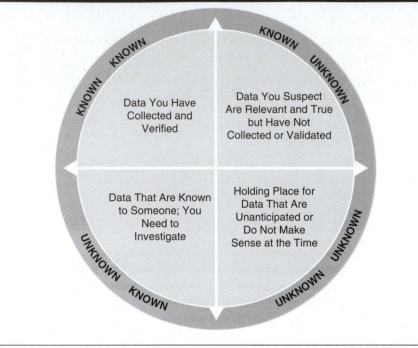

Source: Copyright 2020 Pherson Associates, LLC. All Rights Reserved.

don't know."[3] This provides a category or holding space for unanticipated or unexpected information or for things that just do not make sense at the time (see Figure 8.1).

Sometimes it is useful to consider a fourth category as well—the unknown knowns or what you do not know is known. This category consists of information—often from other disciplines—that provides fresh perspective, new insights, or confirmatory precedents for an argument. For example, while researching the behavior of a terrorist group, you might encounter a discussion in a medical journal of how a virus infects an individual and conclude that the process is similar to how a terrorist group tries to erode the fabric of society. Unknown known information can also include information that is generally perceived to be true but cannot be documented, such as a political leader who is known to have amassed his fortune through corrupt practices even though no documentation can be found to support the allegation.

- *Scan sources for a purpose.* Source selection should be deliberate (see Figure 8.2). Analysts need to understand who or what has directly observed the information being reported and whether an indirect source's reporting will be satisfactory. Wayne Booth, Gregory Colomb, Joseph Williams, and colleagues identified three uses for sources that can guide your selection process in *The*

FIGURE 8.2 ■ Tips for Screening Potential Sources

TIME IS PRECIOUS: TIPS FOR PROCESSING A POTENTIAL SOURCE QUICKLY

1. Skim the source structure, looking at the following:

   • Title, table of contents, or section headings

   • Abstract, executive summary, or preface

   • Topic sentences

   • References or bibliography

2. Summarize the main claims and supporting data.

3. Scan for key themes, concepts, and compelling items of evidence.

4. Relate them to your question and to one another.

Craft of Research, a classic resource that has recently been updated a decade after the deaths of its original authors:[4]

1. *Reading for problems.* This can help you form and hone your framework and understanding of the issue. Are there controversies, gaps, or contradictions that need to be resolved? Are there questions that your clients might not have had the time or insight to have articulated?

2. *Reading for arguments.* You need to know the logical arguments that have been made regarding the question you are trying to answer so that you can compare your data, find areas of agreement and disagreement, identify new areas for inquiry to get a better answer, and formulate your own arguments.

3. *Reading for data and support.* One of the main reasons for developing intelligence sources is to gather credible evidence. When screening, however, analysts must look for data and claims that both support an argument and that contradict or is inconsistent with it.

• *Set browsing boundaries.* Browsing—whether in the library, in a database, or on the internet—is fun for ever-curious analysts and critical to discovering novel insights and clarifying ways to think about hard problems. One of the biggest pitfalls, however, is becoming mired in the search process. Much analytic work, particularly that involving any kind of intelligence analysis, depends on quick reaction to short deadlines. Now that we can access contents of libraries from the comfort of our homes, aimless browsing for information of potential value can eat up valuable time.

Set limits for browsing in your production schedule and write down your search topics and how they evolve. It might help to categorize them by the type or function of the information you seek. Are you looking for facts, evidence, indicators, arguments, views, or observations that answer your intelligence question, help formulate or test hypotheses about future events, or lead you to other relevant information? To get that information, look for reliable sources that support, clarify, or challenge your view of what is going on.

- *Avoid satisficing.* Drawing conclusions based on the first data you find due to its ready availability is known as *satisficing*, and this is not a criterion for solid source selection. Particularly if deadlines are short, analysts are tempted to take shortcuts and judge the value of data by using criteria that are simply "good enough." They will mine databases that are familiar, easy to access, and have produced good results in the past. Avoid these temptations by taking a few minutes to think through your search and your selection criteria, checking to make sure you are not merely pursuing the course of least resistance.

- *Get out of your inbox.* Engage in Outside-In Thinking.[5] Seek data sources outside those that that normally arrive in your inbox or mailbox, or from other information feeds. Figure 8.3 contains a list of some readily accessible sources of information to spur your thinking. Limiting yourself only to those sources that populate your inbox can introduce bias into your analysis.

- *Levy requirements and seek information to fill gaps.* In the intelligence profession, analysts are encouraged to task human or technical collectors to get missing information. In academic and other analytic fields, reach out to experts and others who are developing technologies, methods, and insights that can take your work forward.

Understanding Source Strengths

Primary sources have a direct proximity to the topic or phenomenon being ana-lyzed, while secondary sources are one or more steps removed. Secondary sources com-ment on or draw from primary sources. Some people assume that primary sources are more reliable than secondary ones, but that is not always so. Direct observers may not be knowledgeable of what they are observing—such as a civilian observing a military event or a technology demonstration—or they may be eyewitnesses who get it wrong because they are reflecting mindsets, suggestions, or even stress.

David Schum, whose work we will discuss more in Chapter 9, developed a useful schema to think about the various types of sources you will be choosing among to sup-port your analytic argument.[6]

- *Tangible evidence.* Tangible evidence reflects direct observation and consists of such material as original documents, pictures, or physical objects (see Figure 8.4). These items can be supplemented with explanations from experts or technology sensors or other data. For example, after the March 2010 attack on the South Korean ship *Cheonan*, pieces of the torpedo used were found. Markings on the torpedo were identical to those on known North Korean torpedoes.

- *Authoritative records.* Authoritative records are generally regarded as credible (see Figure 8.5). In addition to such scientific data as the periodic table of elements and tidal charts, government records such as birth and

FIGURE 8.3 ■ Readily Accessible Sources of Information

Internet

- Search engines such as Google and Safari

- Sites of government ministries, nongovernmental organizations (NGOs), corporations, educational institutions, and private organizations that publish finished reports and other documents

- Dynamic reporting, including wikis, blogs, and news feeds

- The deep or dark web, including proprietary, password-protected, and subscription-based databases

- Social media sites through which users create online communities to share information, ideas, and other content, including Twitter, Instagram, and YouTube

- Image, video, and mapping sites

Open Source Media

- TV and radio broadcasts

- Newspapers

- Grey literature (conference proceedings, white papers, and other documents only available in hard copy)

Open Source Publications

- Books, handbooks, and reference materials

- Academic journals and magazines

- NGO publications

Government Publications

- Periodic government publications, surveys, and census reports

- Individual reports by cabinet agencies and other local and national government offices

Human Source Reporting

- Intelligence Community (clandestine sources)

- Law enforcement (informants)

- Academic and other subject matter experts

- Interviews and surveys

Diplomatic and Foreign Liaison Reporting

- Reporting from any part of a foreign government

- Reporting from international organizations

Intercepted Communications

- Spoken, written, typed, or faxed imagery

- Classified or unclassified systems

Imagery

- Classified or unclassified systems

FIGURE 8.4 ■ Tangible Evidence

Strengths	Weaknesses
Is primary source	Not always accessible
Can be authenticated	Can be faked before acquisition
Can be secured from tampering	Susceptible to sensor malfunction or error
Can aggregate data with data from other sources	Can be subject to data misinterpretation
If a journal, it is better if peer reviewed	May not have quality controls

FIGURE 8.5 ■ Authoritative Records

Strengths	Weaknesses
Is primary source	Not always accessible
Can be authenticated	Can be faked before acquisition
Can be secured from tampering	If unsecured, can be tampered with

death certificates, property records, and motor vehicle records are part of this category. A word of caution is needed, however. In this age of Digital Disinformation, we should always consider the possibility that the database may have been corrupted by hackers or by foreign adversaries. If analysts believe this could have happened, they should seek out other ways to validate the information most critical to the analysis.

- *Testimonial evidence.* Testimonial evidence consists of reports of a development, conversation, or event by an observer or participant in the activity (see Figure 8.6). This type of evidence can be directly observed or secondhand (obtained from someone else). Legally, secondhand reporting can be called *hearsay* evidence.

- *Circumstantial evidence.* Circumstantial evidence is not direct evidence but conclusions that rest on some observations plus assumptions the analyst has made (see Figure 8.7). For example, the pieces of the North Korean torpedo found in the area where the attack on the *Cheonan* occurred are assumed to have been involved in the attack on the ship. The pieces were found in the area weeks after the ship suffered the damage.

- *Negative evidence.* Negative evidence can be used to disprove a hypothesis (see Figure 8.8). Consider the circumstances surrounding the attack on the South Korean ship. The question of whether North Korea was preparing additional attacks arose. Negative evidence of North Korean plans for

FIGURE 8.6 ■ Testimonial Evidence	
Strengths	**Weaknesses**
Is primary or secondary source	Is subject to observer's reliability, access, expertise, objectivity, observational sensitivity, and cultural perspective
Often easier to collect than technological or data-driven information	Can be intentionally deceptive or unintentionally mistaken or misinformed

FIGURE 8.7 ■ Circumstantial Evidence	
Strengths	**Weaknesses**
Is based on observation	Is indirect evidence
Is available based on investigation	May be based on incorrect assumptions

FIGURE 8.8 ■ Negative Evidence	
Strengths	**Weaknesses**
Helps narrow range of possibilities	Is indirect evidence
Is inverse of tangible evidence	Needs to demonstrate its relevance to the hypothesis or cause-and-effect relationship

FIGURE 8.9 ■ Missing Evidence	
Strengths	**Weaknesses**
If explicitly identified, helps guard against errors	Hinders analysis
	Is usually hard to collect. If it were easy, it probably would have been collected already.

additional attacks was the absence of a stepped-up alert status for North Korean troops along the demilitarized zone separating North and South Korea.

● *Missing evidence.* Missing evidence is evidence that one would expect if a hypothesis were to be proven but which has not yet been found (see Figure 8.9). The search for Saddam Hussein's weapons of mass destruction (WMD) did not find evidence of such a program. If evidence had been found, it would have been considered proof of the existence of a WMD program. The absence of such information after a thorough search is now considered to be evidence that a WMD program did not exist at the start of the US invasion of Iraq in 2003.

Planning for Source Collection

Analysts should plan ahead to ensure they sample and access a broad range of sources that cross information domains. One of our colleagues teaches her students a five-step process for a successful intelligence collection effort:

1. Define the problem, target, topic, or issue as specifically as possible.

2. Craft a specific and realistic set of priority intelligence requirements.

3. Identify entities or resources that may have intelligence that can be used to satisfy the requirements.

4. Execute an engagement plan for contacting the sources, ensuring that contact mechanisms fit with the sources' preferences for doing business. This is particularly important in cross-domain communications where analysts will be dealing with organizations that have different policies, lexicons, communications channels, and culture.

5. Organize the collected sources through a target network model or spreadsheet to track how the information relates to the issue.[7]

Selecting Sources

When selecting sources to support your analytic claims and judgments, the most valuable ones are usually:

- Most directly relevant to the scope and purpose of the analysis

- Recent enough to be timely and unique

- Reflective of a declared point of view

- Appropriately expert or sophisticated

- Not further removed than a primary or secondary source

How do you know when you have enough sources? Most analysts start the drafting stage of their products with far more sources than they will end up using. You will be adding new sources and information and sloughing off those that are weaker or less interesting as you write. The goal is to find the fewest sources with the best information to make your case.

In some cases, analysts know that the information or insights they need to write their paper exists in field offices but has not been appropriately documented or reported. Usually, officers in the field element are more than willing to share their knowledge but are too busy performing their primary tasks and unable to find the time to write up a report. In such instances, the analyst should consider interviewing the field officers directly and preparing a written report of each conversation. In this way, the information the analyst needs will get "into the system," and he or she can be confident that the information needed to write the paper is documented and reported through appropriate channels.

Using Sources Appropriately

Sourcing and references are proof that analysts know their topic well and are critical to providing the facts or authoritative references to support their assessments (see Chapter 12). By providing references to others' work, the analyst gives credit to their contributions in helping understand difficult issues.

- *Attribute the source accurately.* Use direct quotations, summaries, or paraphrases that precisely reflect the source's context, including the intent, scope, and confidence in the information or the argument. Paraphrasing or expressing the source's information or perspective in your own words ensures that your product flows smoothly. Direct quotations are an effective way to draw attention to a particularly apt turn of phrase or to link source reporting to evidence in your argument. Make sure you clarify any points of agreement or disagreement so you are not "cherry picking," or selecting only data that make your case while ignoring other data that do not.

- *Avoid "copy and paste" and other forms of plagiarism.* Plagiarism—or using someone else's work as your own without citation—is a cardinal sin in analysis. The best way to avoid it—whether of an article or source report—is to identify your framework and plan up front so you are conscious of your original concepts, organization, and assessments. You can then work through your sources, crediting those you use for insights or evidence in your work. The standard for what is common knowledge and not original is a subjective one, but it is applied conservatively in most analytic communities.

Our dependence on computers and soft-copy documents makes us particularly vulnerable to unintentional plagiarism. The "copy" and "paste" functions enable us to quickly transfer and store data nuggets in files and notes, sometimes without adequate reflection of the source.

Whether such practices are holdovers from sloppy academic habits or result from the press of time, no excuses can be tolerated for plagiarism in analytic products. Editors may not know all the sources you consulted, but your peers, coordinators, and sometimes even your knowledgeable consumers will recognize copycat phrases or arguments. Many institutions also employ software engines that will detect plagiaristic practices. Your peers and your clients are counting on you to accurately portray source reporting, quoting the source document if necessary to get the substance and tone right.

- *Understand copyright restrictions.* Using someone else's materials for your work—articles, images, maps, sound and video recordings, web pages—almost always involves copyright protections that govern use and requires permission from the owner in advance of the use. Make sure you know the procedures your organization has in place for using or getting permissions to use these types of sources in your products.

- *Track and review sources over time.* For each issue, analysts are well advised to maintain a spreadsheet or database to track sources according to type, date, and strengths or weaknesses. Review the sheet periodically. Record source details as you conduct your research rather than waiting until you have completed the draft. This will greatly reduce the amount of time spent on writing citations.

Intelligence Community Source Standards

All argument claims eventually stand or fall based on the veracity of the cited sources. Most intelligence community agencies have disseminated specific guidance for evaluating and using sources. Key US Intelligence Community (IC) documents include the following:

- "Intelligence Community Directive 203: Standards of Analytic Tradecraft" sets out expectations for judging the quality and reliability of sources.[8]

- "Intelligence Community Directive 206: Sourcing Requirements for Disseminated Analytic Products" establishes Director of National Intelligence (DNI) requirements for IC-disseminated products to ensure consistent and structured sourcing information.[9]

The directives require that original, underlying sources be used in authoritative disseminated analysis to ensure the protection of sensitive sources and methods. Most of these standards direct that sources do the following:

- Be included as endnotes

- Include all appropriate descriptors

- Be summarized in a prominently displayed source summary statement that concisely describes the strengths or limitations of the key information used in the analysis

- Be retained for the record in a fully sourced copy

- Be appropriate for the classification level

Writing Source Summary Statements

Source Summary Statements, as currently used in the US Intelligence Community, provide concise summaries of the key source information used in the product. They do the following:

- Highlight specific information that describes the intelligence collection disciplines and diversity of information used

- Describe the underlying sources, identifying assumptions about the sources and relating how their information fits into the analysis

- Address strengths or limitations, including inconsistencies and gaps; potential for bias and deception; and degree of confidence in the information and judgments based on that information

Source Summary Statements can be woven into the text of the product, be part of the scope note, or appear in a separate text box. A formula for writing a good Source Summary Statement includes an initial sentence summarizing the type and quality of sources underpinning the product's analytic judgments, a second sentence characterizing the nature and quality of sources supporting the product's key assessment, subsequent sentences describing sources of lesser importance and highlighting unique characteristics of particular sources or analyst concerns about sourcing, and a concluding sentence discussing intelligence gaps.

KEY TAKEAWAYS

- Developing good practices for finding the right information will not only save time but will help ensure that the paper or briefing is tightly focused on the primary message.

- Analysts should first determine what type of information is needed to answer the question and support one's argument. The next step is to focus on what is knowable and how to get needed information that is comprehensive, detailed, up-to-date, and free of bias.

- When focusing on the information that will answer their question, analysts should first identify what is known and knowable and determine options for finding out what is not known.

- Analysts benefit from establishing guidelines to keep them on track and guard against aimless browsing. They should check what they know and do not know, scan potential sources deliberately with a purpose, and set limits on the amount and scope of browsing.

- By scanning easily accessible sources quickly and efficiently, analysts can move beyond their inboxes for information and expertise and avoid settling for the first set of adequate sources.

- Primary sources have a direct connection to the issue or phenomenon but may not be accurate or reliable because of their mindsets, suggestions, or even stress. Secondary sources comment on or make observations based on a primary source.

- Sources can be divided into tangible evidence, authoritative records, testimonial evidence, circumstantial evidence, negative evidence, and missing evidence.

- Sources should be appropriately attributed and quoted or paraphrased to avoid plagiarism.

- Sourcing and Source Summary Statements are the US Intelligence Community's means to be accountable for how sources are used in intelligence reporting and judgment.

CONSIDERING THE CASE STUDY

Review Case Study V, "Puzzling Food Poisonings in Germany."

- Where should you look to find authoritative information about the food poisoning outbreak reported in Germany?

- As you start your research, what is known and what additional information is needed?

- What are examples of primary and secondary sources used in this case study?

- What tangible evidence is used in this case study? Is the case based mostly on

tangible or testimonial evidence? Which is the more trustworthy?

NOTES

1. Two books that provide general overviews of sources are Robert Clark, *Intelligence Analysis: A Target-Centric Approach*, 6th ed. (Washington, DC: CQ Press/SAGE, 2019) and Mark Lowenthal and Robert Clark, *The 5 Disciplines of Intelligence Collection* (Washington, DC: CQ Press/SAGE, 2015).

2. United States Department of Defense, Office of the Secretary of Defense, "News Transcript: DoD Briefing—Secretary Rumsfeld and Gen. Myers," February 12, 2002, http://archive .defense.gov/Transcripts/Transcript .aspx?TranscriptID=2636.

3. Office of the Secretary of Defense, "News Transcript: DoD Briefing."

4. Wayne C. Booth et al., *The Craft of Research,* 4th ed. (Chicago: University of Chicago Press, 2016).

5. See Richards J. Heuer Jr. and Randolph H. Pherson, *Structured Analytic Techniques for Intelligence Analysis*, 3rd ed. (Washington, DC: CQ Press/

SAGE, 2021), Chapter 9 on Reframing Techniques, Outside-In Thinking, 191–194.

6. David A. Schum, *The Evidential Foundations of Probabilistic Reasoning* (Evanston, IL: Northwestern University Press, 2001), 114–120.

7. Jorhena Thomas, "Collection Planning: A Cross-Domain Approach," *Journal of Mediterranean and Balkan Intelligence* (December 2017): 59–71.

8. Office of the Director of National Intelligence, "Intelligence Community Directive 203: Analytic Standards," January 2, 2015, http://www.dni.gov /files/documents/ICD/ ICD%20203%20Analytic% 20Standards.pdf.

9. Office of the Director of National Intelligence, "Intelligence Community Directive 206: Sourcing Requirements for Disseminated Analytic Products," January 22, 2015, http://www.dni.gov /files/documents/ICD/ICD%20206 .pdf.

9 CAN I TRUST THE SOURCES?

SETTING THE STAGE

Access and reliability traditionally have been the primary attributes used for source evaluation by military and civilian intelligence agencies.

- *Access* refers to whether or not the source has personally observed the event or object.

- *Reliability* usually is based on whether previous reporting by the source has later proved to be accurate.

Source descriptions in most intelligence reports include an assessment of both these factors, either numerically or in narrative format. When this information is not known, the source will be described as untested or of unknown reliability. These are essential criteria, but the authors believe that analytic units both in the government and the private sector should employ a more robust set of criteria when validating sources.

The British have used the Admiralty Grading System to assess the reliability and the credibility of the information they receive (see Figure 9.1).[1] This grading system has been used widely for many years by other members of NATO, including

FIGURE 9.1 ■ United Kingdom Intelligence Grading Criteria			
Reliability of Source		**Credibility of the Information**	
A	Completely reliable	1	Confirmed by other sources
B	Usually reliable	2	Probably true
C	Fairly reliable	3	Possibly true
D	Not usually reliable	4	Doubtful
E	Unreliable	5	Improbable
F	Reliability cannot be judged	6	Truth cannot be judged

Source: Reproduced with the permission of the UK government.

the US Army.[2] Each intelligence product receives an alphanumeric rating reflecting the organization's level of confidence in the source material based on experience or other information from the same source. For example, reporting judged *probably true* from a *usually reliable source* is given a B2 rating. The use of two scales versus one scale captures circumstances in which a solid source could produce bad information.

When the Canadians updated their *Joint Intelligence Manual* in 2011, they continued to use the Admiralty Grading System but included two useful charts defining terms to describe the reliability of sources and credibility of information (see Figure 9.2).[3] The descriptions of what each term means were taken from the US Army manual.[4] The Canadian manual recommends that the ratings be based on three criteria:

1. The subjective judgment of the evaluator

2. Experience with previous information provided by the same source

3. Knowledge of the capabilities of the particular sensor system when the information is provided by a sensor

In 2012, the Canadian Joint Forces developed the Source Reliability and Information Accuracy Rating Matrix for incorporation into the Social Network Analysis (SNA) tool set used by the Canadian Forces School of Military Intelligence.[5] The matrix lists five distinct criteria analysts can use to determine a source's reliability and establishes how many of these criteria must be met to warrant a specific credibility rating (see Figure 9.3).[6] It identifies five other criteria for establishing information accuracy, along with instructions on how many of these criteria must be met to qualify for a specific level of information accuracy. The Canadians then conducted research to scientifically validate this expanded schema that should improve how intelligence practitioners use the Admiralty Grading System.

The UK police developed a 5x5x5 system for the rating and handling of Information Intelligence Reports (see Figure 9.4). It retains the two 5-point rating scales for rating the reliability of sources and the credibility of the information but provides different descriptors.[7] It includes an additional 5-point scale for managing the dissemination of the report. The 5x5x5 evaluation process was introduced under the National Intelligence Model to replace the "rule of thumb" evaluation process and to make the storage and use of intelligence auditable. It is described in the Management of Police Information Guidelines published by the National Policing Improvement Agency (NPIA) in 2006.[8] The 5x5x5 system has also been adopted by the Australian police.

(Text continued on page 132)

FIGURE 9.2 ■ Canadian Source Reliability and Information Credibility Rating Scales

Rating Reliability of Source	Description
A. Completely reliable	No doubt of authenticity, trustworthiness, or competency; has a history of complete reliability
B. Usually reliable	Minor doubt about authenticity, trustworthiness, or competency; has a history of valid information most of the time
C. Fairly reliable	Doubt of authenticity, trustworthiness, or competency but has provided valid information in the past
D. Not usually reliable	Significant doubt about authenticity, trustworthiness, or competency but has provided valid information in the past
E. Unreliable	Lacking in authenticity, trustworthiness, and competency; history of invalid information
F. Reliability cannot be judged	No basis exists for evaluating the reliability of the information
Rating Credibility of Information	**Description**
1. Confirmed by other sources	Confirmed by other independent sources; logical in itself; consistent with other information on the subject
2. Probably true	Not confirmed; logical in itself; consistent with other information on the subject
3. Possibly true	Not confirmed; reasonably logical in itself; agrees with some other information on the subject
4. Doubtful	Not confirmed; possible but not logical; no other information on the subject
5. Improbable	Not confirmed; not logical in itself; contradicted by other information on the subject
6. Truth cannot be judged	No basis exists for evaluating the validity of the information

Source: Reproduced with permission of the Canadian government.

FIGURE 9.3 ■ Canadian Source Reliability and Information Accuracy Rating Matrix

Source Rating Scale	Source Reliability Rating	History of Reliability	Source Authenticity/ Bona Fides	Source Objectivity	Source Access to Info	Source NOT Vulnerable to Manipulation	Meets Number of Criteria
A	Reliable	Yes	Yes	Yes	Yes	Yes	All 5
B	Usually reliable	Yes	Yes or No	Yes or No	Yes or No	Yes or No	History, plus 3
C	Fairly reliable	Yes	Yes or No	Yes or No	Yes or No	Yes or No	History, plus 2
D	Not usually	Yes or No	Yes or No	Yes or No	Yes or No	Yes or No	2 of 5
E	Unreliable	No	Yes or No	Yes or No	Yes or No	Yes or No	NA
F	Cannot be judged	No basis exists for evaluating the reliability of the source					

Notes:

1. To be rated "A," the source's authenticity / bona fides must be verifiable, and the source's history of reliability must be verifiable post-factum or by independent verifiable means.
2. To be rated "A" or "B," the source's reporting must always be reliable, with no significant errors.
3. To be rated "C," the majority of the source's reporting must be accurate and actionable.
4. To be rated "D," a minority of the source's reporting may still be accurate and actionable.

Information Rating Scale	Information Accuracy Rating	Independent Verifiable Means	Source Subject Competency	Logical	Practical and Plausible	Consistent	Meets Number of Criteria
1	Confirmed	Yes	Yes	Yes	Yes	Yes	All 5
2	Probably true	No	Yes	Yes	Yes	Yes	4
3	Possibly true	No	Yes or No	Yes or No	Yes or No	Yes or No	3
4	Doubtfully true	No	Yes or No	Yes or No	Yes or No	Yes or No	2
5	Improbable	No	Yes or No	Yes or No	Yes or No	No	0 or 1
6	Cannot be judged	No basis exists for evaluating the validity of the information					

Source: Reproduced with permission of the Canadian government.

FIGURE 9.4 ■ UK Police 5x5x5 System for Evaluating Intelligence Reports

Source and information/intelligence evaluation to be completed by submitting officer

	A	B	C	D	E
Source evaluation	Always reliable	Mostly reliable	Sometimes reliable	Unreliable	Untested source
	1	2	3	4	5
Information/ intelligence evaluation	Known to be true without reservation	Known personally to the source but not to the person reporting	Not known personally to the source but corroborated	Cannot be judged	Suspected to be false

Handling code to be completed by the evaluator on receipt and prior to entry onto the intelligence system

	1	2	3	4	5
To be reviewed on dissemination	**Default:** Permits dissemination within the UK police service **and** to other law enforcement agencies as specified [See guidance]	Permits dissemination to UK non-prosecuting parties. [Conditions apply, see guidance]	Permits dissemination to (non-EU) foreign law enforcement agencies. [Conditions apply, see guidance]	Permits dissemination within originating service/agency only: specify reasons and internal recipient(s). Review period must be set. [See guidance]	Permits dissemination but receiving agency to observe conditions as specified. [See guidance on risk assessment]

LOOKING MORE DEEPLY

Both experience and academic research demonstrate that the process of assessing the credibility of a source is more complex than looking only at source reliability and information credibility. David Schum, who extensively researched and wrote on this subject at George Mason University before his passing in 2018, posited that credibility varies depending on whether one is evaluating tangible or testimonial evidence.[9]

Evaluating Tangible Evidence

Tangible evidence includes documents, objects, charts, and images that can be directly examined by someone to see what is revealed. Schum distinguished between *real tangible evidence*, which is an actual object, and *demonstrative tangible evidence*, which includes such items as diagrams, maps, and market reports that represent or illustrate tangible objects (see Figure 9.5).

FIGURE 9.5 ■ Source Credibility Criteria and Associated Questions		
Tangible Evidence Reporting Criteria		**Associated Questions**
Real Tangible Evidence	**Authenticity**	– Is the object or event what it is represented to be? – Could the object have been tampered with or the image manipulated in some way?
Demonstrative Tangible Evidence	**Authenticity**	– Is the illustration or representation what it is represented to be? – Could the illustration or representation have been altered or adjusted in some way?
	Reliability of Sensing Mechanisms	– Would the sensing mechanism yield the same information if used again under the same conditions? – Is the sensing device reliable? Is the output provided by the sensor always consistent with the input?
	Accuracy	– Does the illustration or representation accurately capture the event or object? – Is the illustration or representation contradicted or confirmed by other facts?
Human Source Reporting Criteria		**Associated Questions**
Competence	**Access**	– Did the source actually see, hear, or do the event being reported? – Did the source have direct access to the information?

Human Source Reporting Criteria		Associated Questions
	Expertise	– Is the source a practiced or trained observer? – Did the source understand the events well enough to provide an intelligent account of the events? – Has the source been responsive to earlier questions we asked?
Credibility	**Objectivity**	– Is there reason for the source to report what he or she expected to see instead of what he or she observed? – Is there reason for the source to report what he or she wished to see instead of what he or she observed? – How long ago did the observation take place?
	Veracity	– What do we know about the source's character and honesty? – Is what the source is saying consistent with what the source reported in the past? – Is the source subject to outside influences or manipulation? – Is there independent confirmation of what the source reported? Are there any other facts that contradict it?
	Observational Sensitivity	– Does the source have a reputation for being a good observer? – What is the source's track record for accurate observations? – Could the conditions under which the observation occurred have influenced what was reported?
	Cultural Perspective	– Could the source's cultural heritage have influenced how the source perceived the event? – Could the source's cultural heritage have influenced what the source thought was appropriate or inappropriate to report?

Sources: This chart is based on information drawn from publications by David Schum, the Office of the Director of National Intelligence, and Pherson Associates.

The credibility of real tangible evidence is determined by a single criterion: authenticity. The key issue is whether the authenticity of the document can be confirmed and if the chain of custody is well established. These criteria are often paramount in law enforcement cases.

Three measures determine the credibility of demonstrative tangible evidence:

1. Authenticity

2. The reliability of the sensing mechanism

3. The accuracy of the representation

A reliable sensor generates the same report when observing the same phenomenon over time. For example, a machine that tests blood should generate the same report every time that sample of blood is tested. Checking the accuracy of reports is essential but often overlooked as deadlines approach—a practice that can prove highly embarrassing when a mistake is discovered at a later date. To guard against this, nurses, for example, frequently ask patients to confirm their date of birth before giving the doctor the patient's chart or test results. Surgeons will also ask the patient where the surgery is to be performed—or even to mark the spot with a marker pen on their body—before putting the patient under anesthesia.

Assessing Testimonial Evidence

In the world of intelligence analysis, far more energy is devoted to assessing the credibility of testimonial information, which is defined as reporting derived from human sources, informants, or assets. As Schum rightly noted, the use of only two criteria to establish the quality of human source reporting—access and reliability—is far too simplistic and can often be misleading.

In the American court system, testimonial evidence is first evaluated in terms of two criteria:

1. The *competence* of the reporter or observer

2. The *credibility* of that source

We believe the same standard should be applied in assessing the reliability of sources in all fields of analysis, especially intelligence analysis.

Competence and credibility are independent factors. A competent observer, for example, may have reason to provide misleading information, and an incompetent observer could just as easily provide accurate or inaccurate information to please the questioner. As Schum and Morris state, "Competence does not entail credibility, nor does credibility entail competence."[10] Deciding that we can believe a source because the source has good access is a non sequitur; the source with excellent access could also be purposefully trying to mislead to influence the behavior of the receiver or to promote a personal agenda. Intelligence collectors will often indicate when they believe a source is providing information in an effort—genuine or pernicious—to influence the recipients of the report.

Whether sources are competent or qualified to provide the information is measured in terms of their *access* to and understanding of the events being observed. In the intelligence world, access is a highly valued commodity. Such understanding or knowledge is usually designated by the term *expertise*. The value of a source having direct access to an event—for example, by attending a meeting of senior policy officials or a board of directors meeting—has little utility if the source does not understand what is being discussed or the implications of what has been decided.

Schum listed three factors for evaluating the credibility of a source: (1) the *objectivity* of the reporter; (2) the *veracity,* sincerity, or truthfulness of the source; and (3) the *observational sensitivity* of the source under the conditions of observation. Evaluating a source or an informant based on these criteria usually requires that the source has an established track record of reporting. This process of evaluation can be accelerated, however, if those in contact with the source are aware of the criteria and ask good questions of the source, such as, "What was happening when you observed that?" or "Did you agree with what she said?"

One of the authors of this book, Randolph Pherson, added one final criterion to this list: *cultural perspective.* A source's cultural heritage and exposure to the world can also influence how that source reports what he or she observed. Many Americans have little sense of history. However, what happened a hundred years ago will frequently influence how a European interprets recent events. Moreover, cultural heritage can influence what a source is comfortable reporting to a receiver of the information. In some cultures, specific topics are taboo and simply are not discussed even among close colleagues or family members.

Eastern cultures are more likely than Western cultures to view developments in a broader context. Empirical studies have shown that those from Eastern cultures tend to focus on the overall environment, while Westerners are more attentive to the particular actions taking place within the scene.[11] This means, for example, that Americans may do a better job of reporting the specific sequence of events when a fight broke out, while a Japanese observer would provide a more accurate rendition of the setting, who else might have witnessed the fight, and the participants' approximate ages.

In assessing the value of a particular source, analysts should take care not to confuse the credibility of the collector with the credibility of the source. A transcript of a conversation that has been snatched from the airwaves, for example, usually provides an accurate representation of the specific conversation. In some circumstances, however, this may not be true if the translation is incorrect or the speaker suspects the conversation may be intercepted and is intentionally spreading disinformation. Similarly, the fact that a reliable newspaper has reported allegations levied by a public figure at a public meeting does not mean that the charges are necessarily true; in some circumstances, the public figure may be purposefully dissembling to promote a personal agenda.

Distinguishing Subsources

Another common trap is the failure to differentiate between the source and the subsource. The source's reliable description of what was said does not necessarily mean that the person the source was quoting was providing credible information. Analysts must recognize—and alert their readers if appropriate—that their reliable source provided no insight into whether the original source—the subsource—is a credible reporter. An analyst should always give equal weight to evaluating the credibility of the primary subsource as well as the source who transmits the information.

Identifying Cyber Sources

Source attribution and evaluation when conducting cyber analysis can be a particularly vexing problem. The first step is to understand the context of the cyber activity. The US National Manager for Cyber in the Office of the Director for National Intelligence (ODNI) has prepared a Cyber Threat Framework to assist analysts in this task.[12] The framework captures the adversary life cycle from *preparation* of capabilities and targeting to *engagement* with the targets to establishing and expanding the *presence* on target networks, to the creation of *effects and consequences* from theft, manipulation, or disruption. The National Manager for Cyber has created a model of the process to increase situational awareness and establish a shared ontology that enhances information sharing.

The next step is to establish attribution for a cyber operation. This is a difficult but not an impossible task. To help with this process, the US Intelligence Community has identified several key indicators to evaluate and determine responsibility for a cyber attack.[13]

- *Tradecraft.* Behavior frequently used to conduct a cyber attack or espionage. An attacker's tools, techniques, and procedures can reveal attack patterns, but these unique tradecraft indicators diminish in importance once they become public and other actors can mimic them.

- *Infrastructure.* The physical and/or virtual communication structures used to deliver a cyber capability or maintain command and control of capabilities. Attackers can buy, lease, share, and compromise servers and networks to build their infrastructure.

- *Malware.* Malicious software designed to enable unauthorized functions on a compromised computer system, such as key logging, screen capture, audio recording, remote command and control, and persistent access.

- *Intent.* An attacker's commitment to carry out certain actions based on the context. Covert, deniable cyber attacks often are launched against opponents before or during regional conflicts or to suppress and harass enemies of the state.

- *Indicators From External Sources.* Reports from private industry, the media, academia, and think tanks can provide relevant data or share hypotheses about the perpetrators.

The US Intelligence Community has identified three practices that can aid in the identification of cyber attackers:

- *Looking for Human Error.* Almost all cyber attribution successes have resulted from discovery and exploitation of the attackers' operational security errors. If the report on first glance looks too good to be true, this should serve as a signal to look more closely for anomalies, inconsistencies, or errors in the reporting.

- *Timely Collaboration, Information Sharing, and Documentation.* Attribution efforts benefit from combining the expertise of regional, political, and cybersecurity analysts and the collaboration of network defenders, law enforcement, private cybersecurity firms, and victims.

- *Rigorous Analytic Tradecraft.* Analysts may start with a set of plausible actors in mind, based on the nature of the cyber incident, the targets, and the context but must be careful to avoid cognitive bias.

The US Intelligence Community also recommends three best practices for presenting analysis related to cyber attribution:

1. Delayering the attribution assessment

2. Providing a confidence level

3. Identifying information gaps

An attribution assessment should indicate whether the incident was an isolated event, who was the likely perpetrator, what was the motivation, and whether a foreign government was involved.

Dealing With Deception

In intelligence analysis, law enforcement, military operations, and the business world, adversaries or competitors often try to deceive us about their intentions, capabilities, and activities. Government officials frequently try to mislead foreign governments about their negotiating positions, goals, and objectives. In business and commerce, firms seek to hide their plans from competitors until they are ready to unveil a new product or project. Corporations carefully protect proprietary financial and technical information from competitors and sometimes release disinformation overstating their accomplishments or disguising their future plans.

Such practices all fall under the rubric of deception, which is defined as an effort to influence perceptions, decisions, and actions of another to the advantage of the deceiver. Deception can cause an individual to take—or not to take—a specific action. If the adversary or competitor has much to gain or lose in any situation, or the organization stands to gain large benefits or incur substantial losses, the likelihood is strong that an enemy or a rival will try to engage in deceptive practices.

Analysts should always be sensitive to the potential for deception and disinformation but will find it difficult to remain alert at all times. Malcolm Gladwell in his most recent book, *Talking to Strangers*,[14] demonstrates using examples ranging from counterintelligence failures to law enforcement misjudgments that humans default to believing others are telling the truth because it is the most efficient way to move through life. Drawing on research by University of Alabama professor Tim Levine, Gladwell observes that humans are particularly bad at judging truthfulness in "mismatches," situations in which dishonest people are attempting to appear honest or when the honest are believed to be dishonest.

Furthermore, most analysts must process large amounts of data and often hundreds of reports every day, looking for information or insights that could influence their lines of argument. This is a challenging task in and of itself. Requiring an analyst to simultaneously assess the value of each specific item of information as to whether it could be deception strains the cognitive capacity of the brain and can paralyze the analytic process.

The best way to deal with this dilemma is to identify those circumstances under which deception or disinformation is most likely to appear or most likely to pose the greatest threat. Once such circumstances are identified, analysts have the duty to pause and critically examine the information to determine whether or not deception or disinformation is present.[15]

Gladwell recommends exercising mindfulness when dealing with new information; "listen more, stay humble and never rush to judgment."[16] At the same time, analysts should take care not to go overboard in questioning data, being too curious, and avoiding coming to closure. Sometimes Occam's Razor really does apply.

Analysts should be most concerned about the possibility of deception or disinformation in the following situations:[17]

- The analysis hinges on a single key piece of information.

- The potential deceiver has a history of being deceptive or misleading.

- Data are received at a critical time when those involved have a great deal to gain or to lose.

- Accepting the new information would require the policymaker or decision maker to expend or divert significant resources.

- Accepting the new information would cause the analyst to alter a key assumption or key judgment.

- The adversary or the competitor could track its adversary's behavior and decision-making process through an established feedback channel.

Critical thinkers must bring all their skills to bear on examining the veracity of the information whenever deception might be present. When analysts evaluate information and make judgments, they need to consider whether the information can be corroborated, whether it can be confirmed by other independent sources, or whether key pieces of information are missing.

Analysts should also do a reality check to ask themselves if the information appears plausible and makes sense. Is the information confirmed by or consistent with known facts? Does it appear to be fair and objective or does it appear to be biased? Is the information internally consistent or is it self-contradictory? Are there obvious errors, anomalies, or inconsistencies in the reporting? Is there sufficient detail to support the judgment?

Analysts have found the following seven rules of the road helpful for dealing with deception and disinformation:[18]

1. Avoid overreliance on a single source of information, as was the case with the German liaison human source known as "Curveball" who provided incorrect reporting on the Iraqi weapons of mass destruction program.[19]

2. Seek the opinion of those closest to the subject or the event.

3. Be suspicious of sources or subsources who have not been seen or for whom it is unclear how they obtained the information.

4. Do not rely exclusively on what someone says (often described as *testimonial* or *verbal intelligence*); instead seek tangible, material evidence that can be confirmed.

5. Look for a pattern where on several occasions a source's initial report appeared correct but later turned out to be wrong. On closer examination, the source's explanation for the error was plausible but weak, appearing as though the source was stretching to come up with an excuse.

6. Know the limitations as well as the capabilities of the potential deceiver.

7. Generate a full set of plausible hypotheses at the outset of a project—including a deception hypothesis, if appropriate.

The source evaluation factors discussed here are critical to overcoming deception. What is the motivation of a human source? What is the source's track record for providing credible, valid reports? Can the source provide documentation? Do statistics come from a reliable source?[20] If technical means of collection were used, how sensitive are the sensors and have they been calibrated correctly? Does the adversary have the capability to identify and deceive technical equipment?

Recognizing Propaganda

Much the same case can be made in dealing with propaganda and its more recent manifestation, Digital Disinformation. Analysts should be alert to the possibility of

FIGURE 9.6 ■ Is This Propaganda?

HOW TO IDENTIFY PROPAGANDA: RED FLAGS

The Publication

- Is it known for extremist views?

The Source

- Is it an obscure "institute" or academic and likely a mouthpiece for a special interest group?
- Where does it get its funding?
- Who are the directors?
- What are their backgrounds?

The Content

- Does the document have a strong emotional aspect?

  a) Ominous, stirring, or patriotic music and images

  b) Association of a person, event, or idea with something hated or feared (e.g., Nazis)

  c) Use of slogans (e.g., "blood for oil," "cut and run," "united we stand")

  d) Use of virtue words (e.g., *peace, happiness, security, wise leadership, freedom, liberty*)

- Is the reasoning poor?

  a) Illogical (or nonintuitive) relationships between concepts

  b) Sweeping conclusions from mere anecdotal evidence

  c) Issue framed to favor one point of view

  d) Irrelevant or questionable data

  e) Vague, undefined terms

- Do you see evidence of false or missing information (telling only half of the story)?

- Is there oversimplification?

  a) Simple answers to complex social and political questions

  b) Blame assigned to an individual or group (i.e., scapegoating)

  c) Misleading stereotypes or labels

  d) Blanket statements

- Is the aim of the article to persuade?

  a) Cites or associates prominent figures to a position, idea, argument, or action

  b) Repeats ideas until they are accepted as truth

  c) Presents ideas as the view of the majority (so get on the bandwagon)

  d) Implies that opposition (to author's premise) would be unpatriotic, undemocratic, or inhumane

Source: Reproduced with permission of the Canadian government.

propaganda and other deliberate attempts to deceive, especially when dealing with materials obtained over the internet and grey literature consisting of handouts, flyers, and pamphlets that are not formally published. Canadian analysts have developed a useful checklist for evaluating whether a document is likely to be propaganda (see Figure 9.6).[21] Many of these questions are equally useful in assessing the validity of information acquired on the internet, as discussed in Chapter 10.

KEY TAKEAWAYS

- The credibility of real tangible evidence is determined by authenticity. The credibility of demonstrative tangible evidence is determined by two additional measures: reliability and accuracy.

- The value of information derived from human sources—testimonial evidence—is determined by two criteria: competence and credibility. Competence is measured in terms of access and expertise. Credibility is based on objectivity, observational sensitivity, sincerity, and cultural perspective.

- These six criteria for evaluating human sources provide a much better measure than the traditional duo of access and reliability.

- Do not confuse the credibility of the collector with the credibility of the source.

- If a source is credible, it does not necessarily follow that the subsource is credible.

- Analysts should be most concerned about deception and disinformation when the judgment hinges on a single source, the analysis is the basis for making major resource decisions, those involved have a great deal to gain or to lose, or the adversary or competitor is likely to have a feedback channel.

CONSIDERING THE CASE STUDY

Review Case Study V, "Puzzling Food Poisonings in Germany," to examine the quality of the sourcing.

- What demonstrable tangible evidence is presented in this case? How would you rate its credibility?

- Several individuals and institutions are quoted in this case study. How would you rate their competence and credibility?

- Are there any examples where the credibility of the collector could be confused with the credibility of the source?

- Were any subsources used whose credibility was not established?

Review Case Study II, "Russian Disinformation: Lessons Learned From the MH17 Shootdown" to explore the issue of deception.

- Which of the six reasons for being concerned about deception might be relevant to the story of the MH17 shoot down?

- Would the Russians have reason to deceive other countries about who shot down the airline? How was this reflected in their propaganda campaign?

- Would Russia have reason to deceive the world about whether it was interfering in the 2016 US presidential elections? How did they pursue this disinformation campaign?

- What questions should analysts have asked when first receiving reports

that Russia was responsible for the shootdown?

- Which of the seven rules of the road would be most useful in assessing whether the spike in inaccurate social media reporting in the lead-up to the November 2016 US presidential election was deception?

NOTES

1. Ministry of Defence, *Understanding and Intelligence Support to Joint Operations*, Joint Doctrine Publication 2-00, 3rd ed., August 2010, chap. 3, 20–21, fig. 3.6 .

2. NATO Standardization Agency, *Allied Joint Intelligence, Counter Intelligence, and Security Doctrine*, Allied Joint Publication 2, December 2003, 1-3-7, 1-3-8; Chief of Defence Staff, "Joint Intelligence Doctrine," in *Joint Intelligence Manual*, May 2005, 2-1; and US Army, "Document and Media Exploitation Tactics, Techniques, and Procedures," in *U.S. Army Document and Media Exploitation Manual*, TC 2-91.8, June 8, 2010, tables 4-1 and 4-2.

3. Chief of Defence Staff, *Intelligence*, Canadian Joint Forces Publication 2.0, August 2011, 3-7, 3-8.

4. US Army, "Human Intelligence Collector Operations," in *21st Century U.S. Military Manuals*, FM 2-22.3, September 2006, part 4, app. B, http://armypubs.army.mil/doctrine/DR_pubs/dr_a/pdf/fm2_22x3.pdf.

5. Canadian Forces School of Military Intelligence, "Sources and Information Rating Matrix," in *Social Network Analysis (SNA) Toolset*, Version 1.0 (working draft), March 13, 2012.

6. Sources for Figure 9.3 are US Army, "Document and Media Exploitation";

Canadian National Defence, "Joint Intelligence Doctrine," B-GJ-005-200/FP-000, May 21, 2003, chap. 2, table 2-1; and Office of the Director of National Intelligence, Denial and Deception Workshop, Ottawa, Canada, September 2008.

7. UK College of Policing, "How to Complete a 5x5x5 Form and Relevant Supplements" (unpublished manuscript), http://library.college.police.uk/docs/APPref/how-to-complete-5x5x5-form.pdf.

8. Rory Dunne, "The 5x5x5 System," *UK Crime Analysis Blog*, November 26, 2010, http://ukcrimeanalysis.blogspot.com/2010/11/5x5x5-system.html.

9. David A. Schum, Gheorghe Tecuci, and Mihai Boicu, "Analyzing Evidence and Its Chain of Custody: A Mixed-Initiative Computational Approach," *International Journal of Intelligence and Counterintelligence* 22 (2009): 298–319.

10. David A. Schum and Jon R. Morris, "Assessing the Competence and Credibility of Human Sources of Intelligence Evidence: Contributions From Law and Probability," *Law, Probability, & Risk* 6, nos. 1–4 (2007): 247–274.

11. Carey Goldberg, "Differences Between East and West Discovered in People's Brain Activity," *The Tech On-line*

Edition 128, no. 9 (Cambridge: MIT, March 4, 2008).

12. Office of the Director of National Intelligence, "A White Paper on the Key Challenges in Cyber Threat Intelligence," October 30, 2018, https://www.dni.gov/index.php/cyber-threat-framework.

13. Office of the Director of National Intelligence, *A Guide to Cyber Attribution*, September 14, 2018, https://www.dni.gov/files/CTIIC/documents/ODNI_A_Guide_to_Cyber_Attribution.pdf.

14. Malcolm Gladwell, *Talking to Strangers: What We Should Know About People We Don't Know* (New York: Little, Brown, 2019).

15. For a detailed checklist, analysts can use to detect possible deception, see Randolph H. Pherson and Richards J. Heuer Jr., *Structured Analytic Techniques for Intelligence Analysis*, 3rd ed. (Washington, DC: CQ Press/SAGE, 2021), 170–174. The checklist walks analysts through a consideration of motive, opportunities, and means (MOM); past opposition practices (POP); manipulability of sources (MOSES); and evaluation of evidence (EVE). The Canadian Chief of Defence Intelligence, Director General Intelligence Production, has added a fourth category, source naivety (SON), that asks several questions, some of which are reflected in Heuer and Pherson's EVE category: (1) Is it just that the well-meaning source is naïve? (2) Might the source be attempting to influence operational plans or policy to advance a personal agenda? (3) Is the source evangelically fervent about the subject under discussion? (4) Does the source subscribe to "nonmainstream" beliefs? and (5) Might the source simply be trying to please you or the interlocutor? The Canadian model is taken from Gudmund Thompson, "Aide Memoire on Intelligence Analysis Tradecraft" (Ottawa, ON, Canada: Chief of Defence Intelligence, 2009).

16. Gladwell, *Talking to Strangers*.

17. The information used in this section was taken from Pherson Associates training materials (www.pherson.org).

18. These criteria were derived from Richards J. Heuer Jr., "Cognitive Factors in Deception and Counterdeception," in *Strategic Military Deception*, ed. Donald Daniel and Katherine Herbig (Oxford: Pergamon Press, 1982) and Michael I. Handel, ed., *Strategic and Operational Deception in the Second World War* (New York: Routledge, 1987).

19. Bob Drogin, *Curveball: Spies, Lies, and the Con Man Who Caused a War* (New York: Random House, 2007).

20. A more extensive discussion of how best to deal with quantitative data and statistics can be found in Chapter 17.

21. Developed by John Pyrik for use in the Canadian Interdepartmental Intelligence Analysis Learning Program. Published in Thompson, "Aide Memoire on Intelligence Analysis Tradecraft."

10 HOW SHOULD I ASSESS THE RELIABILITY OF INTERNET INFORMATION?

SETTING THE STAGE

The internet has changed the way we research and, according to a study by Columbia University scholars, is even changing the way we store and recall information, making us less likely to focus on remembering the information itself and more on where to find it should we need to use it.[1] The advantage of this shift is that it helps us deal with information overload. The disadvantage is that it places a much heavier burden on analysts who use internet sources to be organized and meticulous about tracing and verifying information posted on websites and other internet-based media. Anyone can record an article, make a claim, or cite a supposedly authoritative source for purposes that range from ignorance and carelessness to nefarious deception (see Chapter 9).

While intelligence analysts are more critical consumers of information than the general population, even they are not immune from receiving broadcast emails from colleagues purporting to provide stunning new insights that a simple check of Snopes .com or other myth-busting source will show is a fabrication, misrepresentation, or falsehood. Although none of us is likely to ignore an information burst that resonates emotionally or reinforces personal viewpoints, source-evaluation practices should protect us from using and proliferating bad information.

The internet is an information force multiplier; it allows us to access more information from more sources in more locations worldwide (see Figure 10.1). The challenge is to sort the wheat from the chaff because on the internet the processes for evaluating the credibility of a report usually are lacking. The internet, in essence, is a newspaper without an editor, a publisher without a fact checker, or an academic journal without peer review. Those motivated to express themselves online are writing about their interests and passions, so the potential for bias, manipulation, and fakery are high. The trade-off is that the internet has the advantage of timeliness and offers rapid and wide dissemination. Reliable reporters from news outlets, bloggers, and tweeters can broadcast information and opinions far more quickly than hard-copy journals, books, or libraries.

The goal, however, remains the same: to identify and validate sources on the internet that are credible, present factual information accurately, and clearly support claims and assertions. The dangers of unattributed or manipulated internet content are real but often offset by the richness of the content. The challenge is to use the internet as a tool to authenticate and corroborate both the content and those who are producing it.

FIGURE 10.1 ■ Best Use of the Internet

Some of the most valuable sources provided by the internet achieve the following:

- Alert analysts to new developments, events, opinions, or trends

- Provide excellent information on interest group opinions, platforms, priorities, and plans

- Enable quick access to reliable, well-known journals and publications, some of which require subscription fees or registration

- Offer immediate access to materials or books for downloading before they appear in libraries

- Increase availability to materials from government and academia that can only be found on the internet

LOOKING MORE DEEPLY

When seeking to validate information obtained from the internet, we strongly recommend the following best practices:

Assessing the Author

- *Use content from named authors or organizations.* Beware of internet content that does not specifically identify the people or organizations who created or consolidated it. The information may be true, but you will have difficulty validating the information without being able to check credentials. Do not use anonymous information in your analysis.

- *Investigate credentials.* Take advantage of the power of the internet to review websites for the author; biographical data relating to experience and expertise; references and reviews of publications; and affiliations with companies, universities, or nonprofit organizations. Beware of individuals or sites that do not have contact information.

- *Assess qualifications and point of view.* Critically appraise the author's qualifications to write on the topic and consider what opinions you might expect him or her to espouse based on his or her qualifications and affiliations. Distinguish between the author and an organization that might be sponsoring the posting. How well are the authors' or sponsors' perspectives reflected? Do they affect your understanding of their facts and arguments?

- *Determine the author's access and reliability.* With the increase in ordinary citizens becoming the first to report news, consider an author's access to information. Is the author a primary or secondary source? If he or she is claiming firsthand knowledge, scrutinize the claim for accuracy. Examine social media sites for time/date/location stamps. Are there other sources who witnessed the same event claiming similar information? Does the story appear plausible? Have others reported the same event? Is the author capturing new information or simply repackaging someone else's?

Evaluating the Site

- *Consider site sponsorship.* Where is the site located—in what country—and who is the owner/administrator of the site? Who is responsible for the accuracy of the information on the site? How often is it updated? The website's uniform resource locator (URL) address can help you check the type of organization, where and to whom the URL is registered, and the country affiliation. Websites that end in *.gov, .mil,* or *.edu* can be validated as government or accredited educational institutions with a set of standards for the sourcing, use, and review of information used on the site. Remember that a site name (particularly with the *.com* or *.net* code) may not belong to the well-known institution it appears to cite. Always beware of political bias and remain alert to links to sponsors or contributors that might not be subject to professional standards. The designator *.org* often is selected by nonprofit organizations whose content can range from excellent to awful depending on their agenda and biases.

- *Evaluate the intention of the site.* The reason given for the page's creation can help you judge its content. Is it intended to inform, instruct, explain, influence, or persuade someone to act? Is the author intending to engage the general public, novices, or experts? What can you tell about the professionalism of the information providers from the quality of the site design, organization of the content, or amount of care given to avoiding grammatical, typographical, and spelling errors?

- *Distinguish between opinion and verifiable information.* Is the information fact, opinion, or propaganda? Is it identified as such? Does the author declare any affiliation or bias and avoid language that rouses emotion? Is the information sourced and can those sources be validated? Has it been reviewed or validated by other reputable sources? Is another version of the information available through libraries, organizations, or other off-internet sources? If the site has multiple authors, each of the authors needs to be vetted to ensure legitimacy and accuracy.

- *Check for currency of information and links.* Is a date identified for the information? Does the site have an indication of when it was last updated or whether it is kept up-to-date? What kinds of additional information and sources are linked? Does their relationship to the subject or purpose of the site shed additional light on potential bias? Are any of the links dead ends? Are there any partnerships or relationships to other entities mentioned on the site or linkages to external parties? Make sure you know when links take you from one site to another.

- *Evaluate the source over time.* Organizations, news outlets, and URLs can be bought and sold, change their political leanings, or employ new journalists, all of which can affect the quality of the information found on the site. Keep a log of the sites that are regularly used with a short blurb about the background and the unique attributes of the information gleaned from each site for easy reference. Routinely check with sites like Whois.net to determine ownership and contact information. Sites like Archive.org may provide helpful information about a site's history.

● *Always be critical of internet information.* Remember that websites can be altered or disappear without notice, through inattention, accident, or malevolent hacking. Download a screen shot or print a hard copy of information that is key to your analysis.

Figure 10.2 provides a useful checklist developed by the Canadian government for conducting just such an investigation.[2] The checklist prompts the analyst to look beyond what appears on the computer screen and try to determine the possible biases and agendas of the owners or authors of the website.

FIGURE 10.2 ■ Canadian Checklist for Evaluating Internet Sources		
Name of Website:		**Assessed Reliability**
URL / Address:	http://	Low 1 - 2 - 3 - 4 - 5 High
1. Type	☐ Advocacy ☐ Business ☐ Info/Ref ☐ News ☐ Personal ☐ Entertainment	
Meta-Tags: Who are they trying to attract to their website (*view/source*)? Key words?		
Older Versions: How did the site evolve? (check *www.archive.org*)		
2. Content	How reliable is the information? ☐ Reliable ☐ Can't say ☐ Unreliable	
Accuracy – Errors of fact or logic – Misspellings, poor grammar – Incorrect dates		
Authority – Author unqualified, uncited – Poor reputation – Sources undocumented		

(Continued)

FIGURE 10.2 ■ (Continued)	
Objectivity – Any blatant bias (terms, etc.)? – Persuasive aim? – Single or multiple point of view? – Any sponsors or advertising?	
Currency – Out-of-date references – When was it last updated? – Any dead links? (also check *www .brokenlinkcheck.com*)	
Coverage – Any significant omissions?	
3. Owner/Author	
Full legal company name: – Check links to copyright and privacy statements.	
Who registered the domain?	
Who incorporated the company? Officers/directors?	
4. Affiliations and Associations	
Who do they link to? Shared premises? Tip: Google phone numbers and addresses.	
Who links to them? – Nature of association – Effect on credibility	
What do others say about them? Google names. Check for urban legend, hoax, or fraud.	
Is it consistent with similar sites?	

Source: Used with permission of the Canadian government.

Many universities publish similar lists for evaluating the quality and credibility of internet content.[3] Most of these lists focus on the following key areas for investigation:

- Authority: credentials of author or host of site

- Purpose and intended audience

- Objectivity

- Accuracy/reliability/credibility

- Timeliness of information

- Documentation: citations and quality of links

Figure 10.3 provides a list published by Georgetown University for its students that is comprehensive in addressing all the key issues to explore.[4]

FIGURE 10.3 ■ Georgetown University Guide for Evaluating Internet Content

Author

- Is the name of the author/creator on the page?

- Are his/her credentials listed (occupation, years of experience, position, or education)?

- Is the author qualified to write on the given topic? Why?

- Is there contact information, such as an email address, somewhere on the page?

- Is there a link to a home page?

- If there is a link to a home page, is it for an individual or for an organization?

- If the author is with an organization, does it appear to support or sponsor the page?

- What does the domain name/URL reveal about the source of the information, if anything?

- If the owner is not identified, what can you tell about the origin of the site from the address?

Note: To find relevant information about the author, check personal home pages on the web, campus directory entries, and information retrieved through search engines. Also check print sources in the library reference area; Who's Who in America, Biography Index, and other biographical sources can be used to determine the author's credentials.

Purpose

Knowing the motive behind the page's creation can help you judge its content.

- Who is the intended audience?

  ○ Scholarly audience or experts?

  ○ General public or novices?

(Continued)

FIGURE 10.3   ■   (Continued)

- If not stated, what do you think is the purpose of the site? Is the purpose to

  ○ Inform or teach?

  ○ Explain or enlighten?

  ○ Persuade?

  ○ Sell a product?

Objectivity

- Is the information covered fact, opinion, or propaganda?

- Is the author's point-of-view objective and impartial?

- Is the language free of emotion-rousing words and bias?

- Is the author affiliated with an organization?

- Does the author's affiliation with an institution or organization appear to bias the information?

- Does the content of the page have the official approval of the institution, organization, or company?

Accuracy

- Are the sources for factual information clearly listed so that the information can be verified?

- Is it clear who has the ultimate responsibility for the accuracy of the content of the material?

- Can you verify any of the information in independent sources or from your own knowledge?

- Has the information been reviewed or refereed?

- Is the information free of grammatical, spelling, or typographical errors?

Reliability and Credibility

- Why should anyone believe information from this site?

- Does the information appear to be valid and well-researched, or is it unsupported by evidence?

- Are quotes and other strong assertions backed by sources that you could check through other means?

- What institution (company, government, university, etc.) supports this information?

- If it is an institution, have you heard of it before? Can you find more information about it?

- Is there a non-web equivalent of this material that would provide a way of verifying its legitimacy?

Currency

- If timeliness of the information is important, is it kept up-to-date?

- Is there an indication of when the site was last updated?

Links

- Are links related to the topic and useful to the purpose of the site?

- Are links still current, or have they become dead ends?

- What kinds of sources are linked?

- Are the links evaluated or annotated in any way?

Note: The quality of web pages linked to the original web page may vary; therefore, you must always evaluate each website independently.

Source: Georgetown University Research Guides, https://www.library.georgetown.edu/tutorials/research-guides/evaluating-internet-content.

Detecting Digital Disinformation

The growing use of the internet and social media platforms to manipulate popular perceptions for partisan political or social purposes has made democratic processes increasingly vulnerable in the United States and across the world. Largely unencumbered by commercial or legal constraints, international standards, or morality, proponents of Digital Disinformation[5] have become increasingly adept at exploiting common cognitive limitations such as Confirmation Bias, Groupthink, Vividness Bias, and Judging by Emotion.

Perpetrators of Digital Disinformation compose compelling and seemingly coherent narratives that usually dismiss inconsistent evidence and ignore basic rules of logic. The primary objective of digital deceivers is to provide incorrect information in a seemingly persuasive format that confirms the readers' biases and either hardens mental mindsets or sows apathy or disbelief in the ability to know truth.[6] Uncritical readers will often believe they have "found the truth" when actually they are functioning as both victims and perpetrators of cognitive bias, misapplied heuristics, and intuitive traps.

Digital Disinformation can take several forms. In a 2019 study, the European Parliamentary Research Service identified seven common forms of "information disorder":[7]

- *Satire* or *Parody* with no intention to cause harm

- *Misleading Content* to reshape perceptions

- *Imposter Content* when impersonating a genuine source

- *Fabricated Content* designed to deceive or do harm

- *False Connection* when headlines, visuals, and images misrepresent the content of the story

- *False Context* when genuine content is mixed in to support a false narrative

- *Manipulated Content* when genuine information or imagery is manipulated to deceive

The key distinguisher is intent. Is the perpetrator of the information consciously trying to misinform in an effort to change one's understanding of an issue and ultimately to change that recipient's behavior? Purposeful misinformation, conspiracy theories, deception, and active measures have been used by activists and nation states to influence people in these ways for decades, if not centuries.[8] Such efforts at perception management appear to have had greater impact in recent years due to the following:

- The breadth and volume of misinformation has become staggering, owing to the power of social media platforms.

- The speed of the spread of disinformation is breathtaking as stories can quickly go "viral," spreading to millions of readers. An MIT study in *Science* documents that false rumors travel across the internet six times faster than factual stories.[9]

- People appear to be increasingly seeking simple answers to complex problems. Social network platforms usually present information in simplified form, which makes the message more digestible but far less nuanced—and often inaccurate. The Pew Foundation's 2018 report found that most people are concerned about getting misinformation from social media but rely on the convenience of the sites.[10]

The incentives for digital deceivers to leverage social media platforms to manipulate popular perceptions have also increased dramatically because due to the following:

- Millions of people can be reached almost instantaneously.

- Few perpetrators are held accountable for their posts.

- Perpetrators can micro-target their messages to those most easily swayed and open to persuasion.

Moreover, knowledge of someone's social media profile greatly facilitates the process of identifying how best to package misinformation to reinforce that person's thinking. With the explosive growth in the use of social media platforms and databases, the use of such micro-targeting strategies has proven increasingly effective in product marketing and more recently in political campaigns.

Recognizing one's vulnerability to Digital Disinformation is insufficient for mitigating the threat. A more productive strategy is needed—one that involves the use of critical thinking strategies and Structured Analytic Techniques. People are less likely to be deceived if they make it a habit to evaluate the quality of the evidence used to support a claim and ask what other credible, alternative narratives could explain what has occurred.

These four Structured Analytic Techniques are particularly effective in helping counter the impact of Digital Disinformation:[11]

- *Key Assumptions Check.* Making explicit and questioning the assumptions that guide an analyst's interpretation of evidence and the reasoning underlying a judgment or conclusion.

- *Analysis of Competing Hypotheses.* The evaluation of information against a set of alternative hypotheses to determine the consistency/inconsistency of each piece of data against each hypothesis and the rejection of hypotheses with much inconsistent data.

- *Premortem Analysis* and the *Structured Self-Critique.* Providing systematic processes to use brainstorming and checklist procedures to identify critical weaknesses in an argument and assess how a key analytic judgment could be spectacularly wrong.

The United Kingdom has created a mnemonic, SHARE, to help analysts spot potential disinformation and make sure they are not spreading harmful content whenever they forward an email or retweet a message. The SHARE mnemonic stands for **S**ource, **H**eadline, **A**nalyse, **R**etouched, **E**rror (see Figure 10.4).[12]

FIGURE 10.4 ■ The UK SHARE Checklist

Before you like, comment, or share online, use the SHARE checklist to make sure you're not contributing to the spread of harmful content.

 Source

Make sure that the story is written by a source you trust, with a reputation for accuracy. If it's from an unfamiliar organisation, check for a website's 'About' section to learn more.

 Headline

Always read beyond the headline. If it sounds unbelievable, it very well might be. Be wary if something doesn't seem to add up.

 Analyse

Make sure you check the facts. Just because you have seen a story several times, doesn't mean it's true. If you're not sure, look at fact-checking websites and other reliable sources to double check.

 Retouched

Check whether the image looks like it has been or could have been manipulated. False news stories often contain retouched photos or re-edited clips. Sometimes they are authentic, but have been taken out of context.

 Error

Many false news stories have phony or look-alike URLs. Look out for misspellings, bad grammar, or awkward layouts.

Source: Courtesy of the UK Government.

What About Wikipedia?

Intelligence organizations, like most academic institutions, do not allow the citation of Wikipedia as a source because it is a tertiary aggregation of information from a variety of sources, some of which are not attributable. Articles in Wikipedia are communally produced and of varying quality. The theory is that a community of people of varying educational backgrounds and expertise in the field, but highly interested in a particular topic, will contribute to the knowledge bank of a subject. Over time, these articles will be enriched from the community of contributors. Contributors are encouraged to cite sources for reference but are not required. This makes portions of the content unverifiable.

The good news is that Wikipedia is a potential source of some of the most recent information, provides hyperlinks to sources not available through traditional means or native languages, and has a gigantic pool of active researchers and writers. The bad news is that much of the text is not authoritatively reviewed or fact checked by known experts; however, a self-organizing group oversees the system, editing and monitoring it for vandalism and inappropriate content.

Wikipedia advises researchers to take some time to understand both the strengths and weaknesses of the site, including the social processes, links, references, and associated research aides. Our advice is to use Wikipedia as a thought provoker, concept creator, and source generator but never as single or authoritative source. In sum, one UK journalist writes,

> The general message with Wikipedia is that here, on the face of it, is what we know. But it's up to you to click on those links and citations and decide whether the information comes from sources you ultimately trust and are happy with. Wikipedia shouldn't be anyone's final stop when it comes to seeking knowledge, but rather the gateway to us being able to make up our own minds.[13]

Using the Internet as a Tool to Spur Nontraditional Thinking

As we noted in Chapter 8, unfocused browsing allows our brains to absorb more pieces of discrete information that can enrich our mental frames and sensitize us to new and different ways of thinking about our issues. Searching for a wider span of content on

> "The inconvenient reality is that people and their products are messy, whether produced in a top-down or bottom-up manner. Almost every source includes errors. . . . Many nonfiction books are produced via an appallingly sloppy process. . . . In this author's opinion, the flap over Wikipedia was significantly overblown, but contained a silver lining: people are becoming more aware of the perils of accepting information at face value. They have learned not to consult just one source. They know that authors and editors may be biased and/or harbor hidden agendas. And, because of Wikipedia's known methodology and vulnerabilities, it provides opportunities to teach (and learn) critical thinking."
>
> —Paula Berinstein
> *Information Today*[14]

our issue allows us to use information that is not validated to expand our view of what is possible. It can help us break the rigid barriers of our fact-based analysis and prompt more imaginative thinking about circumstances and factors that might change trajectories.

While most analysts work long days tracking current developments, absorbing information, and writing about their issues, they also force strict limitations on the time permitted for reflection and thinking. Searching should have specific goals, one of which is the development of categories, factors, drivers, and indicators that can have an impact on the topics under study. In this way, internet sources—whether validated or not—have a role to play in our structured thinking. They help us find outliers, potential disrupters or tipping points, and insights for Red Hat Analysis or understanding others' points of view.[15]

Using Multiple Streams of Media to Validate Information

Blogging. The emergence of blogs for personal and professional use has spurred social networks to share common interests. Bloggers may be professionals or simply writers with a passion for a given topic. They may cite research to advance their cause but lack the formal educational credentials or life experiences expected of experts in the field. This makes the job of assessing the author extremely important.

Sometimes it is not the blog itself that interests the researcher but the comments that follow. Blogs can spur a community of people "talking" to one another on the open internet, a rich source of information for the researcher. The participants may use pseudonyms that preclude vetting their qualifications or identities, but their thoughts, ideas, and comments may provide useful insights and spur more creative and imaginative thinking. Tumblr alone is estimated to have more than 470 million registered blog accounts as of October 2019.[16]

Microblogging. Services such as Twitter represent a partial exception to traditional sourcing principles. Postings on microblogs, which are often anonymous and lack detail, can provide notice of sudden events or crisis situations, such as natural disasters, outbreaks of violence or repression, or terrorist attacks. In these situations, immediate, on-the-ground knowledge is important, not expertise provided by an informed observer with a long track record of accurate analysis. This can come later. The number of postings reporting the same event and the number of postings recirculated can provide confirmation of information about natural disasters or manmade crises.[17]

Tweets can provide rapid and valuable information on the extent of earthquake damage and whether emergency services are capable of responding. One word of caution, however. When a natural disaster occurs, using information from Twitter and other social media reporting sites to allocate emergency relief resources can open the door to people overreporting the extent of damage to gain access to more resources. Analysts should be alert to whether and when such behavior is starting to occur.

Hashtags. The use of hashtags takes the concept once used by programmers of tagging metadata behind the scenes and uses it to draw those searching for content on the internet into the user's site. Given the dynamic activity of users on the internet, hashtags allow the content on blogs, microblogs, or other social media to become highly searchable in almost real time. Hashtags may be one word, an amalgamation of words, or a compilation of words. Hashtags are generally short in length but convey a unique, memorable perception of the situation.

As the use of hashtags has gained popularity, so has the use of analytic tools to interpret their popularity to determine who is using them, how they are being used, and what exactly people are saying along with the hashtag. The use of a hashtag alone does not constitute a useful piece of data; more is not always better. The use of blogs, microblogs, images, or videos that contain hashtags can help analysts develop a storyline over time, understand the geographic implications of a real-time event, or develop an understanding of the sentiment of those responding.

Images and videos. Prominent search engines and individual sites such as YouTube and Flickr allow for image and video searching. Hashtags have decreased the amount of time needed for—and increased the accuracy of—a search, but just gathering information is not sufficient. Analysts must keep in mind how the information will be used. What is the most critical information? What is the storyline? Analysts should recognize, however, that information provided about ongoing political crises can come from both proponents and opponents of specific issues. An image or video is usually the best means of independently verifying unsourced or poorly sourced narrative reports in the event of a natural disaster or street demonstration. But even these images can be manipulated by photoshopping or using other software tools. The challenge is to determine the value of anonymous postings in examining developments in evolving economic or political situations.

Mapping imagery. These tools allow analysts to map the location of a specific place, object, or even person's whereabouts on a map containing a street view, satellite image, or a road map. One of the most commonly used sites on the internet is Google Maps. Analysts can use these maps to help determine if the source's story is plausible. Satellite imagery can help determine proximity to a location or elevation considerations. Street mapping can help analysts determine distance between locations or address security concerns for a location. Use of mapping imagery is not without its limitations, however. Just as with the image and video precautions mentioned above, analysts should exercise the same precautions here. Additionally, users generally only get a small snapshot of an area at one specific point in time.

As the internet evolves, the methods and modes for collecting and disseminating information from it will continue to evolve. Analysts are responsible for properly vetting and sourcing the authors and the information. They must substantiate their findings with additional sources and corroborate information gathered from visual references, which are particularly easy to modify.

Words of Warning

The ease of use of internet information underscores bad habits that analysts must discipline themselves to avoid. Some of these were raised in Chapter 8 but bear repeating here to make sure the message is clear:

- "Copy and paste" is plagiarism and is unacceptable.

- An internet site that has used an author's text or artist's image in violation of the creator's copyright is not good enough for a citation. Text should be posted with the author's permission. If there is any doubt, work from and cite the print rather than the internet version.

- The answers to the problems of today are not hidden in Google but must be discovered through solid analytic research and reasoning.

KEY TAKEAWAYS

- The internet provides rich and timely content that should be treated with extreme care because it is unevaluated and may have little or no quality control, depending on the website.

- Analysts should always approach internet content with a critical eye and limit the sources cited to those with known credentials or sponsorship or those previously investigated. Careful examination of the purpose of the site is necessary, along with distinguishing fact from opinion.

- Vulnerability to Digital Disinformation can be mitigated by evaluating the quality of the evidence and sources and considering alternative explanations. Structured Analytic Techniques that can aid in this process include Key Assumptions Check, Analysis of Competing Hypotheses, Premortem Analysis, and Structured Self-Critique.

- Wikipedia should not be used as a source, but some articles may be helpful in finding current information and references on a given topic.

- Analysts should take advantage of internet tools like blogs and microblogs for individual views on breaking news and browsers and search engines to spur nontraditional and imaginative thinking.

- Images, videos, and mapping can support the analytic process by helping to develop or refute the plausibility of circumstances surrounding an event.

CONSIDERING THE CASE STUDY

Review Case Study II, "Russian Disinformation: Lessons Learned From the MH17 Shoot Down."

- Which internet sources used in this case study should be investigated more closely?

- Complete the Canadian Checklist for Evaluating Internet Sources shown in Figure 10.2 for the most suspect internet source.

- Do any of the exceptions to traditional sourcing rules apply to the sourcing used in this case study?

NOTES

1. Betsy Sparrow, Jenny Liu, and Daniel M. Wegner, "Google Effects on Memory: Cognitive Consequences of Having Information at Our Fingertips," *Science* 333, no. 6043 (August 5, 2011): 776–778, https://science.sciencemag .org/content/333/6043/776.full.

2. This checklist was developed by the Canadian government to assist its analysts in evaluating the credibility of web-based sources. It is published in Gudmund Thompson, "Aide Memoire on Intelligence Analysis Tradecraft," (Ottawa, ON, Canada: Chief of Defence Intelligence, 2009) and used with the permission of the Canadian government.

3. Examples of such checklists can be found at "Learn About Evaluating Sources: Five Criteria for Evaluating Web Pages," CCCOnline Library, https://ccconline.libguides.com/c.php ?g=242130&p=1609638; "Evaluating Websites: A Checklist," University of Maryland, University Libraries, https://www.wlps.org/view/2678.pdf; "Evaluating Resources," University of California, Berkeley, Library, http:// guides.lib.berkeley.edu/evaluating -resources; "Evaluating Information," Johns Hopkins University, Sheridan Libraries, http://guides.library.jhu.edu /c.php?g=202581&p=1334997.

4. "Georgetown University Guide for Evaluating Internet Content," Georgetown University Research Guides, https://www.library .georgetown.edu/tutorials/research -guides/evaluating-internet-content.

5. Efforts to purposefully mislead or misinform have also been described as "Fake News," "False News," or "Agenda-Driven News." The phrase most often used in the public domain is Fake News, but the inaccurate use of this term to describe any critical news reporting has undermined its usefulness.

6. Rob Brotherton, "Five Myths About Conspiracy Theories," *Washington Post*, January 17, 2019, https://www .washingtonpost.com/outlook/five -myths/five-myths-about-conspiracy -theories/2019/01/17/0ef1b840-1818 -11e9-88fe-f9f77a3bcb6c_story.html.

7. "Automated Tackling of Disinformation," Panel for the Future of Science and Technology European Science-Media Hub, European Parliamentary Research Service, Scientific Foresight Unit (STOA), PE 624.278, March 2019, 7, https://www .europarl.europa.eu/RegData/etudes /STUD/2019/624278/EPRS_STU (2019)624278_EN.pdf.

8. The term "active measures" refers to actions taken by the Soviet Union, and later Russia, beginning in the 1920s to influence popular perceptions through propaganda, false documentation, penetration of institutions, persecution of political activists, and political violence, including assassinations. For more information, see the testimony of General (ret.) Keith B. Alexander, US Congress, Senate, Committee on Intelligence, *Disinformation: A Primer in Russian Active Measures and Influence Campaigns*, 115th Congr., 1st sess., March 30, 2017, https://www .intelligence.senate.gov/sites/default /files/documents/os-kalexander-033017 .pdf.

9. Soroush Vosoughi, Deb Roy, and Sinan Aral, "The Spread of True and False News Online," *Science* 359, no. 6380 (March 9, 2018): 1146–1151, https:// science.sciencemag.org/content/359 /6380/1146.

10. Elisa Shearer and Jeffrey Gottfried, "News Use Across Social Media Platforms 2018," Pew Research Center, September 10, 2018, http://www .journalism.org/2018/09/10/news-use -across-social-media-platforms-2018/.

11. Randolph H. Pherson, *Handbook of Analytic Tools and Techniques*, 5th ed. (Tysons, VA: Pherson Associates, 2019), 5, 9, 19, 31, 43, 53.

12. "SHARE Checklist," Her Majesty's Government, 2020, https:// sharechecklist.gov.uk/.

13. David Barnett, "Can We Trust Wikipedia? 1.4 Billion People Can't Be Wrong, *Independent*, February 18, 2018, https://www.independent.co.uk/news /long_reads/wikipedia-explained-what -is-it-trustworthy-how-work-wikimedia -2030-a8213446.html.

14. Paula Berinstein, "Wikipedia and Britannica: The Kid's All Right (and So's the Old Man)," *Information Today* 14, no. 3 (March 2006), www.infotoday .com/searcher/mar06/berinstein.shtml.

15. For more information about Red Hat Analysis, see Randolph H. Pherson and Richards J. Heuer Jr., *Structured Analytic Techniques for Intelligence Analysis*, 3rd ed. (Washington, DC: CQ Press/SAGE, 2021), 198–203.

16. Statista: The Statistics Portal, "Cumulative Total of Tumblr Blogs From May 2011 to October 2019 (in Millions)," 2019, http://www.statista .com/statistics/256235/total-cumulative -number-of-tumblr-blogs/.

17. Evgeny Morozov, "Think Again: The Internet," *Foreign Policy*, May/June 2010, 40–44.

WHAT IS MY ARGUMENT?

Making solid arguments based on firm evidence and logic is at the heart of critical thinking. After compiling and evaluating the relevant evidence, one of the first steps is to critically examine the key operating assumptions and identify those that clients can depend on to justify the decisions they make. Analysts need to recognize unsupported assumptions as early as possible to avoid relying on them when building an analytic framework. Many unsupported assumptions turn out to be key uncertainties that require additional research and collection.

Before even starting to write, analysts should think about how best to construct their argument. As they conduct their research and sit down to outline their drafts, analysts should ask themselves,

- What is the key message?

- What are the strongest arguments or claims that will support this primary thesis?

- What is the best evidence to buttress these claims?

More sophisticated analysts will consider how best they can portray their argument as a story or illustrate it with examples or graphics. Enriching the argument with stories or visuals will make it more compelling and deepen understanding of the underlying dynamics. This increases the chances the analysis will stick with the reader in the coming days, months, and years.

When formulating the line of analysis, be sure to consider alternative explanations—or at least the null hypothesis—especially when generating evaluative or estimative products. This helps ensure that you do not fall victim to dangerous cognitive biases and intuitive traps and risk being wrong when it matters the most. If all can agree that there is no single uncontested history of what has happened in the past, then why should anyone hold analysts to the standard of predicting only one version of the future? Analysts who master the discipline of instinctively generating multiple explanations of observable phenomena and considering multiple future scenarios usually are more proficient at developing robust analytic frameworks, identifying boundaries, avoiding logical fallacies, and escaping outdated mental models and mindsets.

The practice of constructing competing scenarios and incorporating alternative views into a draft offers one of the best defenses against the pressures of politicization. Structured Analytic Techniques can provide a rigorous—and objective—foundation from which to view the data, identify conflicting or unsupported assumptions, and explore the evidentiary and logical basis for competing lines of analysis. If analysts can structure arguments in ways that help protagonists—and clients—focus on the key evidence and the underlying logic rather than argue over competing conclusions, they have done their job well.

Even the most rigorous analysis, however, is subject to error. In the intelligence profession, most experienced analysts aspire to be right more than 60 percent of the time. Given the frequent lack of data and the complexity of topics they cover, this is not an unreasonable standard. To meet or exceed this standard, however, you must carefully check your work before it goes out the door. Few would argue that discovering a major error or vulnerability before editing is far better than having to explain errors in analysis months after the paper is published to your peers, supervisors, or even a congressional committee. Good critical thinkers know well that conducting a Premortem Analysis will always take less time than responding to inquiries from postmortem investigators—and it is far less stressful.

11 ARE MY KEY ASSUMPTIONS WELL-FOUNDED?

SETTING THE STAGE

Most analytic judgments are based on a combination of evidence and assumptions that influence how information is interpreted.[1] An *assumption* is defined as something that is taken for granted or that is accepted as true or as certain to happen.[2] A good critical thinker knows that some assumptions are unfounded, and all assumptions must be examined critically. The challenge is that our cognitive processes make it difficult to discover or articulate our own assumptions.

The key to overcoming this cognitive obstacle is to employ a process that helps make the implicit explicit. The individual or the team needs to "put on a different hat" that forces the analyst or the team to think more critically and examine suppositions and biases—including some that they may not even know are influencing the analysis. A structured technique known as the Key Assumptions Check provides that vehicle.

LOOKING MORE DEEPLY

The Key Assumptions Check is a systematic effort to make explicit and question the working assumptions that guide an analyst's interpretation of evidence and reasoning about any particular problem. Such assumptions are usually necessary and unavoidable as a means of filling gaps in the incomplete, ambiguous, and sometimes deceptive information that comprises the analyst's data set. They are driven by the analyst's education, training, and experience. They also can be strongly influenced by the organizational context in which the analyst works.

> "Euclid taught me that without assumptions there is no proof. Therefore, in any argument, examine the assumptions."
>
> —E. T. Bell
> Author and Research Mathematician[3]

A Key Assumptions Check helps analysts avoid analytic traps, generate new insights, and discover knowledge gaps. Moreover, it is easy to use. Most analysts have difficulty identifying their own assumptions because many are rooted in sociocultural beliefs that are held unconsciously or so firmly that they are assumed to be true and not subject to challenge. Nonetheless, identifying key assumptions and assessing the overall impact the assumptions exert on the analysis are critical parts of a robust analytic process. In addition, the technique often uncovers hidden relationships and reduces the chance of surprise should new information render old assumptions invalid.

The process of conducting a Key Assumptions Check is relatively straightforward in concept but often challenging in practice. In developing a list of key assumptions, work from the prevailing analytic line or lead hypothesis back to the key factors that support it. The Key Assumptions Check can be conducted at any point in the analytic process. Most analysts prefer to conduct the check as they begin their analysis to avoid having to reorganize a draft or reconceptualize a section after discovering a faulty assumption late in the process. Reviewing the list of assumptions as you complete the project enables you to see if they still hold up or need to be modified because of new information that was acquired or events that occurred while you were drafting (see Figure 11.1).

"When key assumptions and critical data are not challenged, the result at best is poor analysis; at worst, it becomes the explanation for why we have stumbled into another major intelligence failure."[4]

—Randolph H. Pherson
"Overcoming Analytic Mindsets: Five Simple Techniques"[5]

Being open-minded is essential when conducting a Key Assumptions Check. Involve others less familiar with the topic who can openly challenge the operating assumptions of the group. Based on the authors' experience in facilitating key assumptions exercises, around one in four key assumptions usually collapses on careful examination.

FIGURE 11.1 ■ Stop! Recheck Assumptions

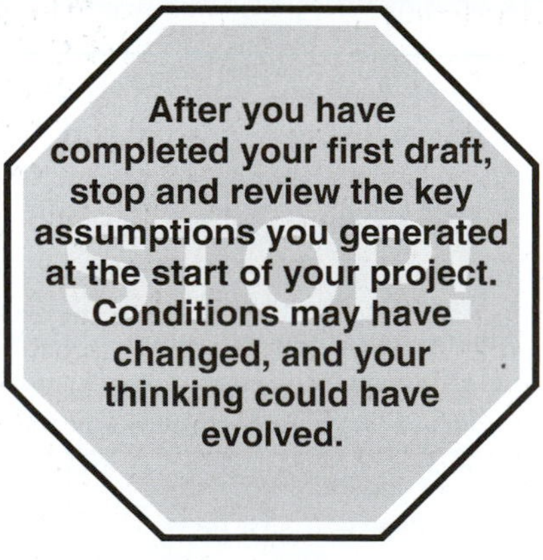

After you have completed your first draft, stop and review the key assumptions you generated at the start of your project. Conditions may have changed, and your thinking could have evolved.

FIGURE 11.2 ■ Key Assumptions Check Worksheet		
Key Assumption	**Rationale**	**Rating: Solid (S), Caveated (C), or Unsupported (U)**
1		
2		
3		
4		
5		
6		
7		

Solid: An assumption that is basically solid.
Caveated: An assumption that is correct with some caveats.
Unsupported: An assumption that is unsupported or questionable.

The Key Assumptions Check involves an eight-step process. Figure 11.2 provides a template.

The eight steps are as follows:

1. Gather a small group of individuals who are working the issue, along with a few "outsiders." The primary analytic unit already is working from an established mental model, so the outsiders are needed to bring other perspectives.

2. Ask participants to bring a list of assumptions to the meeting. If not everyone has a list, start the meeting with a silent brainstorming session. Ask each participant to write down several assumptions on index cards.

3. Collect the cards and list the assumptions on a whiteboard or easel for all to see.

4. Elicit additional assumptions. Work from the prevailing analytic line back to the key arguments that support it. Use various devices to help prod participants' thinking. Ask the standard journalistic questions: Who, What, How, When, Where, and Why.

    a. Phrases such as *will always, will never,* or *would have to be* suggest that an idea is not being challenged and perhaps should be.

    b. Phrases such as *based on* or *generally the case* usually suggest that a challengeable assumption is being made.

5. After identifying a full set of assumptions, critically examine each assumption. Ask,

    a. Why am I confident that this assumption is correct?

    b. In what circumstances might this assumption be untrue?

    c. Could it have been true in the past but no longer be true today?

    d. How much confidence do I have that this assumption is valid?

    e. If it turns out to be invalid, how much impact would this have on the analysis?

6. Place each assumption in one of three categories:

    a. Basically solid and well supported

    b. Correct with some caveats

    c. Unsupported or questionable—the key uncertainties

7. Refine the list, deleting those assumptions that do not hold up to scrutiny and adding new assumptions that emerge from the discussion.

8. Consider whether any unsupported assumptions or key uncertainties should be converted into collection requirements or research topics.

One technique analysts can employ to decide which category to assign to an assumption is to ask, "Can a decision maker or policymaker make decisions about moving resources or people based on this assumption?" If the answer is "yes," then the assumption can be rated as *supported*. If the answer is "it depends," then the assumption merits a rating of *with caveats* and the caveat or caveats need to be recorded. If it would be inappropriate or hard to justify the movement of people or resources based on the assumption, then the assumption should be rated as *unsupported*.

One mistake some analysts make is not distinguishing among assumptions, assessments, and information or intelligence reporting (see Figure 11.3). The key is to decide what is reporting and what is analysis in your own mind. Then be careful to present it as either reporting or analysis in your writing.

A Key Assumptions Check can prove valuable at any time in the drafting process. While most assumptions checks focus on substantive conclusions and the underlying analysis, checking assumptions about the quantity and credibility of the sourcing used to support the analysis can also reap major dividends.

FIGURE 11.3 ■   Distinguishing Among Information, Assumptions, Judgments, and Assessments

A classic mistake many novice analysts make is confusing information or reporting with key assumptions, judgments, and assessments.

- *Information* consists of all the facts relevant to the case or the situation. The information describes what has happened or is happening and summarizes all the relevant reporting on the subject.

- *Assumptions* guide an analyst's interpretation of evidence and reasoning about any particular problem and are often taken for granted.

- *Judgments* are short sentences that highlight the most significant analytic points in a paper. They should include both facts and analysis—the "What" and the "So What." Good key judgments identify a trend, point out what is new, or explain the meaning of the facts cited in the paper. They should be presented in order of importance with the most relevant judgment first. Use of the word because is a key indicator that the sentence contains a judgment. A summary usually describes what is discussed in a paper; a judgment conveys the purpose or main message of the paper. Drafting a set of key judgments is a critical skill as these judgments often may be the only part of the document a client has time to read.

- *Assessments* are judgments about unknowns such as the following:

  ○ Who is or will be involved

  ○ What will happen

  ○ When it will take place

  ○ Where it will occur

  ○ Why it is occurring or will occur

  ○ What the implications are or will be

  ○ How it is likely to evolve

Separating information from analysis or distinguishing reporting from assumptions, judgments, and assessments can be done in a variety of ways. The easiest approach is to first present the information or reporting and then draft a follow-on paragraph or paragraphs that contain the analysis and key judgments. Another strategy is to meld the reporting and the analysis into a series of paragraphs that tell a coherent story but identify the analysis with bold type. The key is to distinguish what is reporting and what is analysis in your own mind and be explicit about presenting this in your analysis.

Do not assess what is known or has already been reported to have occurred. For example, one would not assess that hackers are using the internet to exploit children and advertise child pornography, but one would assess that use of the internet by hackers for this purpose is growing and becoming more sophisticated.

KEY TAKEAWAYS

- Identifying key assumptions and assessing their validity are critical parts of a robust analytic process.

- If an assumption is solid or supported, then policymakers and decision makers can make resource decisions based on this assumption.

- Experience has shown that one in four key assumptions is unsupported when subjected to critical examination.

- An unsupported key assumption often becomes a key uncertainty that should be resolved through additional research or intelligence collection.

- A judgment often contains the word *because*. Analysts must not confuse key judgments and key assumptions with information or reporting.

CONSIDERING THE CASE STUDY

Review Case Study V, "Puzzling Food Poisonings in Germany."

- At the outset of this case, what key assumptions were reporters (and analysts) making about the outbreak of *E. coli* in Germany? How many were supported, in need of caveats, and unsupported?

- Were one in four key assumptions unsupported, as is usually the case?

- How would a Key Assumptions Check have helped German officials working this case?

- If a Key Assumptions Check had been conducted, what key uncertainties would have been identified suggesting priority topics for investigation?

NOTES

1. The information used in this chapter was taken from Pherson Associates training materials (www.pherson.org). A discussion of the Key Assumptions Check and how it relates to other Structured Analytic Techniques can also be found in Randolph H. Pherson and Richards J. Heuer Jr., *Structured Analytic Techniques for Intelligence Analysis*, 3rd ed. (Washington, DC: CQ Press/SAGE, 2021), 132–138.

2. The first definition for the word *assumption* is provided by Merriam-Webster at www.merriam-webster .com/dictionary/assumption; the second definition is provided by the *Oxford English Dictionary* at http:// oxforddictionaries.com/definition/ assumption.

3. E. T. Bell, "What Mathematics Has Meant to Me," republished in *Harmony of the World 75 Years of Mathematics* magazine, eds. Gerald L. Alexanderson and Peter Ross (Washington, DC: Mathematical Association of America, 2007).

4. Randolph H. Pherson, "Overcoming Analytic Mindsets: Five Simple Techniques," presentation to the National Security and Law Society, Emerging Issues in National and International Security, March 21–22, 2005, Washington College of Law, American University, Washington, D.C.

5. Pherson, "Overcoming Analytic Mindsets."

12 CAN I MAKE MY CASE?

SETTING THE STAGE

The crux of the analytic process is making sense of and deriving knowledge from data. Most human brains do this naturally with varying degrees of facility, but some have difficulty putting the pieces together to create a meaning that is greater than the sum of its parts. Many of our students, for instance, have trouble extracting the "So What" from separate pieces of data that together might indicate drug cartel violence transcending a border or an attack plan nearing an operational state. They get stuck on the tactical meaning of the individual sources and cannot rise above the facts to identify and warn of impending danger.

Our job as analysts is to give our clients insights that they do not receive from other sources. We are expected to interpret complex events. Our primary task is to characterize the forces and factors that drive events so decision makers can quickly understand what is going on and decide what actions they should take in response. The means by which we communicate what we know is by making a case or telling a story.

> **Palin:** Well, an argument's not the same as contradiction.
> **Cleese:** It can be.
> **Palin:** No it can't. An argument is a connected series of statements to establish a definite proposition.
> **Cleese:** No it isn't.
> **Palin:** Yes, it is! It 'tisn't just contradiction!
>
> —Michael Palin and John Cleese
> "The Argument Clinic," *Monty Python's Flying Circus*

LOOKING MORE DEEPLY

Analytic products quite simply are what philosophers and logicians call logical arguments or lines of reasoning. They are vehicles that deliver analysts' thinking about what is true and what is not. The process of getting to the argument often includes what philosophers refer to as *dialectic*—a type of conversation in which analysts challenge one another to come up with the best answers to implicit or explicit questions asked by their clients.

The prospect of building an effective argument can be daunting, particularly if you are breaking new analytic ground or exploring future trends. The process can flow more easily if you follow the Analyst's Roadmap (see the inside back cover of this book). The analytic context or framework (see Chapter 3) and the AIMS process (see Chapter 4) guide you in setting the parameters for your argument. Your Concept Paper (see Chapter 4) steers you in planning your product, selecting research methods, and assembling supporting evidence.

As we have discussed earlier, the purpose of analysis is to break an issue into its components. The function of synthesis is to build knowledge by combining and comparing the parts with other things, looking at the relationships among the parts, and assessing the totality of the system. The argument will put it all together to answer the client's questions and array the best evidence to support key points.

Building an Analytic Argument

An argument is made up of a set of statements. One statement constitutes the conclusion; it should be supported logically by the other statements. The conclusion is based on reasonable evidence, connected to observable fact, and characterized by clear, traceable, and fair thinking. Here is a step-by-step approach:[1]

- Take a few minutes to ground yourself.

  o Review your AIMS (see Chapter 4).

  o Refine your question and scope out a reasonable answer or range of possible answers (see Chapter 2).

  o Consider the main types of evidence that are most relevant to that answer (see Chapter 8).

  o Anticipate the questions and objections your reader might have to your evidence and answer.

- Based on your preparatory work, make an assertion or claim.

- Back it with supporting, observable evidence.

- Link the two with reasons why the data are relevant to the claim. The claim and the reasons can usually be connected by the word *because* (see Chapter 17 for the importance of *because* in probability statements and levels of confidence).

- Acknowledge other views and differences and provide evidence and reasons why you do so.

- Refine your claims, reasons, and evidence.

This process appears disarmingly simple but can quickly become complex when you have more than one question or multiple claims. Your highest-order claim (or thesis if you are writing a report in college) is supported by reasons, which can become subclaims themselves and then are supported by their own reasons. The interconnected claims and reasons must eventually be based on evidence or assumptions. In the end, an argument is only as sound as the evidence that supports it.

> "Forgotten were the elementary rules of logic, that extraordinary claims require extraordinary evidence and that what can be asserted without evidence can also be dismissed without evidence."
>
> —Christopher Hitchens
> Author and Journalist, *Slate*, October 2003

If your evidence is clearly and directly illustrative of your reason and claim, then your argument consists of laying out the facts and generalizing them as reasons that support the claim. A common example of this is inferring fire (claim) when we see smoke (evidence) because (reason) smoke only occurs when there is fire. Another example is as follows:

Claim: Gangs pose an increasing threat to public safety in our community.

Reason 1: They are moving into suburban neighborhoods as well as urban areas.

Evidence: New markings and gang-related violence are appearing in suburban neighborhoods as well as urban areas.

Reason 2: They are undertaking a broader range of activities.

Evidence: Primary drug distributors are moving into the trafficking of weapons and illegal immigrants.

Reason 3: More gangs are working internationally, taking advantage of the internet.

Evidence: Recent activity has been reported on northern and southern borders as well as new connections with foreign drug-trafficking organizations and intercepted, incriminating email communications.

In analytic products, however, the relationships more often are not straightforward. The evidence may be ambiguous or clients may interpret it in different ways depending on their mindsets and experience. It may consist of weak indicators that are consistent with more than one scenario. This places the burden on analysts to characterize convincingly the reasons that link the evidence to the claim. How analysts bridge this conceptual gap provides the basis on which their clients evaluate the quality of their reasoning and evidence and builds client trust in the analyst's expertise, understanding of their needs, and answers to their questions.

The best way to learn how to produce effective analytic arguments is to practice doing them. Anthropologist Rob Johnston in a study of professionals in intellectually demanding fields, such as intelligence analysts, astronauts, and anesthesiologists, identified six stages for developing expertise: (1) studying cases, (2) identifying patterns within cases, (3) generalizing patterns across cases, (4) formulating hypotheses, (5) creating models, and (6) testing models.[2] He found that developing expertise takes seven to ten years working with increasingly complex cases. The length of each stage depends on the individual's skills and the complexity of the issue.

Based on our experience teaching and mentoring new analysts, we offer the following advice and admonitions to guide the development of expertise in argumentation:

- *Set in your mind the structure of claims, reasons, and evidence.* The terminology gets confusing because the words can be used in different ways (see Figure 12.1).[3] Using the parts of an argument not only will simplify structuring your product but also aid you in reviewing your paper and the work of others.

- *Make sure your claims, reasons, and evidence are specific and significant.* Busy clients scan products for "news they can use" and skip over vague and generalized terminology that does not add to their knowledge base. Test your claims by assessing the significance of their opposites or showing them to your colleagues.

- *Include appropriate qualifications.* Each component of your argument should reflect how you have dealt with the limitations of knowledge or other conditions by explicitly identifying your assumptions (see Chapter 11) or certainties (see Chapter 17).

- *Avoid reasons that are opinions or unlinked to evidence.* We recall vividly the frustration of one manager who bemoaned that his analysts did not understand that their "personal opinions were not analysis." Opinions are based on beliefs, emotions, and intuition. Analysis may reflect some of those, but only after linking them with evidence and consciously considering alternatives.

- *Enrich your argument by reflecting the broader context and the work of others.* In academic research, this can be done through lengthy citations and references, but in most analytic writing it must be done succinctly and often indirectly.

The Role of Formal Logic

Many critical thinking courses discuss deductive and inductive thinking and the basics of formal logic but often fall short in clarifying how these concepts make a difference in day-to-day analysis. We know of one organization that required analysts in their performance reviews to identify specific examples of products that employed deductive and inductive reasoning, but the organization later gave up the practice. That does not mean that the principles defined by the Greek philosopher Aristotle some 2,300 years ago are not fundamental to good thinking, but the measurement of

FIGURE 12.1 ■ Elements of an Argument

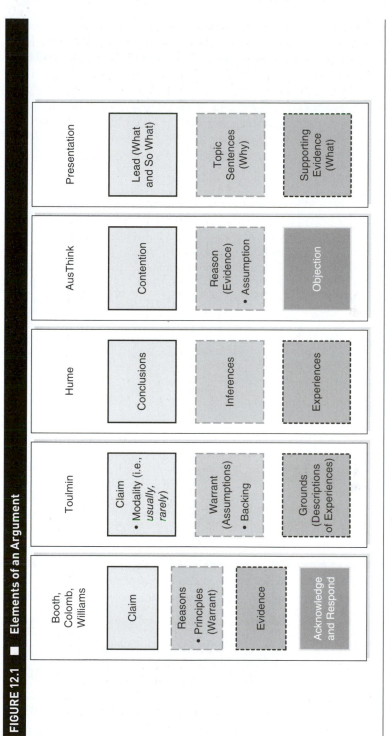

Booth, Colomb, Williams	Toulmin	Hume	AusThink	Presentation
Claim	Claim • Modality (i.e., *usually, rarely*)	Conclusions	Contention	Lead (What and So What)
Reasons • Principles (Warrant)	Warrant (Assumptions) • Backing	Inferences	Reason (Evidence) • Assumption	Topic Sentences (Why)
Evidence	Grounds (Descriptions of Experiences)	Experiences	Objection	Supporting Evidence (What)
Acknowledge and Respond				

Source: Copyright 2020 Pherson Associates, LLC. All Rights Reserved.

successful analytic products is based on the utility of the product for the client rather than on the type of logic employed.

The two types of formal logic, induction and deduction, help us understand how to connect claims and their support.

- *Deduction* reaches a general conclusion (or claim) based on specific and complete evidence (or premises). If the evidence is true, the claim must be true.
    Example:

    Evidence: Selling drugs is an illegal activity.

    Evidence: John is selling drugs.

    Claim: John is committing an illegal activity.

- *Induction* arrives at a generalized conclusion or claim from observed and incomplete evidence. The claim is outside the known facts and is possibly or probably true but could be false. The "inductive leap" is what gets the analyst from the known truth of the evidence to the claimed truth of the conclusion. Example:

    Evidence: Videotape shows an unidentified person trying to enter a sensitive facility.

    Evidence: A lock on a door of the gate shows signs of tampering.

    Claim: The facility is being targeted for attack.

For most analysts, few if any of our analytic arguments are deductive. We rarely have the luxury of complete information in which only one answer can be true. Furthermore, the point of analytic argumentation is to posit and support claims because they have the possibility of supporting more than one plausible alternative. Inductive reasoning helps us as analysts understand how the patterns and trends we observe as part of our experience or research can be true, but it also reminds us that we may be missing critical data or neglecting to consider the full range of alternatives.

Scholars over the past 150 years have broadened the field of argumentation beyond the rigid principles of formal logic to guide us in accounting for the complexities of our changing world. While lengthy discussion of argumentation theory is beyond the scope of this book, two concepts warrant attention because they are frequently mentioned in analytic training courses and reference books.

- *Abduction* is referred to as a third kind of logical reasoning that is useful to analysts in testing hypotheses. Abductive reasoning starts with a set of facts, based on which the analyst develops a hypothesis that, if true, would provide the best explanation for those facts. In the 19th century, logician Charles Sanders Peirce identified abduction as part of the scientific method. The purpose of abduction is to generate the guesses or hypotheses whose consequences can be derived by deduction and evaluated by induction. This is

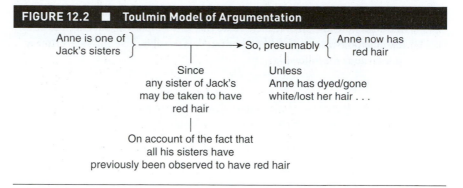

FIGURE 12.2 ■ Toulmin Model of Argumentation

Source: Copyright ©2003 Stephen E. Toulmin. Reprinted with the permission of Cambridge University Press.

an important concept for investigators, diagnosticians, and analysts who have reason to believe a certain precondition can explain the conclusion.[4] Example:

Evidence: The grass has been wet every time it has rained.

Evidence: The grass is wet.

Claim: It must have rained.

- The Toulmin model is the basis for the argument framework used in this chapter. The terms—and indeed those used in most contemporary argument texts—are based on 20th-century philosopher Stephen Toulmin's updating of the classical model to account for contextual differences in relating an argument's claims and support (see Figure 12.2).[5] Toulmin introduced the term *warrant* to describe the belief, supposition, or principle that explains how the evidence supports the claim. Whether or not you need to state this explicitly depends in part on how intuitively obvious or commonly accepted your reason is for your claim. Analysts need to reconsider these connections when thinking through their article from the reader's perspective (see Chapter 16).

Matching Arguments and Analytic Purpose

How an analyst frames the issue depends on the nature of the problem and the purpose of the product. The arguments used in most intelligence writing reflect one or more of the types on the Analytic Spectrum (see Chapter 5 and Figure 5.4).

- *Descriptive Analysis* includes arguments that are data driven, reactive to events, and answer five of the journalist's standard six questions (the Five Ws and an H). Descriptive analytic products summarize and report information about an event, person, entity, or phenomenon but may also generalize by relating data presented to broader patterns and trends. The primary task for the analyst is to convince the client that the information relayed is an accurate and current rendition of reality. To do that, the supporting data need to be as unambiguous, accurate, and authoritative as possible. The analysts' primary tools include the following:

o   Expert knowledge

o   A variety of credible sources that are appropriately characterized in terms of authority and accuracy throughout the product

o   Data displays, such as tables and graphs, in appropriate formats and scales

o   Examples of verified facts or representatives of the verified facts that led to the conclusion

Reports and summaries may not be considered arguments in the classic sense, but analytic products should always contain the implications—the "So What"—and evidence to support these implications in order to answer clients' questions and needs. They usually rely on factual claims from indirect sources that also require corroboration or support. This means that the broader or more speculative the facts and implications presented, the greater the range of evidence required to support them. Acknowledging and accounting for exceptions or contradictory evidence is as critical to the clients' acceptance of reports and summaries as it is for other types of analytic products.

Generalizations are the result of inductive reasoning in which we observe something a few times and assume based on our incomplete information that it happens often or all the time. Clients must see claims for generalizations as plausible and reasonable. Generalized claims are supported by identifying a number of verifiable examples. If the generalization has a descriptive or factual purpose, the examples will be facts. If, on the other hand, it involves explanatory or cause-and-effect relationships, then the examples will be relationships. The more far-reaching the generalization, the more examples will be needed to support it.

Statistics are quantitative generalizations that draw conclusions about large sets of data based on smaller, but carefully defined, representative samples. Statistics support the likelihood of the generalized claim but do not prove it because the data are only a representative sample. Statistics can provide data and gravitas to the analysis, but too many tables or charts can weigh down the product and detract from the claims. We recall one report that illustrated this point well; it was peppered with superfluous line graphs but lacked a simple pie chart that would have illustrated the main claim.

Example of Descriptive Analysis:

Claim: An unknown anarchist with the online pseudonym BORDERControL is trying to organize cyber attacks to take place from March 15 to 25 to protest immigration reform legislation coming to a vote at the end of March.

Reason 1: BORDERControL is encouraging others to stage cyber attacks that would draw attention to the cause.

Evidence: Hackers have been observed stealing email addresses, flooding web servers, defacing websites, and disrupting communications and financial systems.

Evidence: BORDERControL specifically cited as targets the emails of US Senators and Representatives as found on their campaign websites; the military; other unnamed government entities; unnamed industries that use immigrant labor; and news services.

Reason 2: BORDERControL is trying to rally hackers to the cause via a presentation titled "Electronic Civil Disobedience and the Border."

Evidence: A press release calls for sympathizers to meet on March 10 but does not provide a venue.

- *Explanatory Analysis* includes arguments that are slightly less reactive and slightly more conceptually driven than descriptive arguments. They answer the journalist's "Why" question and identify the relationships between facts, events, observables, and trends. They often assert that one thing happened as a result of one or more other observables. A successful causal argument uses both direct and indirect evidence to establish the relationships and the reasonable arguments that one event caused another to happen. The broader or more ambiguous the relationship, the stronger the evidence required to substantiate the claim. The link between the two events often cannot be absolutely verified, but a successful causal argument leaves no doubts about the validity of the link.

The degree of justification depends on the analytic intent. A full causal explanation for an effect requires the analyst to identify and support a number of causes, both direct and indirect, that might have an impact. For example, if the claim is that the price of oil will rise in the next quarter, the evidence would be that winter is approaching (increasing the demand for heating oil), instability in the Middle East is growing (undercutting supply), and two US refineries were just closed for repairs due to hurricane damage (further undercutting supply).

To assign responsibility, the analyst needs to address the most immediate causes that relate to the effect. Analysts should always try to "look around the corner" to determine the future implications of current events. This means analysts should also consider the remote causes of current situations.

Both necessary and sufficient causes can be cited to establish the relationship.

- *Necessary causes* are those in which the result could not have happened without the cause. For example, the acoustic effect of thunder does not occur without the electrostatic discharge of lightning. Being a mammal is necessary to be a human, but it is not sufficient.

- *Sufficient causes* are those that might have caused the event, but other factors may have contributed as well. For example, erratic driving is sufficient for a police officer to stop a car, but it could result from a number of causes.

- *Potential causes* can be clustered or chained so that in combination they contribute to the cause (see Figure 12.3). They can also be defined as Indicators and arrayed against various scenarios to determine which are most diagnostic or helpful in distinguishing among the scenarios.[6]

FIGURE 12.3 ■ Causes of Economic Growth and Slowdown

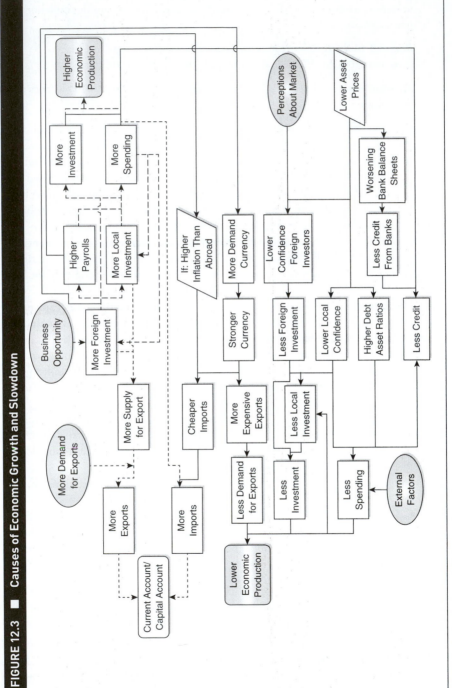

Source: Stock Trend Investing, www.stocktrendinvesting.com.

In addition to defining the types of causes, explanatory arguments can contain

- *Analogies to compare relationships.* Analysts must be sure the phenomena are equivalent and that the key factors are the same in both cases. When people are involved, motive must be established to keep from making unwarranted assumptions about actions.

- *Clues as to the certainty of the relationship.* Words and phrases such as *caused*, *resulted in*, *produced*, or *were responsible* reflect relationships characterized by certainty. When the relationships are less certain, analysts should use words and phrases such as *contributed to*, *facilitated*, and *influenced*.

Example of Explanatory Analysis:

Claim: Escalating rivalry between the Sinaloa and Juarez drug cartels in Juarez has led to increased violence on the US side of the border in El Paso, Texas.

Reason 1: Drug-related violence by the cartels has surged in El Paso.

Evidence: Five people were murdered at a local drug rehabilitation clinic this week; the Juarez cartel has targeted drug rehabilitation facilities in other border cities, but this is the first in El Paso.

Evidence: The Sinaloa cartel attempted to move drugs across the border in daylight. Trucks crossing the border eluded capture by driving at high speed and firing automatic rifles at customs officers.

Reason 2: The cartels are attempting to establish "drug safe houses" in El Paso to backstop operations as they vie to control drug activity in the region.

Evidence: Law enforcement and customs officers discovered three tons of marijuana and a cache of small arms in a ranch house outside El Paso and arrested four men connected with the Sinaloa cartel.

Evidence: Another rancher nearby was reported missing.

Evidence: Government officers have begun visiting properties outside of El Paso in response to reports of a greater cartel presence there.

- *Evaluative analysis* includes an argument with the intent to assess or to establish the meaning or implications of the issue or event by making judgments on key questions. Is the threat increasing or decreasing? Is the risk higher or lower? Is the weapon operational or not? Is the government stronger or weaker?

The critical part of an evaluation is detailing clear and precise definitions of a reasonable and complete set of criteria to use in the appraisal. The best way to achieve this is by using criteria that have assumed common values, identifying their effect, citing authoritative sources, and comparing them to known facts. The analysts' assessments are based on their own expertise and the logic and power of the attributes used to establish the criteria. If the criteria are commonly recognized or linked to reputable sources or other well-established expertise, then the analytic judgment will be well received.

Example of Evaluative Analysis:

> ***Claim:*** The loosely organized hacking movement known as the Collective is increasing efforts to build capability to attack industrial control systems. While no targets appear to have been damaged, growing familiarity with the systems could quickly lead to operational attacks.
>
> *Reason 1:* Collective members have posted threats on the internet against several industrial plants in the Midwest. (Intent: threatening statements)
>
> *Evidence:* Website announcement of a threat against a water treatment plant in Arkansas; calls appear on the internet encouraging people to organize protests against energy companies.
>
> *Reason 2:* Collective members are seeking information about industrial software systems and showing knowledge of system security controls. (Intent: building knowledge)
>
> *Evidence:* Twitter posts share results of browsing for information on specific software and code that would enable access.
>
> *Reason 3:* No evidence of actual attacks but some indications of increasing capabilities.
>
> *Evidence:* There are no postings of malicious activity or reports from potential targets. Internet discussion covers vulnerabilities of control systems operations and design, showing growing sophistication.

- *Estimative Analysis* addresses the question, "What happens next?" It usually forecasts one or more possible scenarios. In such future-oriented projections, analysts typically base their arguments on available data and historical precedent but must rely more heavily on creative brainstorming and logical reasoning to form their analysis. The essence of producing solid estimative analysis is to first identify a set of the key drivers that are most likely to shape the future. Some of these drivers are fairly constant, such as demographic trends, but others can be extremely volatile, such as popular sentiments, civil–military tensions, or the quality of leadership. Both types of drivers are needed to inform good estimative analysis, but most of the analytic ferment should revolve around the key uncertainties.

Cause-and-effect relationships argued in Explanatory Analysis might form the basis for a future in which the same relationship among actors continues. For example, political analysts may argue that particular factors present before an election were influential in determining the election results and the same factors are likely to produce a similar outcome in future elections. Or a doctor tells his patient that the results of a series of medical tests indicate the presence of disease. In the future, similar test results would point to the same disease.

A good critical thinker knows intuitively that there is always more than one credible potential future. Solid estimative analysis will provide several future trajectories and include signposts or indicators to tip off the client about which of the various futures is beginning to emerge.

Two other characteristics of good estimative analysis are the capacity to bound future trajectories and inform clients of circumstances about which they do not need to be concerned. Policymakers and decision makers are accustomed to hearing what could go wrong from intelligence and security analysts, but rarely are they told that they do not need to waste intellectual capital and resources worrying about a particular development. Warning about what might go wrong is a core function for many analysts, but often the policymaker or corporate decision maker would rather hear what can be done to make things work better or improve the profit line.

Example of Estimative Analysis:

Claim: The United States will become less dependent on nuclear energy in the next decade.

Reason 1: Nuclear energy will become increasingly expensive relative to other sources.

Evidence: The price of natural gas is already coming down with the discovery of new repositories.

Reason 2: New alternatives to nuclear energy will emerge.

Evidence: The government and private industry are investing substantial sums of research and development funds to make current alternative energy sources cheaper and are aggressively looking for others.

Techniques for Scoping Your Argument

The more robust your argument and evidence, the more credible you appear to your client. Our own model for how to produce quality analysis was our first division chief, who expected his analysts to stop and think through what was new and significant about their issue and then type out flawlessly a one-page current intelligence article. He could do this on a manual typewriter with no typographical errors. While he made this look simple, the process he followed internally was obviously more complex. We have learned over the years a variety of techniques to help develop, track, and evaluate our arguments before we sit down to draft a product.

- A *topic sentence outline* is an easy way to plan the main points and flow of your product, to identify and understand the argument in another's written argument, or to evaluate your own argument once you have a written draft (see Figure 12.4). Western students are taught to begin paragraphs with topic sentences, but some Western and non-Western writers of arguments may place the main point later in the paragraph. The following steps can assist in making a topic sentence outline:

FIGURE 12.4 ■ Topic Sentence Outline of the Declaration of Independence

DECLARATION OF INDEPENDENCE

When, in the course of human events, it becomes necessary for one people to dissolve the political bands which have connected them with another, and to assume among the powers of the earth, the separate and equal station to which the laws of nature and of nature's God entitle them, a decent respect to the opinions of mankind requires that they should declare the causes which impel them to the separation. **[SCOPE NOTE]**

We hold these truths to be self-evident, that all men are created equal, that they are endowed by their Creator with certain unalienable rights, that among these are life, liberty, and the pursuit of happiness. **[PRIMARY ASSERTION]**

Such has been the patient sufferance of these colonies; and such is now the necessity which constrains them to alter their former systems of government. **[EVIDENCE SUPPORTING VIOLATION OF PRIMARY ASSERTION]**

In every stage of these oppressions we have petitioned for redress in the most humble terms: our repeated petitions have been answered only by repeated injury. **[PRIMARY ATTEMPT TO ADDRESS VIOLATIONS]**

Nor have we been wanting in attention to our British brethren. **[SECONDARY ATTEMPT TO ADDRESS VIOLATIONS]**

We, therefore, the representatives of the United States of America, in General Congress, assembled, appealing to the Supreme Judge of the world for the rectitude of our intentions, do, in the name, and by the authority of the good people of these colonies, solemnly publish and declare, that these united colonies are, and of right ought to be free and independent states. **[FINAL CONCLUSION]**

- o Write what you think will be your topic sentences or—if you have the written product—copy or highlight the first line of every paragraph.

- o Condense these lines into the three components: conclusions or claims, reasons, and evidence.

- o If the argument is not clear, generate or scan the document for additional claims, reasons, and evidence, adding them to the outline.

- o Rearrange the lines, if necessary, to make a clear argument.

- o Identify any gaps that remain in the argument.

● *Argument Maps,* like the topic sentence outline, evaluate the argument by separating the claims and evidence, but they do so graphically so it is easier to think about complex issues and share with others the reasoning behind the conclusion.[7] An Argument Map visualizes the argument parts as a tree diagram that starts from a conclusion or claim, branches to reasons (which may become subclaims) and evidence that support or conflict with one another, and ends when the components represent beliefs or suppositions rather than factual evidence. These suppositions are the argument's key assumptions; the mapping process provides a logical and systematic way to identify them (see Figure 12.5).

The technique is most useful before a product is written to ensure no holes exist in the argument. It is also a good way to evaluate the strength of the evidence and to determine if the argument can be made more effectively or elegantly.

Like other techniques, such as Multiple Scenarios Generation, Argument Mapping can be very complex and take a long time to complete, or it can be a quick way to check the quality of your work. Analysts should be able to evaluate and justify the arguments in their products.

Argument Mapping requires some training and practice to ensure you are doing it correctly, but commercial software can greatly ease the process. Using sticky notes on a whiteboard can also work well in more informal sessions. Color-coding as follows can also be effective:

- o   State the conclusion or main claim, placing it at the top of the tree.

- o   Link the reasons and warrants with green lines to the conclusion.

- o   Connect the evidence with green lines to the reasons each supports.

- o   Identify the objections, challenges, or counterevidence, linking them with red lines to the reasons or evidence in the case of counterevidence they oppose.

- o   Specify rebuttals, if any, with orange lines. An objection, challenge, or counterevidence that does not have an orange-line rebuttal suggests a flaw in the argument.

- o   Evaluate the argument for clarity and completeness, ensuring that red-lined opposing claims and evidence have orange-line rebuttals.

- ●   *Venn Analysis* is a visual technique that helps analysts explore the logic of arguments by graphically displaying relationships among classes through overlapping circles. The overlaps indicate elements of separate groups that have something in common. This technique is useful in organizing and conveying similarities and differences among categories of items, as shown in the diagram of critical thinking skills presented in Figure 12.6.

Commercial office software and freeware offer Venn diagram templates that create the overlaps automatically. The process is simple:

- o   List the classes and members of each class.

- o   Make a series of circles that overlap where classes have members in common.

When applied to argumentation, Venn Analysis can be used to reveal invalid reasoning or validate the soundness of an argument. The technique also helps analysts organize their thinking, look for gaps in logic, or examine the quality of an argument.[8]

FIGURE 12.5 ■ **Argument Map of Osama bin Laden's Declaration of War Against the United States, 1996**

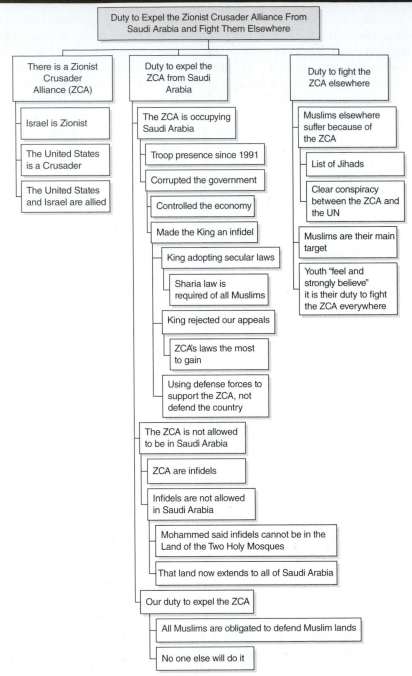

Source: Cynthia L. Storer.

FIGURE 12.6   ■   Venn Diagram of the Components of Critical Thinking

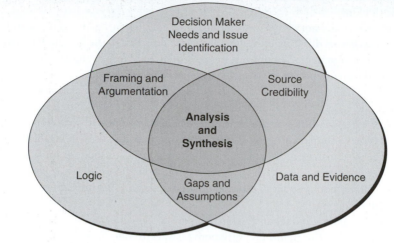

Source: Copyright 2020 Pherson Associates, LLC. All Rights Reserved.

- *Storytelling* is a powerful mental organizer that has been part of human intellectual tradition since the cavemen, but it is rarely mentioned as a specific analytic technique. Just as business planners, doctors consulting with patients, and lawyers addressing juries use narrative to make their forecasts, diagnoses, and arguments compelling and easier to understand, a good analyst should create storylines for their clients, generate scenarios, and ponder "What Ifs" (see Figure 12.7).

Narrative engages the entire brain—logic, emotion, and imagination—drawing on memories of past experiences, culture, and learning. Researchers have shown that the brain visualizes the entire "chunk" of data in a story-based picture that is recalled more easily than disparate pieces of information. When the story is incomplete, we fill in the

FIGURE 12.7   ■   Comparing Analysis and Storytelling Elements

Analysis	Storytelling
Who	Characters
What, How	Plot
When, Where	Setting
Why	Theme
So What	Goal

gaps by relating the story to our personal experience. The downside is that stories reflect our personal biases, but the upside is that they can help us smooth rough spots in our analytic thinking.

For analysts, the story is a narrative framework for presenting or organizing information or, as legal writing expert Kenneth Chestek describes it, the "scaffold on which you hang your argument."[9] In contrast to the left-brained Five Ws and an H, storytelling has analogous elements that speak to the right side of our brain.

Stephen Denning identifies eight types of stories for business leaders, of which two are particularly useful for analysts: knowledge-sharing stories are about problems, and future stories are about forecasting, scenarios, and vision.[10] Cornell professor Daphne Jameson came to similar conclusions after observing language used in business meetings, noting that managers preferred narrative to deal with conflicts, to unify groups, and—most interesting—to share reasoning on complex issues.[11] Managers turned to stories rather than abstract arguments or statistical measures in part because they allowed more context.

Narrative and traditional analysis share many of the same key attributes, suggesting they are left-brain or right-brain variations on ways to communicate complex information. Effective stories include the following characteristics:

- Have a key point or takeaway

- Include vivid detail that will be remembered

- Grab attention with a strong beginning

- Are structured to flow through several short segments

- Keep sentences simple with minimal dependent clauses

Recognizing Spurious Argumentation

Most analysts are not and will probably never be formal logicians, but they should be able to distinguish a solid argument from a weak one. We encourage our students to practice by reading and listening to arguments, then evaluating why they are effective or fallacious. Newspaper op-ed pages can provide good examples of well-reasoned analysis, and advertisements, political campaigns, and much cable television commentary can provide stunning examples of how arguments can be poorly formed, unsupported, and misused.

"In formal logic, a contradiction is the signal of defeat: but in the evolution of real knowledge it marks the first step in progress toward a victory."

—Alfred North Whitehead (British Mathematician and Philosopher)
Science and the Modern World, 1925[12]

Analysts can avoid common logical errors by carefully defining the terms they use and rejecting unfamiliar, ambiguous, or controversial terminology. Some words can become "hot buttons" for those who are seeking to politicize or sensationalize analysis, particularly if a sensitive assessment is leaked to the public through the media or internet. Our public discourse today is replete with fallacious reasoning and even intentionally disseminated disinformation, but we rarely hear interlocutors or commentators address the quality of the argumentation rather than react to the content. We can take this opportunity to practice identifying the spurious argumentation as a way to improve our own logic skills.

Logical fallacies involve a flawed relationship between an argument's claim and its supporting facts or logic. Using old or outdated information—even when more up-to-date information is lacking—is an obvious example of an unacceptable practice. Being aware of the types of common fallacies helps analysts avoid them by revealing the logical disconnect between their premises and conclusions. The fallacies that are most problematic for analysts involve arguments in which the evidence is logically irrelevant to the conclusion or fails to provide sufficient evidence for the conclusion.

- *Circular argument* (or tautology) uses the claim or conclusion as part of the supporting argument.

Example: President Reagan was a great communicator because of his ability to speak compellingly to the American people.

- *Inadequate sampling* occurs when the sample used as a measure to draw a conclusion is too small.

Example: I think the just-released movie will become a big hit based on the three people we interviewed leaving the theater.

- *Hasty generalization* uses a general claim based on insufficient or unrepresentative evidence. It often includes stereotypes and words like *all, every, always,* and *never.*

Example: Deaths from drug overdoses have doubled in the past three years. Therefore, more Americans than ever are dying from drug abuse.

- *False analogy* supports an argument with evidence that is not essentially similar.

Example: If we can crack the genetic code, we should be able to find a cure for the common cold.

- *False dichotomy* occurs when a set of opposing forces or possibilities is reduced to only two options, misrepresenting the complexity of the situation.

Example: It must be either my way or the highway.

- *Non sequitur* asserts a logical relationship between a conclusion and a premise where none exists. The conclusion does not follow the premise.

Example: Joe Smith is a devoted father; therefore, he will be an excellent governor.

- *Post hoc, ergo propter hoc* (Latin for "after this, therefore because of this") claims that if an event preceded another, it must have caused the subsequent event to occur.

Example: Since Chief Jones took office, the crime rate has decreased by 7 percent. Chief Jones should be applauded for reducing the crime rate.

- *Slippery slope* relates the first and last steps in a causal chain when the intervening steps have not occurred.

Example: I didn't get the job I applied for, so I guess I should forget about a career as an analyst.

- *Distraction* (or *Red herring*) brings irrelevant points to distract attention from the issue being argued.

Example: If we build a fence along the entire border, the illegal immigration problem will be solved.

- *Ad hominem argument* (Latin for "to the man") targets the person making the argument rather than the argument.

Example: Brown's argument for political reform is worthless because he is on his third marriage.

- *Ad populum argument* (Latin meaning "to the people") uses popular behavior or opinion to argue a point rather than citing factual evidence.

Example: Most people approve of the new traffic rules; therefore, they must be working.

- *Appeal to authority* occurs when the opinion of a recognized expert is automatically seen as valid.

Example: Reverend Jones said we should picnic in the shade so this is our only option.

KEY TAKEAWAYS

- Analysts convey their thinking to their clients by arguments or sets of statements that contain a conclusion supported logically by the other arguments or statements.

- Arguments are natural follow-ons to frameworks, the AIMS process, and—for longer products—Concept Papers.

- The best way to learn how to generate effective arguments is to practice!

- Analysts should pay particular attention to their claims, reasons, and evidence and make them specific and significant.

- Analysts almost always use inductive thinking because their data are incomplete; this means they are always vulnerable to being wrong.

- How to frame the argument depends on whether the analyst is engaged primarily in descriptive, explanatory, evaluative, or estimative analysis.

- Topic sentence outlines and Argument Maps are good techniques for scoping an argument.

- Storytelling is an underused, but powerful, thought organizer.

- Some of the most dangerous logical fallacies to avoid are false analogies, *ad hominem* arguments, hasty generalizations, false dichotomy, and *post hoc, ergo propter hoc* arguments.

CONSIDERING THE CASE STUDY

Review Case Study I, "Uncharted Territory: Conflict, Competition, or Collaboration in the Arctic?"

- What is the primary assertion made by the analyst in this case study? What key evidence and logic does the analyst provide to support this claim?

- What are two key secondary assertions and the key evidence and logic used to support the claims?

- Are any contrary views or evidence presented that would challenge the key assertion or the secondary assertions that you identified?

- Can you find examples of each type of analysis—descriptive, explanatory, evaluative, and estimative—as they appear in the case study?

- Can you find any examples of logical fallacies in the case study?

NOTES

1. The discussion on argument is informed by a number of works on argumentation but is principally drawn from Pherson Associates training materials (www.pherson.org); Louis M. Kaiser and Randolph H. Pherson, *Analytic Writing Guide* (Reston, VA: Pherson Associates, 2014); Wayne C. Booth et al., *The Craft of Research*, 4th ed. (Chicago: University of Chicago Press, 2016); Joseph M. Williams and Gregory G. Colomb, *The Craft of Argument*, 3rd ed. (New York: Pearson Education, 2007); Stephen E. Toulmin, *The Uses of Argument*, 2nd ed. (Cambridge: Cambridge University Press, 2003); Frans H. van Eemeren et. al., *Fundamentals of Argumentation Theory* (Mahwah, NJ: Lawrence Erlbaum, 1996); and Katherine J. Mayberry, *Everyday Arguments* (Boston: Houghton Mifflin, 2009).

2. Rob Johnston, *Analytic Culture in the US Intelligence Community: An Ethnographic Study* (Washington, DC: Center for the Study of Intelligence, 2005), https://www.cia.gov/library /center-for-the-study-of-intelligence/csi -publications/books-and-monographs /analytic-culture-in-the-u-s -intelligence-community.

3. The word *claim* can refer to the main claim that underpins the product or to subclaims. *Reasons,* when supported by other reasons, become claims in themselves. *Warrants* provide additional backing for reasons, connecting a reason to a general consequence of a general circumstance (i.e., fire results from smoking debris, or animals flee when they sense danger). For a single source with more detailed treatment of argumentation,

we recommend Booth et al., *The Craft of Research*.

4.   Williams and Colomb, *The Craft of Argument*, 235–242.

5.   Stephen E. Toulmin, *The Uses of Argument* (Cambridge: Cambridge University Press, 2003).

6.   For a discussion of Indicators, see Randolph H. Pherson and Richards J. Heuer Jr., *Structured Analytic Techniques for Intelligence Analysis*, 3rd ed. (Washington, DC: CQ Press/SAGE, 2021), chap. 9, 289–303.

7.   This discussion and the technique conventions are based on information from the Austhink website, www.austhink.com/critical/pages/argument_mapping.html.

8.   Pherson and Heuer, *Structured Analytic Techniques*, 112–117.

9.   Kenneth D. Chestek, "The Plot Thickens: The Appellate Brief as Story," *Journal of the Legal Writing Institute* 14 (2008): 131.

10. Stephen Denning, *The Leader's Guide to Storytelling: Mastering the Art and Discipline of Business Narrative*, 2nd ed. (San Francisco: Jossey-Bass, 2011).

11. Daphne A. Jameson, "Narrative Discourse and Management Action," *Journal of Business Communication* 38, no. 4 (2001): 476–511.

12. Alfred North Whitehead, *Science and the Modern World* (New York: Simon & Schuster, 1997), 187. This book was originally published in 1925.

13 DID I CONSIDER ALTERNATIVE HYPOTHESES?

SETTING THE STAGE

Generating and testing hypotheses is a core reasoning skill. It is used by critical thinkers when confronting challenging issues for which the risk of error is great and reliance on intuition shaped by past experience and knowledge could generate the wrong answer.

Analysis of a complex issue must start with a set of alternative explanations or hypotheses that can be tested against the known evidence or relevant information.[1] A hypothesis is a potential explanation or conclusion that is to be tested by collecting and presenting evidence. It is a declarative statement that has not been established as true—an educated guess based on observation that needs to be supported or refuted by more observation or through experimentation.

Alternative hypotheses help explain what could have occurred in the past much as scenarios provide alternative trajectories of what could occur in the future. Both processes benefit from the use of indicators to validate past events or anticipate future ones. Key distinctions between the two are based on provability and availability of data. Hypotheses can be disproved based on available data, but no tangible "evidence" exists for evaluating which future scenario is most likely to be proved correct.

By applying the scientific method, a good critical thinker knows that a hypothesis cannot be proved true based solely on the evidence that supports it because the same evidence could be consistent with other competing hypotheses or additional evidence might be discovered in the future. Science dictates that the best way to establish the most credible hypothesis is to proceed by finding evidence that can refute or disconfirm alternative hypotheses. A single item of evidence that is shown to be inconsistent with a hypothesis can be sufficient grounds to dismiss that hypothesis. For example, if a suspect has a strong alibi, prudent investigators will immediately shift their attention to other suspects. The most tenable hypothesis is the one with little or no disconfirming information.

LOOKING MORE DEEPLY

Generating multiple hypotheses at the start of a project helps analyst avoid several cognitive pitfalls, including jumping to conclusions; being overly influenced by first impressions; *satisficing*, or selecting the first explanation that appears to work; and opting for the answer that elicits the most popular support or is preferred by the boss. Figure 13.1 provides a list of key characteristics of a good hypothesis.

FIGURE 13.1 ■ Components of a Good Hypothesis

A good hypothesis meets the following criteria:

- Is testable and falsifiable

- Is written as a definite statement, not as a question

- Is based on observations and knowledge

- Predicts the anticipated results clearly

- Contains a dependent and an independent variable—a "What" and a "Why." The dependent variable is the phenomenon being explained, and the independent variable does the explaining.

The practice of generating multiple hypotheses also adds value by creating a robust set of bins into which analysts can pour their information as they proceed with their analysis. For example, when assessing the status of Iraq's weapons of mass destruction (WMD) programs prior to the Iraq War in 2003, intelligence analysts were working basically from only two hypotheses: The Iraqi regime had substantial programs and had successfully hidden large amounts of WMD, or it had only modest programs and possessed more limited amounts of WMD. The missing hypothesis was the null hypothesis—that Saddam Hussein had ended all WMD programs and no WMD stockpiles were there to be found. As history demonstrated, this third or null hypothesis later proved to be the correct one.

Unfortunately, substantial evidence was available at the time that was consistent with the null hypothesis, but analysts did not have a bin for this data and the reporting was mostly overlooked. Positing a null hypothesis that WMD stockpiles had been removed would have enabled analysts to argue that the lack of compelling evidence to the contrary meant that the null hypothesis merited consideration as a plausible alternative to the two existing hypotheses.

Creativity in Critical Thinking

Generating a full set of hypotheses and asking the right questions (see Chapter 2) are two parts of the critical thinking process that scream for creativity, fueled by imagination. This is what enables analysts to move beyond the data to explore the probabilities and possibilities—the insights—that will support and inform decision maker plans and actions. The 9/11 Commission's[2] criticism of the intelligence analysis leading up to the unprecedented plane attacks as a "failure of imagination" has served as the impetus to develop tools and techniques to improve quality and collaboration, but it also reinforced the tried-and-true tradecraft practices long taught in the community.

In developing strategies to incorporate creativity into their analytic processes, analysts can draw a lesson from Steve Jobs, who stressed the concept of creativity as "just connecting things" or making new associations among what is already known. The more diverse and wide-ranging thinking from which the connections are drawn, the more likely the solution is to move beyond the obvious. He further explained his thinking in a 1996 *Wired* magazine interview:

> When you ask creative people how they did something, they feel a little guilty because they didn't really do it, they just saw something ... they were able to connect experiences they've had and synthesize new things ... they were able to do that [because] they've had more experiences or they have thought more about their experiences than other people.... A lot of people ... haven't had very diverse experiences. So they ... end up with very linear solutions without a broad perspective on the problem.[3]

His perspective was certainly nothing new. August Ada King, daughter of Lord Byron and author with Charles Babbage of the first paper on computer science more than a 150 years earlier in 1841, also defined imagination as combinations leading to new connections, stressing that the connections are novel and bring the abstract to the real world. She wrote,

> First: it is the Combining Faculty. It brings together things, facts, ideas, conceptions, in new, original, endless, ever varying, Combinations. It seizes points in common, between subjects having no very apparent connexion, & hence seldom or never brought into juxtaposition. Second: It conceives and brings into mental presences that which is far away, or invisible, of which in short does not exist within our physical & conscious cognizance.[4]

Creativity as a Mindset. Research shows that creativity is not a "personality" type or trait, but more like what some characterize as a "mindset" or even a "process," which means we can all develop and improve our creative thinking skills.[5] Popular literature tends to simplify brain theory in portraying analysts as left-brained because they are logical, methodical, and verbally oriented and artists as right-brained, creative, spontaneous, and visually oriented. However, brain imaging studies such as one performed by University of Utah researchers in 2013 found no evidence of preferential use of left or right brain hemispheres but that individuals prefer to use one region of their brains for certain functions, which they called lateralization.[6] In examining neural activity in and between 7,000 regions of the brains of 1,011 subjects, the images showed heavy activity in certain key regions, but on average both sides of the brain were equal in neural networks and activity.

Another conclusion drawn from neural research supports the notion from Dual Process theory (see Chapter 5 for its application in System 1 and System 2 thinking) that creativity is a two-stage process in which innovative ideas are first generated and then evaluated for originality and utility.[7] The implication is that an individual's creativity may be inhibited by their "inner critic," which more strictly evaluates their ideas. In addition, Carol Dweck cites "wide agreement" among 143 creativity researchers that the "number one ingredient in creative achievement ... was exactly the kind of perseverance and resilience produced by the *growth mindset"* (see Chapter 1).

"Integration is creativity."

—Susan A. Gordon
Former Principal Deputy Director for National Intelligence

Brain function is an integration or synthesis of both hemispheres' primary functions, which means humans could not function if the two hemispheres did not talk to each other. The concept of weighing the dominance of one side over the other suggests the benefits of balancing the two to take full advantage of intellectual strengths. For instance, if the predominance of logic and argumentation in the intelligence community implies that the left brain might be more dominant in the population and culture, then a solution could be to increase effectiveness by shifting or balancing that dominance with practice to strengthen the weaker side.[8]

Strategies to Stimulate Analytic Creativity. The demand for analytic thinking and creativity skills is on the rise, according to the World Economic Forum's *The Future of Jobs Report 2018*[9] (see Figure 13.2). Analysts can use the insights from research and what we already know about structured analytic thinking to develop and improve our skills by understanding the breadth and diversity of the issue environment, seeking insights from other disciplines and concepts, and combining concepts in different ways. To operationalize these concepts, try the following:

1. *Conceptualize the breadth of the environment by creating a frame that enables you to imagine the whole.* The easiest way to do this is to create for your problem two spectra of key drivers, or factors that will influence, shape, or affect the outcome of an activity, the development of the issue, or which alternative scenario is most likely to emerge.

- Generate the drivers by answering questions such as

   o   What explains this activity?

   o   Is this the beginning of a trend?

   o   Does the problem or pattern extend beyond my particular issue?

- The most important part is to define meaningful end points for the drivers; that is what will enable imagining the whole picture.

- Multiple Scenarios Generation[10] calls for generating stories for each of the quadrants. The benefit of defining a model in this way is that the matrix incorporates positive and negative aspects so nothing should be a total surprise.

The example in Figure 13.3 from Globalytica's *Analytic Insider* is a matrix, generated in 2016 to help understand the potential impact of US elections, then revisited in March 2019. It demonstrates that creating a frame can focus on the issue rather

FIGURE 13.2 ■ Demand for Analytic Innovation and Creativity Is Increasing

Today, 2018

Analytic thinking and innovation

Complex problem solving

Critical thinking and analysis

Active learning and learning strategies

Creativity, originality, and initiative

Attention to detail, trustworthiness

Emotional intelligence

Reasoning, problem solving, and ideation

Leadership and social influence

Coordination and time management

Trending, 2022

Analytic thinking and innovation

Active learning and learning strategies

Creativity, originality, and initiative

Technology design and programming

Critical thinking and analysis

Complex problem solving

Leadership and social influence

Emotional intelligence

Reasoning, problem solving, and ideation

Systems analysis and evaluation

Declining, 2022

Manual dexterity, endurance, and precision

Memory, verbal, auditory, and spatial abilities

Management of financial, material resources

Technology installation and maintenance

Reading, writing, math, and active listening

Management of personnel

Quality control and safety awareness

Coordination and time management

Visual, auditory, and speech abilities

Technology use, monitoring, and control

FIGURE 13.3 ■ Anticipating Potential Trajectories for US Elections

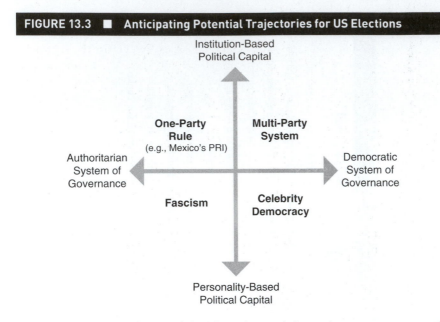

than the emotion or politics and that the technique helps analysts gain perspective by stepping away from any personal view of the problem.[11]

2. *Adapt other models and perspectives to your problem.* Once you imagine the whole, you need to continue to adapt your drivers and model to be more meaningful and sophisticated. For instance, it is not enough to identify "the economy" as a key driver. Ask yourself,

- What are the factors about the economy that make a critical difference? Are the economic influences due to a specific industry, a change in supply chain or routes, availability of natural resources, or trade relationships?

- Do I need to think more deeply about my key assumptions?

- What do the data I have tell me about evolving trends and the data I do not have tell me about the gaps and unknowns?

Try thinking of your problem in terms of different models. One of the authors still maintains a sheet from a training class at the beginning of her career that listed dozens of different topics to spur associative thinking. Peter Schwartz in *The Art of the Long View*[12] noted that a habit that had stood him in good stead was to read fringe literature about technology and change because that is where he would see the first evidence of a trend or a change.

"Old ideas can sometimes use new buildings. New ideas must use old buildings."

—Stephen Johnson
Where Good Ideas Come From: The Natural History of Innovation[13]

For example, Paul Stares and Mona Yacoubian were two of the first to draw epidemiological comparisons between terrorism and "a mutating virus or metastasizing cancer." They argued in a *Washington Post* editorial that this "promising new approach" would "encourage us to ask the right questions," "help us view Islamist militancy as a dynamic, multifaceted phenomenon," and "encourage us to devise a comprehensive, long-term strategic approach to countering the threat."[14]

3. *Ask questions that help you think about the situation differently, specifically those that help you probe what might be wrong about your data or observations, not what is right.* A version of the Premortem Analysis and Structured Self-Critique (see Chapter 15) will help you challenge your assumptions and observations and help identify potential causes of error that previously had been overlooked. It mimics the two processes of creativity in two ways:

- By reframing questions, the exercise typically elicits responses that are different from the original ones. Asking questions about the same topic, but from a different perspective opens new pathways in the brain.

- By asking participants to identify weaknesses, the process encourages different views and legitimizes dissent.

As Stephen Johnson reminds us, "Being right keeps you in place. Being wrong forces you to explore."[15] Looking for the inconsistencies in your data can help analysts do the following:

- Identify the most diagnostic information.

- Focus on disconfirming evidence.

- Flag areas of disagreement or agreement.

- Challenge preconceived ideas.

- Highlight the potential for disinformation or deception.

Classic Methods for Generating Hypotheses

More tactically, analysts have traditionally relied on three methods for generating hypotheses:[16]

1. *Situational Logic.* Analysts consider all the known facts and underlying forces at work at that particular time and place and then postulate several plausible alternative explanations consistent with what is known. This strategy requires analysts to pay careful attention to identifying and checking their key assumptions because they usually work with ambiguous, deficient, and possibly deceptive data.

2. *Applying Theory.* Analysts ask if the current situation is similar to other cases of the same phenomenon. For example, did the shootings follow a pattern of past serial killers? Do the economic indicators suggest the same dynamic as past

double-dip recessions? This approach can be very efficient because large amounts of data are not required, but it also allows analysts to ignore potential key evidence.

Analysts need to be alert to generalized models and theories that may not apply to the specific or unique characteristics of their problem or that require specialized qualitative or quantitative expertise. By understanding the issue framework, analysts can build a conceptual model that identifies the most relevant factors to assess similarities and differences with other theories or models.

3.   *Historical Analogy.* Analysts compare current events to what has happened in the past, either in their personal experience or in history. A potential trap with this method is to assume that both situations are equivalent in most respects and that the dynamic will produce the same outcome. Several senior government officials fell into this trap, for example, when they compared efforts to reconstruct Afghanistan and Iraq after the US invasions post-9/11 to efforts by the United States to rebuild Germany under the Marshall Plan after World War II.[17] Another trap to avoid is latching on to the first analogy that comes to mind or one that fits with existing views. This trap is best avoided by requiring that the analyst come up with multiple analogies before settling on the one that best fits the situation. The resulting hypotheses can serve a variety of purposes, including these:[18]

- Exploring the particulars of a specific case, such as potential causes of unrest or why a situation may be developing.

- Demonstrating similar dynamics across a set of similar situations. This is particularly helpful when an analyst has only limited data with which to work.

- Viewing a problem from different perspectives or disciplines. For example, different hypotheses for explaining the behavior of a drug cartel could be generated by trying to explain the pattern of activities in terms of economics, politics, geography, or logistics.

Structured Techniques for Generating Hypotheses

Three Structured Analytic Techniques—Simple Hypotheses, Quadrant Hypothesis Generation, and the Multiple Hypotheses Generator—are designed specifically for generating hypotheses.[19] These techniques are among several that help analysts generate hypotheses by using creative brainstorming and reframing approaches (see Figure 13.4).

1.   *Simple Hypotheses.* This approach uses a structured brainstorming technique that employs sticky notes to identify key forces and factors, array them into affinity groups, and label each group. The labels then are converted into a set of alternative hypotheses. This process helps ensure that a comprehensive set of hypotheses is generated, but it is necessary to check to ensure that the hypotheses are mutually exclusive.

2.   *Quadrant Hypothesis Generation.* This technique works best when there are two easily identified driving forces that will determine the outcome of an issue. The technique arrays the two drivers on a 2×2 matrix with one driver representing

FIGURE 13.4 ■ SATs for Generating Hypotheses

WHAT STRUCTURED ANALYTIC TECHNIQUES APPLY?

Techniques for generating multiple hypotheses include the following the following:

- Simple Hypotheses
- Quadrant Hypothesis Generation
- Multiple Hypothesis Generator®
- Delphi Method
- Quadrant Crunching™
- Foresight Techniques

the x-axis and the other driver representing the y-axis. The analyst then generates four distinct hypotheses that satisfy the requirements of each quadrant of the matrix by describing the end state that would be shaped by the two drivers.

3. *The Multiple Hypotheses Generator*. This technique uses the Five-Ws-and-an-H strategy (the journalist's classic questions of Who, What, How, When, Where, and Why) to generate a robust set of mutually exclusive permutations that can be evaluated and rated for their plausibility. Analysts review the list of possible hypotheses, discarding those that make little sense or are unlikely. They then select those they believe are most deserving of attention. If time is short or resources dear, then the list of credible hypotheses to consider can be limited to a few. If time is less pressing and resources are available, the analyst can expand the list of candidate hypotheses to consider.

Weighting the Hypotheses

Generating a set of alternative or competing hypotheses is of little value if rigor is not used to evaluate each hypothesis to determine which provides the best explanation of the process or activity under study. Classic factors used to evaluate hypotheses are motive, intent, capability, and whether it makes logical sense.

Analysts often test their hypotheses by using a form of reasoning called *abduction* (see Chapter 12). Abductive reasoning starts with a set of facts, evidence, or relevant information. The analyst then examines each hypothesis in the context of these facts, looking for the hypothesis that best explains the available facts. Because of the complexities inherent to most intelligence analysis and the novelty of most analytic tasks, conclusive proof or refutation of a hypothesis is a rare event.

Structured Analytic Techniques that provide a more systematic way to test hypotheses include Analysis of Competing Hypotheses, Deception Detection, Argument Mapping, and Diagnostic Reasoning.[20]

- *Analysis of Competing Hypotheses (ACH)* is the application of Karl Popper's philosophy of science to the field of intelligence analysis. Popper asserts that analysis should start with multiple hypotheses and proceed by rejecting or eliminating hypotheses for which inconsistent data exist and tentatively accepting only those hypotheses that cannot be refuted.

This approach to hypothesis testing—looking for inconsistent data to disprove a hypothesis rather than compiling all the evidence to make the best case in support of a hypothesis—can bring great efficiencies into the analytic process. It takes only one or a few items of compelling inconsistent data to discard an entire hypothesis from serious consideration. If analysts are sensitive to this fact, their research and analysis can be much more tightly focused and efficient.

● *Deception Detection* consists of a set of checklists analysts can use to assess whether sources, informants, opponents, or competitors are attempting to mislead them or hide important information. The checklists focus on motive, opportunity, and means (MOM); past opposition practices (POP); manipulability of sources (MOSES); and evaluation of evidence (EVE). The inclusion of a deception hypothesis also is highly recommended for those using Analysis of Competing Hypotheses.

Deception is most likely to occur in the following scenarios:

o   The potential deceiver has a history of using deception, such as the Russian and Cuban governments.

o   Key information is received at a critical time when either the recipient or the deceiver has a great deal to lose or gain—for example, when the fraudulent documents surfaced showing that Iraq had imported yellowcake from Niger as US president George W. Bush was trying to make the case for a US invasion of Iraq.

o   The analysis hinges on a single item of information or a single key source, such as the source code-named "Curveball" during the buildup to the US invasion of Iraq.

o   Accepting the information would cause the client to alter an assumption or redirect substantial resources; this happened when fake Allied intelligence reporting collected by the Germans in the run-up to the Normandy invasion in World War II caused them to misposition their troops.

o   The potential deceiver is known to have a reliable feedback channel—a problem for many law enforcement units suspected of being penetrated by drug trafficking organizations.

● *Argument Mapping*, as discussed in greater detail in Chapter 12, is used to test a single hypothesis through logical reasoning. The process starts by writing down a testable hypothesis or tentative analytic judgment and then arraying all the evidence and arguments that support or refute the hypothesis or judgment. This is accomplished by arraying boxes hierarchically below the initial statement and indicating which support and which refute the original statement (see Figure 13.5). If all the branches that support a hypothesis can

FIGURE 13.5 ■ Argument Map: Will the Reserve Bank of Australia Raise Interest Rates?

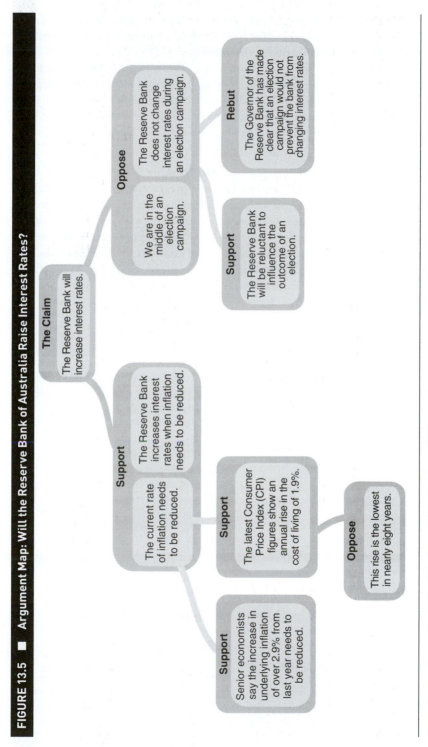

The Claim

The Reserve Bank will increase interest rates.

Support

The current rate of inflation needs to be reduced.

Support

The Reserve Bank increases interest rates when inflation needs to be reduced.

Support

Senior economists say the increase in underlying inflation of over 2.9% from last year needs to be reduced.

Support

The latest Consumer Price Index (CPI) figures show an annual rise in the cost of living of 1.9%.

Oppose

This rise is the lowest in nearly eight years.

Oppose

The Reserve Bank does not change interest rates during an election campaign.

We are in the middle of an election campaign.

Support

The Reserve Bank will be reluctant to influence the outcome of an election.

Rebut

The Governor of the Reserve Bank has made clear that an election campaign would not prevent the bank from changing interest rates.

Source: Argument map using Rationale software at http://www.austhink.com.

be refuted at some point in the evidence chain, then the hypothesis should be discarded. If not, the claim or hypothesis is supported, assuming no new disconfirming information comes to light.

Argument Mapping helps analysts to both clarify and organize their thinking. It also helps analysts recognize assumptions and identify gaps in logic or available knowledge. This visualization technique makes it much easier for analysts to think about a complex subject and enables both analysts and their clients to focus on the most critical information, key assumptions, and all the branches of a logic tree.

● *Diagnostic Reasoning* applies hypothesis testing to the evaluation of a new development, the assessment of a new item of information, or the reliability of a source. The method is to write down the value of an item of evidence or posit the reliability of a source and then brainstorm all the ways the assessment could be wrong. The next step is to critically examine if any of these contrary views is credible and what that implies for the initial assertion. One benefit of using the technique is that it reduces the chance of surprise by ensuring that at least some consideration is given to alternative conclusions.

KEY TAKEAWAYS

● Considering alternative explanations and generating multiple hypotheses is critically important when confronting complex issues in which the risk of error is great and dependence on intuition might lead to wrong conclusions.

● The analyst cannot prove that a hypothesis is true but can only establish that it is the most credible hypothesis by finding facts that refute alternative hypotheses.

● Creativity is key to developing a full set of hypotheses and key questions. It involves making new connections among facts, models, or concepts and making the abstract concrete.

● Analysts can develop their creative skills by identifying the spectra that frame their issue, adapting other models and perspectives to their problem, and asking questions that help them think about the situation differently, particularly about what might be wrong about the data or assumptions.

● Multiple hypotheses can be generated by employing situational logic, identifying historical analogies, and applying models or theories.

● The Analysis of Competing Hypotheses (ACH) methodology offers analysts an efficient way to process data by looking for inconsistent data to disprove competing hypotheses rather than compiling all the evidence to make the best case in support of a single hypothesis.

● ACH was designed to help analysts think systematically about a problem, not to generate solutions.

● Argument Mapping is another powerful thinking tool in part because it exercises both the left (logic) and the right (visualization) sides of the brain.

● The Diagnostic Reasoning technique forces analysts to consider alternative conclusions by consciously applying hypothesis testing to the evaluation of new information or sources.

CONSIDERING THE CASE STUDY

Review Case Study V, "Puzzling Food Poisonings in Germany."

- Were sufficient alternative hypotheses concerning the origin of the infection considered?

- Was sufficient attention paid to whether it was a version of a known strain of *E. coli* or an unknown strain?

- Which of the strategies for developing creativity might have helped analysts frame this problem?

- Which technique—situational logic, identifying historical analogies, or applying models or theories—would be most appropriate in generating alternative hypotheses in this situation?

- How would an ACH exercise have helped analysts work this problem?

NOTES

1. This chapter is drawn in part from Randolph H. Pherson and Richards J. Heuer Jr., *Structured Analytic Techniques for Intelligence Analysis,* 3rd ed. (Washington, DC: CQ Press/ SAGE, 2021), 146–154 and 272–276 as well as from Pherson Associates instructional materials (www.pherson .org).

2. *The 9/11 Commission Report: Final Report of the National Commission on Terrorist Attacks Upon the United States,* July 22, 2004, http://govinfo.library .unt.edu/911/report/index.htm. A hard copy of the report was published by W. W. Norton in 2005.

3. Gary Wolf, "Steve Jobs: The Next Insanely Great Thing," *Wired*, February 1, 1996, https://www.wired .com/1996/02/jobs-2/.

4. Betty A. Toole, *Ada, the Enchantress of Numbers* (Mill Valley, CA: Strawberry Press, 1992), Kindle.

5. Greg Satell, "Set the Conditions for Anyone on Your Team to Be Creative, *Harvard Business Review*, December 5, 2018, https://hbr.org/2018/12/set-the -conditions-for-anyone-on-your-team -to-be-creative.

6. J. A Nielson et al., "An Evaluation of the Left-Brain vs. Right-Brain Hypothesis With Resting State Functional Connectivity Magnetic Resonance Imaging," *PLOS ONE* 8, no. 8, e71275, https://doi.org/10.1371 /journal.pone.0071275.

7. See studies such as Naama Mayseless and Shimone Shamay-Tsoory, "Unleashing Creativity: The Role of Left Temporoparietal Regions in Evaluating and Inhibiting the Generation of Creative Ideas," *Neuropsychologia* 64 (November 2014): 157–168 and Paul T. Sowden, Andrew Pringle, and Liane Gabora, "The Shifting Sands of Creating Thinking: Connections to Dual-Process Theory," *Thinking & Reasoning* 21, no. 1 (February 2015): 40–60.

8. We thank colleague Todd Sears for comments on brain function that led us to Iain McGilchrist's *Master and His Emissary: The Divided Brain and the Making of the Western World*, 2nd ed. (New Haven, CT: Yale University Press, 2019), which sensitizes readers to the influence of perceptions of right and left "brained-ness" on culture and society. Other books, such as Robert

Sapolsky's *Behave: The Biology of Humans at Our Best and Worst* (New York: Penguin, 2017), also reinforce the importance of integration.

9. World Economic Forum, *The Future of Jobs Report: 2018*, September 17, 2018, http://www3.weforum.org/docs/WEF _Future_of_Jobs_2018.pdf.

10. These techniques are described in more detail in Chapter 9 of Pherson and Heuer, *Structured Analytic Techniques*, 272–276.

11. Randolph Pherson, "Is the United States Heading Toward Radical Political Change?" *Analytic Insider* 6, no. 1 (March 2019), http://www .globalytica.com/analytic-insider-blog/.

12. Peter Schwartz, *The Art of the Long View: Planning for the Future in an Uncertain World* (New York: Bantam, Doubleday, Dell, 1991).

13. Stephen Johnson, *Where Good Ideas Come From: The Natural History of Innovation* (New York: Riverhead Books, 2010).

14. Paul Stares and Mona Yacoubian, "Terrorism as a Virus," op-ed, *Washington Post*, August 23, 2005.

15. Johnson, *Where Good Ideas Come From*.

16. This section is drawn from Richards J. Heuer Jr., *Psychology of Intelligence Analysis* (Washington, DC: Center for the Study of Intelligence, 1999), republished by Pherson Associates (Reston, VA: Pherson Associates, 2007), and Pherson Associates instructional materials.

17. David Ekbladh, "The Marshall Plan Mystique," *Peace and Conflict Monitor*, April 14, 2003, www.monitor.upeace .org/archive.cfm?id_article=13; and David Rohde and David E. Sanger, "How a 'Good War' in Afghanistan Went Bad," *New York Times*, August 12, 2007, www.nytimes.com/2007 /08/12/world/asia/12afghan.html ?pagewanted=1.

18. This perspective on generating hypotheses is drawn from "An Intelligence Analysis Primer: Six Steps to Better Intelligence Analysis," *Global Futures Forum* (March 2008), 25.

19. These techniques are described in more detail in Pherson and Heuer, *Structured Analytic Techniques*, 146–154. As of the publication date, the Multiple Hypotheses Generator˚ software was in the process of being hosted and is not currently available.

20. These techniques are described in more detail in Chapter 7 of Pherson and Heuer, *Structured Analytic Techniques*, 129–179.

14 HOW DO I DEAL WITH POLITICIZATION?

SETTING THE STAGE

Concern over the potential for politicization of intelligence analysis—and for analysis writ large—must be taken seriously. The charge most commonly levied in the media is that the analytic community tailors its analysis to make it more palatable to senior policy officials. In recent years, the opposite charge has been levied—senior US decision makers have labeled Intelligence Community analysts as members of the "Deep State" intent on undercutting their policy agendas.

According to Jack Davis, a former national intelligence officer (NIO) for Latin America and accomplished mentor of analysts,

> A politicized and therefore unprofessional assessment can be defined as an analytic deliverable that reflects either (1) the analyst's motivated effort to distort facts and judgments to support, or *oppose*, a specific policy, political entity, or general ideology, or (2) a conspicuous, even if unmotivated, disregard for sound tradecraft standards that produces similarly distorted outputs that could affect the policymaking process.[1]

Richard Betts expands on this concept, noting that politicization can be both top-down (when officials try to make intelligence analysis conform to policy) or bottom-up (when analysts imbue their product with their own political biases).[2] Top-down politicization occurs when policymakers "cherry pick" their evidence, trumpet questionable reporting that supports their views, fabricate or distort information to support their policy agendas, or task analysts to conduct research and produce analysis that will support their policy agenda.

Dennis J. Gleeson, a former director of strategy in the Directorate of Analysis in the US Central Intelligence Agency (CIA), notes that top-down politicization can result in serious costs as experienced prior to and following the US invasion of Iraq in 2003. Vice president Dick Cheney's repeated visits to the CIA asking the same questions multiple times and in different ways, for example, had a chilling effect on the analytic workforce. More recently, Gleeson observes: "By trying to shape analysis to support his administration's world view, [US president Donald] Trump is creating the conditions for committing our country to courses of action that have the potential to be as costly or disastrous."[3]

The most pernicious—and we suspect the most likely—form of bottom-up politicization is the tendency of analysts to self-censor. This rarely happens but can occur if an analyst decides not to write an article because the recipient would not like the story being told or because including certain information could put his or her organization in a bad light. When discussing the role of intelligence in the 2003 Iraq War, Paul Pillar, a former NIO for the Middle East, cited the sugarcoating of unwelcome analysis as a particularly bad form of politicization.[4]

Many—including Sherman Kent, who headed the Office of National Estimates at the CIA in its formative years—contend that the best way to avoid politicization is to keep the analyst and the policymaker separated to avoid any potential that the analyst's objectivity might be compromised.[5] The problem with this approach is that intelligence analysts can become so disengaged from the policy community that they can no longer provide effective support.

Providing timely analysis is an ODNI (Office of the Director of National Intelligence) analytic standard, and compliance requires interacting with policymakers to know with what issues they are wrestling and how soon decisions must be made. Analysts in the business sector face similar dilemmas when their key findings are perceived by management to not support corporate goals or to document the need for actions that would reduce profitability.

If the senior decision makers are inclined to discount or ignore the intelligence analysis, this should not be a reason for not continuing to generate a stream of solidly reasoned and well-evidenced intelligence products. The audience for good analysis is much broader than just the White House, including not only those at the working levels and others in the analytic community but the public and the US Congress.

LOOKING MORE DEEPLY

A better way to avoid the pitfalls of politicization is to build an analytic culture that actively promotes two key principles: analytic objectivity and integrity.[6] Analysts must come to work every day knowing that their task is to do the best they can to explain why things happen—and that how they frame their argument has to be independent of any political consideration or business imperative. This point is made explicit in the CIA's ethos statement: "We are truthful and forthright, and we provide information and analysis without institutional or political bias."[7] Betts has come to much the same conclusion in his writings, concluding that "the irrevocable norm must be that policy interests, preferences, or decisions must never determine intelligence judgments."[8]

Carmen Medina, former deputy director for intelligence at the CIA, observed in 2007 that analysts should not regard integrity and neutrality as the same thing or assume that one is dependent on the other. Neutrality implies some distance from the client, whereas integrity rests on the willingness to provide the most complete answer even if it is not what the client wants to hear. She explains, "Neutrality cannot be used to justify analytic celibacy and disengagement from the customer. If forced to choose between analytic detachment and impact on policymaking, the 21st century analyst must choose the latter."[9]

One strategy for dealing with politicization is to provide alternative interpretations of the evidence, posit multiple hypotheses, and generate alternative scenarios when trying to anticipate what the future will bring. As NIO for Latin America, Randolph

Pherson was often asked by policymakers, "What do you think I should do?" Over time, he learned that the best response was to say,

> Three options are available to you. Here are the upsides and the downsides of each option based on the community's assessment of how each option is likely to play out. And this is our level of confidence in the intelligence reporting that supports our assessment of each of these options. I defer to you to decide which option to choose or recommend to your superiors.

Most policymakers appreciate analytic inputs and will factor them into their thinking. Analysts should keep in mind, however, that decision makers must also consider the analysis in the context of what they have learned from other sources, the policy implications of each option, and the amount of risk they are prepared to take. Analysis can inform their judgments, but it rarely determines what is decided.

Robert M. Gates laid out this dilemma in 1992 in a message to CIA analysts after he survived a bruising confirmation battle to become director of Central Intelligence (DCI). He said,

> Unwarranted concerns about politicization can arise when analysts themselves fail to understand their role in the process. We do produce a corporate product. If the policymaker wants the opinion of a single individual, he or she can (and frequently does) consult any one of a dozen outside experts on any given issue. Your work, on the other hand, counts because it represents the well-considered view of an entire intelligence community. Analysts . . . must discard the academic mindset that says their work is their own.[10]

The challenge for editors and managers of analysts is to shape an analyst's draft to make it more focused and compelling in ways that are consistent with the available evidence and not motivated by policy concerns. As Betts describes the process, "If done properly, managers' editing should be a form of benign politicization, bringing intelligence 'into the realm of politics' without corrupting it."[11]

The growing use of videos, visualizations, and other digitalized forms of electronic communication poses even greater challenges to analysts. As newspaper editors know well, choosing which picture of someone to publish is often seen as a political act, especially if an unflattering image is chosen. A political rally can be depicted as a success if the camera zooms in on the candidate and a tight circle of enthusiastic supporters or a disaster if the camera zooms out to show that most of the room is occupied by empty chairs.

Far less attention has been paid to what constitutes bias in the selection of an image than in written text. Substantial energy is being devoted in today's world to manipulating and photoshopping images for posting on the internet to support political or ideological objectives.

A growing concern is a new technology that almost anyone can use to create increasingly convincing—but false—sound clips, videos, and photos. "Deepfakes," which are media that have been digitally altered through artificial intelligence techniques, pose a major risk for both individuals and democratic institutions. Laymen now can plug a photograph or video clip into prewritten code and produce an extremely realistic, lifelike false image or false video. Deepfakes are inherently hard to detect and, so far, society is largely ill-equipped to deal with them.

Incentives to post Deepfakes on social media are likely to grow as politicians and perpetrators of Digital Disinformation seek to enflame passions surrounding highly divisive issues such as immigration, ethnic differences, and, especially in the United States, abortion and gun safety. Deepfakes pose a major challenge to the precepts of liberal democracy because

- massive groups of people can be reached almost instantaneously;

- deepfakes can be micro-targeted, focusing on those most easily swayed and open to persuasion; and

- perpetrators are rarely held accountable for what is posted.

In addition, perpetrators of Deepfakes—and Digital Disinformation writ large— are increasingly adept at manipulating perceptions by exploiting common cognitive biases, misapplied heuristics, and intuitive traps. Examples that the Russians and others have leveraged to promote their agendas include Confirmation Bias, Groupthink, Vividness Bias, and the Anchoring Effect.

This increased use of video, graphics, and other digitized images in analytic products will require new metrics for assessing digital objectivity. Managers will need to be more proactive in reviewing all phases—and all forms—of analytic production to ensure that analytic integrity is not compromised. Supervisors of analysts must also resist the temptation when pressures mount and deadlines approach to short-circuit the role of analysts in the production process. More important, they need to constantly reinforce the perception that analysts are responsible for tracking their products through the often-multiple stages of the editorial and review process to ensure that analytic tradecraft and standards have not been compromised along the way.

Relating Critical Thinking to Politicization

The need to protect against politicization extends to every element of critical thinking. For example, analysts should ask, "Who is my client?" to help them conceptualize a tightly focused paper, but they must not tailor the analysis or the message to make it more palatable to that client.

When one of the authors served as NIO for Latin America, he often encountered situations when the State Department was at odds with the Defense Department or the White House. When delivering intelligence products that were requested by one agency or department, he always sent a copy of the paper to policy counterparts in other agencies to ensure that everyone in the policy community was working off the same baseline of intelligence information (see Figure 14.1).

Such procedures also serve as a practical check on analytic objectivity. For example, if analysts are uncomfortable sharing with the State Department how they answered a question for the Defense Department, then they need to consider whether basic analytic standards (see Chapter 3) have been compromised.

Most debates surrounding the potential for politicization center around our second critical thinking element: What are the key questions? The primary concern is whether

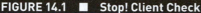

FIGURE 14.1   ■   Stop! Client Check

If you are reluctant to send a paper to a key policymaker or decision maker that you drafted in response to another policymaker or decision maker's question, then you need to stop and recraft the analysis.

clients have attempted to politicize the product by asking leading questions or have framed an issue in such a way to ensure that the response will best serve their political agenda. Analysts should take responsibility for ensuring that the right question is being answered. This can be accomplished either by explaining to the client why the question needs to be rephrased or by raising the level of analysis to provide broader perspective while still answering the specific question asked.

Prior to the US invasion of Iraq, the White House was accused of trying to politicize intelligence reporting when senior policymakers kept pressing the Intelligence Community to find out where Iraq's weapons of mass destruction (WMD) were located. Many Intelligence Community professionals argued that the more appropriate question would have been, "What is the status of Iraq's WMD programs?" The first version of the question makes an implicit assumption that such weapons exist; the second formulation is moot on the existence of weapons stockpiles.

The Silberman-Robb WMD Commission found no evidence of politicization, concluding that "no analytic judgments were changed in response to political pressure to reach a particular conclusion."[12] The example illustrates, however, the importance of putting any request for analysis in the proper framework. Policymakers and decision makers must function in a political environment and can easily fall into the trap of asking analysts for more ammunition to defend their policies. The analytic community— analysts and managers alike—has the duty to identify such requests for what they are and craft responses that address the questions in a more appropriate analytic context.

"The administration used intelligence not to inform decision-making, but to justify a decision already made. It went to war without requesting—and evidently without being influenced by—any strategic-level intelligence assessments on any aspect of Iraq. . . . If the entire body of official intelligence analysis on Iraq had a policy implication, it was to avoid war—or, if war was going to be launched, to prepare for a messy aftermath."

—Paul Pillar,
Former National Intelligence Officer for the Middle East[13]

Using Structured Techniques to Depoliticize the Analysis

Structured Analytic Techniques can help counter the pressure to politicize analysis whether the pressure comes from the client or the analyst (see Figure 14.2). The techniques accomplish this task by establishing a more rigorous context in which to address the question and by creating a transparent audit trail of how the answer was generated. If charged with generating a politicized response, analysts can show the accuser how they derived their judgments and ask to be shown where in that process the analysis lacked objectivity.

Structured Analytic Techniques can serve as a tool for dealing with politicization because they establish a systematic baseline from which to view the data in a more objective fashion, help reframe the analysis to avoid conflict over a particularly contentious point, or present multiple explanations ensuring that everyone's perspective is addressed in the overall analysis. As analysts become more familiar with these techniques, the challenge will be learning to apply them rigorously in the political heat of the moment.

The following techniques have proven particularly useful in mitigating the pressures of politicization:

- Analysis of Competing Hypotheses and other matrices array the data so each item of relevant information can be evaluated for how it contributes to the analysis. Assumptions inherent in how the information is rated or interpreted can also be identified and challenged.

- Multiple Hypothesis Generation provides the opportunity to view the issue from a wider range of perspectives. Use of the Multiple Hypotheses Generator® or Quadrant Hypothesis Generation helps ensure that all possible alternatives get attention and that the final set of hypotheses is both comprehensive and mutually exclusive.

FIGURE 14.2 ■ SATs for Countering Politicization

WHAT STRUCTURED ANALYTIC TECHNIQUES APPLY?

Techniques for dealing with politicization include the following:

- Analysis of Competing Hypotheses
- Multiple Hypothesis Generation®
- Foresight Analysis
- Indicators
- What If? Analysis
- Argument Mapping
- Mutual Understanding
- Joint Escalation
- Nosenko Approach

● A well-done Foresight analysis can include scenarios that approximate how a senior policymaker views the issue as well as several contrary or even counterintuitive perspectives. The inclusion of at least one scenario consistent with the policymakers' vantage point provides recipients with an anchor for the analysis and makes it easier to understand other perspectives in terms of how they relate to their baseline scenario.

● Indicators Generation, Validation, and Evaluation are powerful tools for countering political bias. If agreement can be obtained on what constitutes a good set of validated indicators for determining whether something will occur, then a person who is convinced that Scenario X will occur has little ground to argue if all the indicators for that scenario do not emerge and indicators for an alternative scenario do.

● A good set of indicators also protects analysts from charges their analysis is politically biased. Most policymakers find it compelling if analysts can say, "These are the indicators we developed six months ago that would warn such a development was going to happen. Now most have emerged, confirming our analysis." The analysts' case is even stronger if they had also developed a list of indicators to show that the event was not going to emerge and most or all of those indicators had not occurred.

● Often, a highly contentious debate (either among analysts or between analysts and decision makers) can be defused by use of What If? Analysis. The key to What If? Analysis is to reframe the argument by saying, "Let us assume the issue we now are arguing about has been resolved in this way a year from now. How did that happen? Who had to do what so that events transpired in that way?" The description of what had to happen can then be translated into a series of indicators of what should be monitored to see if the asserted outcome will actually occur. The technique allows analysts to circumvent a particularly contentious and sometimes emotional debate by moving beyond the immediate and often unresolvable issue to focus on more fundamental forces and factors.

● The value of Argument Mapping is that it ensures all views are represented. Any argument made for a position can be rebutted publicly on the map, and all arguments and evidence that anyone deems relevant can be included on the map. If assumptions are suspected to be politically biased, a box supporting that position can be added and others can counter with boxes describing contrarian or counterbalancing forces.

Policy Prescription and Opportunities Analysis

The relationship between the intelligence analyst and the policymaker differs from culture to culture. In Canada and the UK, for example, analysts often work closely with policymakers, providing direct support to the decision-making process. In the United States, the relationship is usually more distant.[14] Two factors largely contribute to the difference: the substantial disparity in the size of the intelligence bureaucracies and the intellectual histories of each country.

- The US intelligence and policymaking communities dwarf those found in Canada, the United Kingdom, and all other countries. Analysts are more likely to be separated from their clients both geographically and organizationally.

- The US Intelligence Community has been influenced heavily by the views of Sherman Kent, who observed more than sixty years ago that if analysts get too close to their policymaking and action-taking clients, they will be in danger of losing the independence of mind and the substantive depth and analytic expertise that enables them to make a distinctive professional contribution to national security.[15]

In 1996, The Commission on the Roles and Responsibilities of the United States Intelligence Community concluded that the question of how close analysts should get to policymakers was real but manageable.[16] It asserted that the need to present the "unvarnished truth" to policymakers is at the core of every analyst's tradecraft training and ethos and that this mitigates the potential for bias. Jack Davis, who testified before the commission, framed the issue in this way: "If an intelligence analyst is not in some danger of being politicized, he is probably not doing his job."[17] According to Davis, the mission of intelligence analysts is to "apply in-depth substantive expertise, all-source information, and tough-minded tradecraft to produce assessments that provide distinctive value-added to policy clients' effort to protect and advance US security interests."[18]

In his role as NIO for Latin America, one of the authors quickly learned the value of establishing close working relations with his principal clients in the policy community. Even more important was the realization that access to key policymakers was greatly enhanced if he could provide useful insights and actionable intelligence in addition to the traditional warnings and worst-case assessments intelligence analysts are best known to generate. Over the years, a pattern developed where the author learned that US national interests were best served when he managed to balance the number of warning messages he delivered with an equal number of helpful insights that policymakers could use to advance their policy objectives.

A strategy of providing policymakers and decision makers with assessments that evaluate both the opportunities and the risks of various policy options they might be considering will be valued by most policymakers.[19] The analyst's role is to help decision makers shape the future. This requires that analysts not only warn about what bad things the future might bring but also identify forces and factors the decision maker can influence to optimize national interests or policy objectives. Such opportunity-oriented assessments, or opportunities analysis, should focus on how to mitigate bad scenarios from unfolding and how to enhance the prospects for positive developments to occur.[20]

For opportunities analysis to be effective, it must be timely, provide new insights or a new frame for understanding a problem, and be specific enough to offer actionable options that policymakers or decision makers can implement. Analysis crafted to support a decision that arrives after it has been made obviously is useless. A more important distinction, however, is that opportunities analysis should be offered in time for a decision maker to fashion a new course of action that capitalizes on the analytic insights to exploit a perceived opportunity or to prevent an unwanted outcome. In addition, the decision maker must believe that the analysis comes from a trustworthy source and is intended to serve the overarching national security interest or corporate goals, not support a parochial policy agenda.

A major caveat for analysts is never to cross the line between offering useful ideas and expressing personal views of which ideas most deserve to be implemented. When asked to provide an assessment of the risks and benefits of various policy options, analysts must never be seen as promoting personal agendas or reflecting personal political preferences. The ability to provide analysis that is universally deemed objective in an increasingly politicized environment is highly valued. Almost everyone whom decision makers engage is an advocate. The information most of their sources provide is almost always intended to influence their decisions, not make them smarter.

In the world of most policymakers, the intelligence analyst is a rare commodity: someone who knows the facts, will actually point out knowledge gaps, and is motivated only by the desire to help them make the best-informed decision possible.

Engaging Policy Officials

Traditional Policy Support. If an analyst has developed a close and trusting relationship with a policymaker, several techniques can be employed to maintain objectivity and ensure integrity in the exchange. Savvy policymakers who know how to use intelligence analysis will look to analysts as an unparalleled source for actionable information as well as analytic insight.

- *The Rule of Three.* When asked to make a recommendation, say that there are three ways to approach the issue. Lay out the information, intelligence, and logic that supports each approach and let the policymaker decide which makes the most sense. If pressed to offer a recommendation, you can state the likelihood of success you believe the analytic community would assign to each option (often using percentages as discussed in Chapter 17).

- *Critique Existing Options.* If several policy options are under consideration, provide an analysis of the likelihood of success for each predefined option, but be sure to emphasize the quality of the sourcing as well as any key information gaps. If no one has yet to articulate existing policy options, ask the decision maker to articulate them and then critique the list he or she provides.

- *Bring a Friend.* Pre-brief a more junior policymaker or subordinate (the executive officer or someone who works the account) and ask them to attend the briefing with you. If the policymaker asks, "What should I do?" or "What do you recommend?" simply turn to the junior official, who probably has anticipated the question, and let her or him answer it. The officer most likely will complement your analysis with a set of policy options for seizing new opportunities or mitigating the adverse developments that you have mentioned.

Briefing Officials With Fixed Mindsets. The primary task of an analyst is to help policymakers and other decision makers make good decisions based on the best available information and the most compelling logic. This task becomes more challenging, however, when the recipient of the analysis bases his or her decisions on preestablished, firmly held, and often immutable precepts or world views. Such individuals are usually more interested in imposing their view on the world—or on the environment in which they operate—than trying to understand it better. They see data as useful ammunition they can cite to demonstrate the correctness of their approach or predispositions. Information that contradicts their view is usually quickly dismissed or simply ignored.

When asked to provide analytic support to individuals with such strongly held views, many of whom could be described as ideologues, a successful analyst will take time to develop different strategies for communicating the analytic message.

- *Broaden the context.* When an official asks for specific information or intelligence to justify his or her position, frame the response in a broader context, providing the recipient with the data directly relevant to the request as well as any associated information and analysis that is contradictory. Offer up the pros and the cons in a comprehensive framework to enable the decision maker to act based on a fully informed set of facts and analysis.

- *Focus on strategic drivers.* Take the initiative to generate an "arms-length" strategic view of the situation, identifying key drivers and establishing an overarching framework for understanding the dynamics at play. Once such a framework is established, tactical disagreements over how to interpret specific items of information become far easier to resolve.

- *Employ structured techniques.* Rely more heavily on Structured Analytic Techniques—such as Indicators, Argument Mapping, Deception Detection, Analysis of Competing Hypotheses, and Premortem Analysis—that can demonstrate in a compelling way how the official can avoid becoming the victim of a mental mindset or a cognitive trap.

Analysts should never refrain from providing hard-hitting, objective, and well-supported analysis, even when the message is likely to be poorly received. However, be mindful that challenging a decision maker's views directly is inappropriate and almost always counterproductive. Usually such conversations will make the client more obdurate and less likely to seek analytic support in the future.

Briefing "Novice" Decision Makers. In recent years as the level of political polarization has increased in the United States—and throughout much of the world—analysts have been challenged with learning how to support a different type of policymaker: highly partisan, senior decision makers who see the world in terms of "us versus them," rely heavily on nontraditional commercial and private sources of information, and do not understand the basic roles and missions of law enforcement and the intelligence community. Providing analytic support to this new breed of novice decision maker requires a reframing of the roles and responsibilities of the analyst.

- *Redefine Your Primary Client.* When dealing with novice decision makers, the concept of the White House—or the Presidency, Privy Council, or Chancellor's Office—as the primary client for intelligence analysis needs to be revisited. The intelligence community needs to expand the scope of analytic support beyond the highest offices of leadership in their nations to a much broader array of decision makers, legislators, and even the public.

- *Establish Analytic Baselines.* The primary mission becomes the need to establish a baseline description of what is happening in the world (and why) for the national security community writ large.

- *Reset Priorities.* The traditional core functions of warning and counterintelligence remain critical, but additional attention is needed in two areas:

  ○ Providing strategic perspective on global trends, such as climate change and cyber threats

  ○ Ferreting out and actively countering the impact of conspiracy theories and Digital Disinformation

- *Protect Sources.* In an era of novice decision makers, greater emphasis must be given to ensuring sources and methods are not compromised. Novice decision makers often are ill-informed or even oblivious to the importance of determining the quality of sourcing. They usually are not familiar with the technical language that has evolved to characterize the quality of a source and less aware of the need not to reveal sources and methods.

The best briefing strategy to adopt is to define the question or issue carefully, putting it in terms that the recipient can process and absorb. Unfortunately, in these circumstances, opportunities analysis is likely to become a casualty of the times. If trusted relationships cannot be established with senior decision makers, then any effort to generate new ideas is likely to be met with suspicion; the recipient will almost always assume that the analyst is trying to achieve his or her own personal agenda.

When dealing with both ideologues and novice decision makers, one of the worst mistakes an analyst can make is to self-censor. Self-censorship can take two forms. First, is tweaking the analysis to make it more acceptable to the client in the hope of retaining access and sustaining a dialogue. Second, and more pernicious, is to not address a certain topic because the views of the analytic community differ from those of the client. Often the justification given for not writing an article is that the policymaker or decision maker would not read the article or would quickly dismiss the analysis. Analysts, however, should never discount the possibility that a combination of hard facts and sharply drawn analysis that competes with a decision maker's views may over time allow the policymaker to "discover" on his or her own the merit of a contrary view.

In the end, it all comes down to maintaining an analytic culture of direct engagement with the client, coupled with a deeply ingrained culture of objectivity and integrity. Intelligence community managers need to constantly reinforce this culture in speeches and at office offsites. Senior leaders need to incentivize such behavior through personal example. They should also actively monitor analyst interactions with policymakers, praising those who walk these fine lines the best.

KEY TAKEAWAYS

- Politicization can take two forms: (1) top-down when the policymaker attempts to influence the analytic line and (2) bottom-up when the analytic community tailors its analysis to make it more palatable to senior policy officials.

- The most pernicious, and probably most widespread, form of bottom-up politicization is the tendency of analysts to self-censor.

- Analysts are a rare commodity because they are not advocates; they are motivated by the desire to help the policymaker or decision maker make the best decisions possible. Decision makers who understand this key distinction will benefit the most from what the community can produce.

- The increased use of video, Deepfakes, and other digitized images in analytic products will require new metrics for vetting sources and assessing digital objectivity.

- Structured Analytic Techniques are effective in dealing with politicization

  because they can provide a systematic baseline from which to view the data, reframe the analysis, or present alternative views that capture the perspective of all key stakeholders.

- Those who provide analytic assessments to traditional policymakers or decision makers should strive to balance the amount of bad news they deliver with an equal portion of opportunities analysis that decision makers can use to advance their objectives.

- Analysts need to reframe how to relate to highly partisan and novice decision makers who do not fully understand the intelligence mission and distrust the leadership of the IC by generating a sound baseline product for consumption by the broader national security community.

- The best defense against the pressures of politicization is to build an analytic culture based on objectivity and integrity and to provide alternative views.

CONSIDERING THE CASE STUDY

Review Case Study VI, "The Case of Iraq's Aluminum Tubes."

- Did the author present a balanced picture of Iraq's Weapons of Mass Destruction program?

- What cognitive biases, misapplied heuristics, and intuitive traps did the analysts fall prey to in assessing the status of Saddam Hussein's Weapons of Mass Destruction program?

- What Structured Analytic Techniques could the author have employed to better deflect any charge of politicization?

- The article was written for a traditional decision maker. How would you organize it differently if the client was an ideologue or a novice decision maker?

NOTES

1. Jack Davis, "Tensions in Analyst-Policymaker Relations: Opinions, Facts, and Evidence," Sherman Kent School for Intelligence Analysis, *Occasional Papers* 2, no. 2 (January 2003), 10, https://www.cia.gov /library/kent-center-occasional-papers /vol2no2.htm.

2. Richard K. Betts, *Enemies of Intelligence: Knowledge & Power in American National Security* (New York: Columbia University Press, 2007), 67.

3. Dennis J. Gleeson, "The High Cost of Politicizing Intelligence," *The Atlantic*, February 25, 2017, https:// www.theatlantic.com/politics/archive /2017/02/the-high-cost-of-politicizing -intelligence/517854/.

4. Paul R. Pillar, "Intelligence, Policy, and the War in Iraq," *Foreign Affairs* 85, no. 2 (March/April 2006): 22.

5. Sherman Kent, *Strategic Intelligence for American World Policy* (Princeton, NJ: Princeton University Press, 1949), 195–201.

6. These two principles are well represented in analytic standards promulgated for analysts in the United States. The ODNI's Office of Analytic Integrity and Standards lists "Objective" and "Independent of Political Consideration" as the first two of five IC Analytic Standards. See the Office of the Director of National Intelligence, "Intelligence Community Directive 203: Analytic Standards," January 2, 2015, http://www.dni.gov /files/documents/ICD/ICD%20203 %20Analytic%20Standards.pdf.

7. Central Intelligence Agency, "CIA Vision, Mission, Ethos, and Challenges Statement," November 1, 2018, https:// www.cia.gov/about-cia/cia-vision -mission-values.

8. Betts, *Enemies of Intelligence*, 75.

9. Carmen A. Medina, "What to Do When Traditional Models Fail: The Coming Revolution in Intelligence Analysis," *Studies in Intelligence* 46, no. 3 (April 14, 2007), https://www .cia.gov/library/center-for-the-study -of-intelligence/csi-publications/csi -studies/studies/vol46no3/article03 .html.

10. Robert M. Gates, "A Message to Analysts: Guarding Against Politicization," address to CIA personnel reprinted in *Studies in Intelligence* 36, no. 5 (March 16, 1992): 9, https://www.cia.gov/library/center -for-the-study-of-intelligence/kent-csi /volume-36-number-1/pdf/v36i1a01p .pdf.

11. Betts, *Enemies of Intelligence*, 77.

12. Commission on the Intelligence Capabilities of the United States Regarding Weapons of Mass Destruction, *Report to the President of the United States* (Washington, DC: Government Printing Office, March 31, 2005), 188, https://www.gpo.gov /fdsys/pkg/GPO-WMD/pdf/GPO -WMD.pdf.

13. Pillar, "Intelligence, Policy, and the War in Iraq," 22.

14. Jack Davis, "Improving CIA Analytic Performance: Analysts and the Policymaking Process," Sherman Kent School for Intelligence Analysis, *Occasional Papers* 1, no. 2 (September 2002): 2, https://www.cia.gov/library /kent-center-occasional-papers /vol1no2.html.

15. Sherman Kent also cautioned in *Strategic Intelligence* that too much distance between the policymaker and the analyst would make intelligence irrelevant, concluding that this was more dangerous than allowing the analyst to get too close to the policymaker.

16. Commission on the Roles and Responsibilities of the United States Intelligence Community, *Preparing for the 21st Century: An Appraisal of US Intelligence* (Washington, DC: Government Printing Office, March 1, 1996), https://www.govinfo.gov/app/details/GPO-INTELLIGENCE.

17. Davis, "Improving CIA Analytic Performance," 7.

18. Davis, "Tensions in Analyst-Policymaker Relations," 9.

19. Davis, "Tensions," 10–11.

20. Davis, "Tensions," 9.

15 HOW MIGHT I BE SPECTACULARLY WRONG?

SETTING THE STAGE

Intelligence failures are often attributed to inadequate information collection, analytic misjudgments, and policy errors, but spectacularly wrong judgments typically result from failures of analysis.[1] The cause can be insufficient data, a failure to overcome mental models and cognitive pitfalls, a lack of imagination, reliance on unsupported assumptions, faulty reasoning, or the failure to consider alternative hypotheses and outcomes. Using critical thinking skills and Structured Analytic Techniques is the best way to overcome most of these barriers to good analysis.

Even the most rigorous analysis, however, combined with the best and latest data, is subject to error because of the impossibility of accounting for all the factors influencing decisions by leaders and other key individuals and groups. The raw material underlying an analytic judgment consists of data and reasoning. When the data are ambiguous, fragmentary, transitory, or deceptive, the analysis can be wrong. This is often the case in the intelligence world when the data represent only a fraction of the information needed for a comprehensive analysis.

Similar problems exist when the opposite condition prevails, and the analyst is overwhelmed with a mass of data. In such circumstances, the challenge is to isolate the relevant information necessary to conduct the analysis. Arraying those data in an orderly and logical fashion adds to the challenge. Time constraints almost always pose an additional obstacle.

Information challenges are compounded by cognitive problems and the limitations of the human mind. Our perception of facts is often clouded because we begin observing events in early stages when the situation is not clear yet and the facts are sketchy. We persist in our early judgments because we are quick to accept confirming data and to ignore or reject data that are inconsistent with our lead hypothesis. In analyzing data, we tend to discern patterns early, jump to conclusions, ignore contradictory information, and take other mental shortcuts. If we do not array our data systematically, reason logically, avoid common fallacies, and test our assumptions by considering alternatives, we risk making flawed judgments.

Because the natural tendency of analysts is to build mental models, we often fail to anticipate unexpected events. Past experience can blind an analyst to a newly emerging situation. Failure to consider a complete set of alternative hypotheses or outcomes can desensitize us to critical new information pointing to an alternative explanation. If the analyst does not have a robust set of bins in which to organize the data, critical information can fall through the cracks and not be factored into the final analysis. Major discontinuities cannot be foreseen if they have not been imagined.

LOOKING MORE DEEPLY

Given these vulnerabilities, analysts should assume that they will be wrong at times. For example, if an analyst has decided that four actions are likely to happen and likely is defined as meaning the judgment will be correct in three of the four instances, then logic would argue that one of the four analytic judgments will be wrong.[2]

This suggests that analysts should adopt the practice of exploring whether and under what circumstances they might be wrong every time they draft a product or present a major analytic judgment (see Figure 15.1). Although many techniques can be used for challenging judgments, this chapter focuses on two reframing techniques, Premortem Analysis and Structured Self-Critique. This pair of techniques provides the most effective and most comprehensive approach for discovering how one might be spectacularly wrong.

The motivation for conducting a Premortem Analysis and a Structured Self-Critique is straightforward. Would you prefer to learn that you might be spectacularly wrong *before* your product is edited or *after* it is published when you are invited to explain to a congressional committee or commission conducting a postmortem where you went wrong? Few analysts would have difficulty answering that question, particularly if conducting a Premortem Analysis and a Structured Self-Critique requires only a few hours and preparing for a postmortem investigation can take days, weeks, or even months. Although most analysts and managers would agree that a Premortem Analysis and a Structured Self-Critique should be done for all products, many end up skipping this step because of pressures to publish. The best way to overcome this obstacle is to decide when to schedule the Premortem Analysis and Structured Self-Critique session when you begin to write the product or to require it as part of the production process.

If writing a short product, the best time to conduct a Premortem Analysis is right before you submit it for editing or review. With a longer or more complex assessment, the best time is after you have completed your research and sketched out what the

---

FIGURE 15.1 ■ SATs for Challenging Your Analysis

WHAT STRUCTURED ANALYTIC TECHNIQUES APPLY?

Techniques for challenging one's analytic judgments include the following:

- Premortem Analysis
- Structured Self-Critique
- Red Team Analysis
- What If? Analysis
- High Impact/Low Probability Analysis
- Delphi Method
- Argument Mapping

product will say, but before you begin the tedious process of drafting the product or building the PowerPoint slide deck.

When launching the Premortem Analysis, the most important first step is to invite all the drafters and key stakeholders involved in the production process to participate in a brainstorming session. For short products or products that follow an established format, a Premortem Analysis could consist of no more than a five-minute phone call or a meeting where everyone stands for five-to-ten minutes while a short checklist is reviewed.

For most products, a short electronic or in-person brainstorming session will suffice. The facilitator should set the stage for the session by saying,

> Let's assume that the product has been published or the briefing has been delivered and X months or years have passed. Unfortunately, time has shown that the key analytic judgments in the product were fundamentally wrong, and we have spectacularly failed in our assessment. How can we explain what went wrong in our analytic process?

The facilitator or group leader then asks the participants to write down their best two or three ideas on index cards. After five minutes of silence, they pass their cards to the facilitator, who records them on a whiteboard or easel and invites the group to discuss which potential explanations are most concerning and require follow-on action. The group then decides how the vulnerabilities can best be addressed—for example, by conducting a Key Assumptions Check, a Deception Detection analysis, or an Asset Validation assessment.[3] The session should conclude with a list of key potential vulnerabilities and an action plan for how to address the problems uncovered by the Premortem Analysis brainstorming session.

> "In the end, a premortem may be the best way to circumvent any need for a painful postmortem."
>
> —Gary Klein
> *Harvard Business Review*[4]

The second step is to conduct a Structured Self-Critique. The Premortem Analysis exercise focuses on leveraging right-brain activities to identify potential problems in the analysis; the Structured Self-Critique is more of a left-brained activity that requires the team to evaluate the product against a list of known mistakes analysts have made in the past. Figure 15.2 illustrates six of the most significant questions that should be addressed in conducting a Structured Self-Critique. A more comprehensive list of questions that the group should address includes the following:

- Have alternative explanations or hypotheses been considered?

- Was a broad range of diverse opinions solicited?

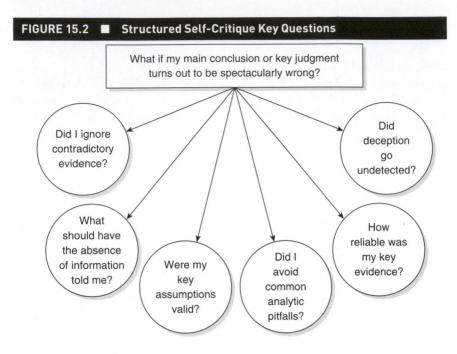

FIGURE 15.2 ■ Structured Self-Critique Key Questions

- Were key assumptions identified and critically examined? Were unsupported assumptions identified? Did the group consider how this could change the analysis?

- Was any evidence that might disprove the lead hypothesis or key analytic judgment ignored, misinterpreted, or rejected because it was not consistent with the main line of analysis?

- Are there any significant information gaps? Have we considered how the lack of these data could have influenced the key analytic judgments?

- Is there missing evidence that one would expect to see in the regular flow of information? Does its absence suggest that someone might be trying to deceive us?

- Are there any anomalous items of evidence that have been rejected as not important because they were initially believed to be insignificant to the line of analysis?

- Have we ignored whether alterations in the larger environment driven by technology, globalization, or economic, social, environmental, or political change could be contributing to what has happened or will be happening?

- Does the analysis assume that the leader of the adversary government, group, or company will act rationally and not be driven by personalistic criteria?

- Does the topic involve an unfamiliar culture or subculture, and do we know how this might affect that culture's decision-making process?

- Does the government, company, or competitor have a motive, opportunity, or means to engage in deception to influence the organization's policies or change its behavior?

Analytic units will often add questions to this list that are tailored to their specific work environment. Usually the first items on this list are examples of past errors that the unit does not want to repeat. This is called learning from your mistakes. Most analysts can easily recall when they made a major mistake, and they will remember not to do it again.

A bigger challenge is to remember past "near misses." These are incidents when the analyst or the organization either got it wrong, but no one noticed, or almost got it wrong, but the error was not critical to the analysis at the time (see Figure 15.3). Peter Madsen of Brigham Young University and Robin Dillon and Catherine Tinsley of Georgetown University describe them simply as "outcomes that could have been worse but for the intervention of good fortune."[5]

A good example came in a December 2019 article in *Science*, "How Saving the Ozone Layer in 1987 Slowed Global Warming."[6] The article explained how scientists had discovered that the Montreal Protocol, an international agreement to ban the use of chlorofluorocarbons (CFCs), had helped reverse the depletion of the ozone layer, with the attendant result of making the projected average temperature on Earth 1°C cooler by 2050. Congressional approval for the protocol was reached despite concerted opposition from the chlorofluorocarbon industry. In 1988, the head of DuPont testified before the US Congress that "scientific evidence does not point to the need for dramatic CFC emission reductions. There is no available measure of the contribution of CFCs to any observed ozone change."[7]

Implementation of the protocol despite the initial opposition thus contributed to significantly mitigating the impact of global climate change. Scientists have recently discovered that in regions such as the Arctic, the *avoided warming* will be as much as 3 to 4°C. The findings were made inadvertently when a team of scientists set out to quantify how the Montreal Protocol had affected atmospheric circulation around Antarctica. The new finding that the Montreal Protocol will prove to have much greater impact on global warming than the Kyoto Agreement—which was aimed directly at greenhouse gases—will be seen by most of the world as much-needed good fortune. Failure to implement the protocol could have caused substantial, unanticipated damage to the global environment.

Figure 15.3 relates another example of how lessons can be learned from near misses. A key takeaway from both examples is that such near misses should not be treated as successes but as *failures* that were barely avoided. Careful examination of the causes of a near miss can provide exceptional insights into future vulnerabilities that need to be corrected. That does not regularly happen, according to Dillon and Tinsley's earlier research, because "people have a natural tendency to see near misses as successes rather than as indicators that something is wrong."[8]

FIGURE 15.3 ■ The North Anna Earthquake: A Nuclear Near Miss?

When a major 5.8 magnitude earthquake centered in Mineral, Virginia, hit the US East Coast on August 23, 2011, Dominion Power's North Anna Nuclear Power Plant was only eleven miles from the epicenter.[a] The earthquake shut down the two nuclear power reactors, and three of four diesel generators started up to supply electricity to the safety systems. Fortunately, a fifth backup generator was brought on line to replace the broken generator that suffered a coolant leak.[b] The initial reaction to this was, "Good news! A nuclear disaster similar to what occurred at Japan's Fukushima Daiichi plant the previous March has just been averted!"

But no one anticipated that one of the diesel generators would not work. What would have happened if all four, or even two or three, of the generators failed when the earthquake hit? The plant was designed to survive an earthquake of a magnitude of 5.9 to 6.1, which suggests the event qualified as a very fortunate near miss.[c] The near miss gave Dominion Power the opportunity to review its safety standards and make appropriate adjustments. As analysts, we also need to learn from our near misses and use techniques such as the Structured Self-Critique to ensure that we do so.

a. "Dominion's North Anna Power Station Restores Offsite Power," *Dominion News*, August 23, 2011, http://dom.mediaroom.com/news?item=71825.

b. "UPDATE 3-Quake Raises Safety Concerns as US Nuclear Plant Shut," Reuters, August 23, 2011, http://www.reuters.com/article/quake-usa-nuclear-dominion-idUSN1E77M1N320110824.

c. Waldo Jaqueth, "Did We Dodge a Bullet With Lake Anna?" cvillenews.com, August 23, 2011, http://cvillenews.com/2011/08/23/quake-nuclear-plant/.

Their research using data from 1990 to 2007 showed that airlines successfully learn from near misses only when two conditions are met:

- The near miss falls into a recognized category
- That category is recognized to have previously caused accidents

But if near misses do not fit into a recognized category or one that is currently seen as dangerous, airlines may be squandering opportunities to collect useful, safety-relevant information that could be gained from those other types of near misses. This argues strongly for including a list of near misses in any Structured Self-Critique checklist.

A Structured Self-Critique can be conducted in three ways:

1. Make a list of past mistakes and near misses and review it to determine if the same mistake is being made again.

2. Create a list of potential mistakes that should be avoided, drawing from preestablished lists of generic mistakes, and ask if any of these mistakes are being made again.

3. Create both lists and meld them into a single master list.

A homeland security manager who had recently received instruction on the pre-mortem process decided to implement the first option in an effort to raise awareness in his unit, which had substantial turnover, to keep it from making the same mistakes. To drive his point home, he posted a Premortem Analysis list on the door to his office so that everyone would see it every time they entered his office.[9]

After reviewing these Structured Self-Critique checklists, analysts should also reassess their level of confidence in their key judgments. The final step is to develop an action plan for investigating any shortfalls that were discovered, make changes as necessary to the analysis, and reevaluate the mainline judgments.

The value of the premortem approach is best described by Gary Klein, who first developed the technique:

> The premortem doesn't just help teams to identify potential problems early on. It also reduces the kind of damn-the-torpedoes attitude often assumed by people who are overinvested in a project. Moreover, in describing weaknesses that no one else has mentioned, team members feel valued for their intelligence and experience, and others learn from them. The exercise also sensitizes the team to pick up early signs of trouble once the project gets under way.[10]

KEY TAKEAWAYS

- Even the most rigorous analysis is subject to error; that is the human condition.

- Fixing the analysis in a product before it is published is always smarter than having to explain later why errors occurred.

- Conducting a Premortem Analysis and a Structured Self-Critique may take a few precious hours of an analyst's time but could save weeks or months of labor if a postmortem is ordered.

- A Premortem Analysis and Structured Self-Critique should be scheduled at the beginning of every project and made a routine part of the production process.

- Analysts should tailor the list of Structured Self-Critique questions to their work environment, adding examples of their own past mistakes and near misses.

- For shorter products, the best time to conduct a Premortem Analysis and a Structured Self-Critique is right before submitting the product for editing.

- For longer products, the best time is after the analyst concludes the research and sketches out the product, but before beginning the tedious process of drafting.

- Near misses are failures that were narrowly avoided. They should be identified and included in the Structured Self-Critique list to identify vulnerabilities that can be corrected.

CONSIDERING THE CASE STUDY

Review Case Study VI, "The Case of Iraq's Aluminum Tubes."

- Imagine yourself conducting a Premortem Analysis of the case study. Assume that your preliminary analysis is that the aluminum tubes were acquired to support Iraq's Weapons of Mass Destruction program.

  o Consider each of the Five-Ws-and-an-H questions as it relates to the case study and write down your response to each in a sentence or two: Who, What, How, When, Where, and Why. Conduct a brainstorming session asking how each of the answers you generated for each question might be spectacularly wrong.

o   Decide what additional work needs to be done to explore potential alternative explanations and whether any key judgments need to be adjusted.

● Conduct a Structured Self-Critique of the analysis in the case study, focusing in particular on the following questions:

o   Have sufficient alternative explanations or hypotheses been considered?

o   Was a broad range of diverse opinions solicited and factored into the analysis?

o   Were key assumptions identified and critically examined? Were unsupported assumptions identified? Did the group consider how this could change the analysis?

o   Are there significant information gaps? Have we considered how the lack of data could have influenced the key analytic judgments?

o   What might have been learned if we had spent more time trying to put ourselves in Saddam's shoes and understand what motivated his actions?

NOTES

1. The information used in this chapter was taken from Pherson Associates training materials (www.pherson .org).

2. Donald P. Steury, ed., *Sherman Kent and the Board of National Estimates: Collected Essays* (Washington, DC: CIA Center for the Study of Intelligence, 1994), 133. Sherman Kent is quoted as defining *probable* as 75 percent plus or minus 12 percent.

3. Asset validation is a formal process used by intelligence collectors to assess the credibility of a source based on his or her past record of reporting.

4. Gary Klein, "Performing a Project Premortem," *Harvard Business Review*, September 2007, http://hbr.org/2007 /09/performing-a-project-premortem /ar/1.

5. Peter Madsen, Robin L. Dillon, and Catherine H. Tinsley, "Airline Safety Improvement Through Experience With Near-Misses: A Cautionary Tale," *Risk Analysis* 36, no. 5 (May 2016): 1054–1066.

6. Alvin Stone, "How Saving the Ozone Layer in 1987 Slowed Global Warming," *Science*, December 9, 2019, https://www.science.unsw.edu.au/news /saving-ozone-layer-1987-slowed-global -warming.

7. "Du Pont: A Case Study in the 3D Corporate Strategy" (Greenpeace position paper, September 1997), https://studylib.net/doc/8335223

/du-pont--a-case-study-in-the-3d
-corporate-strategy.

8. Catherine H. Tinsley, Robin L. Dillon, Peter M. Madsen, "How to Avoid Catastrophe," *Harvard Business Review*, April 2011, https://hbr.org/2011/04 /how-to-avoid-catastrophe.

9. Story related to Randolph H. Pherson by a Customs and Border Patrol unit manager who was taking a Globalytica workshop on Managing Analysis.

10. Klein, "Performing a Project Premortem."

HOW DO I CONVEY MY MESSAGE EFFECTIVELY?

The impact of your analysis is largely determined by the organization, clarity, and credibility of your argument. The more tailored your product is to your client, the more impact it will have.

Good writing is a function of good thinking. If you find yourself struggling to craft a sentence or a paragraph, you probably do not have enough information to work with or have not thought through your argument clearly enough.

- Good journalists and intelligence writers always put the bottom line up front, presenting the most essential information first and the least important last.

- The title and lead paragraph should convey your key message, addressing both the "What" and the "So What."

- Each paragraph should begin with an analytic topic sentence and have one main point. Each section, paragraph, and sentence should move your story and argument forward in a clear, direct, and convincing way.

The Iraq weapons of mass destruction fiasco provided a painful reminder of the need to convey probabilistic judgments and levels of confidence in a rigorous way. Always follow a probabilistic statement with a "because" phrase citing the key factors supporting that judgment. Source Summary Statements can also be powerful tools for conveying the credibility of sources and levels of confidence to the client in the most efficient way possible.

Graphics can relay your message in a much more compelling way than any narrative. They can save the reader time by capturing large amounts of data in a single chart and, more important, can add meaning by illustrating key relationships, trends, or boundaries. Good critical thinkers can summarize an entire paper in a single one-page infographic; the process also helps reveal potential gaps in their knowledge and expose new relationships or lines of argument.

A sloppy draft suggests a sloppy thinker. The only way to avoid this is to run a spell check and a grammar check *and* proofread your paper in hard copy before it leaves your hands. If you establish a reputation for handing in polished drafts, reviewers will look forward to getting your papers and will return them faster.

16 IS MY ARGUMENT PERSUASIVE?

SETTING THE STAGE

Persuasion is simply an effort to evoke a change in someone's attitude or behavior. While persuasion in contemporary advertising or political campaigning has taken on the meaning of unethical or false manipulation, the techniques of persuasion are neither inherently good nor evil. They can be used to advance noble or pernicious goals. Persuasion is both a science and an art, the practice of which can be improved with awareness, knowledge, and practice.

In intelligence analysis, persuasion is convincing your readers or audience to believe what you are saying and to trust your skill in accurately portraying events, context, and potential. You are not appealing to their emotions, even though they may react emotionally to your work depending on their level of stress and whether they agree with you in the first place. Your ability to convince your client is based on your credibility and trustworthiness as a knowledgeable and fair thinker and on the logic and comprehensiveness of your argument. For those who took rhetoric in school, this translates as relying on *ethos* and *logos* rather than *pathos*.

> "The truth isn't the truth until people believe you, and they can't believe you if they don't know what you're saying, and they can't know what you're saying if they don't listen to you, and they won't listen to you if you're not interesting, and you won't be interesting unless you say things imaginatively, originally, freshly."
>
> —William Bernbach,
> American Advertising Executive[1]

LOOKING MORE DEEPLY

You want to produce analysis that gains your clients' confidence and convinces them that your argument is a reliable base on which they can act. In the best of all possible worlds, they will be able to grab what they need from your assessment and apply it quickly. You are part—and are seeking to become an essential part—of what enables them to be effective in their jobs.

Your Credibility and Their Needs

Much of your ability to affect your clients is based on their perception of your credibility as the producer of valuable analysis. This principally depends on how they perceive you, including your reputation and authority, your body of work, and your current message.

- Are you and your organization known and respected by your audience?
- Is your credibility buttressed by recent accomplishments and contributions?
- Does your client appreciate your views and perspective?
- Is the message you are presenting clear and compelling?
- Is it delivered well and in a way that is easy to understand?

To maximize the impact of your analysis, you need to understand how your clients process information and are influenced by it (see Figure 16.1). The genesis of academic research on persuasion stems from the study of propaganda during World War II, but it provides a solid foundation for understanding how our consumers receive and perceive our work. Based on the work of Yale professor William McGuire and others, we know that information recipients who have been exposed to messages progress through a series of steps, as follows, before they are influenced to act.[2]

- Pay attention to the message.
- Comprehend the message.
- Accept the message.
- Retain the message.

"Making the simple complicated is commonplace; making the complicated simple, awesomely simple, that's creativity."

—Charles Mingus
American Jazz Bassist and Composer[3]

FIGURE 16.1 ■ Criteria Your Client Might Use to Evaluate Your Arguments

When your client reads your paper, he or she should be asking,

- Is the central claim (the "What" and the "So What") clear and relevant to my interests?
- Does the structure of subclaims expand and enrich the central claim?
- Is supporting evidence reasonable, relevant, and concrete?
- Does it take into account conflicting evidence or interpretations of the same evidence?
- Is it easy to translate it into my frame of reference and responsibility?

We can influence the first two steps through production and dissemination of effective analytic products, but the second two are largely dependent on the interests and abilities of your clients (see Chapter 1).

- Their familiarity with your topic will determine whether you need to include basic information; the complexity of the topic will determine whether your claims are simpler or more technical.

- Their opinion of your work will determine whether you provide more or less support for your points and how you take account of their views.

- Their interests and choice in whether they have to read or want to read your analysis will determine your "hooks" or attention grabbers.

- What they have to do with the information will determine whether you should lay out opportunities, implications, or prospects for action.

Techniques Relevant to Analysis

Five techniques often cited in the advertising literature can be used effectively by analysts to make their arguments more persuasive.

1. *Simplicity or elegance.* Simplicity makes your argument more comprehensible. The easiest way to "**K**eep **I**t **S**imple, **S**tupid" (KISS) is to limit the number of substantive arguments. Your client will appreciate it if you show your sophistication through the simplicity of your argument.

2. *Similarity.* Your clients will be more likely to pay attention to your analysis if they believe you understand their situation and their needs. You most likely will not be able to connect personally with most of your clients, but you should strive to be known for work that resonates with them. For instance, the authors now spend far less time meeting with senior government officials one-on-one, but many thank us when they meet us because they appreciate what we teach based on our knowledge of their general expectations.

3. *Reciprocity.* We are more likely to be influenced by someone who has given us something, either tangible or intangible, and we feel obliged to repay what another person has provided. The speed with which we respond to or the empathy with which we anticipate our client's needs reflects beneficially on our products and our value. Listening can be a form of reciprocity; an audience who is listened to tends to be more receptive.

4. *Contrast.* What we see and believe in a situation depends to a great extent on what we have encountered immediately prior to that situation. Furthermore, we tend to exaggerate the differences between two adjacent events. Relating our analysis to hot issues on our client's platter makes our analysis stand out from other information sources and provides analysts with the opportunity to point out areas in which the decision maker can act differently and better.

5. *Scarcity.* Opportunities appear more valuable when their availability is limited. Information that is scarce, new, or exclusive should be stated early in the analysis to establish a strong reason for people to listen. Clients tend to listen more carefully if they know they can use your analysis to head off something bad as opposed to just benefiting from something good. For example, when one of the authors asked a senior decision maker why he assiduously read the current intelligence produced by the US Central Intelligence Agency (CIA) every day, the decision maker's response was not that he learned new information or gained new insight but that he needed to know what others in the government were being told in order to defend current policy.

Avoiding Common Pitfalls

Analysts are plagued by multiple challenges that make it hard to come up with cogent, compelling, and comprehensive arguments every day. The questions we are trying to answer and the issues we are trying to address are by definition weighty and complex. If not, decision makers would not need our advice. Our dynamic world changes and overlaps in ways that make it difficult to be expert or familiar with all the data, players, technology, and possibilities, even if we maintain an explicit data framework. Crises and disruptive changes force managers to reassign analysts from areas in which they have years of expertise to others in which they have nothing other than the data flowing into their inbox.

> "Everything should be made as simple as possible, but not simpler."
>
> —Albert Einstein

Here are a few questions you can ask yourself to avoid some of the most common traps.

- *Familiarity.* Have you limited yourself to information and sources with which you or your clients are already familiar? They may not be the most effective or authoritative on a different issue.

- *Out-of-date information or concepts.* Did your quick searches for framing structures and data lead you to sources and citations that are not the latest? They may have been overtaken by more recent data, concepts, or discoveries.

- *Satisficing.* Have you collected just enough data to be able to deliver your product? Accounting for alternative views, placing the issue in a larger context, or contrasting information may change or lend richness to your piece.

- *Oversimplification.* Have you restricted yourself to only the most elemental arguments and basic data? Simplicity can be your best friend if you have a handle on your issue and data; it can be your worst enemy if you are a neophyte masquerading as an expert.

- *Mismatched data or interpretations.* Have you taken data or interpretations from a known issue and applied them to a dynamically evolving situation? Many compared the US military engagement in Afghanistan to the previous Soviet occupation of that country, but it was a different event in a different time. You need to look for the unusual or new factors that are influencing change.

- *Not consulting with colleagues who have broader perspectives.* Have you run your analysis by more experienced colleagues who may have worked or be working on your issue or a similar issue? Baseline data and tacit knowledge about how we have failed or succeeded in previous analytic efforts is not usually explicitly shared except through networking, mentoring, and collaboration (see Chapter 6). This is one of your greatest protections against being wrong.

- *Vagueness.* Have you given your piece multiple reads—or practiced your briefing—to identify vague or ambiguous language or gaps in logic? If we are not clear in our argument or information, we cannot be clear with our readers. Review your analysis several times to replace vague claims or words with concrete ones that provide a clear image of what you are saying (see Chapters 12 and 19).

In the end, your client is best served if you build a coherent structure for your analysis; do not expect your reader to join you conceptually on the second floor if you have not established the foundation and initial building blocks for your analysis. We have been in meetings in which common understanding of extraordinarily difficult issues was built through a process of identifying the initial framework then addressing the evidence piece by piece. This resulted in a more sophisticated and jointly shared body of information that is better able to address a wider variety of challenging and forward-looking problems.

Beware that models are just that: representations of our best understanding of our issue at one point in time (see Chapter 7). They approximate the reality of the issue but are not the reality. They can be valuable in providing a tether in time to support your efforts to look to the future, whether at what might happen in the next day or the next several decades. Your success in convincing your client to believe your analysis will always come back to your production of clear analysis on relevant topics that can be quickly understood and used.

Your Message in a Digital Medium

In today's digital world where clients may be receiving products on tablets, computers, or even phones, analysts must pay as much attention to the persuasive aspects of the medium as well as to their logical argument.[4] They must be active members of a collaborative team that includes the digital environment and graphic designers, data scientists, and environment curators to consider user engagement and experience.

User Engagement. How do we connect with three types of readers?

- *Quick readers* or *browsers* look at the headlines or titles, read the summary or first paragraph, and look at the visuals.

- *Substantive readers* look at the headlines or titles, read the summary, look at the visuals, then read the subheads.

- *Encyclopedic readers* potentially read everything but want to be able to come back to the subject to learn more or to answer questions.

Web-based readers look at products in a Z pattern, which accommodates the *browsers* and *substantive readers*. Layering information is key to accommodating the *encyclopedic readers*.

User Experience. How do we sustain the story over time? What are the elements that are enduring? Does the analytic content contain the elements of a good story (see Chapter 12)? Are we taking full advantage of digital communications, using the CREATE model to make products more user friendly and memorable (see Chapter 19)? In addition to the questions we considered to understand our client (see Chapter 1), analysts should also ask the following about the clients they serve digitally:

- *Can they access the material?* Not all clients have the same technology or the time to search for what might be most interesting for them to read. Can they easily adjust font size and other reading preferences?

- *Do they have choices in how to get to layered information?* Scrolling, buttons, pull-down menus, and hyperlinks provide options in helping clients access the information that is most valuable to them.

- *Does it work and is it intuitive?* Is the technology reliable and is a continuing story laid out so the client knows where to go every time?

- *Can the client find it again?* Are the key words or tags common rather than arcane or clever?

- *Are the details inspired or distracting?* Does each element add to the story or just add bells and whistles?

- *Do we have metrics to help us understand the client's engagement and how we can improve the experience?* Digital formats provide an unprecedented opportunity for soliciting direct feedback in terms of what materials are accessed most often. This can be a valuable supplement to traditional metrics of tracking follow-up questions or actions taken based on what they have read.

"Foot Stomping" the Basics. The fundamentals of intelligence analysis peppered throughout this book apply just as well in digital production with even greater premium on brevity and clarity that enables clients to "grab it and go."

- *Substance.* Titles and leads are still important. Summaries are even more important because many users will not scroll beyond the first screen.

- *Supporting materials.* Digital environments enable use of the full range of attention-getting materials for multisensory experiences to help you make your case. When you pick the visual, you pick the story. How can you use a variety of images to illustrate your argument? Can you make them interactive?

  o   Who? Pick a photo or video.

  o   What? Use a map or flyover video.

  o   When? Draw a timeline.

  o   Why? Pick a diagram or picture.

  o   How? Outline the process.

- *Perceptions and cognitive bias.* The variety of illustrations and user engagement in digital environments heightens the care and consideration we must give to the supplementary materials we select. First, take care to make sure you are not a potential victim of Digital Disinformation. Testing a visual is a good idea to ensure accuracy and because not all people see the same thing in a picture or illustration. We can easily reinforce stereotypes or beliefs about people, issues, or developments unintentionally if we are not sensitive to the unspoken messages our clients might derive from visualizations. Nonverbal communication can trigger reactions that are more emotional than intellectual, reflecting the unconscious work view and cognitive biases that individuals develop to make sense of their environment and prepare them to take action. Knowing our own and our clients' cognitive "bins" for categorizing people, places, or things is essential when selecting supplementary illustrations.

KEY TAKEAWAYS

- The impact of the analysis is determined in large part by the credibility of the analyst as the author and that of the organization that published the article.

- To maximize their impact, analysts must understand how their clients process analysis and are influenced by it.

- The more tailored the product is to the client, the more impact it will have.

- Concepts used in the advertising world, such as simplicity, similarity, reciprocity, contrast, and scarcity, can be used effectively by analysts to make their arguments more persuasive.

- Analysts must take particular care not to fall into the traps of satisficing, using out-of-date or mismatched information, oversimplification, and vagueness.

- Analysts should not expect a client to join them on the second floor of their argument if they have not built a firm conceptual foundation on the first floor.

- Enabling clients' analytic understanding of digital analytic production requires attention to how different users are engaged and whether they are easily able to get to the information they need.

- Digital, rather than hard-copy, production places even greater emphasis on analytic basics for brevity and clarity, provides greater opportunity for multisensory supplemental illustrations, and requires careful attention to ensure that materials do not encourage or reinforce biases.

CONSIDERING THE CASE STUDY

Review Case Study I, "Uncharted Territory: Conflict, Competition, or Collaboration in the Arctic?" Assume you have been asked to write an intelligence assessment of the prospects for conflict in the Arctic region in the next decade.

● What might be the primary thesis or argument of the paper?

● How could you establish credibility in making this argument?

● Which of the five techniques often used in advertising might you rely on the most to make the argument?

● To which of the seven common traps discussed in the chapter might you be most susceptible?

● How could you most effectively make your argument in a digital environment?

NOTES

1. William Bernbach, quoted in *Hey, Whipple, Squeeze This,* ed. Luke Sullivan (Hoboken, NJ: John Wiley, 2008), 6.

2. William J. McGuire, "Personality and Attitude Change: An Information-Processing Theory," in *Psychological Foundations of Attitudes,* ed. A. G. Greenwald, T. C. Brock, and T. M. Ostrom (New York: Academic Press, 1968), 179–180.

3. Charles Mingus, "Creativity," *Mainliner* 21, no. 5 (1977): 25, quoted by W. H. Starbuck and P. C. Nystrom, "Designing and Understanding Organizations," in *Handbook of Organizational Design,* vol. 1 (New York: Oxford University Press, 1981), 9.

4. Most of the information in this section is derived from the Introduction and Chapter 2 of Rubén Arcos and Randolph H. Pherson, eds., *Intelligence Communication in the Digital Era: Transforming Security, Defence and Business* (London: Palgrave Macmillan, 2015).

17

HOW SHOULD I PORTRAY PROBABILITY, LEVELS OF CONFIDENCE, AND QUANTITATIVE DATA?

SETTING THE STAGE

Analysts owe each client their best recitation of what they know and what they think. After reviewing all the available data, reexamining the line of reasoning, and considering alternatives, analysts also need to give their readers some idea of the likelihood that their analytic judgments will turn out to be correct. This is most often done with terms such as *likely*, *most likely*, and *almost certainly*. Analysts sometimes will give a numerical percentage, such as *a 60 percent chance*, reflecting the strength of their data and the soundness of their reasoning.

In the wake of the 9/11 terrorist attacks, analysts have begun to document the level of *confidence* they have in their sources and in the *accuracy* of their judgments. This is a different process, and it often gets mixed up with the concept of probability.[1] Analysts can confuse the difference between providing an assessment of a 60 percent chance of an event occurring and recording their levels of confidence in that judgment, which is based on the credibility of the available data and persuasiveness of the line of reasoning. For example, an analyst could be 70 percent confident in assessing that an event has a 60 percent chance of occurring based on incomplete data, or 95 percent confident in that same judgment that an event has a 60 percent chance of occurring based on a more robust set of evidence.

When presenting quantitative data and statistical analyses, analysts need to be particularly careful to avoid displaying the data in biased ways and to fully document how the figures were derived. Analysts need to apply their critical thinking skills when collecting data and assessing how accurately others present their data.

LOOKING MORE DEEPLY

One of an analyst's primary tasks is to assess human behavior. Such assessments reflect one's views of the strategic situation as well as the intellectual and emotional makeup of leaders and their supporters and adversaries. Analytic judgments take into account key players' motivations, ambitions, psychological strengths and weaknesses, and views on strategic issues—none of which can be measured precisely. Analysts must also consider organizational constraints and other influences on a leader's decision making to formulate their subjective judgments of the likely behavior of leaders or the direction of the national economy.

Because of all the uncertainties that must be factored into a product, analysts need to give their clients an overall assessment of the probability that they are correct. In providing these estimates, analysts can present either a verbal or numerical estimate. Verbal statements—such as *almost certainly, highly likely, probable, better than even, 50/50 chance*—give the readers some idea of the analysts' sense of the potential predictive accuracy of their judgments. Once again, analysts must avoid conflating the assessment of *it is highly probable that this will happen* with the concept of *it is highly probable that I am right that it is highly probable this will happen*.

Past experience—buttressed by research studies—cautions, however, that the meaning clients assign to such words of probability can vary substantially from what was intended. How clients interpret such words will be influenced by their own—and often differing—experiences with the use of such words as well as their personal preferences. In a study on measuring perceptions of uncertainty often cited in the US Intelligence Community and summarized in Figure 17.1, NATO officers assigned a probability percentage to the word *probable* ranging from 25 to 90 percent. The same group of officers assessed the phrase *highly likely* as carrying a probability ranging from 50 to 95 percent. On the other end of the spectrum, the phrase *little chance* received probabilities ranging from 2 to 35 percent.

We have replicated this experiment hundreds of times in the classroom with the same results.[2] Invariably, students will allocate percentages ranging from 30 to 85 percent to the phrases *probably* and *most likely*. The wide range of percentages given would indicate that these words mean very different things to different people—raising the question of what information of value is actually being communicated.

Efforts to standardize the range of uncertainty associated with such words have met with limited success. Over a half-century ago, Sherman Kent proposed a schema for standardizing ranges of uncertainty that has yet to catch on as a universal standard despite its underlying logic (Kent's proposals are represented by the shaded boxes in Figure 17.1). Several US Intelligence Community agencies have tried to deal with this phenomenon by publishing tables of probability ranges similar to that generated by Kent, but these often are disregarded by the reader.

One of the difficulties can be demonstrated in how one interprets the word *probable*. In the classroom exercises cited previously, students were asked if the word *probable* can be used to represent a probability of less than 50 percent. In all instances, more than half of the class confidently answers "no." In almost every class, however, a small group of students—10 or 20 percent—answer just as vigorously "yes." They explain that not all situations involve a choice between only two options. If, for example, five independent options are being considered and the likelihood of each option is 5, 20, 15, 35, and 25 percent, respectively, then the option with 35 percent likelihood should be considered the single most probable outcome. In this case, however, the outcome of "not the 35 percent outcome" is more probable than the 35 percent outcome or any of the other specific outcomes under consideration. We find that students often have difficulty differentiating between single most probable outcomes and most probable outcomes.

How one defines probabilistic terms can also vary depending on the profession. For example, the National Weather Service has assigned a probability to the word *likely* of 80 to 90 percent while respondents in one of their studies determined that recipients

FIGURE 17.1   ■   Measuring Perceptions of Uncertainty: NATO Officers and Sherman Kent

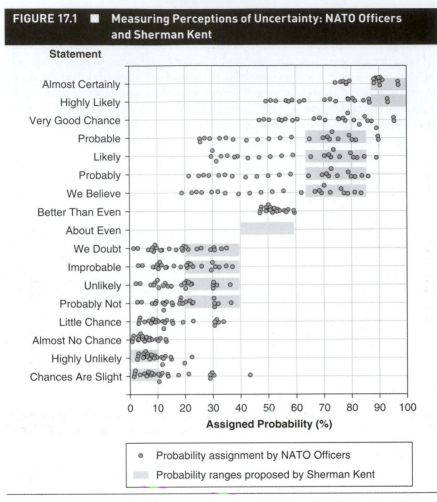

Sources: Sherman Kent, "Words of Estimated Probability," in *Sherman Kent and the Board of National Estimates: Collected Essays,* ed. Donald P. Steury (Washington, DC: Central Intelligence Agency, Center for the Study of Intelligence, 1994); Scott Barclay et al., *Handbook for Decision Analysis* (McLean, VA: Decisions and Designs, 1977).

of their reports only equated it to an average of 62.5 percent. In another study, practicing physicians assigned a probability of 70 to 73 percent to the word likely.[3]

A further complication is that even if the producers of the analytic product reach consensus on what probabilistic language to employ, recipients of the document or briefing may either subconsciously or consciously interpret the phrase in a way more consistent with or supportive of their desired preference or outcome. For example, the client will often translate a term such as *likely* as meaning 70 or 80 percent if that is a desired outcome, but as only 50 or 60 percent if the outcome is not desired.

Following the 9/11 attacks on the United States and the incorrect Iraq weapons of mass destruction (WMD) National Intelligence Estimate (NIE), the National Intelligence Council (NIC) started publishing a probability chart showing the relative probabilities of key terms as depicted in Figure 17.2.[4] The NIC chart arrayed key terms from least to most likely without assigning specific percentages.

Charles Weiss in a 2012 study on communicating uncertainty noted that intelligence analysts are not alone in wrestling with this problem:

- Scientific advisers have a tendency to paper over their differences with ambiguous language, to use general qualifiers when their scientific assertions are not thought to be adequately proven, and to fear that any admission of uncertainty would undercut the basis of a policy recommendation.

- Lawyers must deal with levels of uncertainty when describing the strength of evidence presented in a court. Does the evidence prove guilt "beyond a reasonable doubt," or does it only support a "reasonable belief"?[5]

In Figure 17.3, Charles Weiss compares the scales of uncertainty used in the Kent scale, by the director of national intelligence (DNI), in the climate change scale

---

FIGURE 17.2 ■ US National Intelligence Council Probability Scale

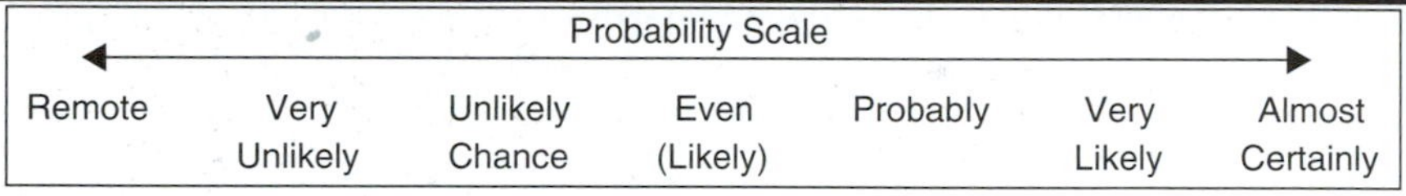

Probability Scale

←——————————————————————————————————→

Remote	Very Unlikely	Unlikely Chance	Even (Likely)	Probably	Very Likely	Almost Certainly

Source: Reproduced with permission of the US government.

FIGURE 17.3 ■ Scales of Uncertainty Used in Intelligence, Science, and Law

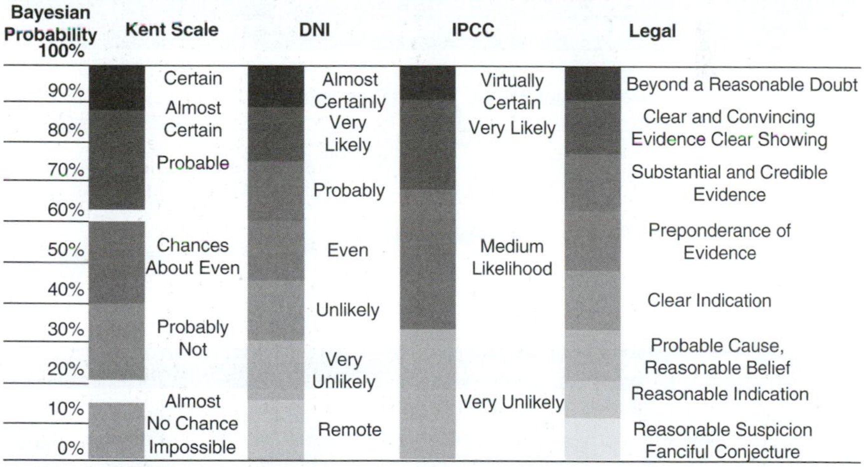

Bayesian Probability 100%	Kent Scale	DNI	IPCC	Legal
90%	Certain	Almost Certainly	Virtually Certain	Beyond a Reasonable Doubt
80%	Almost Certain	Very Likely	Very Likely	Clear and Convincing Evidence Clear Showing
70%	Probable			Substantial and Credible Evidence
60%		Probably		
50%	Chances About Even	Even	Medium Likelihood	Preponderance of Evidence
40%				Clear Indication
30%	Probably Not	Unlikely		Probable Cause, Reasonable Belief
20%		Very Unlikely		Reasonable Indication
10%	Almost No Chance	Remote	Very Unlikely	Reasonable Suspicion
0%	Impossible			Fanciful Conjecture

Source: Adapted from Weiss, Charles. (2008). "Communicating Uncertainty in Intelligence and Other Professions." *International Journal of Intelligence and CounterIntelligence* 21. 57–85. 10.1080/08850600701649312

Note: Weiss's figure, "Scales of Uncertainty," contains errors, which are corrected in Figure 17.3.

developed by the Intergovernmental Panel of Climate Change (IPCC), and in the legal scale used by lawyers in categorizing the persuasiveness of the evidence they present to a jury.[6] A comparison of all four scales shows how different professions have dealt with the need to define levels of uncertainty in similar ways.

In 2010, the Defense Intelligence Agency (DIA) expanded the NIC's scale to create two scales of likeliness expressions ranging from *impossible* to *certain* (see Figure 17.4). One scale focuses on likelihood and the other on probability. DIA also added a caveat that, in the rare circumstance when likelihood cannot be assessed, analysts should use terms such as *may*, *could*, *might*, and *possibly*.[7] The word *could*, for example, would be used appropriately in an article describing the source of a cyber attack that could have been launched by a foreign country or by a lone hacker. The problem is that it can be extremely challenging to pin down the origin of most cyber attacks.

In the United Kingdom (UK), analysts have been provided with a Probability Yardstick to use in their intelligence products.[8] The yardstick arrays a probability range against a standardized qualitative term (see Figure 17.5).[9] What is intriguing about the UK probability ranges is that a conscious decision was made to insert gaps between each level. The intent is to discourage analysts from trying to draw too fine a line in generating percentages and to remind recipients of their intelligence products that the terms are not intended to make precise distinctions.

Canadian intelligence analysts have also wrestled with this problem. The chief of defence, Director General Intelligence Production, opted to array probabilistic terms on a scale from no chances in ten (*will not, no prospect*) to ten chances in ten (*will, is certain*), as shown in Figure 17.6.[10] The chart contains a caution that the numbers on

---

FIGURE 17.4 ■ US Defense Intelligence Agency Likeliness Expressions and Confidence Levels

Impossible							Certain
Remote	Very Improbable	Improbable	Even Chance	Probable	Very Probable	Almost Certainly	
Will Not	Very Unlikely	Unlikely		Likely	Very Likely	Will	

Source: Reproduced with permission of the US government.

FIGURE 17.5 ■ UK Probability Yardstick

Fraction	1/20 1/10	1/5	1/4	1/3 2/5	1/2 5/9	3/4 4/5	9/10 19/20
	remote chance	highly unlikely	unlikely	realistic possibility	likely or probable	highly likely	almost certain
Percent	5% 10%	20%	35% 40%	55%		80% 90% 95%	
0%		25%		50%	75%		100%

Source: Professional Development Framework for all-source intelligence assessment, reproduced with permission of the UK government.

FIGURE 17.6 ■ Canadian Probability Terms

As intelligence analysis is seldom based on perfect knowledge, Chief of Defence Intelligence (CDI) uses specific probabilistic words to express the likelihood of an assessed development or event. The number scale is not intended to suggest precision, but should be used as a guide to understanding the relationship of the terms to one another.

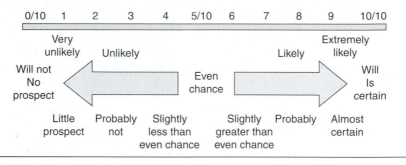

Source: Reproduced with permission of the Canadian government.

the scale are "not intended to suggest precision, but should be used as a guide to show the relationship of the terms to one another."

Interchangeable use of the terms *probably* and *likely* could also confuse recipients of analytic products. In the 1950s and 1960s, *probably* was the dominant term used by the US National Intelligence Council but *likely* has become the dominant term in the 1990s and 2000s.[11] In weather forecasting, there is a large variance in the use of the word *likely* while in the medical profession use of the term *probable* has shown much more consistent results. In a 2008 Mercyhurst College study, the authors recommend against use of both terms interchangeably, arguing that their research has shown that versions of *likely* should be used and that the term *probably* should not be used. The same study noted that over the decades the NIC has shifted from use of estimative words such as *we estimate* and *we believe* to *we judge* and *we assess*.

Reflecting extensive research on the use of probabilistic language terms from the 1950s to the early 2000s, a master's degree candidate at Mercyhurst College built a new scale based on seven words of estimative probability. It resembles much of what Kent and the NIC published but refines the phraseology and differs somewhat in the percentage ranges (see Figure 17.7). The percentile ranges are broken down into groups of 15 percent, except for the middle range of "chances a little better/little less," which was assigned only 10 percent, and the bands at the two extremes of the upper and lower ranges, which were assigned 14 percent. Certainty or impossibility—terms that are rarely conveyed in intelligence assessments—are represented at the top and bottom of the new scale and occupy only 1 percent of the range.[12]

When using probabilistic language, analysts should be alert to two common traps often encountered in using verb forms.

1. Try to minimize use of modal verbs[13] such as *could* or *might* because sentences that contain them usually convey little useful information to the reader.

FIGURE 17.7 ■ Kesselman List of Estimative Words

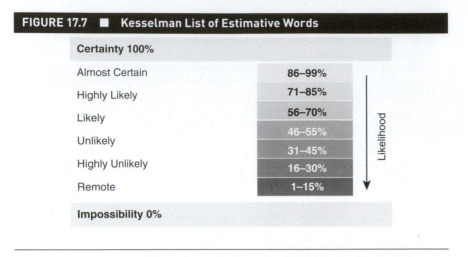

Certainty 100%

Almost Certain	86–99%
Highly Likely	71–85%
Likely	56–70%
	46–55%
Unlikely	31–45%
Highly Unlikely	16–30%
Remote	1–15%

Likelihood

Impossibility 0%

Source: Rachel F. Kesselman, "Verbal Probability Expressions in National Intelligence Estimates: A Comprehensive Analysis of Trends From the Fifties Through Post 9/11" (master's thesis, Mercyhurst College, 2008), 62, https://www.gwern.net/docs/statistics/bayes/2008-kesselman.pdf.

2. Avoid using two probabilistic phrases in the same sentence—for example, by saying that "something *might* happen because the following conditions *are likely* to occur." The better phrasing is to state that "something *might* happen because the following conditions *are present*" or "something *will* happen *if* the following conditions occur." Similarly, a 50 percent chance of a 30 percent chance is nothing more or less than a 15 percent chance.

Analysts should also be alert to when they are mixing modal terms (i.e., *may, might, could* express the possibility of occurrence) with probabilistic terms (i.e., *probably, likely, unlikely* express the likelihood of occurrence).

● Using two modal terms in the same sentence usually presents no problem. For example, saying, "A political coalition *might* form because a hung parliament *is possible*" works because the cause (a hung parliament) and the effect (a political coalition) both have a *possibility* of occurring or not occurring (the choices are "yes/no" or, mathematically speaking, "1/0").

● Including a modal term and a probabilistic term in the same sentence can confuse meaning because an event that *is possible* ("yes" or "1") is no longer *impossible* ("no" or "0") so by definition has a probability greater than zero. The sentence "A political coalition *might* form because a hung parliament *is likely*" makes little sense because we have already stated the effect (a political coalition) *is possible* so the *probability or likelihood* of the cause (a hung parliament) is irrelevant. Note that the coalition would result *because* of the hung parliament, but it is the effect of its *possibility* and not the *likelihood*.

- Modal terms chained to probabilistic terms, however, can be meaningful in some contexts. For example, if we know that the government is capable of authorizing defensive measures in the event of an impending attack, an analyst could meaningfully say, "Defensive measures *might* be taken because an attack *is likely*." In this case, we are certain about the *possibility* that the government can take the measures, but we are uncertain about the *likelihood* that it will do so.

One strategy for dealing with this environment of chronic imprecision when using probabilistic language is to substitute numbers for words. The authors have encountered many decision makers in the military who preferred the use of percentages to represent probability. Usually percentages of probability are conveyed in deciles, stating that an event has a 20, 30, or 60 percent chance of occurring. This approach helps the drafter avoid the well-established imprecision of narrative probability terms, but it often is faulted for conveying more precision than the evidence or the situation would warrant.

A good technique for assessing the soundness of a percentage probability judgment is to ask, "What is the probability percentage of this hypothesis being wrong?" If the probability percentage of the hypothesis being wrong and the probability percentage of the hypothesis being right do not add up to 100, then the analyst needs to rethink the assessment.[14]

Another solution is to present probability ranges by saying, for example, that an event has a 20 to 40 percent chance of occurring instead of making a point prediction. Such an approach is recommended only when the analyst has sufficient information to justify establishing a distinct upper boundary as well as a lower boundary for the estimate. However, simply distributing probabilities over a range (for example, by saying something is somewhere between 20 and 40 percent probable) is meaningless and should be treated—in every respect—the same as saying something has a 30 percent chance of occurring. To illustrate, if you have a 50 percent chance of a 90 percent outcome *and* a 50 percent chance of a 10 percent outcome, it is exactly the same as a 50 percent chance of something happening. Similarly, a uniform distribution between 10 to 90 percent is exactly the same as 50 percent, with no distinguishing features on any theoretical level. In addition, providing a wide range, for example, of 20 to 70 percent is more likely to confuse than to educate the client.

In presenting numerical probability estimates, analysts and clients must understand that analytic judgments cannot convey the same degree of mathematical precision as rolling dice or dealing cards from a deck. Nor can they provide the same degree of precision as a factory's estimate of the likely percentage of defective products after accumulating years of production data. This is especially true for analytic judgments that deal with one-time events or events that have no directly comparable precedent.

A strategy that one of the authors believes worked well in presenting judgments in National Intelligence Estimates he drafted is to substitute bettor's odds for percentages. For example, instead of saying something was almost certainly going to occur, the analyst would say the event had a 9-in-10 chance of occurring. Similarly, an event an analyst might assign a rough probability of 30 percent would be portrayed as having a 1-in-3 chance of succeeding.

Bettor's odds[15] appear to be more effective in conveying probabilistic assessments because they convey an implicit risk calculation that is more likely to resonate with the decision makers who assess risks daily as part of their jobs. Moreover, most people are more accustomed to dealing with odds than with percentages, and they usually are interpreted more accurately than percentages. One downside is that users of bettor's odds can easily overstate low probabilities with statements like "only 1 chance in 1,000."

In his book *Calculated Risks,* Gerd Gigerenzer, a cognitive psychologist at the Max Planck Institute for Human Development in Berlin, explores how people miscalculate risk and uncertainty.[16] He makes a strong case for recasting conditional probabilities in terms of natural frequencies—simple counts of events—rather than the more abstract notions of percentages, odds, or probabilities. He argues that it is easier to comprehend the sentence, "Based on recent studies, eight out of every 1,000 women have breast cancer" than the statement, "The probability that a woman has breast cancer is 0.8 percent."

In tests Gigerenzer conducted of German and American doctors presenting a problem involving conditional probabilities, an overwhelming percentage got the answer wrong when using percentages. When he replaced the percentages with natural frequencies, nearly all of them got the correct answer, or close to it.[17]

The best strategy for dealing with probabilistic judgments is to follow the probability statement (regardless of whether one uses a word, a percentage, or a set of odds) with the word *because* and a response to complete the sentence. For example, "We believe the event is *highly likely* to happen *because* two necessary conditions are present, and a key driver is gaining strength." The remainder of the paragraph or the section should explore these three significant reasons in more detail.

By providing clients with explicit language laying out why a specific word or percentage was selected, they can make their own independent calculations of the probability of the event occurring. This approach also allows clients to track the accuracy of the assessment over time, monitoring the situation to see if the arguments for its being right are growing stronger or weaker.

Levels of Confidence

The key to presenting levels of confidence is to state not just how confident you are as an analyst but why you are confident. The formula is similar to the one used to document probability statements. For example, "We judge with *high confidence* that the following will happen *because* we have two independent sources stating this is the intent of the key decision makers."

A good example of this was the confidence assessment included at the end of the US Intelligence Community's key judgment regarding the extent of Russian interference in the 2016 US elections:

> We assess Russian president Vladimir Putin ordered an influence campaign in 2016 aimed at the US presidential election. Russia's goals were to undermine public faith in the US democratic process, denigrate Secretary Clinton, and

harm her electability and potential presidency. We further assess Putin and the Russian government developed a clear preference for president-elect Trump. We have high confidence in these judgments.[18]

If, on the other hand, the analyst or the producing organization has low confidence in a particular source or judgment, then it is important to state what additional information or what additional events must transpire to increase the level of confidence. It is not a failure to declare low confidence when forecasting future possibilities that might result from the interplay of dynamic forces and factors.

As previously noted, the US Intelligence Community (IC), as a result of the 9/11 attacks and Iraq WMD estimate, has mandated in IC Directive 203 on analytic standards (see Figure 3.8) that analysts describe their level of confidence in judgments and assessments.[19] Most intelligence agencies use definitions of high, medium, and low levels of confidence, similar to those provided in Figure 17.8.[20] While the sets of definitions parallel each other closely, the NIC formulations focus more on an analyst's confidence in the estimative judgments provided in the paper. The definitions used by law enforcement organizations, including the Federal Bureau of Investigation (FBI) and Department of Homeland Security (DHS), usually are tied more to levels of confidence in the sourcing.[21]

DIA stands out from most other agencies in that it has taken a more rigorous—and highly commendable—approach to defining confidence levels by establishing three distinct metrics (see Figure 17.8):

1. The strength of the knowledge base, reflected in part in the quality of the sources

2. The number and importance of key assumptions used to fill key information gaps

3. The strength of the underlying logic, measured in part by the use of analytic techniques

These metrics are then used to assess the analyst's level of confidence along three dimensions:

1. From uncorroborated to well-corroborated information

2. From many to minimal assumptions

3. From mostly weak to strong logical inferences[22]

We caution that repeatedly describing confidence levels in most paragraphs of an article or estimate can diminish the readability of a document. This problem can be overcome by including an overall summary of levels of confidence in a text box (see Chapter 8). In parts of the US Intelligence Community, these text boxes are referred to as Source Summary Statements. They summarize the author's evaluation of the credibility of the sources and analytic judgments in the article. If placed at the beginning of a document

FIGURE 17.8 ■ US Intelligence Community Confidence Level Definitions

NATIONAL INTELLIGENCE COUNCIL (NIC)

Our assessments and estimates are supported by information that varies in scope, quality, and sourcing. Consequently, we ascribe high, moderate, or low levels of confidence to our assessments, as follows:

High Confidence generally indicates that our judgments are based on high-quality information, and/or that the nature of the issue makes it possible to render a solid judgment. A "high confidence" judgment is not a fact or a certainty, however, and such judgments still carry a risk of being wrong.

Moderate Confidence generally means that the information is credibly sourced and plausible but not of sufficient quality or corroborated sufficiently to warrant a higher level of confidence.

Low Confidence generally means that the information's credibility and/or plausibility is questionable, or that the information is too fragmented or poorly corroborated to make solid analytic inferences, or that we have significant concerns or problems with the sources.

FEDERAL BUREAU OF INVESTIGATION (FBI)

High Confidence: Direct or high-quality intelligence from multiple sources or from a single highly reliable source, such as high-quality imagery, human intelligence, or signals intelligence. High confidence generally indicates that the FBI's judgments are based on high-quality information or that the nature of the issue makes it possible to render a solid judgment.

Medium Confidence: Indirect or derived intelligence from multiple sources or from a single reliable source. Medium confidence generally indicates that the information is interpreted in various ways, that the FBI has alternate views, or that the information is credible and plausible to render a solid judgment.

Low Confidence: Little or no information available, intelligence from untested sources, or for which there is little or no corroboration. Low confidence generally means that the information is scant, questionable, or very fragmented; that it is difficult to make solid analytic inferences; or that the FBI has significant concerns or problems with the sources.

DEPARTMENT OF HOMELAND SECURITY (DHS)

High Confidence generally indicates that judgments are based on highquality information from multiple sources or from a single highly reliable source, and/or that the nature of the issue makes it possible to render a solid judgment.

Moderate Confidence generally means that the information is credibly sourced and plausible, but can be interpreted in various ways, or is not of sufficient quality or corroborated sufficiently to warrant a higher level of confidence.

Low Confidence generally means that the information's credibility and/or plausibility is questionable, the information is too fragmented or poorly corroborated to make solid analytic inferences, or that DHS and the FBI have significant concerns or problems with the sources.

Source: Reproduced with permission of the US government.

and read first, the Source Summary Statement helps the reader more efficiently assess the significance of the information and judgments as they read the article.

Given the subjective nature of assessing levels of confidence, conveying levels of confidence graphically is often preferable. For example, key judgments can be portrayed in a text box or matrix and the level of confidence associated with each key judgment can be indicated with symbols, colors, or degrees of shading. The same approach works well when presenting a list of indicators or a list of key assumptions.

When information is conveyed in a matrix, a final column can be added on the right with the letters *H*, *M*, or *L* or three different icons to convey high, medium, or low levels of confidence for what is represented in each row. Alternatively, the cells in the matrix can be shaded with different colors. In this case, it is important to choose appropriate shades—for example, a deep red would be a poor choice to represent *low* given the intensity of the color. In our experience, various shades of purple or blue are the most effective, in part because they work for people who are color blind.

Quantitative Data and Statistics

When writing, reading, or reviewing papers that contain quantitative analysis, remember these ten rules of the road for presenting or interpreting quantitative data and statistics:[23]

1. Be cautious in making categorical claims and skeptical when you come across products that do so. We live in an uncertain world and rarely can something be actually "proven" or "disproven."

2. Openly acknowledge the uncertainty inherent in any study by listing up front the key assumptions that underpin the analysis. Papers that do so usually merit serious attention.

3. Pay attention to how data are collected and the context in which the research was conducted. Be wary of convenience sampling. Be more trustful when random sampling and double-blind testing are used. Samples should be large enough to justify conclusions and representative of the entire population.

4. Do not make the common mistake of comparing raw numbers without adjusting for expected baseline differences. For example, California obviously has more car accidents than Arizona because California has many more cars. A more reasonable comparison would be accidents per person in each state. Similarly, trends in dollars should always be reported with adjustments made for inflation.

5. Account for the fact that data often lose relevancy over time. Based on the experience of practitioners, a reasonable standard is that data used for forecasting should be no more than three to six months old, data used in medical research should be no more than two years old, and sources used to support national security analysis should be no more than five years old. Obviously, these time frames will vary depending on the circumstances, but

as the world becomes increasingly complex, we can expect these time frames to become ever shorter.

6. When presenting judgments based on percentages, ask if the contrapositive is also true; often it is not. For example, if *X* is 70 percent, is it true that *Not X* is 30 percent? This may not be the case if the remaining 30 percent constitutes *Y*, *Z*, and *K*. When dealing with circumstances where only *X* or *Not X* can be true, ask yourself the following question: "If *X* is 70 percent, am I equally comfortable with saying *Not X* is 30 percent?" If not, then the 70 percent estimate needs to be adjusted.

7. Determine or be explicit in stating whether the *average* is the *mean* (the sum of figures divided by the number of figures), the *mode* (the figure that appears the most frequently), or the *median* (the figure in the middle where half the figures are larger and half are smaller). In a normal distribution (the bell curve), the *mean*, *mode*, *and median* tend to be about the same. In nonstandard distributions, however, these values can vary widely given the same set of data.

8. Note if categories have been aggregated to present an unusually large number by connecting a stream of terms with the word *or*. For example, "Seventy percent of oversized men report being physically assaulted, denied employment, or insulted because of their size."

9. Understand that quantitative studies may not show *causation* but may show *correlation* (see additional discussions on causation and the Analytic Spectrum in Chapter 5 and Chapter 7). Two variables can be correlated in several different ways:

    - *X* may cause *Y*.

    - *Y* may cause *X*.

    - *X* and *Y* may affect each other.

    - *Z* (a totally different variable) may cause *X* and/or *Y*.

For example, ice cream sales are correlated with drownings in many parks. Do ice cream sales cause drownings? Or do drownings cause ice cream sales? Or does a third factor (warm temperatures) create the conditions for both?

10. Know the meaning of statistical significance: that a result is unlikely due merely to chance. The conventional (and arbitrary) threshold for declaring statistical significance is a probability of less than 5 percent or a *p*-value less than 0.05. With large sample sizes, you often will see statistically significant results, especially if there is a relationship between the variables; small sample sizes often do not yield statistical significance. Statistical significance does not mean practical significance. To declare practical significance, you need to determine whether the size of the difference is meaningful.[24]

KEY TAKEAWAYS

- Both analysts and clients vary widely in the meanings they assign to probabilistic terms such as *likely* or *probably*.

- The best way to convey a level of likelihood is to follow the probabilistic word, percentage, or bettor's odds with the word *because* and a response to complete the sentence that includes a list of key factors that support the judgment.

- A good technique for assessing the soundness of a numeric probability judgment is to check to see if the percentage of a hypothesis being wrong and the percentage of it being right add to 100.

- The key to presenting levels of confidence is for analysts to state not just how confident they are as analysts but why they are confident.

- A Source Summary Statement is a powerful tool for giving readers an overall sense of an analyst's level of confidence and the quality of the sources used to support the analysis before they start reading the paper. It also helps the analyst reduce visual clutter in the main document.

- Take care when presenting statistics and quantitative data and be even more skeptical when interpreting what you read.

CONSIDERING THE CASE STUDY

Review Case Study VI, "The Case of Iraq's Aluminum Tubes."

- How would you assess the chances that Iraq procured aluminum tubes to use in its nuclear centrifuges for the purposes of developing a nuclear bomb? What words, percentages, or bettor's odds would you assign to this judgment?

- What is the rationale behind your choice of a word, a percentage, or bettor's odds in the answer you provided above? In other words, if you added the word *because* to the end of the preceding

sentence, what reasons would you give to complete the sentence?

- What level of confidence do you have in the sources used to support the analysis on whether Iraq procured aluminum tubes for use in its nuclear centrifuges for the purposes of developing a nuclear bomb?

- What level of confidence do you have in your overall assessment regarding the overall status of Iraq's Weapons of Mass Destruction programs?

NOTES

1. The information used in this chapter is adapted from Pherson Associates training materials (www.pherson.org).

2. Most of the exercises were conducted with US Intelligence Community analysts, although similar results were

recorded in classes taught elsewhere in the US government and in the private sector. One hypothesis that needs to be explored is whether such differences are more prominent among English speakers as opposed to those speaking other languages.

3. Rachel F. Kesselman, "Verbal Probability Expressions in National Intelligence Estimates: A Comprehensive Analysis of Trends From the Fifties Through Post 9/11" (master's thesis, Mercyhurst College, 2008), 62, https://www.gwern.net/docs/statistics/bayes/2008-kesselman.pdf.

4. In the wake of the 9/11 attacks on the United States and the Iraq WMD fiasco, all National Intelligence Estimates published by the National Intelligence Council now include introductory material describing the NIC's methodology in providing probabilistic language and describing levels of confidence. The estimate *Iran: Nuclear Capabilities and Intentions* (November 2007), for example, includes a section on probabilistic language titled "National Intelligence Estimates and the NIE Process" as well as a text box titled "What We Mean When We Say: An Explanation of Estimative Language." The NIE and the introductory language can be accessed at http://www.dni.gov/files/documents/Newsroom/Reports%20and%20Pubs/20071203_release.pdf.

5. Charles Weiss, "Communicating Uncertainty in Intelligence and Other Professions," *International Journal of Intelligence and CounterIntelligence* 21, no.1 (June 13, 2012): 63–69, http://dx.doi.org/10.1080/08850600701649312.

6. Weiss, "Communicating Uncertainty," 61. Weiss' figure, "Scales of Uncertainty," contains errors that are corrected in Figure 17.3.

7. Defense Intelligence Agency, "What We Mean When We Say: An Explanation of Estimative Language," May 18, 2010, chart of "Likeliness Expressions and Confidence Levels"; used in courses Pherson Associates teaches for US Intelligence Community analysts.

8. Ministry of Defence, "Understanding and Intelligence Support to Joint Operations," Joint Doctrine Publication 2-00, 3rd ed. (August 2010), 3–23.

9. Professional Head of Intelligence Assessment (PHIA), "The PHIA Probability Yardstick," in *Professional Development Framework for All-Source Intelligence Assessment* (January 2019), 29.

10. Gudmund Thompson, "Aide Memoire on Intelligence Analysis Tradecraft" (Ottawa, ON, Canada: Chief of Defence Intelligence, 2009).

11. Kesselman, "Verbal Probability Expressions," 67.

12. Kesselman, 71.

13. Modal verbs of probability (*may, might, could*) allow the expression of an opinion or guess about *possibility* when the answer is not known for sure. *Probability* or likelihood expresses the chances something will happen, often in percentages or terms like *likely, probably, or unlikely.*

14. We are indebted to Richards J. Heuer Jr. for suggesting this commonsense technique for adding rigor to the use of probabilistic statements.

15. Poker champion Annie Duke in *Thinking in Bets: Making Smarter Decisions When You Don't Have All the Facts* (New York: Penguin Random House, 2018), asserts that thinking about uncertainties like betting triggers thinking more closely about beliefs, focuses us more objectively on accuracy and outcomes, and tamps down resistance to new information. She also advocates the use of thinking techniques like backcasting and the premortem.

16. Gerd Gigerenzer, *Calculated Risks* (New York: Simon & Schuster, 2002).

17. Steven Strogatz, "Chances Are," *New York Times,* April 25, 2010,

http://opinionator.blogs.nytimes
.com/2010/04/25/chances-are/.

18. Office of the Director of National
Intelligence, National Intelligence
Council, "Assessing Russian Activities
and Intentions in Recent US
Elections," Intelligence Community
Assessment 2017-01D, January 6,
2017, ii, https://www.dni.gov/files/
documents/ICA_2017_01.pdf.

19. Office of the Director of National
Intelligence, "Intelligence Community
Directive 206: Sourcing Requirements
for Disseminated Analytic Products,"
https://www.dni.gov/files/documents/
ICD/ICD%20206.pdf

20. Office of the Director of National
Intelligence, National Intelligence
Council, "What We Mean When
We Say: An Explanation of
Estimative Language," a text box
that follows the Scope Note in the
National Intelligence Estimate,
"Iran: Nuclear Capabilities and
Intentions," November 2007, www
.dni.gov/press_releases/20071203_
release.pdf. The text box is used
in courses Pherson Associates teaches
for US Intelligence Community
analysts.

21. The definitions of DHS and FBI levels
of confidence are used in courses
Pherson Associates teaches for US
Intelligence Community analysts.

22. Office of the Director of National
Intelligence, National Intelligence
Council, "What We Mean When We
Say." This text box is used in courses
Pherson Associates teaches for US
Intelligence Community analysts.

23. These rules of the road were derived
from multiple sources, including
Pherson Associates training materials;
Daniel Levitin, *The Field Guide to Lies:
Critical Thinking in the Information
Age* (New York: Penguin, 2018);
Darrell Huff, *How to Lie With Statistics*
(New York: W. W. Norton, 1982);
Neil A. Manson, "How to Lie With
Statistics: Lessons for Intelligence
Analysts," presentation to the Five Eyes
Conference (Oxford: University of
Mississippi, March 17, 2015); Jeffrey
Sauro, "What Does Statistically
Significant Mean?" *Measuring U*
(blog), October 21, 2014, http://www
.measuringu.com/blog/statistically-
significant.php.

24. Sauro, "What Does Statistically
Significant Mean?"

18 HOW CAN GRAPHICS SUPPORT MY ANALYSIS?

SETTING THE STAGE

Incorporating graphics into an assessment or article helps analysts make a compelling case by conveying information more vividly. Graphics and visuals serve two main functions:

1. Summarize data so they are more easily absorbed by the reader

2. Show relationships that add meaning to the data

Large amounts of data can be conveyed extremely efficiently in a well-designed graphic or video. For example, a bar graph or line chart enables readers to immediately comprehend trends or patterns, and infographics allow readers to absorb large amounts of data and relationships quickly. Senior officials and managers can use—and often rely on—graphics to understand underlying dynamics, make accurate comparisons, and draw conclusions in a matter of seconds. Often a cartoon or a photograph can convey a message far more effectively than a paragraph of text.

The old adage that "a picture is worth a thousand words" was never more obviously demonstrated than during the Cuban missile crisis in 1962. On October 15, 1962, the CIA provided the White House with detailed imagery identifying Soviet nuclear missile installations under construction on the island of Cuba (see Figure 18.1).

| FIGURE 18.1 ■ Soviet Missiles in Cuba |

Source: Photo12/Universal Images Group via Getty Images.

FIGURE 18.2 ■ Missiles on Soviet Freighter

Source: Bettmann/Contributor/Getty Images.

Subsequent images showed missiles on the decks of Soviet freighters headed to Cuba (see Figure 18.2). The pictures provided undeniable evidence that the Soviets were intent on establishing a missile base in Cuba, ninety miles off the coast of Florida. US officials debated several military options, and President John F. Kennedy opted for a naval blockade against Soviet ships carrying missile equipment. Eventually, the Soviets withdrew the missiles and nuclear war was averted.[1]

Each analytic discipline claims its own favorite techniques for representing data with graphics.

- *Economic data* readily lends itself to tables, matrices, bar charts, line graphs, pie charts, and other more advanced forms of graphical display.

- *Military analysis* is often illustrated with maps, photographs of equipment, overhead photography, and three-dimensional terrain models.

- *Political data* offers a somewhat greater challenge but often includes photographs of leaders, imagery of demonstrations, tables of polling data, statistical displays, annotated maps, flow charts, and other schematics.

In all cases, the best graphics do not just summarize the data but tell stories about what the data mean in support of the analytic conclusion.

LOOKING MORE DEEPLY

As the world becomes increasingly digitized and images are instantaneously transmitted across continents in matters of minutes or seconds, the power of graphics and visual representations is accelerating rapidly across the globe. Photographs documenting the flow of migrants into Europe from Syria and several other countries in 2015 told a powerful story with which no text-based news report could compete. Similarly, vivid videos of beheadings conducted by the Islamic State in Iraq and the Levant (ISIL) beginning in 2014 and media coverage of the coordinated terrorist attacks in Paris in November 2015 galvanized world opinion against the extremist movement. Video coverage of US president Donald Trump's historic first summit meeting with North Korean leader Kim Jong Un in Singapore in June 2018 had people across the globe riveted to their televisions to see how the two leaders would interact. Similarly, Trump's statement at the joint press conference in Helsinki that he believed Russian president Vladimir Putin when he said Russia did not interfere in the 2016 US elections has been replayed countless times because of the insights it offers on how Trump relates to Putin. Many citizens of the world have now come to expect to see such images as part of their daily news "take."

Tomorrow's consumers of analytic products will be increasingly inclined to seek information on—and gain analytic insights from—digital, interactive, and increasingly hand-held formats.[2] The widespread use of portable devices and multi-touch screens reinforces this trend. The delivery of analysis on a dynamic, digitally based platform offers the benefit of delivering new types of media to the clients. Clients are likely to increasingly expect analytic products to include video clips, animations, interactive maps, infographics, and overhead imagery, including "flyovers" of the landscape. Digitally based presentations will allow analysts to dramatically increase the amount of available information through the inclusion of hyperlinks, but analysts must take care not to overwhelm the reader with additional information they cannot usefully absorb.

Given the innate power of a picture or graphic, analysts should strive to incorporate interactive infographics, videos, and other visualization techniques directly into their products. Dan Roam believes there is "no more powerful way to prove that we know something well than to draw a simple picture of it."[3]

Visual thinking does not come easily to everyone, but it, like many analytic techniques, is developed with practice. Most of us probably were quite good at it as children. When our grandnephew was eight years old, after listening to an adult discussion of this book, he said, "I'm going to draw a cover for it." Ten minutes later he had produced a picture that visualized critical thinking as a person in the midst of a whirl of light bulbs, brains, clouds, and the word *ideas*. For the second edition, he contributed an updated version from his perspective as a twelve-year-old (see Figure 18.3).[4]

Analysts must be careful to apply the same standards of analytic tradecraft in assessing the credibility of the sources providing such images. As advertisers well know, today's technology makes it very simple to edit or crop a picture and adjust an image in ways that do not represent reality. Deepfakes are just beginning to infiltrate the popular consciousness and are likely to be used increasingly—and with great impact—to sow disinformation. For these reasons, pictures or video used in articles must be validated by reputable news organizations or other organizations with established standards for ensuring the authenticity of the image or audiotape.

Graphics for Summarizing Information

The first challenge for the analyst is to create graphics that summarize the data in the most efficient and accurate way possible. Analysts should first ask what type of graphic is best suited to portray what the data are saying. For example, pie charts are

FIGURE 18.3 ■ A Child's Visualization of Critical Thinking

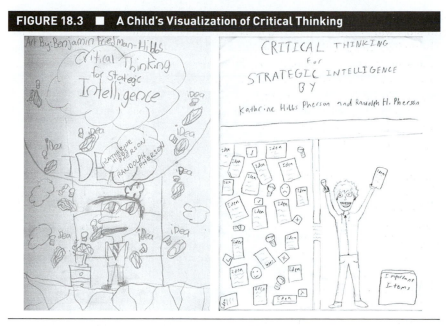

Source: Benjamin Friedman-Hibbs, 2012 (age 8, left), and 2016 (age 12, right). Copyright 2020 Benjamin Friedman-Hibbs. All Rights Reserved.

superb at representing proportions of similar data, such as polling results, at a glance, and line graphs excel at showing trends over time.

Figure 18.4 provides an excellent example of the effective use of graphics to display large amounts of data.[5] In this chart, Ralph Lengler and Martin Eppler from the University of Lugano, Switzerland, have organized one hundred different visualization methods into six different categories using the periodic table of elements as their framework. The six categories are (1) data visualization, (2) information visualization, (3) concept visualization, (4) strategy visualization, (5) metaphor visualization, and (6) compound visualization. Each technique is coded on its task and interaction (an overview, data, or both); whether it represents convergent or divergent thinking; and whether it depicts structure (such as hierarchies and networks) or process (either stepwise cyclical in time or continuous sequential).

To learn more about each of the techniques and their potential uses, visit Lengler and Eppler's website and interact with the chart.[6] When the computer mouse hovers over a specific technique on the chart, an illustration of that form of visualization pops up.

The use of color can greatly enhance visual display, but the analyst should be aware that various societies perceive colors differently (see Figure 18.5). For example, yellow is associated with cowardice in many Western cultures while connoting courage in Japan. Red is the color of mourning in South Africa, but it is the color of good luck in China and is often worn by brides in Eastern cultures.[7] When using colors, analysts should pick a palette in which the intensity of the color matches the intensity of the indicator—for example, using a light color such as pale blue for low and a more intense color such as navy blue for high. We have learned over the years that purple and blue are two of the best colors to use to show multiple levels with increasing degrees of intensity.

FIGURE 18.4 ■ A Periodic Table of Visualization Methods for Management

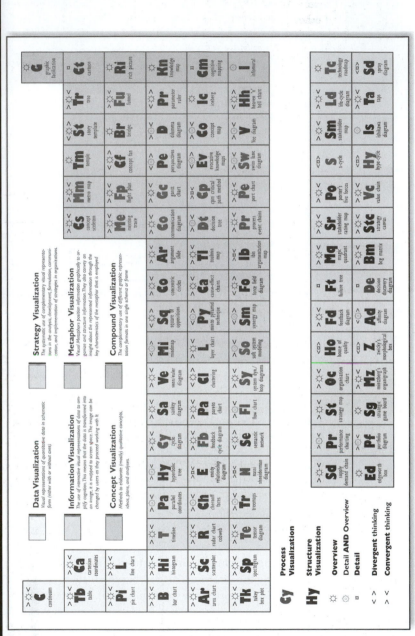

Source: © Prof. Martin J. Eppler, University of St. Gallen, www.visual-literacy.org.

FIGURE 18.5 ■ Stop! Colors Matter

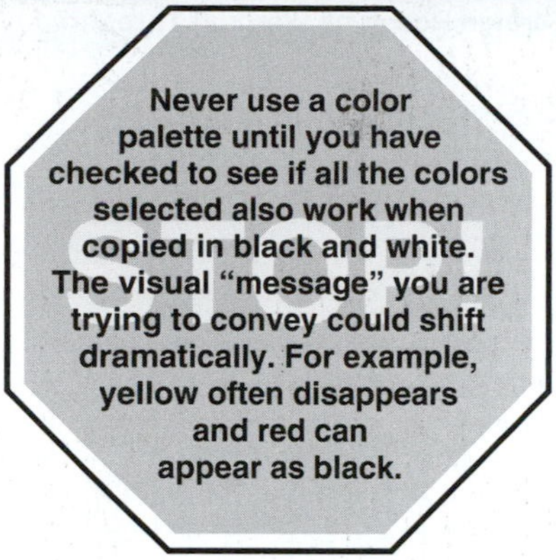

Never use a color palette until you have checked to see if all the colors selected also work when copied in black and white. The visual "message" you are trying to convey could shift dramatically. For example, yellow often disappears and red can appear as black.

Graphics That Add Meaning

The second and greatest challenge is to create graphics that add real meaning to the data. Two classic examples of this are military battle maps annotated with arrows and other colored lines that tell the "story" of the military engagement and overhead imagery that contains small text boxes to focus the viewers' attention on various distinguishing features in the picture.

Even a simple bar graph can convey a powerful message. Figure 18.6, for example, is taken from a study that assesses whether a country's economy is on the verge of collapse.[8] The analysis focuses on current trends in such areas as inflation, balance of payments, and foreign reserves. The bar graph is one in a series that tracks the country's level of foreign reserves but also displays a warning threshold. The message effectively conveyed by the graphic (and extensively supported by an analysis of both quantitative and qualitative trends) is that the country's economy will be vulnerable to collapse as soon as foreign reserves dip below the threshold shown by the dotted line.

Visual representations work much better than text for explaining complex and highly interrelated systems. Figure 18.7 provides a reader at a glance all the factors that should be taken into consideration in trying to ensure that an institution produces high-quality analytic products.[9] Such graphics help the reader capture the entire process in his or her mind and can provide tips as to which factors are the most important by varying the thickness of lines and font sizes.

Ten Do's and Don'ts When Using Graphics[10]

- Ensure that the message of the chart is consistent with ALL the available relevant facts and evidence.

- Let the data speak for itself; avoid obtrusive labels, grid lines, or 3D presentations that distract the reader.

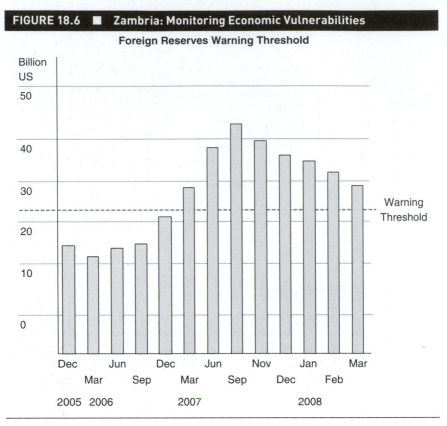

FIGURE 18.6 ■ Zambria: Monitoring Economic Vulnerabilities

Foreign Reserves Warning Threshold

Source: Copyright 2020 Pherson Associates, LLC. All Rights Reserved.

- Make sure the type is legible; usually sans serif type is preferred, but both serif and sans serif can be used if they complement each other. Do not use ALL CAPS, set the type at an angle, use ***bold and italics*** at the same time, knock white type out of a black or colored background, or include hyphenated words.

- When creating a graph, use decimal points for accuracy but round off the numbers to the significant digit to facilitate comparison.

- In setting the scale for the y-axis, use increments that reflect how people naturally count.

- Do not plot more than four lines on a single chart.

- Label the lines on a chart directly; use legends only when space is tight, and the lines intersect repeatedly.

- In bar charts, the width of the bar should be twice the width of the space between the bars.

FIGURE 18.7 ■ **Factors Ensuring Analytic Quality**

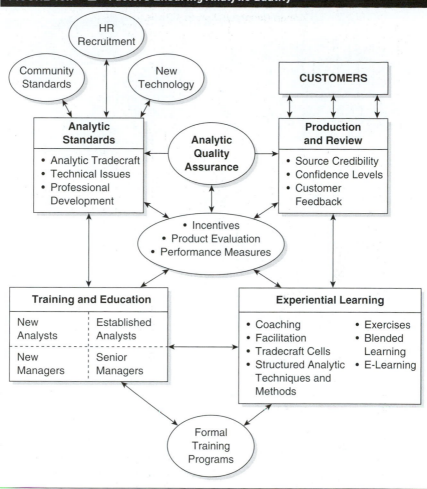

Source: Copyright 2020 Pherson Associates, LLC. All Rights Reserved.

- The shading of bars should move from lightest to darkest; alternating light and dark bars makes the chart hard to read.

- Pie charts should have no more than five slices. The largest value should be at the top to the right and the next largest value should be at the top to the left, followed by the other values on the left in decreasing size.

Five Ways Graphics Can Mislead You[11]

1. The use of *3D drawings* to represent data is often difficult to interpret because of the distorted effect of perspective associated with the third dimension these drawings introduce. The comparison of a 3D pie chart with a regular pie chart

FIGURE 18.8   ■   Comparison of Pie Charts

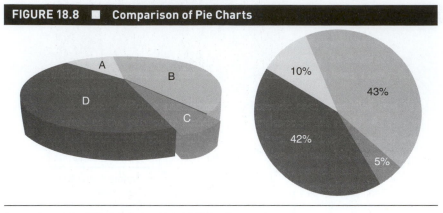

Source: Copyright 2020 Globalytica, LLC. All Rights Reserved.

in Figure 18.8 illustrates this problem. In the 3D version of the chart, the two smaller slices appear about the same size because things that are closer to the reader will appear larger than those in the back. In fact, the rear slice is twice the size of the front slice.

2. *A truncated graph* (also known as a torn graph) has a y-axis that does not start at zero. Truncated graphs can be used to illustrate small differences, but they also can seriously exaggerate the extent of actual change (see the two bar graphs in Figure 18.9 that display identical data). Microsoft Excel will truncate graphs by default if the values are all within a narrow range, and editors will truncate graphs to save space, not realizing how such a display distorts the data.

3. *Changing the ratio* of a graph's dimensions can skew the visual impact of the primary analytic point. Figure 18.10 illustrates how reducing the width by half and doubling the height will show much greater "improvement" or "progress," while reducing the height and increasing the width would suggest

FIGURE 18.9   ■   Comparison of Bar Graphs

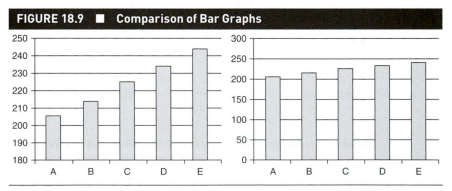

Source: Copyright 2020 Globalytica, LLC. All Rights Reserved.

FIGURE 18.10 ■ Changing the Ratio of Graphs

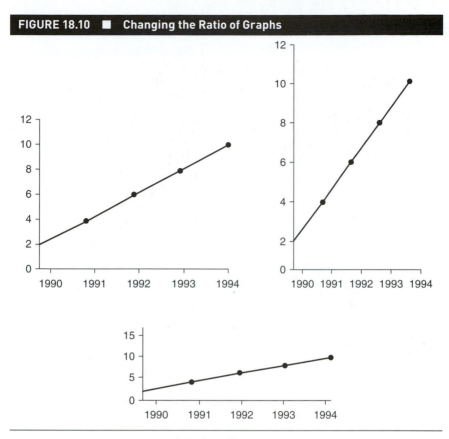

Source: Copyright 2020 Globalytica, LLC. All Rights Reserved.

little change over time. Usually the height of the line represents two-thirds of the chart area.

4. Including *too much data* in a graphic can overwhelm the reader (see Figure 18.11). This can be a particular problem with Link Charts and Venn diagrams. The graphic should not be a data dump but should tell a story the reader can easily follow.

5. Many people are now creating their own maps and posting them on the internet. The first question you should ask is who created the map and for what purposes. Watch out for the following:[12]

   ● Titles that make grand claims but are not supported by the data.

   ● Maps that are not sourced or lack authoritative sourcing.

   ● Heat and density maps that basically simply show where the most people live—in essence, there is more of X if more people live there.

   ● Mapmakers that use size and color to promote their cause or hide inconvenient data.

FIGURE 18.11 ■ Including Too Much Data in a Graphic

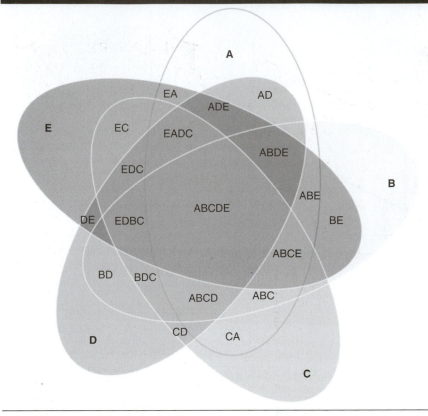

Source: Copyright 2020 Globalytica, LLC. All Rights Reserved.

    ○   Maps that distribute the data in a biased or inappropriate way to make a point or to promote the mapmakers' political agenda. In Figure 18.12, data classes are defined in two different ways in the legends, leading the reader to draw very different conclusions from the map regarding the strength of the Hispanic community in Florida. Which legend is the most objective and should be used?

Summarizing Your Paper in a Single Graphic

Creating graphics can be learning experiences in and of themselves. Crafting a single chart to map the key line of argument in a paper will not only focus attention on the most important points but could reveal gaps in knowledge or logic. By leaving out the details and engaging the topic from a higher degree of abstraction, authors are forced to think more rigorously about how they have organized their product as well as ask themselves what they have left out.

To graphically summarize the key points in the Office of the Director of National Intelligence (ODNI) study on collaboration discussed in Chapter 6 (see Figure 6.1),

FIGURE 18.12 ■ Hispanic or Latino Population in Florida by County

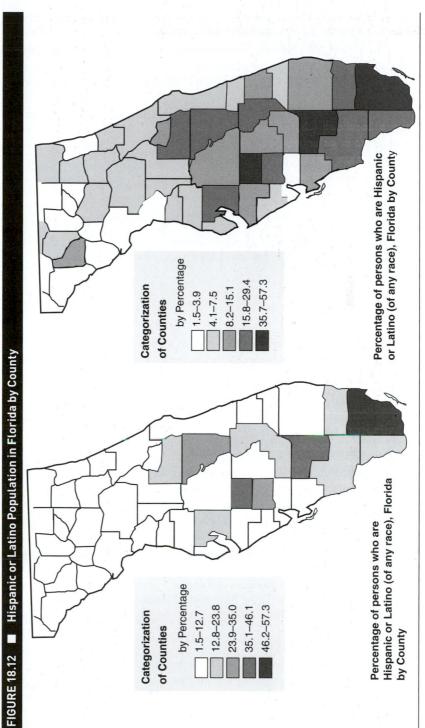

Categorization
of Counties

by Percentage

1.5–3.9
4.1–7.5
8.2–15.1
15.8–29.4
35.7–57.3

Percentage of persons who are Hispanic
or Latino (of any race), Florida by County

Categorization
of Counties

by Percentage

1.5–12.7
12.8–23.8
23.9–35.0
35.1–46.1
46.2–57.3

Percentage of persons who are
Hispanic or Latino (of any race), Florida
by County

Source: Census 2000, prepared with American Fact Finder.

one of the authors needed to show that the commitment of senior leaders to collaboration was essential to the success of every element of the process. For this reason, a large circle was drawn around all three sets of factors and given the label "Command Intent." The message the graphic conveys is that collaboration will not succeed unless the chief executive—in this case the Director of National Intelligence (DNI) himself—is a visible proponent of the process.

Another example of using graphics to summarize the primary message of an article can be found in the case study, "The End of the Era of Aircraft Carriers," in which Figure IV.2 is a dramatic portrayal of how US defense spending grossly outpaces that of any other country. Figure IV.4 captures the basic message of the case study in one picture, depicting how three drivers could spur a significant reduction in the size of the global aircraft carrier fleet.

> "It is not how much space there is, but rather how it is used. It is not how much information there is, but rather how effectively it is organized."
>
> —Edward Tufte
> *Envisioning Information*[13]

The benefits of trying to capture the essence of a book with a single graphic were demonstrated even more starkly in producing a summary graphic for *Structured Analytic Techniques for Intelligence Analysis* (see Figure 18.13).[14] This began simply by arranging the sixty-six techniques discussed in the book into six families. Then, notations were added to show which techniques were most closely related to one another. This process revealed that a distinct subset of techniques shared one common characteristic: They were linked to at least three different families or domains of techniques.

What was most interesting in creating the graphic was that six of the ten techniques that had met this requirement—(1) Cluster Brainstorming, (2) Key Assumptions Check, (3) Multiple Hypothesis Generation, (4) Analysis of Competing Hypotheses, (5) Foresight analysis, and (6) Indicators—were already well established as core techniques in the US Intelligence Community. Three others—Quadrant Crunching™, Premortem Analysis, and Structured Self-Critique—were gaining popularity and showing promise for joining the group. The graphic helped explain why. The process of creating the graphic revealed a heretofore unarticulated rationale for why these techniques had gained such prominence. We suspect that techniques crossing over several domains are used more frequently because they advance critical thinking skills in several different ways.

Planning Ahead

Most seasoned analysts know that graphics can be powerful tools for conveying their message more effectively and presenting key insights in a more efficient manner. With this in mind, analysts will usually plan ahead for what graphics to incorporate into a draft. In some cases, they will even organize a longer article around what graphics are likely to prove most effective in telling the story. For example, if a map is called for to support the analysis, the analyst might ask what information could be depicted on the

FIGURE 18.13 ■ Six Families of Structured Analytic Techniques

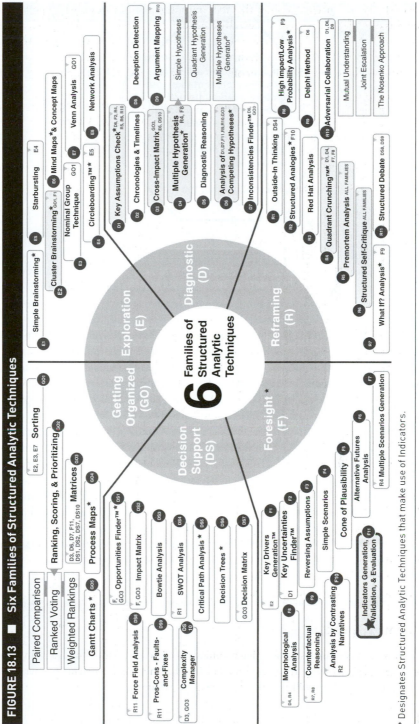

* Designates Structured Analytic Techniques that make use of Indicators.

Source: Copyright 2020 Pherson Associates, LLC. All Rights Reserved.

FIGURE 18.14 ■ Stop! Graphics Must Matter

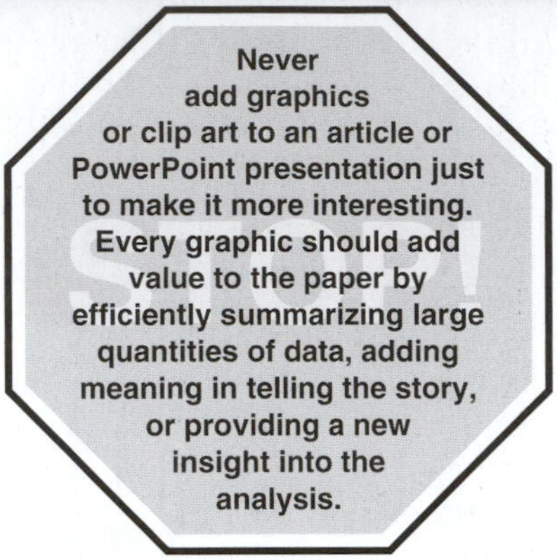

Never add graphics or clip art to an article or PowerPoint presentation just to make it more interesting. Every graphic should add value to the paper by efficiently summarizing large quantities of data, adding meaning in telling the story, or providing a new insight into the analysis.

map to illustrate key analytic points. Another question to ask is whether large amounts of data can be captured in a single matrix or chart, thus alleviating the need to draft several paragraphs or pages of text to summarize all the factual information (see Figure 18.14).

A good rule of thumb in deciding how many graphics to use is to remember that most readers are put off when three or more pages of text contain no graphics to provide visual relief. If analysts have no graphic, table, chart, matrix, or text box to break up a long section of continuous narrative, they should consider finding a picture or adding a quotation. When inserting quotations, rely on authoritative, original sources or established compendia, such as John Bartlett's *Familiar Quotations*.[15] According to our publisher and reflected in our personal experience, a surprising number of quotations listed on internet sites are inaccurate or improperly sourced.

Placement of graphics is both an art and a science. Usually a map or an overarching summary graphic is best located on the facing (even-numbered) page across from the first (odd-numbered page) of the article. This placement helps clients orient themselves in the data and the argument as they begin to read the article. Later in the article, full-page graphics, text boxes, or matrices are best placed on even-numbered pages across from the portions of the text that relate to that graphic. Other considerations for placing graphics in written products include the following:

- The impact of smaller graphics can be optimized by embedding them in the text.

- Larger graphics that take up half a page or one-third of a page usually work best when hung on the top of the page that follows the paragraph in which the graphic was mentioned.

- Oversized graphics or foldouts are usually best placed at the front or the back of an article.

For this book, we opted to provide two summary graphics, one on the inside front cover (The Critical Thinkers Checklist) and another on the inside back cover

(The Analyst's Roadmap), that capture the key points presented in this book. For *Structured Analytic Techniques for Intelligence Analysis*, we included a foldout back cover graphic that organized the sixty-six techniques into six families of techniques: (1) Getting Started, (2) Exploration, (3) Diagnostic, (4) Reframing, (5) Foresight, and (6) Decision Support. When publishing the *Handbook of Analytic Tools and Techniques*, we made the foldout graphic part of the front cover because it provided the reader with a quick way of understanding how the handbook was organized around the families of techniques.[16]

KEY TAKEAWAYS

- Graphics can relay information far more powerfully than any narrative; in an increasingly globalized society, the adage, "A picture is worth a thousand words" is becoming an understatement.

- Graphics can be used both to summarize the data and to add meaning to the data.

- Analysts should never forget that colors connote different things from one culture to another.

- Pay attention to the do's and don'ts for generating good graphics; if you fail to

get the basics right, the graphic will lose its impact.

- The challenge of summarizing an entire paper in one graphic will force authors to think more rigorously about how they have organized the paper and ask what has been left out.

- Before beginning to draft, analysts should consider what graphics are needed and how best they can be used to convey the key message of the paper.

CONSIDERING THE CASE STUDY

Review Case Study IV, "The End of the Era of Aircraft Carriers."

- Did the analyst incorporate an appropriate number of graphics in the article?

- Did any graphic summarize a large amount of information in a single chart?

- Did any graphic add meaning or provide unique insights?

- How well did the author summarize the key message of the case study in a single graphic?

NOTES

1. Lewis Chang and Lewis Kornbluh, "The Cuban Missile Crisis: 1962, The 40th Anniversary," National Security Archive, George Washington University, 2nd ed. (New York: The New Press, 1998), http://www.gwu.edu/~nsarchiv/nsa/cuba_mis_cri/declass.htm; Dino A. Brugioni, *Eyeball to Eyeball: The Inside Story of the Cuban Missile Crisis* (New York: Random House, 1991).

2. See "Introduction: The Changing Intelligence Communications Landscape," in *Intelligence Communication in the Digital Era: Transforming Security, Defence and Business,* ed. Rubén Arcos and

Randolph H. Pherson (London: Palgrave Macmillan, 2015).

3. Dan Roam, *The Back of the Napkin: Solving Problems and Selling Ideas With Pictures* (New York: Penguin, 2009), 3.

4. This graphic was created by Benjamin Friedman-Hibbs at age eight and age twelve to illustrate his concept of critical and analytic thinking.

5. Ralph Lengler and Martin J. Eppler, "Towards a Periodic Table of Visualization Methods for Management," Institute of Corporate Communication, University of Lugano, Switzerland, http://www.visual-literacy.org/periodic_table/periodic_table.pdf.

6. Ralph Lengler and Martin J. Eppler, "Periodic Table of Visualization," www.visual-literacy.org/periodic_table/periodic_table.html.

7. Jennifer Krynin, "Color Symbolism Chart by Culture: Understand the Meanings of Color in Various Cultures Around the World," About.com guide, http://webdesign.about.com/od/color/a/bl_colorculture.htm.

8. This example is taken from Pherson Associates training materials (www.pherson.org). The graphic was derived from an actual study but sanitized for use in classroom instruction.

9. This graphic was created by Randolph H. Pherson and used by Pherson Associates to support work done for several clients.

10. These rules were extracted from Dona M. Wong, *The Wall Street Journal Guide to Information Graphics* (New York: W. W. Norton, 2010). We highly recommend this book, which offers a much more detailed and fully illustrated discussion of "do's and don'ts" for information graphics. Other highly recommended books include

Cole Kussbaumer Knaflic's *Storytelling With Data: A Data Visualization Guide for Business Professionals* (Hoboken, NJ: John Wiley, 2015) and Scott Berinato's *Good Charts: The HBR Guide to Making Smarter, More Persuasive Data Visualizations* (Boston: Harvard Business Review Press, 2016).

11. Information for this section was taken from Pherson Associates training materials (www.pherson.org); Stephen Few, *Show Me the Numbers: Designing Tables and Graphs to Enlighten*, 2nd ed. (Burlingame, CA: Analytics Press, 2012); and Boyce Rensberger, "Slanting the Slope of Graphs," *Washington Post*, May 10, 1995, https://www.washingtonpost.com/archive/1995/05/10/slanting-the-slope-of-graphs/08a34412-60a2-4719-86e5-d7433938c166/.

12. These tips from a professional geographer were taken from Andrew Wiseman, "When Maps Lie," *The Atlantic Citylab*, June 25, 2015, http://www.citylab.com/design/2015/06/when-maps-lie/396761/.

13. E. R. Tufte, *Envisioning Information* (Cheshire, CT: Graphics Press, 1990), 50.

14. Randolph H. Pherson and Richards J. Heuer Jr., *Structured Analytic Techniques for Intelligence Analysis*, 3rd ed. (Washington, DC: CQ Press/SAGE, 2021).

15. Geoffrey Brown and John Bartlett, *Bartlett's Familiar Quotations: Passages and Phrases in Common Use*, 17th ed. (Boston: Little, Brown, 1919), revised and enlarged by Nathan Haskell Dole (New York: Bartleby.com, 2000).

16. Randolph H. Pherson, *Handbook of Analytic Tools and Techniques*, 5th ed. (Tysons, VA: Pherson Associates, 2019).

19 HOW DO I PRESENT MY MESSAGE IN THE MOST COMPELLING WAY?

SETTING THE STAGE

Good writing is good thinking on paper. If you have thought through your framework, your sources, and your argument, the writing will come easily. Pieces that are difficult to write and to read are those that the author wrote too quickly, slapping together a potpourri of related information and thoughts without connective depth or narrative flow.[1]

Analytic articles and briefings must convey a message rather than merely describe information or an incident. The goal is to help the busy reader quickly understand what is new, different, or critical about an issue. Presenting a message that gets your clients' attention, interest, and trust is all about conveying the message up front with clarity, precision, and brevity. What is the value your busy client will get from reading the piece? What is the value the taxpayer or the corporation gets from having you research and write it?

Get used to the fact that your message—captured in the title, lead sentence, or key points—may be the only part of your article that your client reads. You want to be certain that the message is what you want your reader to remember. One of the authors learned as a young analyst on assignment to the White House Situation Room that complex analytic topics have to be simplified if they are to be useful at the highest levels. She learned how to compress any intelligence paper, regardless of its length, into one paragraph. Your clients can always come back for more information when and if they need it. A message—either written or oral—that is well delivered (and perhaps updated and redelivered) sets the stage for the client to take action.

LOOKING MORE DEEPLY

Meaning must be clear to you before you can make it clear to your reader. This is not easy given the variety of services that analysts perform for their clients: We characterize issues and problems, identify trends, anticipate unexpected changes and developments, determine the evidential reliability and value of unevaluated or ambiguous information, extract significant details out of masses of data, and synthesize details into meaningful observations. Different specialties and types of analysis manifest themselves in different products; many have styles, formats, and guidelines all their own. But it all comes down to the message: What are the key analytic insights that can be drawn from the available information?

Your argument's claims should be the same as your message, but this may not be the case if you have not accurately conceptualized your argument with your clients in mind. Beginning to draft your product provides the perfect opportunity to check your message by developing an "elevator speech" after asking yourself, "If I were on an elevator with my client for less than a minute, what would I tell them about my issue?"

Here are the three elements critical to effective presentation of your message:

1. The attention-getting presentation of the message itself

2. Structuring the product so the message is prominently featured and well explained

3. Writing it in a style that is simple, direct, and easy to understand

Scope Note

One common way to set your clients' expectations for your product is through a Scope Note. A clearly crafted Scope Note "tees up" the topic, setting the stage for efficient reading and deciding what action, if any, needs to be taken as a result of the analysis.

An effective Scope Note includes the following:

- A concise statement of the topic and its relevance to the client organization's mission, specifically capturing the essence of its perspective, contribution, or interest

- Intended audiences, stated as specifically as possible

- What readers are expected to do or how they are expected to benefit as a result of receiving the product

- Components and partners who contributed, prepared, or coordinated on it

Some Scope Notes may also address these matters:

- Bounds for the topic—what is included and what is not

- Key information gaps and what is being done to fill them

- The product's relationship to other work on the topic. Is it a follow-on to other assessments? Is it a part of a series?

For instance, a Scope Note might be as simple as this:

This [product] [purpose: warns, highlights, focuses, examines, provides awareness of] [topic of product]. It includes information to assess [specific intended audience] in [undertaking specific action or use of information].

Key Message

No matter what your purpose or product, you communicate the essence of your message in two unambiguous ways—the title and the lead paragraph.

Remember that the formatting of analytic reports will differ depending on the audience and whether a strategic or tactical message is being delivered. Almost all intelligence products adhere to the Inverted Triangle structure, with the bottom line up front. Well-written articles have crisp topic sentences and transition sentences that support the overall storyline. All well-written drafts should have the following:

- *Titles that grab the consumer's attention.* The title is your "contract" with the reader and should match exactly the main point or judgment. You are setting the reader's expectations and mental framework for what will be in the product. You must resist going beyond the data or sensationalizing the conclusion. Make sure the title names the actor or trend and uses an active verb for the "So What." Avoid using subordinate clauses and be brutal in slashing superfluous words.

Try writing the title first to clarify the focus. You can change it as you develop the piece. If you cannot condense your message into a pithy, engaging title, you lack the clear message that is essential for a successful, informative analytic piece. Titles should rarely extend beyond one line.

- *Leads that tell the story in a nutshell.* The lead telescopes in one sentence the "What" and "So What"—highlighting new insights, warnings, changes, and critical implications (see Figure 19.1). It is the key takeaway for the reader. Busy clients often skim materials, reading only the leads, bolded text, or topic sentences. Your lead should use different language than that which appears in the title.

You should expect the lead to be edited many times. Product reviewers and editors bring their own experience and assessment of what they believe will attract clients' attention. The facts and subordinate points that make up the argument or line of reasoning should directly support the lead, providing the substance and content to establish its credibility and significance.

- *Formats that support the required action.* Analytic products have different formats for different organizations, purposes, and decision makers. Military targeting assessments, law enforcement or homeland security bulletins, current

FIGURE 19.1 ■ Leads Accomplish Many Objectives

A LEAD BY ANY OTHER NAME . . .

- Major Claim
- Bottom Line Up Front
- Big Picture
- Core Assertion
- Key Judgment or Key Point
- Statement of Synthesis
- "What" and "So What"

intelligence articles for specific decision makers, and intelligence estimates all may look different but have more in common than might appear on the surface.

We recall a few students in one national agency criticizing intelligence writing instructors for not using organization-specific templates. The students, who were analysts, were so intent on figuring out how to "fill in the blanks" on required forms in their organization that they completely missed recognizing the effective writing principles that apply to any format.

Some organizations highlight or place in bold type or italics major points or conclusions. If you do that on behalf of your organization, be sparing in what you feature. If everything is special, nothing is special.

- Inverted Triangle structure. All intelligence writing is based on the Inverted Triangle model, which organizes the analyst's thinking and information in a logical progression that begins with the most important concept, thought, or idea and descends to the least important point (see Figure 19.2).[2] It follows conventions common to journalism but differs from academic writing in which the logical flow usually presents the researcher's evidence in increasing order of significance and builds to an ending conclusion. This principle of beginning with the most critical information and descending to the least important applies to entire assessments, articles, or paragraphs.

- Bottom line up front (BLUF). Clients not only want the most important information to lead analytic products, they want to know the implications of that information as well. A newspaper article often begins with a factual lead, describing an event and the accompanying Five-Ws-and-an-H: Who, What, How, When, Where, and Why.[3] Busy readers of analysis want the facts and the evidence, but they want the analysis or assessment of the evidence first. They expect to read informed judgments based on experience, collection, and the weighing of the material and sources.

- Paragraphs that start with analytic topic sentences. Each paragraph should have one main point. It begins with an analytic topic sentence, which has a core assertion that will be supported by the remaining sentences in the paragraph. In keeping with the Inverted Triangle model, topic sentences should appear in decreasing order of importance, generality, or detail. Organize your product to avoid repetition of evidence or themes that can confuse your client.

Reviewers will question the assertions in your topic sentences to ensure that you have evidence to support them, have considered alternatives, and have questioned your assumptions. They may also react to the length of your paragraphs. Paragraphs are easiest to digest if they have at least two sentences (an assertion and minimal support) but not more than five. If your sentences are long, include fewer in the paragraph.

- *Transitions that smooth the argument's flow.* Transitional words and phrases help orient the client to where you are in your reasoning. They link

FIGURE 19.2 ■ The Inverted Triangle: Contrasting Ways to Write a Paper

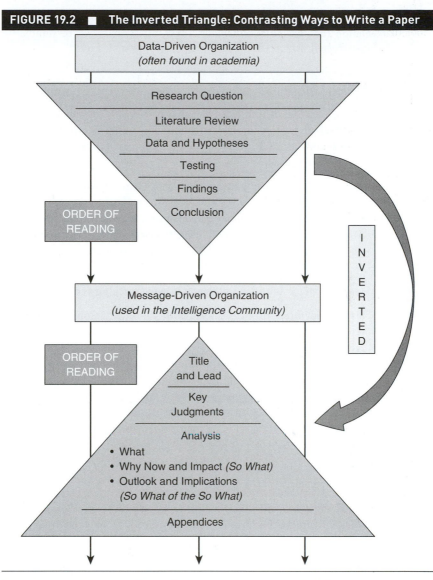

Source: Copyright 2020 *Analytic Writing Guide*, Pherson Associates, LLC. All Rights Reserved.

ideas, paragraphs, or other parts of speech and preview what is coming next. You should consciously look to use them in key locations in your product. Be aware that using too many transitional words is more awkward than using too few. The word *also*, for example, is usually a prime candidate for deletion during editing.

Transitions are more important in written products than in oral briefings where they can be emphasized with voice or gestures. They can emphasize a point (*the most compelling evidence*), compare or contrast (*similarly*, *as opposed to*), clarify or add information (*for example*, *additionally*), enumerate (*next*, *last*), or summarize (*as a result*, *in conclusion*).

Simple and Direct Style

Your clients may be tired of reading. They always will seek the quickest way to understand the critical information in the least amount of time. You owe it to them to convey complex ideas and data so they can grasp the point the first time and not have to ponder what you are trying to say.

- *Clear, precise, and succinct sentences.* You can write clearly if you choose simplicity over complexity. Use short, familiar words and expressions—the fewer syllables the better. For instance, *use* is easier to absorb than *utilize*. Adopt a direct sentence structure in which the actor and the verb are close to the beginning of the sentence. Limit dependent clauses that add detail but dilute your message.

    o **Unclear:** By utilizing an anonymizer, one can surf websites discreetly without leaving a footprint and therefore avoid tracking of cookies.

    o **Clear:** Anonymizer software can help hide your identity on the internet.

Strive for precision in your words and expressions, opting for concrete nouns and verbs that create a clear mental picture in the reader's mind. Avoid vague, abstract, or bureaucratic language that blurs or disguises meaning. Make sure you do your homework and know the facts behind comparison adjectives, such as *high* unemployment or a *moderate* political faction. Be specific in saying what you mean and make sure it means the same thing to your clients.

    o **Vague:** Worsening security problems close to the border will have long-term consequences for the regime.

    o **Specific:** Increasing narcotrafficker attacks on police posts close to the border will prompt the government to request additional foreign support to stay in power.

Make every word count, eliminating "deadwood," or words that are unnecessary to convey your message. Guard against redundancy that can sneak into phrases, such as *too many extraneous words*. Strong nouns and verbs limit the need for modifiers.

- *Active voice.* A verb's voice, or its relationship to the nouns in the sentence, is active when the actor or subject performs the action. This is usually a clearer, more concise, and more interesting sentence structure. A passive sentence structure means that the actor is absent or is the object of the action specified by the verb. Passive voice can be confusing if the reader needs to guess who the actor is. It forces the writer to add words that are weak, including nonspecific pronouns (*there*, *it*), phrases using the preposition *by* to denote the actor, and compound verbs.

Compound verbs consist of a form of the verb *to be* plus a past participle or verb form usually ending in *-ed, -en,* or *-t* (for example, *were increased, was attacked, is approved*).

- o **Passive:** The police obtained the warrant and the suspected terrorist was arrested. (Did the police apprehend the terrorist or did someone else?)

- o **Active:** The police obtained the warrant and arrested the suspected terrorist.

- o **Passive:** Security and speed of access will be improved by the new identity verification system.

- o **Active:** The new identity verification system will improve security and speed of access.

The key to identifying passive voice is finding sentence subjects that are not performing the action in the verb. To make the sentence active, place the actor before the verb and the object after, drop part of the compound verb, or change it to a single, more precise one.

- o **Passive:** The decision to stage the coup was made by the insurgents.

- o **Active:** The insurgents decided to stage the coup.

- o **Passive:** The arrival times are listed on the schedule.

- o **Active:** The arrival times are on the schedule.

- o **Passive:** The directions are shown in this brochure.

- o **Active:** The directions appear in this brochure.

Passive voice is grammatically correct, but because it is less active and more bureaucratic, we seek to minimize it in analytic writing. You can use it when you intentionally want to hide the actor or emphasize the idea over the actor. This is often the case in scientific or resource writing, but it also explains why technical documents often sound formal and boring. In short, use passive voice consciously and sparingly if you cannot find an acceptable active alternative.

- o **Passive:** In FY20, resources for analyst travel were reduced 10 percent.

- o **Passive:** The new analytic product was designed to be read quickly by busy executives.

- o **Passive:** The snake-venom antidote was administered immediately, and the patient made a full recovery.

- ● *Style that follows specific guidelines.* Almost every organization—including our company—has its own style guide. It is an invaluable tool for building a common set of expectations for good writing; conventions for grammar, spelling, and punctuation; and specialized templates and formats. Some of the most common grammar mistakes are discussed in Figure 19.3. Following the style guide can also save significant time in the editing process.

Pay particular attention to your organization's rules regarding punctuation. Few support the well-intentioned but incorrect advice from some grade school teachers to place commas where you pause in reading a sentence aloud. Commas are used primarily to set off items in a series of three or more, before conjunctions such as *but* and *and* that

---

FIGURE 19.3 ■ Top Five Grammar Offenses

Editors say they spend the most time fixing the following grammatical errors:

1. **Misuse of relative pronouns.** A relative pronoun "relates" a subordinate clause to the rest of a sentence: who, whom, that, which.

   ○ Who/whom. *Whom* is always an objective pronoun, *who* is the subjective.

   ○ That/which. *That* is used with restrictive clauses and *which* with nonrestrictive clauses that are set off with commas.

   Correct Examples: From <u>whom</u> did you get the recipe? I selected the lettuce <u>that</u> had the least wilted leaves. He made the salad, <u>which</u> did not taste quite right.

2. **Lack of subject–verb agreement.** Singular subjects need singular verbs, and plural subjects require plural verbs.

   Correct Example: Does <u>anyone</u> in this room <u>claim</u> responsibility for this error?

3. **Disagreement between pronouns and their antecedents.** A pronoun must agree in person, number, and gender to the word, phrase, or clause to which it refers.

   Correct Examples: If <u>a person</u> wants to succeed professionally, <u>he or she</u> must know the rules of the game.

4. **Confusing possessive pronouns and contracted pronouns.** A possessive pronoun substitutes for a possessive noun: *his, hers, yours, its, ours, theirs,* and *whose.* A contracted pronoun is a shortened version of a pronoun plus the verb "is." It's = it+is, who's = who+is. Contractions should be avoided in analytic writing.

   Correct Examples: I don't know <u>whose</u> car that is, but <u>it's</u> in my parking space.

5. **Wrong use of words.**

   ○ Affect/effect

   To effect means "to bring about." To affect is "to do something to."

   ○ Principle/principal

   A principle is a standard, law, or rule. A principal refers to a person in charge.

   ○ Capitol/capital

   A capital can refer to a city that serves as the seat of government, wealth in the form of money or property, or a letter case. A capitol is the physical building in which a legislative assembly meets.

   Correct Examples: *The <u>principal</u> of our school chaperoned a field trip to the <u>capitol</u> and hoped the visit would <u>affect</u> the students in a positive way.*

separate two independent clauses,[4] and to set off introductory and parenthetical clauses. When in doubt, leave it out.

The guidelines provide consistency and a professional appearance to publications and briefings. If your organization does not have specific guidelines, select and follow one of the major guides used in universities or corporations. The most common include the *Chicago Manual of Style* (CMOS) and the citation and format styles of the American Psychological Association (APA) and the Modern Language Association (MLA).

Briefings and Oral Presentations

Briefings are a powerful way to communicate your analytic message.[5] They can be prepared quickly for informal or impromptu presentations and tailored to present to a few individuals in their offices or to hundreds or thousands in an auditorium or in a webinar. Even more important, they allow for interpersonal interaction to stress essential points, answer questions, and solicit client feedback and follow-on tasking.

A first-rate briefing flows out of good thinking and good writing. To make a strong presentation, analysts follow many of the same principles they use to organize their thoughts. They should prepare an outline that suits their or their organization's style. For instance, military briefings often follow set procedures and most organizations have specific briefing templates.

When preparing an oral presentation, take care to do the following:

- Conceptualize, plan, and rehearse your presentation.

- Fit your briefing to client or audience needs.

- Keep your briefing concise and to the point.

- Present your case in a format your audience can easily follow with transitions that help communicate the message.

- Anticipate having less time than scheduled to make your presentation.

- Remember the adage about repetition: Say what you are going to say, say it, and say what you said.

Structuring Your Oral Presentation

Most briefing formats consist of an introduction, a body, and a conclusion tied together with clear transition statements. A general rule of thumb calls for devoting about 10 percent of the time to the introduction, 70 percent to the body, and 20 percent to the conclusion.

- The introduction summarizes for the audience the topic and its significance, the bottom line, and the presentation's organization.

- The body follows the organization you laid out in the introduction and presents your case and information in detail. It substantiates the bottom-line message, clarifying the meaning or importance of key points. It may lead the audience through a chronology or chain of events, specify cause-and-effect relationships, or use stories as illustrations.

- The conclusion reinforces your key points in case listeners have missed any part of the presentation and may recommend actions or follow-on activities.

- Transition statements cue the audience to when, how, and why you are moving to a new topic or segment. They also separate the key points and help the audience follow the organization you promised in the introduction.

- Questions should be anticipated and can be used to explore critical issues in more detail.

Preparing Your Oral Presentation

When preparing briefings, be sure to consider the following questions:

- Who is your audience?
  - What do your listeners already know about your subject and what do they need to know?
  - Do they have the same experience and knowledge or a wide variety of backgrounds?
  - What responsibility do they have for actions that might be taken?
  - Do they have preconceived opinions about the subject or about you?
  - Who in the audience might try to challenge your arguments?
  - Based on the time and circumstance, what might their mood be— welcoming, ready for lunch, tired, worried, enthused?
  - Are they used to formal or casual briefings and exchanges?
- What is the presentational environment?
  - What is the purpose of the meeting? Is it a fact-finding session or a conference?
  - Have you given the briefing before or is this a one-time, tailored presentation?
  - How large is the audience?
  - How much time will you have?
  - Are questions and answers (Q&As) included in your time or does the time limit apply only to the prepared part of the briefing?
  - Are there other briefers? How many briefers will go before you? Are they likely to go over their time?
  - How much time will you need to set up?

- What is your strategy for your presentation?
    - o What do you want to achieve with your presentation?
        - ☐ Do you want the audience to do something or think the way you do?
        - ☐ Do you want to explain something they need to know but do not know much about yet?
        - ☐ Do you want to update them on a situation with which they are already familiar?
        - ☐ Do you want to provide them with information on how to do or achieve something?
    - o What kind of strategy or combination of strategies will be most effective, given your audience, your personality, the situation, and your subject matter?
    - o Do you want to use calm logic, forceful emphasis, friendly informality, respectful formality, or another approach?
- What is your message?
- What are some of the questions your audience is likely to raise and how will you answer them?

Delivering Your Oral Presentation

You can take entire courses on oral presentation, so we consolidate here our most useful tips for delivering successful briefings:

- Always check out the room beforehand. Determine if you will need a microphone. Ensure that your slides and video work and that audio for the microphone or video clips is set at the right volume.

- Present the material clearly and succinctly, engaging your audience from the beginning and holding their attention until the end.

> "Simplicity does not precede complexity, but follows it."
>
> —Alan J. Perlis
> Computer Scientist and First Recipient of the Turing Award[6]

- Deal with anxiety and anticipate problems. Remember that you are there to tell your listeners something they do not know. You are the expert.

- Keep graphics simple and allow the audience to focus on them.

- Never wing it. Always spend time beforehand preparing and rehearsing your briefing.

- Decide ahead of time what you can leave out if the time for your presentation is shortened or you start to run over your time limit.

- Do not be afraid of pauses. They appear to the audience as though you are being thoughtful. Do not fill silence with distracting sounds or unnecessary movements.

- Make eye contact with your audience to establish rapport and assess whether they are attentive and getting the message. Look, but do not stare, directly at an individual on occasion. Try to complete a sentence before you shift your gaze.

- Speak clearly at a moderate pace in short, complete sentences. Avoid verbal trash, such as *ah-ah-ahhhhhhh*, *ummmmmmm*, or *ummmmmmm-ah* as well as sentence enders like "Correct?" or "OK?"

- Vary the pace, volume, and pitch of your voice. Avoid speaking in a low, slow monotone.

- Never apologize for anything connected with your presentation. If something goes wrong, keep your cool, correct the mistake, and move to the next point.

- Never read your briefing. We cannot emphasize this enough. You can read short quotations to ensure accuracy.

- Never make up an answer to a question. If you do not know, say so, make a note, and offer to provide an answer later (see Figure 19.4).

- Never put your hands in your pocket, rattle keys or money, play with your badge or the pointer, pace, or prance about.

Delivering on Digital and Interactive Devices

Digital technologies are fundamentally changing how analysis is disseminated and used by clients. A major transition is underway from delivering analysis by means of static, narrative-based formats to increasingly more dynamic, digitally based modes of presentation. Clients are increasingly seeking to access information through digital, interactive, and multimedia formats. Digitally based multimedia formats offer a

FIGURE 19.4 ■ Good Briefers Are Active Listeners

BE AN ACTIVE LISTENER DURING QUESTIONS AND ANSWERS

1. Acknowledge the speaker's concerns, strengths, feelings, and efforts.
2. Avoid rehearsing your next response while "listening."
3. Suspend judgment.
4. Paraphrase your understanding of the speaker's words.
5. Ask questions for clarification with genuine intent to learn.

dazzling array of options for communicating analytic judgments to decision makers in an effective and highly efficient manner.[7]

With digital delivery, the reader is no longer locked into a specific time to be briefed or to read an analytic product. He or she can vary the amount of time spent processing the information as well as the time of day and the location. Digitally based platforms also offer the opportunity to deliver information in multiple—and more data-rich—formats, such as video clips, infographics, interactive maps and charts, and simulations.

In the coming years, most consumers of analysis will be acquiring their information on mobile devices that allow them to read as little or as much as they want at a time and location of their choosing. Future products will be "user driven," layered with material that explains, defines, expands upon, and visually depicts what is written. This will require drafters to develop presentational tradecraft skills that focus on the following:

- How the analytic product looks (how well do the images convey the story?)

- How the product comes to the reader (what is the user's capacity to access the material?)

- How the product is organized or "unfolds" (is the bottom line up front and supported by solid data and logic?)

CREATE is a simple mnemonic that helps analysts conceptualize a product that takes full advantage of digital communications and the transition to more dynamic modes of content delivery (see Figure 19.5). By applying the basic principles of design

FIGURE 19.5 ■ CREATE: A Guiding Framework

C **Consumer**
Who would be interested in this story?

R **Relevance**
What angle or aspect of the story would resonate with this consumer or get this consumer's attention?

E **Enable the Decision**
How will this story provide insight and understanding to aid decision making?

A **Access**
How will the consumer access this story? In print, on the web, or on a tablet?

T **Time**
When should the consumer read this story? How much time does the consumer have to read this story?

E **Elements**
What elements will help imprint the mental image I want to communicate?

Source: Copyright 2020 Pherson Associates, LLC. All Rights Reserved.

and persuasion found in the CREATE model, analysts can make their products more reader friendly and memorable.

- *Client* refers to the need to have a specific client or customer set in mind for the product.

- *Relevance* spurs the analyst to ask if the needs of all the various clients have been addressed by the product.

- *Enable the Decision* refers to providing an understanding of the "Why" or the "So What" in a way that enables the client to take action.

- *Access* refers to knowing how the client best processes information—for example, if he or she prefers narrative to graphics or interactive exploration to more linear presentations.

- *Time* addresses when the consumer is most likely to read the product and how much time he or she can allot to processing the material.

- *Elements* refers to the kinds of visuals that would be most effective in conveying the story, such as a video, animation, imagery, charts, or a map.

Multimedia products offer the analyst the opportunity to incorporate images that will help make the story more "sticky," or memorable, by providing an image to help frame or illustrate the problem, animation to show exactly how a process is done, a video to capture the determination of the protesters, or an interactive graphic showing how quickly a lethal virus like H1N1 Swine flu, Ebola, or COVID-19 could spread worldwide. Multimedia products should always reflect the four principles of design: *proximity, alignment, contrast,* and *repetition.* The graphic should be placed close to the explanatory text, and the alignment of graphics should be consistent throughout the document or web page. Contrast should be employed to help make important facts or judgments stand out, and repeating similar images based on an overarching design theme can help the reader work his or her way through the presentation or know immediately how to get back to the home page.

KEY TAKEAWAYS

- A good thinker is a good writer. If an analyst has thought through the framework, the sources, and the argument, the writing will come easily.

- Analysts who find themselves struggling to craft a sentence or a paragraph probably do not have enough information or have not thought through their argument clearly.

- Good intelligence writers and journalists always put the bottom line up front (BLUF), presenting the most essential information first and the least important last.

- The title and lead paragraph of the article should tell the story, addressing both the "What" and the "So What."

- Each paragraph should begin with an analytic topic sentence and have one main point. Each section, paragraph, and sentence should move the story forward in a clear and direct way.

- The use of active voice is essential to writing compelling analysis. Passive voice sometimes cannot be avoided, particularly when writing about resources or technical issues, but should be used sparingly.

- A good briefing is built the same way as a well-written article; it has a clear message, develops a simple line of argument, and uses stories to illustrate the key points.

- The transition from delivering analysis by means of static, narrative-based formats to increasingly dynamic, digitally based modes of presentation is fundamentally changing how analysis is generated and consumed.

CONSIDERING THE CASE STUDY

Review Case Study IV, "The End of the Era of Aircraft Carriers."

- Does the title of the article effectively capture both the "What" and the "So What?"

- Is the article organized according to the Inverted Triangle model, which orders the analysis from the most important concept, thought, or idea to the least critical information?

- Do all the paragraphs begin with good topic sentences?

- Is the key message clearly stated?

- How well does the format—a What If? Analysis—work for communicating the basic message?

- What percentage of the sentences is in active voice? Should more sentences be in active voice? If so, which ones?

- If this case study were to be presented in digital format, what multimedia formats would be the most effective in conveying the key points of the analysis?

NOTES

1. The information used in this section was adopted from Pherson Associates training materials (www.pherson.org).

2. This model is represented by many in journalism and the US Intelligence Community as an Inverted Pyramid placing the most important things (specifically the topic sentence or key message of the paper) at the top of an upside-down pyramid. Others have found the image confusing, however, arguing that the supporting evidence should form the base of the pyramid as it provides the foundation for the analysis or the rationale for the topic sentence. Our preference is to use the image of a triangle to mirror how a paper is organized, reflecting the amount of space each section takes up, and then illustrating how this order can be inverted, thereby contrasting a data-driven organization of a paper with a message-driven approach.

3. When listing the five "Ws," the authors group What and How together because the answers often overlap. This order of the five Ws and How also closely resembles the organization of a declarative sentence with an actor, action, and consequence.

4. Independent clauses have subjects and predicates, which means they could stand on their own as a complete sentence.

5.   For a more robust discussion of how to conceptualize, organize, and deliver oral and digital presentations see Randolph H. Pherson, Walter Voskian, and Roy A. Sullivan Jr., *Analytic Briefing Guide* (Reston, VA: Pherson Associates, 2017).

6.   Alan J. Perlis, "Epigrams on Programming," *ACM SIGPLAN Notices* 17, no. 9 (September 1982): 7–13.

7.   Most of the information in this section is derived from the Introduction and Chapter 2 of Rubén Arcos and Randolph H. Pherson, eds., *Intelligence Communication in the Digital Era: Transforming Security, Defence and Business* (London: Palgrave Macmillan, 2015).

20 HOW DO I KNOW WHEN I AM FINISHED?

SETTING THE STAGE

All good analysts, good writers, and critical thinkers know they are not finished when the first draft is completed. The coordination and review process almost always takes far longer than it took to write the paper, but at least two other crucial steps must be taken before beginning the review process—substantive review, self-editing, and/or peer review. Your credibility rests on your ability to catch gaps in logic, unconvincing evidence, misspellings, errors in analysis, errors in fact, and poor grammar in your paper. No matter how solid your logic, your message will not be compelling if you cannot convey it with correct grammar and spelling (see Figure 20.1).[1]

Ideally you should take a day off and focus your mind on something else before going back to review and self-edit your product. Simply distancing yourself from your writing for a period of time will help you catch errors you might otherwise have missed. A good strategy is to ask a colleague, friend, or spouse to peer review your draft. The more important the topic and the more widely it will be distributed, the more critical it is to have others review your draft no matter how serious the time constraints. It is

FIGURE 20.1 ■ Stop! Self-Edit

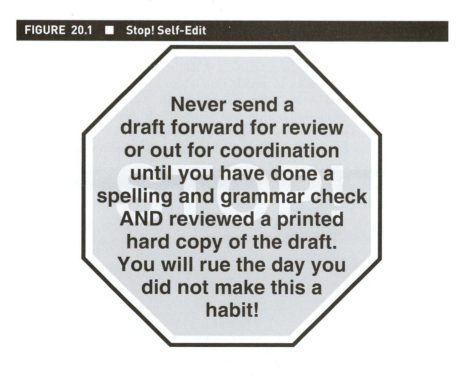

Never send a draft forward for review or out for coordination until you have done a spelling and grammar check AND reviewed a printed hard copy of the draft. You will rue the day you did not make this a habit!

always better to take a few minutes to find your mistakes than to have your boss or hundreds of other people discover them for you!

LOOKING MORE DEEPLY

Substantive Review

The premier techniques for conducting a substantive review of your product are the Premortem Analysis and the Structured Self-Critique, as described in Chapter 15 (see Figure 20.2).[2] Go back and review your key assumptions one more time to ensure that they remain well supported. The reason for this double check is that your thinking may have evolved since you first challenged your assumptions, or the situation has developed in ways that would require you to reassess a key assumption. A Deception Detection check should be done if the analysis is based on a single critical item of information or a stream of reporting from a single source. Finally, conduct a Red Hat Analysis by imagining yourself in the shoes of your client and reread the paper, asking yourself the following questions: "Does this paper satisfy my needs as a senior policymaker or decision maker?" and "What actions would I be likely to take after reading this product?"

Peer Review

Many organizations encourage—or even require—that a draft be peer reviewed before submitting it for formal review. In academia, most journal articles must undergo a rigorous peer-review process before qualifying for publication. Professors or other experts familiar with the topic of the paper will review a draft to ensure proper sourcing, defensible logic, and methodological rigor. In government and the private sector, peer review is most often conducted by colleagues working in the same office.

For peer review to be effective, reviewers should receive a list of instructions or tasks defining what is expected of them in examining the draft. Simply giving your colleague your draft and saying, "Tell me what you think," will often result in getting the draft back the next day with a sticky note saying, "Looks pretty good to me, but I found two typos you need to correct." Such a process only wastes everyone's time. A far better approach is to give peer reviewers the questions you expect them to answer

---

FIGURE 20.2 ■ SATs for a Final Check

WHAT STRUCTURED ANALYTIC TECHNIQUES APPLY?

Techniques you can use when conducting a final check on your analysis include the following:

- Premortem Analysis
- Structured Self-Critique
- Key Assumptions Check
- Deception Detection
- Red Hat Analysis
- Argument Mapping

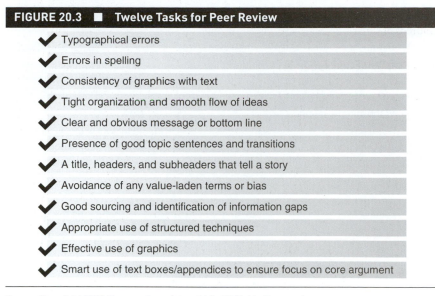

FIGURE 20.3 ■ Twelve Tasks for Peer Review

- ✔ Typographical errors
- ✔ Errors in spelling
- ✔ Consistency of graphics with text
- ✔ Tight organization and smooth flow of ideas
- ✔ Clear and obvious message or bottom line
- ✔ Presence of good topic sentences and transitions
- ✔ A title, headers, and subheaders that tell a story
- ✔ Avoidance of any value-laden terms or bias
- ✔ Good sourcing and identification of information gaps
- ✔ Appropriate use of structured techniques
- ✔ Effective use of graphics
- ✔ Smart use of text boxes/appendices to ensure focus on core argument

Source: Copyright 2020 Pherson Associates, LLC. All Rights Reserved.

or tasks you want them to perform. A list of potential tasks is provided in Figure 20.3. Ideally, drafters will pick three or four tasks on this list that they believe need attention or address the types of mistakes they know they have made in the past. Reviewers can then concentrate their efforts on those areas.

One obstacle analysts often encounter when seeking peer review is that colleagues in their work unit are reluctant to "criticize" their peers. The reluctance can stem from not wanting to be critical of a superior, the desire to avoid antagonizing a friend, or coming from a culture where offering direct criticism is frowned upon. One technique for overcoming this obstacle is to engage all the members of the unit in a brainstorming session to create a list of what tasks a good peer review can accomplish (similar to the list provided in Figure 20.3). Once consensus is reached on the key tasks a peer review can accomplish in their unit, it becomes much simpler to ask a peer to take on a few of the previously agreed-upon tasks in their review. This process also makes the work of the peer reviewer much easier as he or she knows what tasks are most important to focus on when conducting the review.

Editorial Review

We provide several checklists on the following pages for checking the quality of your presentation. You should pick one or two lists that work best for you or are most appropriate to the type of paper you have written. Analysts should plan ahead and carve out time for conducting reviews when constructing production schedules. Each of the checklists has strengths and weaknesses.

- *The Nine Principles of Analytic Writing* (Figure 20.4) apply to any type of written product.[3] If the author can master the application of these principles, the editing, coordination, and review process will greatly accelerate. For longer papers,

FIGURE 20.4 ■ The Nine Principles of Analytic Writing

1. **Determine the context and put conclusions first.**

   Determine the big picture and put the conclusions up front; begin with judgments or findings and then go on to support them. Your busy reader wants to know immediately what your point is.

2. **Know the client's needs.**

   Look at the message and ask yourself: "So What?" Clients look to you to provide insights, judgments that will help them make decisions, and warnings about matters that might require action. Writing serves readers best when it tells them both what they want to know and what they ought to know.

3. **Organize logically.**

   Present the conclusions in a logical and orderly way to avoid confusing the reader and causing unnecessary reiteration. Prepare an outline or draw a sketch to help you organize your ideas and identify any gaps in logic or flow.

4. **Understand formats.**

   Each publication has its own structural design that helps you organize your information. Understand the similarities and differences to develop speed and versatility in packaging the information.

5. **Use precise language.**

   Everyone who reads what you have written should come away with the same message. Choose words and expressions that convey *exactly* what you have in mind. The crucial test is not whether you understand what you have written but whether there is any possibility that the reader might misunderstand.

6. **Economize on words.**

   Strive to achieve brevity and succinctness. Make each word count. Keep sentences short to make the reader's job easier and to enable you to say as much as possible in the available space. Adopt a conversational tone. Avoid redundant language (e.g., *close confidant, unexpected surprise, in close proximity*) as well as rhetoric, colloquialisms, technical jargon, and vague abstractions.

7. **Strive for clarity of thought.**

   Remember that writing is thinking on paper. When the meaning of your writing is not clear, the thoughts behind the words may not be clear. Clarity is the *single most important goal* in writing. To achieve clarity, favor simplicity over complexity and use precise language instead of vague words. This means using short, familiar words. Use adjectives and adverbs sparingly to avoid diluting your judgments.

8. **Use active voice.**

   Use active, not passive, voice. Active voice makes your writing more direct, vigorous, and concise. Structure your sentences so that the subject performs an action and the object receives the action of the verb.

9. **Self-edit your writing and seek peer review.**

   Revising is an essential part of writing. Few writers produce a perfect first draft. Always self-edit your work and never turn in a paper that you have not reviewed in hard copy. Seek out peer review whenever possible; select one of the checklists provided in this book and ask the peer reviewers to use it when editing your paper.

FIGURE 20.5 ■   The Four Golden W Questions

Use the following questions as a review aid when writing a short paper:

1. ***What*** is going on?
   - A question that is often much harder to answer than it looks.

2. ***Why*** is it going on?
   - What are the forces or factors that are driving the issue?

3. ***What*** does it mean?
   - What are the implications of this?
   - How does it impact the policymaker or decision maker?
   - Does it present opportunities to exploit or dangers to avoid?

4. ***What*** can be done about it?
   - What options are available to the decision maker?
   - What leverage can be brought to bear on this issue?
   - What can one do and what will prevent others from acting (and vice versa)?

analysts should plan to take several hours or even a few days to assess whether the draft satisfies all the requirements on the checklist. The good news is that the time an analyst devotes to this task of self-editing will always pay dividends both in terms of reputation and time not lost in review and coordination.

- *The Four Golden W Questions* (Figure 20.5) are most useful when drafting short papers, particularly those that afford the analyst little time to compose the article.[4] They offer the best shoot-from-the-hip solution for exploring information gaps, conceptualizing an assessment, checking the analysis, and organizing the finished product. They parallel the way most people approach an issue, which makes them a great tool for organizing and crafting an easily digestible product. The list leaves out many potential traps while focusing on what is most essential in conveying the key message to the client.

The next three checklists can be used by either the drafter or by an editor—or preferably both.

- *The Evaluating Major Assessments Checklist* (Figure 20.6) provides a comprehensive list of questions that should be answered before disseminating a longer article or intelligence assessment.[5] The list of prepublication questions includes some that may apply in only certain circumstances. The set of postmortem questions is short but just as important.

- Most analysts and editors will recognize comments on the *When to Say No Checklist* (Figure 20.7) that they have thought or actually said out loud in the past.[6] The key is to resist the natural inclination to ignore these flags and send the article forward prematurely for editing or additional review. When tempted to do so, analysts and editors must honestly ask themselves if the paper meets the standards they have set for themselves and, if not, whether the deadline for the paper can be delayed. A delay offers the opportunity to either

FIGURE 20.6 ■ Evaluating Major Assessments Checklist

PREPUBLICATION QUESTIONS

1. Does the message provide specific value (the "So What") to the policymaker? Is the piece insightful, going beyond the obvious?

2. Is the piece relevant to decision maker interests or current concerns?

3. Is the key analytic message presented clearly and prominently? Is the message consistent throughout the piece (e.g., in the title, lead sentence, body, outlook, implications)?

4. Are the judgments supported by well-researched facts and logical reasoning?

5. Is confidence in the judgments clearly and explicitly stated?

6. Does the piece describe the sources and the analyst's level of confidence in them?

7. Does it cite key factors driving outcomes?

8. Does the piece explicitly identify and assess trends?

9. Does it assess what is likely to happen next and provide a clear statement of timing?

10. Is the message consistent with previous products?

11. Is the message new or does it run counter to a previous message?

12. Does the piece provide warning, if appropriate?

13. Does the piece explicitly identify key assumptions? Does it identify the consequences of an assumption being wrong?

14. Does the paper demonstrate a precision of language (i.e., grammar, structure, editing, word usage)?

15. Do the graphics carry the analytic message effectively?

16. Is the piece appropriately multidisciplinary?

If appropriate, does the piece achieve the following:

17. Assess key implications for the client?

18. Describe alternative outcomes and highlight the most likely ones?

19. Indicate opportunities for the consumer to exploit?

20. Identify key information gaps and unknowns?

21. Identify differing views on the key issues? Were any analytic differences presented clearly and prominently?

22. Acknowledge possible deception or disinformation efforts or previously discredited reporting?

POSTMORTEM QUESTIONS

1. Was the piece timely?

2. How did the client react to the piece?

3. Have the judgments proved accurate?

4. Have new forces, factors, or players emerged to change the analysis, and, if so, should the client be notified?

Source: Copyright 2020 Pherson Associates, LLC. All Rights Reserved.

FIGURE 20.7 ■ When to Say No Checklist

Do not send a paper forward for editing or further review if you hear yourself saying,

1. **The paper is probably good enough** . . . Deciding it is much better than when you first saw it, you focus on the improvements rather than the absolute quality standards it must meet.

2. **They can fix it up the line** . . . Passing it up the line so sharper minds at the next level(s) can fix it because you are unable to diagnose the problem or fix it.

3. **Just to be safe, I'd better add** . . . Throwing in more material so no reviewer can say it is not comprehensive. Or, adding a different or firmer analytic judgment so it will be more appealing to readers.

4. **I have reached my limit** . . . Sending the draft forward because you have run out of ideas or energy to attempt more changes—and the authors are at their limit too.

5. **The piece is due, so it is done** . . . Sending an unfinished piece forward, focusing on the imminence of the deadline rather than the quality of the paper.

6. **It is a bad piece, but it had to be coordinated** . . . Succumbing to—or not managing—the coordination process, which can introduce extraneous information or remove essential material.

7. **I need to fix this alone** . . . Not asking for help after editing successive drafts because it would be seen as a sign of weakness.

---

take more time to deal with the problems or to narrow the focus of the paper to avoid having to address the pitfalls you have encountered. And if all that fails, analysts should look to their colleagues and subordinates for help before sending the draft up the line for more senior scrutiny.

● An accomplished critical thinker will be finished only after completing the next—and final—checklist and answering all the questions in the affirmative with confidence. The *Critical Thinker's Checklist* (see inside front cover) provides a succinct but relatively comprehensive overview of what constitutes an excellent analytic product. If time is of the essence, this is the most important checklist to employ.

KEY TAKEAWAYS

- The biggest mistake most analysts make is not doing a careful self-edit in *hard copy* before turning in their drafts.

- Submitting a product with spelling or grammar mistakes marks the analyst as a sloppy thinker no matter how brilliant the analysis.

- For editors, the biggest mistake is failing to learn when to say no and to stop editing a troubled paper.

- It is a lot easier—and a lot faster—to catch and correct one's own mistakes than to process extensive reviewer comments.

- Seek out a peer reviewer and be explicit about the tasks you want him or her to perform.

- If an analyst establishes a reputation for delivering polished drafts, reviewers will give the analyst the benefit of the doubt, will look forward to getting drafts from the analyst, and will return them faster.

- If time is of the essence, an analyst should, at a minimum, complete the Critical Thinker's Checklist (see inside front cover) to double-check the work before it goes out the door.

CONSIDERING THE CASE STUDY

Review Case Study III, "Blackout on the Eastern Seaboard!"

- What potential vulnerabilities would a Structured Self-Critique of the case study reveal?

- How well does the article adhere to Figure 20.4, "The Nine Principles of Analytic Writing"?

- Would Figure 20.5, "The Four Golden W Questions," or Figure 20.6, the

"Evaluating Major Assessments Checklist," provide a more appropriate tool for self-editing this product? What flaws or weaknesses in the case study would use of either checklist reveal?

- What courses of action might the use of the "Critical Thinker's Checklist" (see inside front cover) suggest?

NOTES

1. See Louis M. Kaiser and Randolph H. Pherson, *Analytic Writing Guide* (Reston, VA: Pherson Associates, 2014) for some useful tips and pitfalls to avoid when writing and editing papers.

2. These techniques are described in more detail in Randolph H. Pherson and Richards J. Heuer Jr., *Structured Analytic Techniques for Intelligence Analysis*, 3rd ed. (Washington, DC: CQ Press/SAGE, 2021), 211–221.

3. The original list is found in *Analytic Thinking and Presentation for Intelligence Producers: Analysts Training Handbook* (Washington, DC: Central Intelligence Agency, Office of Training and Education, July 2000), 23–25, https://archive.org/details/CIA_Analytic_Thinking_and_Presentation_for_Intelligence_Analysis_Training_Handbo/page/n13/mode/2up. Versions have been used throughout the US . Intelligence

Community since 2000; the more compressed version of the list appearing in this book was prepared by Randolph H. Pherson in 2011 to serve a broader analytic community.

4. This list was taken from Pherson Associates training materials (www.pherson.org).

5. Various versions of this list have been used throughout the US Intelligence Community for many years; the list was revised by Randolph H. Pherson to serve a broader analytic community.

6. This list was originally developed by David Terry for use by US intelligence analysts and was subsequently refined and revised by Randolph H. Pherson to support broader applications of the list. A more detailed discussion of the list can be found in Walter Voskian and Randolph H. Pherson, *Analytic Production Guide* (Reston, VA: Pherson Associates, 2015).

CASE STUDIES

PART

V

UNCHARTED TERRITORY

Conflict, Competition, or Collaboration in the Arctic?

Rising temperatures and reduced sea ice are creating an uncertain future for the Arctic, an area of some 5.4 million square miles—almost one and a half times the size of the United States.[1] More than 4.2 million people live in the Arctic region (see Figure I.1). This number is projected to grow substantially in the coming years. Climatic shifts in the Arctic are not only spurring changes in demographics but in the demand for natural resources, transportation routes, and economic development.[2]

Armed conflict is not viewed as a serious possibility by most observers, but tensions are evident among the "Arctic Eight"—Russia, the United States, Norway, Sweden, Iceland, Finland, Canada, and Denmark (Greenland).[3] Russia, for example, has warned that countries could be at war within a decade over resources in the Arctic region.[4] The

FIGURE I.1 ■ Population in the Arctic Region (in Thousands)	
North American Arctic:	**769**
United States	649
Canada	120
European Arctic:	**1,339**
Denmark (Greenland/Faroe Islands)	107
Iceland	313
UK (Orkney Islands)	20
Norway	465
Sweden	250
Finland	184
Russian Arctic:	**2,058**
Murmansk Region	842
Yamalo-Nenets Autonomous Areas	588
Arkhangelsk Region	3
Vorkuta/Norilsk/Taimyr Districts	355
Yakutia	37
Magadan Region	163
Koryak/Chukotka Autonomous Areas	70

Source: Pherson Associates, LLC, 2016.

FIGURE I.2 ■ Arctic Eight Memberships

| International Maritime Organization (IMO) | UN Convention on the Law of the Sea (UNCLOS) Commission on the Limits of the Continental Shelf (CLCS) |

European Union (EU)

| Arctic Council (AC) | Barents Euro-Arctic Council (BEAC) |

Arctic Five (A5)

United States	Denmark	Finland
Canada	Norway Russia	Sweden
		Iceland

Arctic Council Observers:
9 international organizations and
12 nongovernmental organizations

China	The Netherlands
France	Poland
Germany	Singapore
India	South Korea
Italy	Spain
Japan	United Kingdom

Arctic Council Permanent Participants:
6 indigenous peoples' organizations

Source: Adapted from "The Arctic Council: Perspectives on a Changing Arctic, The Council's Work, and Key Challenges," Arctic Council, plenary meeting joint memorandum, Anchorage, Alaska, October 21–22, 2015, 3, https://oaarchive.arctic-council.org/bitstream/handle/11374/1527/EDOCS-2698-v1-ACSAOUS201_Anchorage_2015_10-1-1_Multilateral_Audit_Report.pdf?sequence=1&isAllowed=y.

dramatic changes coming to the Arctic, however, also offer major opportunities to develop mutually beneficial collaborative relationships to manage new challenges.

Canada, along with other neighboring Arctic countries, established the Arctic Council in 1996.[5] The council provides a neutral forum for the Arctic Eight to discuss emerging issues or problems that are occurring in the Arctic. China, along with eleven other nations, participates in Arctic Council meetings with permanent observer status (see Figure I.2). On May 12, 2011, at its seventh ministerial meeting, the member states of the Arctic Council signed the first legally binding agreement negotiated under the auspices of the council.[6] The purpose of the Agreement on Cooperation of Aeronautical and Maritime Search and Rescue in the Arctic is to strengthen search and rescue cooperation and coordination in the Arctic.

KEY DRIVERS

How the Arctic evolves over the next decade or so will be determined by a set of key drivers—defined as forces, factors, and events that will dictate how the region actually develops. In 2014, the Arctic Council launched the Adaptation Actions for a Changing Arctic (AACA) project "to assist local decision makers and stakeholders … in developing adaptation tools and strategies to better deal with climate change and other pertinent environmental stressors." The report identified two sets of drivers:

- **Global drivers** that focus on the wider context within which the Arctic is changing. How is the global economy expected to develop? What might the world's population be in 2050? How will global demand for mineral resources change over time? What are the expectations for future global demand for energy? These global factors come with large uncertainty, especially several decades out, yet they set the scene for dramatic change in the Arctic.

- **Arctic drivers** include the changing population of the Arctic region, shipping through Arctic waters, the activities of oil and gas companies, mining, Arctic tourism, and food security.[7]

Overlapping Legal Structures

Several international institutions are engaged in managing the affairs of the Arctic region. In addition to the Arctic Council, the Arctic Eight countries are members of several organizations that have ratified Arctic policies or are in the process of developing Arctic policies, including the United Nations (UN), North Atlantic Treaty Organization (NATO), European Union (EU), Barents Euro-Arctic Council (BEAC), International Maritime Organization (IMO), Commission on the Limits of the Continental Shelf (CLCS), and UN Convention on the Law of the Sea (UNCLOS). The variety of organizations and memberships offer the Arctic states flexibility in how they engage on the Arctic but also present challenges:

- The Arctic Five coastal states—Russia, United States, Norway, Canada, and Denmark (Greenland)—met in Ilulissat, Greenland, in 2008 and in Chelsea, Canada, in 2010. In 2015, they signed a "Declaration Concerning the Prevention of Unregulated High Seas Fishing in the Central Arctic Ocean" in Oslo, Norway.[8]

- The foreign ministers of the six members of the Barents Euro-Arctic Council (BEAC)—Russia, Norway, Sweden, Finland, Iceland, and Denmark (Greenland)—meet once a year. The BEAC was formed in 1993 to promote regional cooperation, secure political stability, and support sustainable development.[9]

- All the countries in the Arctic region belong to the International Maritime Organization (IMO), the United Nations' specialized agency responsible for improving maritime safety and preventing pollution from ships.[10]

- Russia is the only country with territory in the Arctic that is not a NATO member. This could complicate future efforts to peacefully resolve potential conflicts in the region.[11]

An international legal framework exists for governing economic use of the region based on global, customary international law codified in the UNCLOS. The convention obligates states to respond individually and jointly to the new challenges deriving from increasing economic activities.[12]

Norway is the only Arctic state to have defined the outer limits of its continental shelf in the Arctic Ocean. Russia, Canada, and Denmark (Greenland) have started the process of filing claims with the United Nations Commission on the Limits of the Continental Shelf (CLCS).[13] Since the United States has not ratified the Convention on the Law of the Sea, it cannot engage in the process to extend its jurisdiction into the Arctic Ocean.[14]

Although the Arctic countries have not defined their boundaries, they have agreed to recognize Exclusive Economic Zones (EEZs). EEZs allow for Arctic countries to operate 200 nautical miles off the country's coast. Each country has sovereign rights over the land, water column, seabed, and the subsoil in their EEZ. The bulk of oil and mineral resources in the Arctic are believed located in the EEZs.

Growing Access to Natural Resources

The melting of ice in the Arctic Ocean is gradually exposing natural resources to commercial exploitation.[15] Human activity, including shipping, mining, energy exploration, fishing, and tourism, has increased in the Arctic by almost 400 percent over the last decade.[16] The Arctic is estimated to contain about 90 billion barrels of oil, or potentially 13 percent of the world's oil reserves (see Figure I.3). About 41 percent of this oil is projected to be in the Russian Arctic Zone (RAZ). The RAZ is also estimated to contain over one quadrillion cubic feet of undiscovered natural gas—or some 70 percent of all Arctic natural gas.[17]

Potential Upswing in Commercial Fishing

The impact of climate change on commercial fishing in the Arctic Ocean is still unknown. In the high seas of the north, fishing is legal only in the EEZs of the Arctic countries. As ocean temperatures rise, fish are projected to migrate north because of the colder temperatures. On July 16, 2015, the Arctic Five signed the Declaration to

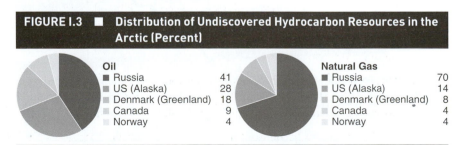

FIGURE I.3 ■ Distribution of Undiscovered Hydrocarbon Resources in the Arctic (Percent)

Oil

■ Russia	41
■ US (Alaska)	28
■ Denmark (Greenland)	18
■ Canada	9
■ Norway	4

Natural Gas

■ Russia	70
■ US (Alaska)	14
■ Denmark (Greenland)	8
■ Canada	4
■ Norway	4

Source: United States Coast Guard Arctic Strategic Outlook (April 2019), https://www.uscg.mil/ Portals/0/Images/arctic/Arctic_Strategic_Outlook_APR_2019.pdf.

Prevent Unregulated Fishing in the Central Arctic Ocean.[18] The declaration acknowledges that "the dramatic reduction of Arctic sea ice and other environmental changes in the Arctic, combined with the limited scientific knowledge about marine resources in this area, necessitate a precautionary approach to prevent unregulated fishing in the area."[19]

Climate change, ocean acidification, and the subsequent changes in marine productivity are likely to affect not only fisheries, but eventually the whole economy in the Arctic. A 2014 study of the effect of carbon dioxide (CO_2) emissions on the economics of marine fishing in the Arctic projects that total Arctic fisheries revenue will increase between 14 and 59 percent by 2050, relative to 2000. Simultaneously, total fishing costs, fishers' incomes, household incomes, and economy-wide impacts in the Arctic are projected to increase. Ocean acidification, however, is expected to reduce potential increases in catch and economic activity. Although the projections suggest that Arctic countries are likely to be "winners" under climate change, in comparison with tropical developing countries, the effects of ocean acidification will lower the expected future benefits in the Arctic.[20]

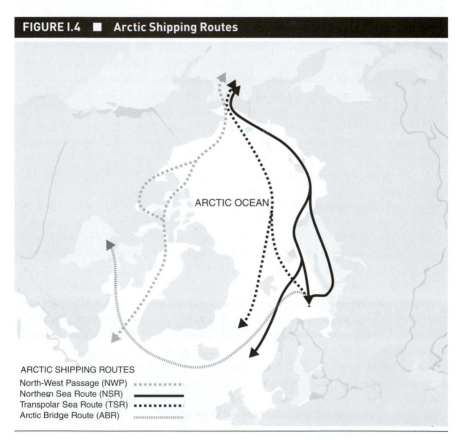

FIGURE I.4 ■ Arctic Shipping Routes

ARCTIC OCEAN

ARCTIC SHIPPING ROUTES
North-West Passage (NWP)
Northern Sea Route (NSR)
Transpolar Sea Route (TSR)
Arctic Bridge Route (ABR)

Source: Adapted from Malte Humpert, The Arctic Institute, Washington, D.C.

New Commercial Shipping Routes

Over the last thirty years, the average extent of decline of sea ice covering the North Pole has been 15 to 20 percent.[21] The Arctic is warming twice as fast as the global average, making climate change's polar effects more intense than anywhere else in the world. Scientists project that the North Pole will see completely ice-free summers by 2030. The melting is making commercial shipping in Arctic waters increasingly possible.[22] By 2030 to 2050, the melting of ice in the Arctic will allow permanent sea passages to open in the Northwest Passage (NWP) and the Northern Sea Route (NSR) (see Figure I.4).[23]

Experts expect that Iceland and Greenland will emerge as major shipping hubs for Arctic Sea routes in the future. If both passages become accessible year-round, cargo could be moved from the Atlantic to the Pacific approximately 40 percent faster than through the Suez Canal.[24] The probability of these routes becoming busier has galvanized Arctic states to improve infrastructure for handling greater maritime traffic.[25]

Countries that do not have territory in the Arctic are also interested in taking advantage of the opportunities presented by melting sea ice. In 2015, China's Ministry of Transport published a paper reflecting growing Chinese interest in using shipping lanes in the NWP and NSR to support economic development.[26]

KEY ROUTES

The Northwest Passage (NWP)

The Arctic waterway surrounding North America is shared by the United States and Canada. This sea route is considered an "international strait" that allows any nation or company unrestricted access. The United States could use the NWP as an alternative to the Panama Canal. However, the NWP is currently frozen for most of the year. If freighters pass through the waterway now, they must be escorted by icebreakers.

The Bering Strait is a natural chokepoint connecting the NWP and the Pacific Ocean. The Strait is relatively narrow and shallow (less than 200 feet deep) with only 60 miles separating Russia from the United States.[27] The strait region is warming more rapidly on average than the rest of the globe, with the largest temperature increases occurring during fall and early winter.

As of 2016, the largest ship to make the passage through the NWP was a luxury cruise ship, the *Crystal Serenity*. The cruise line charged $21,855 per person for the transit. The voyage began on August 15 in Alaska and ended on September 16 in New York, taking thirty-two days. As a condition of travel, the United States and Canada required the cruise ship to be escorted by two helicopters and one icebreaker.[28]

In 1990, the United States and Russia signed the USA-USSR Maritime Boundary Agreement, which confirmed the maritime boundary agreement established by the 1867 convention line.[29] Under this agreement, all mandates of international law apply to the strait. Ships can pass through the waterway without requesting permission from Russia or the United States. Russia, in particular, is interested in shipping cargo through the strait and across the Northern Sea Route (NSR).[30]

The Northern Sea Route (NSR)

Most experts agree that passage through the NSR offers greater commercial advantages than the NWP. During the Cold War, the Soviet Union invested considerable research and development to build infrastructure for the NSR. After the collapse of the Soviet Union, Russia's investment in the NSR declined, but it began rebuilding its Arctic infrastructure a few years ago.

Basic infrastructure is much more developed in the NSR than in the NWP. The infrastructure spans 3,000 miles of Russia's Arctic waterway and includes fifteen seaports from Murmansk to Provideniya. The NSR has a unique advantage because commercial traffic flows north along inland waterways to feed it. By 2030, the Russian government predicts that 80 million tons of freight will pass through the NSR annually.[31] If this prediction proves accurate, the NSR would rival the Suez Canal in total tonnage. However, in 2015 only eighteen ships made the passage, ten of which were registered to Russia.[32]

The Arctic Bridge Route (ABR)

With the retreat of Arctic ice, Russia is showing interest in developing the ABR because it could provide a major shipping route linking Europe to North America. As of 2016, the route was navigable only four months of the year but will become more accessible as the global climate warms. The Arctic Bridge is currently a seasonal sea route approximately 4,200 miles in length connecting the Russian port of Murmansk to the Hudson Bay port of Churchill, Manitoba, in Canada. Churchill is the principal seaport on Canada's northern coast and has rail and air (but no road) connections to the rest of Canada. The port of Murmansk on the ice-free Kola Bay has rail connections to St. Petersburg and the rest of Europe. Murmansk is also linked by road to the rest of Russia.[33]

The Transpolar Sea Route (TSR)

The TSR is the most direct route for transshipments across the top of the world from Russia to Canada, traversing the North Pole. It has yet to attract significant commercial interest because multiyear ice remains a formidable obstacle for most of the Arctic shipping season.[34] Commercial shippers do not anticipate they can use the TSR until the summer of 2030.[35]

KEY PLAYERS

Russia: An Emerging Dominant Presence

Russia undoubtedly has the most to gain from a rapid melting of Arctic ice. The Arctic region is home to over two million Russians; the three largest populated areas are Murmansk, Norilsk, and Vorkuta.[36] This is the largest Arctic population that lives year-round in this frigid environment.

Russian president Vladimir Putin has stated that Russia will "maintain the role of a leading Arctic power."[37] His rhetoric suggests that Russian security and sovereignty will be well defended. Russia has forty icebreakers and eleven under construction (see Figure I.5). Several super ice breakers will be added to the fleet that can break through Arctic ice year around, allowing them to escort European and Asian freighters along the Northern Sea Route. Russia's nuclear icebreakers, which account for 25 percent of its fleet, are operated out of Murmansk, the largest deepwater port in the Arctic. A nuclear icebreaker can cut through ice ten feet in depth.

FIGURE I.5   ■   Arctic Icebreakers

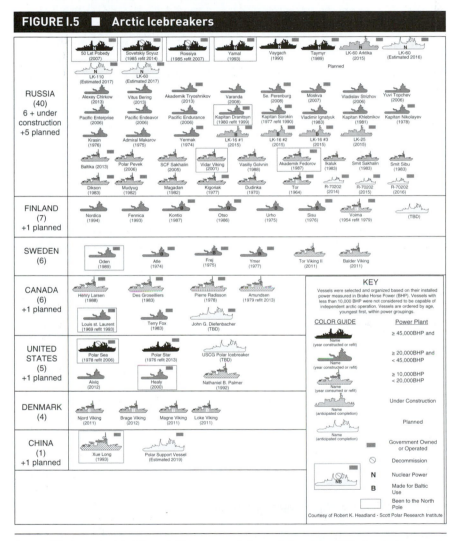

Source: US Coast Guard, Office of Waterway and Ocean Policy data, 2017. An electronic copy of the chart is located at https://www.dco.uscg.mil/Portals/9/DCO%20Documents/Office%20 of%20Waterways%20and%20Ocean%20Policy/20170501%20major%20icebreaker%20chart .pdf?ver=2017-06-08-091723-907.

Russia is developing capabilities to guard its territory and protect its economic interests. Since 2007, Russia has focused on significantly developing resources and military capabilities in the region.[38]

Modernization of its fleet by 2020 is a top priority for the Russian government. Russia's Northern Fleet is located in the Arctic coastal city of Severomorsk. In 2015, Russia conducted fleet exercises that involved 45,000 troops, 41 ships, and 110 aircraft.[39] Russia's submarine forces include nine nuclear-powered ballistic missile submarines (SSBNs); four nuclear-powered guided-missile submarines (SSGNs); thirteen nuclear-powered submarines (SSNs); and seven diesel-electric submarines (SSKs).

In February 2013, President Putin approved Russia's Strategy for the Development of the Arctic Zone, which "aims to implement the sovereignty and national interests of the Russian Federation in the Arctic and contributes to the missions of the state policy of the Russian Federation."[40] The strategy calls for increasing Russia's presence in the Arctic and boosting the region's development by 2020.[41] Russia now has eighteen fully operating bases along its Arctic coastline (see Figure I.6).[42,43]

Russia's claims that the Lomonosov Ridge is part of the Russian continental shelf is a key element of its economic strategy. If the claim were accepted internationally, this would allow Russia to expand its EEZ to the North Pole, nearly doubling the Russian Arctic Zone (RAZ). The claim, however, has not been recognized by other Arctic states. This has not stopped Russia from claiming new areas outside the RAZ. Russia is particularly interested in the potential for exploiting oil, gas, and other mineral

FIGURE I.6 ■ Russia's Militarization of the Arctic

Source: Adapted from multiple sources.

reserves in the Arctic. In 2007, Russia planted a flag under the Arctic ice cap outside its 200 nautical mile limit.

United States: Unfocused and Under-Resourced

The US Department of Defense Arctic Policy states that US national security interests in the Arctic region include "missile defense and early warning; deployment of sea and air systems for strategic sealift, strategic deterrence, maritime presence, and maritime security operations; and ensuring freedom of the seas."[44] In support of this policy, the North American Aerospace Defense Command (NORAD) and US Northern Command (USNORTHCOM) have created an Arctic security framework for keeping the Arctic safe and secure.[45]

The US Navy and the US Coast Guard, however, can muster far fewer resources than Russia in the Arctic region. The United States has only nine military bases in Alaska and Greenland:

- In Alaska, the United States Command (ALCOM) consists of 16,000 regular personnel and 3,700 National Guard and reserve personnel.[46] The US Navy conducts training operations in the Arctic. In March 2016, it deployed two submarines in a five-week training exercise called ICEX.[47]

- In Greenland, Thule Air Base was an active US military base during the Cold War and has the northernmost deepwater port in the world. Thule's mission is to use its global network of sensors to provide warning of missile attack, space surveillance, and space control to NORAD and Air Force Space Command.[48]

The US Navy has described the Arctic as a "low security threat," focusing most of its attention on building partnerships, supporting search and rescue, and scientific research. The *U.S. Navy Article Roadmap 2014–2030* states that "due to the successful policy between Arctic Region Nations—such as the Russia-Norway Barents Sea Agreement—there can be a peaceful use of the Arctic without military force."[49]

The United States has limited infrastructure in the region, lacks a joint military base, and has no heavy icebreaker assets (see Figure I.7).[50] The Pentagon recognized this lack of infrastructure and programmed up to $6 billion for research and development in the fiscal year 2017.[51] The Pentagon's objectives were to bolster US capabilities by providing sailors with the equipment and Arctic technology platforms they need to obtain situational awareness to operate in the Arctic.

The United States Coast Guard has a small Arctic fleet of four icebreakers, consisting of one large icebreaker, the *Polar Star,* and three smaller ones, the *Avig, Healy,* and *Nathaniel B. Palmer.*[52] The *Polar Star* was built in 1976 and is under almost constant repair. The US Coast Guard plans to build only one more icebreaker, the *Polar Sea*; it is proposing to lease icebreakers from private American and Canadian companies to meet anticipated demand.[53]

The apparent US–Russia "icebreaker gap" has spurred some US security experts to urge policymakers and Congress to invest in building more icebreakers.

FIGURE I.7 ■ Russian, United States, and NATO Armed Forces in the Arctic

Russian Armed Forces in the Arctic	USSR in 1980s	Russia in 2010s
Submarines	172	30
SSBNs	39	7
SSBNs in permanent patrol	10–12 (607 in Arctic)	1–2
Aircraft carriers	2	1
Larger ships	74	17
Auxiliary vessels	200	33
Aircraft	400	100
Helicopters	--	40

US and NATO Armed Forces Capable to Operate in the Arctic	US in 1980s	US in 2010s	NATO in 2010s
Submarines	78	33	85
SSBNs	28	6	8
SSBNs in permanent patrol	--	6-8	--
Submarines armed with cruise missile Tomahawks	--	39	--
Aircraft carriers	7	4	6
Larger ships	90	49	100
Ships (Aircraft for landing troops)	24	14	--
Aircraft	700	360	200

Source: Adapted from A. Arbatov, "The Arctic and Strategic Stability," in *The Arctic: Zone of Peace and Cooperation,* ed. A. Zagorski (Moscow: Institute of World Economy and International Relations, Russian Academy of Sciences, 2011), 65–67 (in Russian).

Other experts believe the United States is too far behind Russia's icebreaker capabilities and that future funding should be allocated to more critical US security needs.

Norway: Focused on the Future

Norway has direct access to the Arctic Ocean and is investing heavily in the Arctic and the Barents Sea. It has a population of 5 million with 464,000 living inside the Arctic Circle. Foreign Minister Børge Brende described the Arctic as Norway's most important foreign policy priority. He noted that many countries, including Norway,

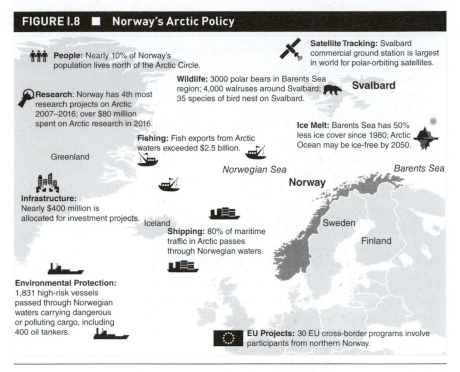

FIGURE I.8 ■ Norway's Arctic Policy

People: Nearly 10% of Norway's population lives north of the Arctic Circle.

Satellite Tracking: Svalbard commercial ground station is largest in world for polar-orbiting satellites.

Research: Norway has 4th most research projects on Arctic 2007–2016; over $80 million spent on Arctic research in 2016.

Wildlife: 3000 polar bears in Barents Sea region; 4,000 walruses around Svalbard; 35 species of bird nest on Svalbard.

Svalbard

Fishing: Fish exports from Arctic waters exceeded $2.5 billion.

Ice Melt: Barents Sea has 50% less ice cover since 1980; Arctic Ocean may be ice-free by 2050.

Greenland

Norwegian Sea

Barents Sea

Norway

Infrastructure: Nearly $400 million is allocated for investment projects.

Iceland

Sweden

Shipping: 80% of maritime traffic in Arctic passes through Norwegian waters.

Finland

Environmental Protection: 1,831 high-risk vessels passed through Norwegian waters carrying dangerous or polluting cargo, including 400 oil tankers.

EU Projects: 30 EU cross-border programs involve participants from northern Norway.

Source: Adapted from "Norway's Arctic Strategy: Between Geopolitics and Social Development," Norwegian Government. 2017, pp. 1–40. Accessed on February 6, 2020.

are looking to the north where new opportunities are opening up and significant challenges need to be met (see Figure I.8).[54]

The Norwegian government has been bolstering its security with large training exercises in the north involving other NATO members and partners.[55] The army has an active military force of 25,800 personnel.[56] In 2016, Norway hosted the first joint training operation involving thirteen nations with 13,800 troops,[57] including 3,000 from the US Army, 6,500 from the Norwegian Armed Forces, and 4,000 troops from eleven allied nations (Great Britain, Germany, the Netherlands, Sweden, Poland, Denmark, Canada, Belgium, France, Latvia, and Spain) as well as some 300 NATO support personnel. In 2018, Norway hosted Exercise Trident Juncture to test NATO's cyber defenses and its ability to operate in cold climates.[58] The exercise involved 50,000 participants from NATO and partner countries, 250 aircraft, and 65 ships.

Norway believes the Arctic ice melt will present new opportunities for economic growth. Eighty percent of Norway's maritime area lies north of the Arctic Circle, and Norwegians control the sixth-largest merchant fleet in the world.[59] Narvik, for example, has great potential as a port city for shipping materials through the NSR. When the Norwegian Ministry of Foreign Affairs published its *Arctic 2030* plan, it said, "The government will give priority to the following five areas: international cooperation, the development of a knowledge-based business sector, knowledge development, infrastructure, and emergency preparedness and environmental protection."[60]

Melting sea ice could significantly expand Norwegian exports of oil, gas, and fish products. The top three Norwegian exports in 2014 were crude petroleum ($45.1

billion), petroleum gas ($43.6 billion), refined petroleum ($6.56 billion), and non-fillet fresh fish ($4.9 billion).[61] The government has begun a dialogue with oil companies to explore whether the oil reserves previously unavailable can be exploited in the future as the ice melts. Norway is partnering with Russia, for example, to gain access to oil reserves in the Barents Sea and the Arctic Ocean. On September 15, 2010, Norway and Russia signed a treaty in Murmansk on Maritime Delimitation and Cooperation in the Barents Sea and the Arctic Ocean.[62]

The Barents Sea appears to be the most accessible, and presumably the least costly, to explore and exploit. According to the US Geological Service, the Barents Sea shelf off Russia and Norway may contain about 11 billion barrels of undiscovered oil as well as 11 trillion cubic meters of undiscovered natural gas."[63]

The quota on the amount of cod that can be taken per year from the Barents Sea was set at 1,000,000 kilos in 2014.[64] This and other fishing quotas may expand as cod and other fish species increasingly migrate north due to the global warming of the oceans.

Iceland: Potential Shipping and Fishing Hub

Iceland, with a population of more than 340,000 in 2020, is located strategically between Europe and Greenland.[65] The island has twenty-six ports that would give it a significant advantage as a potential mega shipping hub when commercial traffic begins to flow through the NWP and NSR. In March 2011, Iceland's parliament launched its Arctic Policy focusing on "climate change, environmental issues, natural resources, navigation, and social development as well as strengthening relations and cooperation with other states and stakeholders on the issues facing the region."[66]

Officials are especially concerned about the impact of climate change on the commercial fishing industry.[67] Exports of fish fillets ($976 million annually) and non-fillet frozen fish ($449 million) are two of its three leading sources of trade revenue, exceeded only by raw aluminum ($1.87 billion).[68]

Rising ocean temperatures can change the migration patterns of fishing stock and spawning grounds, but Icelandic scientists have yet to determine the specific effects on the fishing industry. In 2013, at a global forum on the Arctic Circle in Washington, D.C., Icelandic president Olafur Ragnar Grimsson said "countries beyond the polar region deserved a say in determining the future of the far north."[69]

In 2016, Icelandic diplomats spent a week in Murmansk discussing Iceland's plans for the Arctic.[70] They introduced companies specializing in fishery equipment and services and were briefed by the Russians on tourism opportunities in Murmansk.[71]

Iceland and the United States have longstanding diplomatic ties dating back to the establishment of NATO in 1949.[72] NATO allies are responsible for the defense of the island because Iceland does not have a standing military and cannot defend its borders or airspace.[73] Iceland and the United States entered into a defense cooperation agreement in June 2016 that allows US forces to use Icelandic facilities and commits the United States to maintaining a "resilient" defense plan for the island.[74]

Iceland has become concerned by the potential security threat posed by Russia. On September 22, 2016, three Russian bombers, without announcing or asking for permission, entered Icelandic airspace.[75] These bombers then flew dangerously close to an Icelandic passenger jet. In 2016, the US Navy asked the Department of Defense for funds to repair a former base located in Keflavik. This base had previously been occupied by US forces during the Cold War.[76]

Icelandic relations with China have grown substantially in recent years, involving shipping, trade, oil, and scientific research. In 2012, the Chinese icebreaker *Xue Long* (Snow Dragon) visited Iceland transiting the NSR.[77] The voyage was the first effort by a non-polar icebreaker to transit the Arctic.[78] The *Xue Long* stayed in Iceland for four days and then returned to Shanghai where the Polar Research Institute of China (PRIC) is located.[79] The PRIC is responsible for conducting all Arctic research for China.

In 2013, the director of the PRIC, Huigen Yang, met with Iceland's Minister of Foreign Affairs, Össur Skarphéðinsson.[80] They discussed the future of shipping in the NSR. In those meetings, Yang projected that as much as 10 percent of Chinese cargo destined for Europe—worth about $37 billion annually—could make the transit through the NSR.[81] Iceland has also allowed the China National Offshore Oil Company to explore the waters of Iceland for oil reserves. In 2013, China entered into a free trade agreement with Iceland, its first with a western European state.[82]

Sweden: An Established Presence

Sweden has made it clear that its vision for the future is to focus attention on the environmental, economic, and human dimensions of climate change while striving to keep political tensions low.[83] Approximately 250,000 of Sweden's 9 million people live in a land-locked region inside the Arctic Circle. Sweden does not have access to the Arctic Ocean and relies on Norwegian ports for access. For example, it ships iron ore from the port of Narvik in Norway to the global market.

The Swedish government participates with NATO members and other partners in security exercises, but Sweden is not a member of NATO.[84] It has an active Partnership for Peace relationship with NATO based on a policy of nonmilitary alignment that was established in 1994.[85]

Heightened concerns about Russian military activities in Crimea and its intentions in the Baltic have spurred NATO to step up cooperation with Sweden and Finland in the Baltic region.[86] The Russian incursion into Crimea, in particular, spurred Sweden to establish a new security policy in 2015, redirecting its security focus to the Baltic Sea region.[87]

Sweden's defense posture is built around the concept of total defense, or *totalförsvaret*, which maintains that all Swedish citizens have a responsibility to defend Sweden.[88] The Swedish military has 52,000 full-time personnel, including an Arctic special forces group known as the Lapland Ranger Regiment.[89] These forces operate and train in subzero climates in northern Sweden. Arctic training consists of Arctic survival skills, long-range patrols, and long-distance raids.[90]

Sweden has the second-largest fleet of icebreakers that operate in the Arctic. It has seven icebreakers, one of which is on long-term charter from a private ship owner. The fleet is used to escort ships in the Arctic Ocean and Baltic Sea. Swedish icebreaker services earn Sweden 20 to 40 million euros annually, depending on the winters' severity.[91]

Sweden has been conducting research in the Arctic for almost one and a half centuries. The icebreaker *Oden* is used to escort ships and to carry out the research.[92] In 1991, *Oden* was the first non-nuclear icebreaker to voyage to the North Pole successfully.[93] Diesel-powered icebreakers are better equipped for Arctic research, although nuclear icebreakers are stronger. *Oden* also supported the Canadian government in establishing its Arctic Sea continental shelf claims.[94]

Sweden and Norway are often cited as sharing Europe's longest, oldest, and most peaceful border, reflecting their long history of strong economic and diplomatic ties. Sweden, Norway, Finland, and Northwest Russia also share deep cultural ties as a result of the Sami indigenous population. The Sami, numbering some 70,000 to 100,000, have migrated across Sweden, Finland, Norway, and Russia for thousands of years.[95]

Finland: A Minor Player

Finland has no coastline on the Arctic Ocean. It shares borders with Sweden and Norway, but its longest border is with Russia. Finland has a population of some 5 million people with 184,000 living inside the Arctic Circle, mostly in Lapland. Finland regards the Arctic Council as the most important cooperation forum on Arctic matters.[96]

Finland's Arctic strategy is focused on improving the region's security, environment, economy, infrastructure, and protecting the Sami indigenous peoples. Finland's top exports in 2014 were refined petroleum ($7.6 billion), kaolin coated paper ($5.73 billion) and large flat-rolled stainless steel ($3.36 billion).[97]

Finland is not a member of NATO but has had a Partnership for Peace relationship with that organization since 1994.[98] In 2016, it hosted the forty-fourth multination training operation BALTOPS.[99] The training exercise involved roughly 6,100 maritime, ground, and air force troops.[100] The training exercise took place throughout the Baltic nations. Finland's involvement with NATO, however, has been a longstanding point of friction for Finnish–Russian relations.[101]

Finland has a fleet of seven icebreakers, but most of their icebreakers operate in the Baltic Sea and are not properly equipped to function in the Arctic Ocean.[102] Finland is constructing a new "state of the art" icebreaker that will operate in the Baltic Sea year around.

Canada: Building Capacity

Canada's key security objectives in the Arctic are to protect the sovereignty of indigenous populations, maintain control over its resources, avoid trade vulnerabilities, and preserve jobs for Canadians. More than 100,000 Canadians live above the Arctic Circle.[103] Its vision for the Arctic is "a stable, rules-based region with clearly defined boundaries, dynamic economic growth and trade, vibrant Northern communities, and healthy and productive ecosystems."[104]

Canada and the United States are bound by a bilateral security agreement known as the North American Aerospace Defense Command (NORAD). NORAD was originally established to protect North America from nuclear missile attacks from the Soviet Union. Canada's NORAD contributions are Canadian Armed Forces serving in NORAD-related activities in the United States and Canada. It also has fighter aircraft on alert status that maintain daily operations.[105] If the Arctic becomes a combat zone, the United States has a security obligation to protect and defend Canada's sovereignty.

Canada's Parliament recognizes that the melting ice environment in the Arctic could pose new security threats. For the past fifteen years, Canadian security forces have been rebuilding their military capabilities and presence in the Arctic on land, sea, and air.[106] More recently, the growing Russian presence has served as a catalyst for Canada to reestablish its military presence. The Royal Canadian Army, Navy, and Coast Guard have taken several actions to protect Canadian sovereignty in the Arctic as well as in the EEZ.

- The Canadians have invested in new ships, airplanes, and satellites.

- The Canadian Coast Guard has built an Arctic fleet of fifteen ships (two heavy icebreakers, four medium icebreakers, and nine multipurpose vessels) and two hovercrafts.

- The Royal Canadian Navy is building six offshore patrol vessels ships that can operate in the Arctic. This small fleet has smart capabilities that will give the navy real-time situational awareness in the region.

- The army has strengthened its northern operating ground forces, the Canadian Rangers. The rangers, estimated at 1,850 members, maintain patrols from sixty locations spanning all three northern territories.[107]

- The army is also developing powerful winterized vehicles to give the Rangers greater Arctic combat effectiveness to operate in these cold conditions. The Arctic Light Over Snow Vehicle (ALOS) can patrol in temperatures of –40 degrees Fahrenheit.[108]

Denmark (Greenland): Strategically Positioned

Denmark has maintained control over Greenland for nearly 300 years. Greenland occupies the twelfth-largest land mass in the world, but it has a population of only 58,000. Denmark's colonization of Greenland dates as far back as the year 1775, but over the last few decades Greenland has been seeking to become fully independent.

Denmark has given Greenland more autonomy over domestic policy in recent years, culminating in the Self-Government Act of 2009.[109] As a consequence of this act, the people of Greenland have taken more control over government, and Greenlandic was made the official language of Greenland. Denmark, however, retains control over Greenland's foreign and defense policy and represents it in multination organizations such as the United Nations and the Arctic Council.[110]

Greenland is now entering a period of rapid social transformation, due in equal parts to climate change and the need to acquire funds to support economic and political independence from Denmark.[111] The dominant feature in Greenland's geography is its rapidly melting freshwater central ice sheet, which covers about 1.7 million square kilometers or 80 percent of the island, with an average thickness of 2.1 kilometers.

The melting of the Greenland ice sheet and the erosion of its coastline are exposing rare minerals and allowing greater oil exploration (see Figure I.9).[112]

FIGURE I.9 ■ Greenland's Mineral and Oil Resources

Measured Benefits of Mineral and Oil Extraction

Resource	Calculated Raw Quantity	Calculated Pure Quantity	Unit Value ($)	Total Value ($)	Tax Rate (%)	Greenland's Revenue ($)
Oil	31 billion barrels	31 billion barrels	46–100 ($/barrel) (15-year range)	1.4–3.1 trillion	.53	742 billion–1.643 trillion
Iron	2.3–2.7 billion tons	1.5 billion tons	52.74 ($/ton)	110.754–142.398 billion	.37–42	40.97–59.7 billion
Zinc	133.1 million tons	5.621 million tons	1,724.34 ($/gram)	9.69 billion	.37–42	3.58–4.069 billion
Gold	1.67 million tons	30.06 million grams	372.43 ($/gram)	1.521 billion	.37–42	562.77–638.82 million
Lead	133.1 million tons	735,500 tons	1,720.11 (monthly average)	1.27 billion	.37–42	46.9–533.4 million

Greenland's Total Tax Revenues From Minerals: $742 billion to $1.643 trillion

Source: Adapted from Zachary Abbott, *Natural Resources and Economic Power: The Development-Security Nexus of Greenland* (Carlisle, Pennsylvania: Dickinson College, 2016), 8, https://scholar.dickinson.edu/cgi/viewcontent.cgi?article=1045&context=student_work.

Greenlanders expect the ice melt will allow year-round access to valuable minerals such as gold, zinc, copper, diamonds, platinum, rubies, titanium, and uranium. A rush to mine these minerals could create a major economic boom with a projected value ranging from $742 billion to $1.643 trillion.[113]

The growing accessibility of minerals, however, has stirred debate among Greenlandic politicians over whether the rare earth minerals should be mined. Part of that debate focuses on what role foreign companies should play in extracting these minerals. In 2012, Greenland's parliament passed the Large Scale Act of 2012 that allowed foreign companies to build mines and import cheap foreign labor.[114] Concerns were raised, however, that this would result in a surge of migrants. Former prime minister of Greenland Aleqa Hammond spoke against the bill, stating that "foreign companies should not run off with Greenland's riches, but Greenland should gain from the resources starting day one." She specifically criticized the hiring of Chinese workers.[115]

A year later, the bill was amended to mandate foreign companies to hire Greenlandic workers. The amendment also called for reliance on Greenlandic companies as much as possible.[116] What remains to be seen is what influence foreign companies—particularly those representing Chinese interests—will have in shaping the commercial and political environment in Greenland.

China: A Potential Disrupter

China's approach to the Arctic can be characterized by a strategy of buying into Arctic-related projects and participating in diplomatic organizations such as the Arctic Council.[117] In 2013, China was granted permanent observer status in the Arctic Council. A permanent observer cannot vote but can attend council meetings, submit proposals, and participate in policy discussions. China also is gaining influence through diplomatic relations with the Nordic nations, buttressed by foreign investments, mostly in Greenland.

Former US under secretary of state Thomas Pickering has expressed concern that China's activities have diminished US influence in Greenland and Iceland. "The Chinese government has sought to win political support from the Greenland government in a quiet fashion, using its economic power, patience, and long-term perspective as major leverage."[118]

Some Chinese foreign policy experts believe that president Xi Jinping is expanding the country's foreign policy interests in the Arctic in accordance with China's "One Belt One Road" initiative. The "One Belt One Road" initiative is intended to connect regions from all over the world by building highways, railroads, ports, and shipping lanes. Greenland and Iceland are presumed to be a part of this initiative because of their location within the Arctic in addition to the large amounts of raw mineral deposits in their countries.

Danish diplomats have said Denmark was also willing to work with China to explore new Arctic sea routes. China has expressed strong interest in building stronger ties to Greenland and Denmark.

- On April 24, 2014, president Xi Jinping held talks with Queen Margrethe II of Denmark. China and Denmark subsequently concluded a memorandum of understanding that promotes the development of the Kvanefjeld Project in southern Greenland. Kvanefjeld contains one of the world's largest deposits of rare earth elements and uranium, with scope to increase the resource base substantially.[119]

- In 2016, a Chinese mining company purchased a Danish iron ore mine for $2 billion. Investments of this kind have been known to give China leverage to open dialogues with and establish stronger ties to local governments.

NOTES

1. Charles K. Ebinger and Evie Zambetakis, "The Geopolitics of Arctic Melt," *International Affairs* 85, no. 6 (2009): 1215–1232, https://www.brookings.edu/wp-content/uploads/2016/06/11_arctic_melt_ebinger_zambetakis.pdf.

2. Ebinger and Zambetakis, "The Geopolitics of Arctic Melt."

3. Countries are listed in order of those with largest to smallest populations in the Arctic region (see Figure I.1).

4. Shiloh Rainwater, "Race to the North: China's Arctic Strategy and Its Implications," *Naval War College Review* 66, no. 2 (2013), https://digital-commons.usnwc.edu/nwc-review/vol66/iss2/7.

5. Arctic Council, "Agreement on Cooperation on Aeronautical and Maritime Search and Rescue in the Arctic," ministerial meeting in Nuuk, Greenland, May 12, 2011, https://oaarchive.arctic-council.org/handle/11374/531.

6. Svein Vigeland Rottem, "The Arctic Council and the Search and Rescue Agreement: The Case of Norway," *Polar Record* 50, no. 3 (2013): 284–292, http://citeseerx.ist.psu.edu/viewdoc/download?doi=10.1.1.737.7905&rep=rep1&type=pdf.

7. R. Andrew, *Socio-Economic Drivers of Change in the Arctic*, AMAP Technical Report No. 9 (Oslo, Norway: Arctic Monitoring and Assessment Programme, 2014).

8. Egill Thor Nielsson and Bjarni Mar Magnusson, "The Arctic Five Strike Again," July 30, 2015, http://en.polaroceanportal.com/article/197.

9. Barents Euro-Arctic Council (website), http://www.beac.st/en.

10. International Maritime Organization (website), http://www.imo.org/en/Pages/Default.aspx.

11. Juha Jokela, *Arctic Security Matters*, Report No. 24 (Paris: European Union Institute for Security Studies, June 2015), https://www.iss.europa.eu/sites/default/files/EUISSFiles/Report%2024.pdf.

12. Olav Schram Stokke, "Political Stability and Multi-Level Governance in the Arctic," in *Environmental Security in the Arctic Ocean*, ed. Paul Arthur Berkman and Alexander N. Vylegzhanin (Dordrecht, Netherlands: Springer, 2013), 297–311.

13. *The Great Challenge Of the Arctic: National Roadmap for the Arctic* (Paris: Ministry of Foreign Affairs and International Development, June 2016), http://www.diplomatie.gouv.fr/fr/IMG/pdf/frna_-_eng_-interne_-_

prepa_-_17-06-pm-bd-pdf_cle02695b
.pdf.

14. *The United Nations Convention on the Law of the Sea: A Historical Perspective* (New York: United Nations, Division for Ocean Affairs and the Law of the Sea, 2012), http://www.un.org/ depts/los/convention_agreements/ convention_historical_perspective .htm.

15. Gail Whiteman, ed., *Valuing the Arctic Ice Melt: Final Report* (Rotterdam, Netherlands: Ecorys, 2014).

16. Charles Emmerson and Glada Lahn, *Arctic Opening: Opportunity and Risk in the High North* (London: Chatham House, April 1, 2012), http://library .arcticportal.org/1671/.

17. United States Coast Guard, *Arctic Strategy*, May 2013, https://www .dco.uscg.mil/Our-Organization/ Assistant-Commandant-for-Prevention-Policy-CG-5P/Marine-Transportation-Systems-CG-5PW/ Arctic-Policy-Office/.

18. US Department of State, "Arctic Nations Sign Declaration to Prevent Unregulated Fishing in the Central Arctic Ocean," news release, July 16, 2015, https://2009-2017.state.gov/r/pa/ prs/ps/2015/07/244969.htm.

19. US Department of State, "Arctic Nations Sign Declaration."

20. Lauren V. Weatherdon et al., "Projected Scenarios for Coastal First Nations' Fisheries Catch Potential Under Climate Change: Management Challenges and Opportunities," *PLOS ONE 11*, no. 1 (January 13, 2016): e0145285, https://doi.org/10.1371/ journal.pone.0145285.

21. Dongqin Lu et al., "An Economic Analysis of Container Shipping Through Canadian Northwest Passage," *International Journal of E-Navigation and Maritime Economy*, 1 (2014): 60–72.

22. Jonathan Masters, *The Thawing Arctic: Risks and Opportunities* (Washington, DC: Council on Foreign Relations, December 16, 2013), https://www .cfr.org/backgrounder/thawing-arctic-risks-and-opportunities.

23. "Climate Change." The Arctic Institute. Accessed June 1, 2020, https://www.thearcticinstitute.org/ projects/climate-change/.

24. Halvor Schøyen and Svein Bråthen, "The Northern Sea Route Versus the Suez Canal: Cases From Bulk Shipping," *Journal of Transport Geography* 19, no. 4 (July 2011): 977–983.

25. Marc Lanteigne, *China's Emerging Arctic Strategies: Economics and Institutions* (Reykjavik: Institute of International Affairs, University of Iceland, 2014), http://ams.hi.is/ wp-content/uploads/2014/11/ ChinasEmergingArcticStrategiesPDF_ FIX2.pdf.

26. Xie Cheng, ed., "China Issues Guidance on Arctic Navigation in Northwest Passage," Blogspot, April 22, 2016, http:// arcticnorthwestpassage.blogspot .com/2016/04/china-issues-guidance-on-arctic.html.

27. L. Brigham et al., *Bering Strait Region Case Study*, Institute of the North, http://www.institutenorth.org/assets/ images/uploads/files/5.5-Bering-Strait-Region-Case-Study.pdf.

28. "This Luxury Cruise Ship Will Soon Sail Through the Arctic: Here's What That Means for Alaska," *Anchorage Daily News*, June 12, 2016, https:// www.adn.com/arctic/2016/06/12/ this-luxury-cruise-ship-will-soon-sail-through-the-arctic-heres-what-that-means-for-alaska/.

29. "Agreement With the Union of Soviet Socialist Republics on the Maritime Boundary, June 1, 1990, https://2009-

2017.state.gov/documents/
organization/125431.pdf.

30. Margaret Blunden, "Geopolitics and
the Northern Sea Route," *International
Affairs* 88, no. 1 (2012): 115–129,
https://gdzienemo.files.wordpress.
com/2014/09/geopolitics-and-the-
northern-sea-route.pdf.

31. "Russia Bolsters Arctic Expansion,"
Marine & Commerce (July 2015),
http://www.marineandcommerce.com/
files/mc0715/mc0715_NevaArctic.pdf.

32. "Northern Sea Route Shipping
Statistics," Protection of the Arctic
Marine Environment, Arctic Council,
2020, https://www.pame.is/projects/
arctic-marine-shipping/older-projects/
northern-sea-route-shipping-statistics.

33. Joe Friesen and Unnati Gandhi,
"Russian Ship Crosses 'Arctic Bridge'
to Manitoba," *Globe and Mail Canada*,
October 18, 2007, https://www
.theglobeandmail.com/news/national/
russian-ship-crosses-arctic-bridge-to-
manitoba/article1084466/.

34. Malte Humpert and Andreas
Raspotnik, "The Future of Arctic
Shipping Along the Transpolar Sea
Route," *The Arctic Yearbook: 2012*,
http://www.arcticyearbook.com/
images/Arcticles_2012/Humpert_
and_Raspotnik.pdf.

35. Humpert and Raspotnik, "The Future
of Arctic Shipping."

36. "Population," *The Arctic*, http://arctic
.ru/population/.

37. Lassi Heininen, Alexander Sergunin,
and Gleb Yarovoy, *Russian Strategies
in the Arctic: Avoiding a New Cold War*
(Moscow: Valdai Discussion Club,
September 2014), http://www.uarctic
.org/media/857300/arctic_eng.pdf.

38. Mike Nudelman and Jeremy Bender,
"This Map Shows Russia's Dominant
Militarization of the Arctic," *Business
Insider*, August 7, 2015, http://www

.businessinsider.com/chart-of-russias-
militarization-of-arctic-2015-8.

39. Paul Ames, "Russia's Military Is
Muscling Into the Arctic, Where
Melting Ice Is Freeing Up Resources,"
Public Radio International online,
October 18, 2015, http://www.pri.org/
stories/2015-10-18/russias-military-
muscling- arctic-where-melting-ice-
freeing-resources.

40. "The Development Strategy of the
Arctic Zone of the Russian Federation,"
website of the Government of the
Russian Federation, February 20,
2013," http://www.research.kobe-u
.ac.jp/gsics-pcrc/sympo/20160728/
documents/Keynote/Russian%20
Arctic%20strategy%202013.pdf.

41. "Putin: Russia Has No Plans
to Militarize Arctic," *Sputnik
International*, December 19,
2014, https://sputniknews.com/
military/201412191016043432/.

42. Nudelman and Bender, "This
Map Shows Russia's Dominant
Militarization of the Arctic."

43. Stephen J. Blank, *Russia in the Arctic*
(Carlisle, PA: Strategic Studies
Institute, US Army War College,
2011), https://ssi.armywarcollege
.edu/?s=russia+in+the+arctic.

44. Blank, *Russia in the Arctic*.

45. *A Brief History of NORAD* (North
American Aerospace Defense
Command, Office of History,
December 2013), https://www.norad
.mil/Portals/29/Documents/A%20
Brief%20History%20of%20
NORAD%20(current%20as%20
of%20March%202014).pdf.

46. Siemon T. Wezeman, *Military
Capabilities in the Arctic* (Solna,
Sweden: Stockholm International
Peace Research Institute, March
2012), https://www.sipri.org/

publications/2012/sipri-background-papers/military-capabilities-arctic.

47. "ICEX 2016: Arctic Operations and Scientific Investigations," *Undersea Warfare*, Spring 2016, https://www.public.navy.mil/subfor/underseawarfaremagazine/Issues/PDF/USW_Spring_2016.pdf.

48. "821st Air Base Group Mission," Peterson Air Force Base (website), http://www.peterson.af.mil/Units/821st-Air-Base-Group.

49. *U.S. Navy Arctic Roadmap 2014–2030* (Washington, DC: Navy Task Force Climate Change, February 2014), https://www.navy.mil/docs/USN_arctic_roadmap.pdf.

50. "Arctic and Offshore Patrol Ship Project," Royal Canadian Navy (website), April 19, 2013, http://www.navy-marine.forces.gc.ca/en/fleet-units/aops-home.page.

51. John Liang, "Arctic Spending," InsideDefense.com, September 23, 2016, https://insidedefense.com/insider/arctic-spending.

52. "Major Icebreakers of the World," US Coast Guard chart, https://www.dco.uscg.mil/Portals/9/DCO%20Documents/Office%20of%20Waterways%20and%20Ocean%20Policy/20170501%20major%20icebreaker%20chart.pdf?ver=2017-06-08-091723-907.

53. International Security Advisory Board, *Report on Arctic Policy* (Washington, DC: US Department of State, September 21, 2016), https://2009-2017.state.gov/t/avc/isab/262342.htm.

54. *Norway's Arctic Policy* (Oslo, Norway: Ministry of Foreign Affairs, November 2014), https://www.regjeringen.no/globalassets/departementene/ud/vedlegg/nord/nordkloden_en.pdf.

55. *Norway's Arctic Policy.*

56. Crista Mack, "US Army Warms Up With Norwegian Cold Weather Training Exercise," US Army (website), http://www.army.mil/Arcticle/163535/US_Army_warms_up_with_Norwegian_cold_weather_training_exercise.

57. *Alliance at Risk: Strengthening European Defense in an Age of Turbulence and Competition* (Washington, DC: Atlantic Council), http://publications.atlanticcouncil.org/nato-alliance-at-risk/.

58. North Atlantic Treaty Organization, "Trident Juncture 2108: It Is Happening in the Air, on Land, at Sea, and in Cyberspace," https://www.nato.int/cps/en/natohq/157833.htm.

59. *Norway's Arctic Policy.*

60. *Norway's Arctic Policy.*

61. "Norway: Exports, Imports, and Trade Balance," Observatory of Economic Complexity (website), http://atlas.media.mit.edu/en/profile/country/nor/.

62. Treaty Between the Kingdom of Norway and the Russian Federation Concerning Maritime Delimitation and Cooperation in the Barents Sea and the Arctic Ocean, September 15, 2010, https://www.regjeringen.no/globalassets/upload/UD/Vedlegg/Folkerett/avtale_engelsk.pdf.

63. James Henderson and Julia S. P. Loe, *The Prospects and Challenges for Arctic Oil Development* (Oxford: Oxford Institute for Energy Studies, University of Oxford, November 2014), https://www.oxfordenergy.org/wpcms/wp-content/uploads/2014/11/WPM-56.pdf.

64. Henderson and Loe, *Arctic Oil Development.*

65. World Population Review, "Iceland Population," https://worldpopulationreview.com/countries/iceland-population/.

66. A Parliamentary Resolution on Iceland's Arctic Policy, March 28, 2011, https://www.government.is/media/utanrikisraduneyti-media/media/nordurlandaskrifstofa/A-Parliamentary-Resolution-on-ICE-Arctic-Policy-approved-by-Althingi.pdf.

67. "Icelandic Fisheries," Promoteiceland.com, September 30, 2013, http://www.iceland.is/files/icelandic-fisheries-press-kit-enska-30-sept-2013.pdf.

68. "Norway: Exports, Imports, and Trade Balance."

69. Marc Lanteigne, *China's Emerging Arctic Strategies: Economics and Institutions* (Reykjavik: Centre for Arctic Policy Studies, University of Iceland, November 2014), http://ams.hi.is/wp-content/uploads/2014/11/ChinasEmergingArcticStrategiesPDF_FIX2.pdf.

70. "Visit to Murmansk," http://www.iceland.is/iceland-abroad/ru/english/news-and- events/visit-to-murmansk/8951/.

71. "Visit to Murmansk."

72. North Atlantic Treaty Organization, "Member Countries," http://www.nato.int/cps/en/natohq/topics_52044.htm.

73. International Security Advisory Board, *Report on Arctic Policy.*

74. International Security Advisory Board.

75. Iceland Says Russian Bombers Taking 'Risks' Near Passenger Jets," *Radio Free Europe/Radio Liberty,* http://www.rferl.org/a/iceland-says-russian-bombers-taking-risks-near-passengers-jets/28015577.html.

76. Daniel Kochis and Brian Slattery, *Iceland: Outsized Importance for Transatlantic Security* (Washington, DC: Heritage Foundation, June 2016), http://www.heritage.org/research/reports/2016/06/iceland-outsized-importance-for-transatlantic-security.

77. Trude Pettersen, "Chinese Icebreaker Bound for North Pole," *Barents Observer,* http://barentsobserver.com/en/arctic/chinese-icebreaker-bound-north-pole-23-08.

78. Pettersen, "Chinese Icebreaker Bound for North Pole."

79. Pettersen.

80. Mia Bennett, "The Northern Sea Route: An Iceland–China Link," Foreign Policy Association (blog), March 19, 2013, http://foreignpolicyblogs.com/2013/03/19/the-northern-sea-route-an-iceland-china-link/.

81. Bennett, "The Northern Sea Route: An Iceland–China Link."

82. Omar R. Valdimarsson, "Iceland Is First in Europe to Sign Free Trade Pact With China," *Bloomberg,* April 13, 2013, https://www.bloomberg.com/news/articles/2013-04-15/iceland-is-first-in-europe-to-sign-free-trade-pact-with-china.

83. Valdimarsson, "Iceland Is First in Europe."

84. Valdimarsson.

85. North Atlantic Treaty Organization, "Relations With Sweden," http://www.nato.int/cps/en/natolive/topics_52535.htm.

86. North Atlantic Treaty Organization, "Relations With Sweden."

87. "Sweden's Defense Policy: 2016 to 2020" (Ministry of Defense, Government of Sweden, June 1, 2015), http://www.government.se/globalassets/government/dokument/forsvarsdepartementet/sweden_defence_policy_2016_to_2020.

88. "Sweden's Defense Policy," Government of Sweden.

89. "Sweden's Defense Policy," Government of Sweden.

90. "Arctic Rangers," unofficial web page for Swedish army unit, http://arcticranger.tripod.com/.

91. *Baltic Sea Icebreaking Report: 2015–2016* (Baltic Icebreaking Management, 2016), http://www.baltice.org/app/static/pdf/BIM%20Report%2015-16.pdf.

92. Sweden's Strategy for the Arctic Region (Ministry of Foreign Affairs, Government of Sweden, 2016), http://www.openaid.se/wp-content/uploads/2014/04/Swedens-Strategy-for-the-Arctic-Region.pdf.

93. "Voices," *National Geographic*, June 24, 2014, http://voices.nationalgeographic.com/2014/06/24/oden-icebreaker-pictures-science-environment-ships-sweden-copenhagen/.

94. "Swedish Icebreaker to Help Canada Map Arctic Shelf," *Radio Sweden*, May 26, 2016, http://sverigesradio.se/sida/artikel.aspx?programid=2054&artikel=6440908.

95. Christian Jakob Burmeister Hicks, *Historical Synopsis of the Sami/United Nations Relationship* (Stefansson Arctic Institute, 2000), http://www.thearctic.is/PDF/Synopsis%20of%20Sami-UN%20Relations%20PDF.pdf.

96. *Arctic Strategy* (Prime Minister's Office, Government of Finland, 2013), http://vnk.fi/documents/10616/334509/Arktinen+strategia+2013+en.pdf/6b6fb723-40ec-4c17-b286-5b5910fbecf4.

97. "Finland: Exports, Imports, and Trade Balance," Observatory of Economic Complexity, http://atlas.media.mit.edu/en/profile/country/fin/.

98. North Atlantic Treaty Organization, "Relations With Finland," http://www.nato.int/cps/en/natohq/topics_49594.htm?selectedLocale=en.

99. "BALTOPS 2016," US Naval Forces Europe-Africa/US 6th Fleet (website), http://www.c6f.navy.mil/forces-efforts/baltops-2016.

100. "BALTOPS 2016," US Naval Forces Europe-Africa.

101. "Why NATO Is Still a More Reliable Partner for Finland Than Russia," *Russia Direct*, July 8, 2016, http://www.russia-direct.org/opinion/why-nato-still-more-reliable-partner-finland-russia.

102. "Major Icebreakers of the World," US Coast Guard chart.

103. International Security Advisory Board, *Report on Arctic Policy*.

104. Timothy Wright, "China's Race Towards the Arctic: Interests, Legitimacy, and Canadian Security Implications" (master's thesis, University of Calgary, 2014), http://hdl.handle.net/11023/1889.

105. *Arctic Strategy* (US Department of Defense, 2013), https://www.defense.gov/Portals/1/Documents/pubs/2013_Arctic_Strategy.pdf.

106. Adam Lajeunesse, "The Canadian Armed Forces in the Arctic: Purpose, Capabilities, and Requirements" (policy paper, Canadian Global Affairs Institute), http://www.cgai.ca/canadian_armed_forces_in_the_arctic.

107. "Joint Task Force North Exercises" (Government of Canada, National Defence, Canadian Armed Forces), February 20, 2013, http://www.forces.gc.ca/en/operations-regional-jtf-north/exercises.page.

108. Lajeunesse, "Canadian Armed Forces in the Arctic."

109. "Politics in Greenland," Government of Greenland (website), http://

naalakkersuisut.gl/en/About-government-of-greenland/About-Greenland/Politics-in-Greenland.

110. International Security Advisory Board, *Report on Arctic Policy*.

111. Emma Wilson, *Energy and Minerals in Greenland: Governance, Corporate Responsibility and Social Resilience* (London: International Institute for Environment and Development, 2015), http://pubs.iied.org/pdfs/16561IIED.pdf.

112. Siri Fischer Hansen, trans., *Factsheet Denmark* (Copenhagen: Ministry of Foreign Affairs of Denmark, February 2010), http://www.netpublikationer .dk/um/10180/pdf/web.pdf.

113. Zachary Abbott, *Natural Resources and Economic Power: The Development-Security Nexus of Greenland* (Carlisle, PA: Dickinson College, 2016), https://scholar .dickinson.edu/cgi/viewcontent.cgi?article =1045&context=student_work.

114. Hans Peder Kirkegaard, Md Mehedi Hasan, and Maywand Asif, "Mining and Education in Greenland" (student term paper, Roskilde University, 2012), https://forskning.ruc.dk/ en/studentProjects/mining-and-education-in-greenland.

115. "Greenland.pdf," http://rudar.ruc.dk/ bitstream/1800/16015/1/Greenland .pdf.

116. "Greenland.pdf."

117. Timothy Wright, "China's Race Towards the Arctic: Interests, Legitimacy, and Canadian Security Implications" (master's thesis, University of Calgary, 2014), http:// hdl.handle.net/11023/1889.

118. Jingchao Peng and Njord Wegge, "China's Bilateral Diplomacy in the Arctic," *Polar Geography* 38, no. 3 (July 3, 2015): 233–249, doi:10.1080/10889 37X.2015.1086445.

119. "Greenland Minerals and Energy, China's NFC Sign MOU," *Rare Earth Investing News*, March 25, 2014, https://investingnews.com/daily/ resource-investing/critical-metals-investing/rare-earth-investing/ greenland-minerals-and-energy-chinas-nfc-sign-mou/.

Case Study II

RUSSIAN DISINFORMATION

Lessons Learned From the MH17 Shootdown

On July 17, 2014, Malaysian Airlines Flight 17 (MH17)—en route from Amsterdam to Kuala Lumpur—was thirty miles from the Russia-Ukraine border flying at 33,000 feet when it was shot down by a missile with a Russian-made 9N314M warhead launched from a Russian Buk missile system (see Figure II.1).[1] The Boeing 777 carried 283 passengers and 15 crew members. On board were six persons traveling to an international conference on AIDS in Melbourne, Australia, several distinguished scientists, a young rower from Indiana University, a pioneer in aerospace engineering, an international reporter who covered elections in Ukraine,[2] and eighty children—all of whom perished.[3]

Responsibility for investigating a crash is usually assigned to the state within which an incident occurs, according to the International Civil Aviation Organization. Ukraine initiated the probe but asked the Dutch Safety Board (DSB) to head the investigation because most of the victims were from the Netherlands.[4] The DSB formed a Joint Investigation Team (JIT) composed of representatives from the countries most impacted by the tragedy—the Netherlands, Ukraine, Malaysia, Australia, and Belgium.[5]

FIGURE II.1 ■ Flight Path and Last Flight Data Recorder Point of MH17, Buk Missile Launch Site, and Main Crash Site

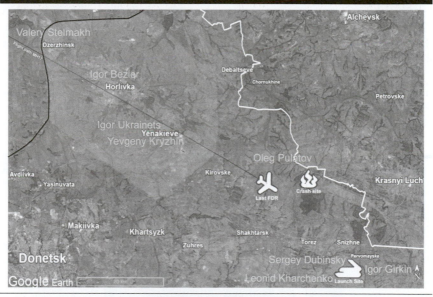

Source: Pherson Associates annotation of Google Earth screenshot.

Note: The frontlines are shown in black, the approximate Bezler-controlled territory is highlighted in light gray, and the administrative border between the Donetsk and Luhansk Oblasts is in white.

Significant evidence was found linking Russia to the downing of MH17. In October 2015, the DSB announced that its fifteen-month investigation confirmed that the missile was a Russian-made Buk missile.[6] In June 2016, the JIT published a photo of a part from a Buk missile found at the crash site.[7] On September 28, 2016, the JIT released its report, which revealed the origin and site of the missile launch, confirmed the weapon type, and presented alternative hypotheses. JIT cited witness testimony, satellite imagery, photographs, and intercepted phone conversations as its basis for confirming that the Buk missile launching platform was manufactured in Russia, transported from Russia to the Ukraine, and returned to Russia an hour after the plane was shot down.[8] The report identified the launch-site location as an agricultural field near Pervomaiskyi, Ukraine, which was controlled by Russian-backed fighters at the time of the incident.[9] The report further elaborated on the JIT statement earlier that year regarding the type of weapon and the methodology used to identify the missile series and system.[10]

The team explored alternative scenarios regarding the source and type of weapon. It ruled out speculation that the downing of the aircraft was a terrorist attack or caused by an explosion originating from inside the plane based on forensic evidence revealed in the investigation. For example, particles of the unique type of glass used for the cockpit windows in a Boeing 777 were found in the bodies of the cockpit crew during the postmortem investigation of the victims. Given that the glass shards were found inside the victims' bodies, the plane had to have been penetrated from outside.[11]

Another hypothesis was that a military aircraft shot down the plane.[12] This scenario was ruled out by evidence collected from radar data, witness testimonies, and forensic data that indicated no other planes were in the air in eastern Ukraine at the time MH17 was struck down.

According to a report issued by the research organization Bellingcat, Russian military veteran Igor "Strelkov" Girkin placed a post on his social media site within minutes of the shootdown saying, "we shot down a Ukrainian military plane." When it became apparent, however, that the plane was a commercial airliner, the post was quickly taken down.[13]

On May 24, 2018, the JIT held a press conference in Utrecht, Netherlands, revealing an image of the Buk TELAR rocket found at the site of the MH17 crash that showed the serial number printed on the rocket (see Figure II.2). At the conference, JIT announced that the missile belonged to the 53rd Anti-Aircraft Missile brigade, a

FIGURE II.2 ■ Buk Missile Found at Crash Site

Source: Robin van Lonkhuijsen/AFP via Getty Images.

Russian brigade based in the western Russian city of Kursk.[14] As a result of this evidence, both the Netherlands and Australia announced they were holding Russia accountable for shooting down the plane.

The JIT compiled a list of one hundred potential suspects who could be held responsible in some way for the disaster. In June 2019, the JIT released the names of four men who it alleged were involved in transporting the missile from Russia to Ukraine and declared them primary suspects in the downing of MH17.[15] International arrest warrants issued by the JIT charged Igor Girkin, Sergey Dubinsky, Oleg Pulatov, and Leonid Kharchenko with the murder of 298 passengers and crew members (see Figure II.3). Girkin, Dubinsky, and Pulatov have served in Russian intelligence or have a history of employment with the Russian military. Kharchenko is a Ukrainian national who lacks a military background, unlike his co-conspirators. He, however, was serving at the time as the commander of a combat unit in eastern Ukraine.

FIGURE II.3 ■ Key Suspects in the Downing of MH17	
Name	**Data**
Igor Girkin, "Igor Strelkov"	• Minister of Defense of the Donetsk People's Republic (DNR) • Was at the front line near launch site the day before shootdown
Sergey Dubinsky	• Girkin's Deputy • Head of GRU DNR • Stationed at GRU DNR HQ, Donetsk • Key figure coordinating transportation of Buk missile to launch site
Oleg Pulatov, "Khalif," "Gyurza"	• Head of 2nd Department of GRU DNR (reconnaissance and special operations) • Guarded missile launcher; first to arrive at crash site • Colonel in DNR, Lt. Colonel in Russian Armed Forces
Leonid Kharchenko, "Krot" (Mole)	• Battalion Commander, subordinate of Pulatov • Member of GRU DNR intelligence unit • Guarded Buk missile, involved in removal of Buk from crash site • Allegedly involved with illegal weapons sales • Ukrainian citizen born in Kostyantynivka, Ukraine
Igor Bezler, "Bes" (Demon)	• Leader of the Bezler group • Separatist leader of the DNR • Recruited in February 2014 by Russian military intelligence to form insurgent groups in eastern Ukraine; returned to Crimea in fall 2014

(Continued)

FIGURE II.3 ■ (Continued)	
Name	**Data**
	• In mid-July, his forces controlled Yenakieve, Dzerzhynsk (Toretsk) and parts of Makiivka; had some units near Donetsk. His stronghold is Hortivka, Ukraine • Known to operate like an "independent warlord" but recognizes the DNR leadership and collaborates with DNR commanders • Former GRU Lt. Colonel (until 2002) • Crimean-born, Russian citizen
Igor Ukrainets, "Minyor" (Sapper)	• Bezler's Deputy, Lt. Colonel in the DNR • Commander of the Minyor Unit (one of Bezler's infantry, and later artillery, units) • Ranking official who accompanied Buk missile launcher through DNR-controlled territory at the time of launch • Served in the Soviet Armed Forces; received special training at artillery school in St. Petersburg • Girkin accused him of desertion and treason in early July 2014 • Ukrainian citizen
Yevgeny Kryzhin	• Member of the Minyor Unit under Ukrainets • Volunteer militant from the Russian Far East • Based in Yenakieve; arrived in Yenakieve on July 13, 2014, smuggling military aid into rebel-held Ukraine for a Russian organization • Originally a medical assistant and in radio communications
Valery Stelmakh, "Naemnik" (Mercenary)	• Member of the Bezler group • Militia commandant of Dzerzhynsk • Major in the Soviet Armed Forces, currently in Russia • First spotted MH17 in Dzerzhynsk and flagged it as a potential enemy aircraft • In an intercepted phone conversation, Stelmakh told Bezler, "A birdie is flying towards you" (towards Horlivka) • Bezler ordered Stelmakh to report this to a higher up and Stelmakh notified Pulatov • Fought in Soviet-Afghan War • Born in Dzerzhynsk in 1955

Source: Copyright 2020 Globalytica, LLC. All Rights Reserved.

RUSSIA'S AGGRESSIVE COUNTERNARRATIVE

Russian officials initially responded to the international community's accusations that Russia was responsible for shooting down MH17 by holding a press conference on July 21, 2014. At the press conference, Russia's Defense Ministry presented radar data that depicted another aircraft flying in the vicinity of MH17 moments before the plane was shot down.[16] The Russian Union of Engineers claimed that a thorough examination of the wreckage showed that the plane was shot down by heat-seeking air-to-air missiles.[17] The Russian media furthered this narrative by crediting the testimony of an unverified source alleged to be a Spanish air traffic controller in Kiev, Ukraine. The supposed witness claimed that MH17 was followed by two Ukrainian fighter jets. The testimony was later discredited.[18]

In August 2015, the Russian tabloid *Komsomolskaya Pravda* released an audio recording of two men impersonating US Central Intelligence Agency (CIA) "agents" who were conspiring to shoot down MH17.[19] The tape contains a number of linguistic inaccuracies such as improper syntax, awkward lexical and prosodic stresses, and other blatant conversational abnormalities, indicating that the men recorded are not native English speakers. The source of the video and the identities of the men in the recording were not provided by the tabloid, strongly suggesting that the Russian government was using one of its media outlets to spread propaganda and disinformation.

When the JIT revealed that the missile was Russian made and the launch platform had been transported from Russia to Ukraine and then back to Russia an hour after the crash,[20] Russian officials admitted that the Buk missile system was manufactured by Russia in 1986. They claimed, however, that the missile had been delivered to a Russian military unit in Ukraine and was never returned to Russia.

In September 2018, Moscow repudiated the international investigators' claims that assigned responsibility for the downing of the aircraft to Russian separatists.[21] At a press conference held by Russia's Ministry of Defense, officials asserted that the evidence of Russia's involvement in the crash was fraudulent. According to the Russian officials, the videos presented by international investigators showing the missile being transported from Russia to Ukraine were fake. They also claimed that Russia had evidence that the videos were falsified.[22]

Russia tried to deflect blame to Ukraine by insisting it had evidence of Ukraine's liability for the crash. Russia claimed to be in possession of an audio recording of a Ukrainian soldier professing to have shot down the plane. Moreover, JIT revealed in June 2019 that a Russian operative was sharing conspiracies on his Facebook profile that the Buk missile launcher was Ukrainian and that the downing was part of a deliberate false flag attack orchestrated by Ukraine, the United States, and Royal Dutch Shell.[23]

An analysis of Russia's response to allegations that it was responsible for the MH17 shootdown reveals a robust program of denial and deception. The Russians tried to reframe the narrative by fabricating a story, deflecting blame, and using details that could not be verified by an external investigation team or, at the very least, would be difficult and time-consuming to disprove. The Russian methodology can be described as the Five D's: **Dismiss**, **Distract**, **Deflect**, **Distort**, and **Distrust**.[24]

- Russia tried to **dismiss** the allegations and **deflect** blame by refocusing attention and claiming it had evidence of Ukraine's involvement.

- The press conferences held two years after the accusations and four years after the crash served to **distract** the international media and the public from other more recent or ongoing crimes.

- Russian officials sought to **distort** the facts by stating that the missile launcher was never returned to Russia despite video evidence of the missile launcher's transport that had been released two years earlier.

- Russian propagandists tried to instill doubt and **distrust** in the investigation by dismissing the video footage as fake and propagating other Digital Disinformation.

This disinformation strategy was also reflected in the methods used by members of the four separatist groups associated with the downing of MH17: the Donetsk People's Republic (DNR); the DNR's military intelligence unit, the Main Intelligence Administration (GRU) DNR; the Bezler Group and its Minyor Unit; and the Vostok Brigade… (see Figure II.4).[25]

The following Sensitive But Unclassified (SBU) phone intercept indicated that the Bezler group was involved:

Naemnik: Nikolaevich …

Bezler: Yes, Naemnik.

Naemnik: A birdman [misspeaks] … **a birdie is flying towards you**.

Bezler: Is a birdie flying towards us?

Naemnik: Yes … [just] one, for now …

Bezler: A reconnaissance [aircraft] or a big one?

Naemnik: Can't see behind the clouds … [it's flying] too high …

Bezler: I see … roger … **report upwards**.[26]

Deflecting Attention From the Bezler Group

Even though the identities of these men were confirmed by international investigators, Bezler continued to deny any involvement with the downing of MH17. The Russian news agency RIA Novosti leaked a conversation involving Bezler who defends himself using elements of the Five D's disinformation strategy as follows:

- **Dismisses** the link between the conversation and MH17 by claiming that the plane referenced in the phone intercept was a different plane.

- **Distorts** the facts by stating, "The Boeing fell in the area of Snizhne. There are 100 [kilo]meters between [Yenakieve and Snizhne], I don't have weapons capable of downing planes at such a distance."[27] The actual distance between the two cities is 43 kilometers.

FIGURE II.4 ■ Associations of Key Actors

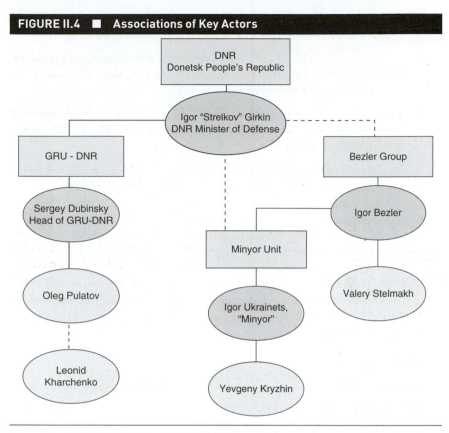

Source: Copyright 2020 Globalytica, LLC. All Rights Reserved.

- **Deflects** attention away from his group by saying he didn't have the weapons capabilities in an effort to **distract** from his connections with equipped militant groups and his role in spotting the plane.

Although the Bezler group may not have been involved with the actual downing of the plane, they were involved with the transportation of the Buk missile as evident from the video recordings later published in the JIT report in 2016.[28] In response to the video, Bezler employed the same disinformation strategy, and **dismissed** the video in a post on his social media account: "I looked through the video, and at 01:31 I had to laugh and from then on I watched it as an animated fiction movie."[29]

The day after the downing of MH17, a member of the Minyor unit, Yevgeny Kryzhin, posted "five points" on his LiveJournal blog attesting to the Minyor Unit's innocence. In his post, Kryzhin

- **Dismisses** allegations against his unit: Kryzhin asserts that the audio recordings of conversations between Minyor members are fake.

- **Distracts** from the Minyor unit's role in the crash by stating that the members of the Minyor group, heard on the SBU recording, were nowhere near the vicinity of the crash at the time.

- **Distorts** the truth: He claims that the group did not have the weapons capabilities required to perform this action.[30]

- **Deflects** and sows **distrust**: Kryzhin accuses the Ukrainians of making fake audio recordings, addressing Ukraine directly saying, "So Ukry [Ukrainians] f*** off with your fakes."[31]

- **Deflects** and **distorts**: A Ukrainian LiveJournal user confronted Kryzhin on the site stating that the separatists have Buks to which he replied, "Only Strelkov has Buks."[32] The unit may not have had the weapons capabilities independently; however, they were working with the DNR, which did have the weapons capability. Furthermore, the Minyor unit was involved with the transport of the Buk.

The JIT countered this strategy by presenting persuasive contrary evidence, specifically by (1) showing that the missile that brought down the plane belonged to the 53rd Russian military brigade and (2) providing video showing that the missile was transported from Russia to Ukraine prior to the attack.

THE WEAPONIZATION OF DIGITAL DISINFORMATION

The weaponization of "internet-based social media platforms" as an information warfare method first emerged in the early 2000s. Russia used it initially to shape domestic public opinion and suppress political opposition.[33] Following the downing of MH17, the Russian government used Digital Disinformation both as a defensive tactic to counter the international community's accusations and to mold popular views of the incident. In recent years, the Russians have modernized their approach to spreading disinformation and have increasingly targeted international audiences.

Targeting the Domestic Population

Russia's first efforts to deflect blame for the downing of MH17 were largely directed internally, using social media and state media outlets to spread disinformation. Russian separatists were heard blaming each other on social media and blaming the Ukrainians on another networking site called LiveJournal and in TV interviews on *Russia Today* (RT). Some separatists even took credit for downing the plane on their own social media accounts. The release of an unconvincing tape of Russian agents impersonating CIA agents by a Russian tabloid almost certainly was directed toward the Russian population because major linguistic imperfections were allowed to appear in the audio.

The Russian government insisted that the perpetrators were independent separatists, even though the key players involved in the downing of the plane had ties to the

Russian military and the GRU. Disassociating the perpetrators of the shootdown from Russian military forces was central to a disinformation campaign designed to preserve domestic support for the Russian military efforts and to promote Russian nationalism.

Targeting the United States With Upgraded Techniques

Over the past decade the Russians have increasingly used disinformation methods, particularly the weaponization of social media, as an offensive tactic in their information warfare operations directed toward the United States. Technological advancements in artificial intelligence (AI), advertising, and the rapidly growing global reliance on social media networks and internet news sources have been exploited aggressively. Russian Digital Disinformation campaigns reflecting the Five-D's strategy to Dismiss, Distract, Deflect, Distort, and Distrust have become increasingly sophisticated and destructive.

Several years before the 2016 US presidential election, Reuters reported that a Russian think tank controlled by the Kremlin, the Russian Institute for Strategic Studies (RISS), generated an elaborate plan to influence the US election campaign. The RISS reportedly recommended that the Kremlin launch a propaganda campaign via social media and that their "social media propaganda effort turn toward undermining faith in the American electoral system by spreading false stories of voter fraud."[34] It also recommended that Russian state-backed global news outlets encourage US voters to elect a president "who would take a softer line toward Russia."[35]

Leading up to the US presidential election in 2016, Russian operatives affiliated with the Internet Research Agency (IRA) used American social media platforms to spread disinformation and divisive propaganda. According to the report of the US Senate Select Committee on Intelligence (SSCI), "Russia-based actors, at the direction of the Russian government, effectuated a sustained campaign of information warfare against the United States aimed at influencing how this nation's citizens think about themselves, their government, and their fellow Americans."[36]

Russia's government has denied involvement with the IRA's interference in the 2016 US election; however, the committee found that there was "significant Kremlin support, authorization, and direction of the IRA's operations and goals."[37] Furthermore, a Russian oligarch known to be a close comrade of president Vladimir Putin, Yevgeny Prigozhin, funneled millions of dollars to IRA operations devoted to engaging with US citizens on social media in 2016.[38]

Just as the Russian government attempted to disassociate itself from the Russian militants who shot down MH17, the Kremlin has continuously **dismissed** any blame for or associations with the IRA's operations and the actions of Russian operatives that impeded US democratic processes by exploiting and manipulating American civic discourse.

Russian trolls targeted Americans by interacting with US citizens through various sophisticated disinformation methods. The goal of this divisive propaganda was to intensify racial, social, and political cleavages within the US population.

Highly skilled Russian disinformationists programmed and deployed bots that repeatedly posted socially divisive and politically polarizing content on US social media sites.

They posted inflammatory and provocative comments to engage US citizens and created and shared **distorted** content on these platforms. The Russian operatives created fake social media accounts that targeted Americans based on sociopolitical demographic factors to influence public opinion on "hot-button" political topics such as race and immigration.[39]

Sixty-six percent of all Facebook advertising content created by the IRA included topics and phrases pertaining to race.[40] The majority of racially divisive content created by the IRA was targeted at African Americans.[41] The IRA created Facebook pages and Instagram, Twitter, and YouTube content geared toward sowing **distrust** in African American audiences.[42] Seeking in particular to target African Americans living in metropolitan areas, Russian trolls used locational targeting methods. Blacktivist, one of the IRA's Facebook pages, received 11.2 million engagements, and half of its top ten Instagram accounts included racial content that was targeted toward African American audiences.[43]

Russian operatives also used Facebook events to promote anti-immigrant rallies in the United States.[44] One technique was to use what the advertising industry calls "dark-post" ads, seen only by the narrow, intended audience. Facebook calls its dark-post service "Unpublished Page Post Ads."[45]

Targeting US Presidential Candidates

A major component of Russia's information warfare strategy to interfere with the 2016 US election and democratic processes was the creation and dissemination of disinformation about the 2016 US presidential candidates. Fake news stories were dispatched through social media by Russian trolls about the US presidential candidates, the Democratic National Committee (DNC), and other US politicians. The Senate Select Committee on Intelligence found that IRA trolls also targeted and disparaged Republican candidates in the primaries including Jeb Bush, Marco Rubio, and Ted Cruz. The trolls' goal was to discredit and **dismiss** any candidate with views and interests counter to those of the Russian government.

On July 22, 2016, three days before the Democratic national convention, WikiLeaks released 19,252 DNC emails.[46] This release and the persistent stream of continuing leaks became a major **distraction** for Hillary Clinton's campaign. Russian GRU hackers, operating under the front "Guccifer 2.0," sent WikiLeaks thousands of DNC emails that they had retrieved by hacking into the DNC's email server.[47]

According to the FBI investigation report, Russian hackers with financial ties to the IRA had roamed through the DNC's network for seven months prior to the release of the hacked messages.[48] In addition, the Russian operatives hacked into Clinton campaign chairman John Podesta's email and delivered hundreds of his emails to WikiLeaks.[49]

During the critical final months of the campaign, Buzzfeed reported that the twenty top-performing false election stories from hoax sites and hyper-partisan blogs generated 8,711,000 shares, reactions, and comments on Facebook.[50] Efforts to sow **distrust** in US political institutions accelerated. According to the SSCI report, Hilary Clinton was especially targeted by Russian Digital Disinformation campaigns to "undermine public faith in the US democratic process, denigrate Secretary Clinton, and harm her electability and potential presidency."[51]

Reinforcing these efforts were other social media posts designed to **deflect**. Following the WikiLeaks release of hacked materials, one fake news story that emerged, commonly known as "Pizza-gate," asserted that one of Podesta's leaked emails revealed records of a child-sex trafficking ring that was, according to this rumor, run by Hillary Clinton out of the basement of a pizza shop in Washington D.C.[52]

The story, which originated on Twitter, was quickly picked up by right-wing entertainment programs such as InfoWars and Breitbart. The story was shared about 1.4 million times by more than 250,000 accounts in the first five weeks following its release.[53] In addition, more than 3,000 accounts tweeted about Pizza-gate five times or more. Experts have concluded that automated bots were largely behind the dissemination of this fake news story.

In response to this fake news story, in December 2016 a man in North Carolina decided to drive to the pizza parlor in Washington, D.C., armed with an AR-15 semiautomatic rifle, a .38 handgun, and a folding knife.[54] He entered the pizza shop determined to "free the abused children he was convinced were being held in the nonexistent basement."[55]

A Twitter account operated by Russian trolls in St. Petersburg used another form of **distraction** by posing as the Tennessee Republican Party with the name @TEN_GOP. It posted a manipulated version of one of the Podesta emails on Twitter that attempted to incriminate Hillary Clinton for the Islamist-militant attacks on the US consulate in Benghazi that resulted in the deaths of four US officials.[56] The Russian news agency Sputnik published an article regurgitating the @TEN_GOP story and used the fake document as the basis for its news article.[57]

Sputnik's retrieval and dissemination of this fake news story provides a good example of Russia's asymmetric information warfare operation. Sputnik's aggressive manipulation of the Benghazi event shows how well Russia attempted to apply the Five D's method to denigrate Hillary Clinton, undermine her credibility, and create overall distrust in the US Government and its processes. The incident was intended to make Hillary and US government institutions appear elusive and to sow **distrust** of Clinton within the American population.

The US House of Representatives formed a select committee to investigate the validity of these accounts relating to the Benghazi incident. After two years of research and hearings and an expenditure of $7 million, the committee released an 800-page report concluding that no evidence could be found indicating that Clinton was culpable regarding the Benghazi attack.[58]

Russia also used the St. Petersburg trolls to create and organize political events on Facebook to sow **distrust** of Clinton. The "Being Patriotic" Facebook group created by Russian trolls organized and promoted political rallies on Facebook.

- One event, titled "Down with Hillary!" was scheduled to occur on July 23, 2016—the day after the first WikiLeaks release.[59]

- Another report showed that Russians had put up a Facebook page encouraging Texas to secede from the United States.[60]

In the final three months leading up to the November election, the number of Digital Disinformation engagements on Facebook pertaining to the election outperformed the number of postings on legitimate news websites.[61] The two most widely shared distortions of information about the two candidates were the claim that Pope Francis had endorsed Donald Trump's campaign and that Hillary Clinton had sold weapons to the ISIS terrorist group in Syria.[62]

RUSSIA'S GROWING DIGITAL DISINFORMATION EFFORTS

Liberal democracies have been targeted by Russian/Soviet active measures and disinformation campaigns since the early 20th century.[63] In recent years, the Kremlin has increasingly leveraged social media to interfere in democratic elections and civic discourse by means of political and ideological manipulation of democracies. In Europe, Russian disinformation has worked its way into the social media feeds of voters in Germany, France, the Netherlands, the United Kingdom, and many other countries (see Figure II.5).

Russian state media outlets, for example, were used to inflame anti-immigrant and anti-refugee sentiment in Western Europe.[64] As stated in the SSCI report,

> We are in the midst of a world-wide internet-based assault on democracy. The Oxford Internet Institute have tracked armies of volunteers and "bots," or automated profiles, as they move propaganda across Facebook and Twitter

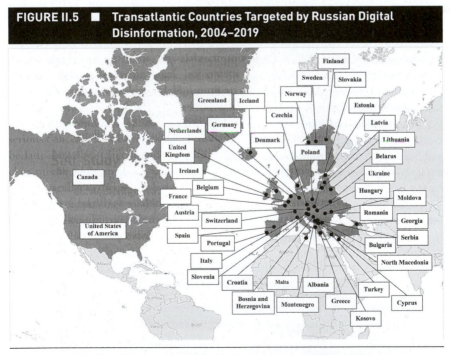

FIGURE II.5 ■ Transatlantic Countries Targeted by Russian Digital Disinformation, 2004–2019

Source: Copyright 2020 Globalytica, LLC. All Rights Reserved.

in efforts to undermine trust in democracy or to elect favored candidates in the Philippines, India, France, the Netherlands, the United Kingdom, and elsewhere.[65]

Russia's Disinformation Campaign in Germany

In Germany, anti-immigrant rhetoric has been aimed at Muslims and refugees from Syria and other parts of the Middle East/North Africa region who began flooding into Europe beginning in 2015. Roughly 5 million (or 25 percent) of the world's refugee population are Syrian refugees.[66] Germany has accepted over 1 million Syrian refugees.[67]

Russia quickly sought to take advantage of the rising anti-immigration sentiments spurred by this influx. A news broadcast on Russia's main news channel claimed that migrants were raping children in Germany. They said a young Russian-German girl named Lisa was kidnapped and raped by Syrian migrants. The segment continued with a blurry video that depicted an assumed Syrian migrant boasting about raping her.[68] It was later discovered that this video had been uploaded to YouTube six years earlier.

German police confirmed that the girl had been reported missing. The Russian foreign minister held a press conference directed toward a Russian audience where he discussed migration problems and referred to the girl in the story as "our girl Lisa."[69] In addition, RT covered several segments on the fear and concerns that Germany's Russian speakers had toward Syrian refugees. According to German Deutsche Welle, women who were filmed in these segments were later found out to be paid television actors.[70]

In addition to targeting Germans with anti-immigration content, Russia sponsored and promoted far-right and white-nationalist parties in Germany. Russia's weaponization of immigration in Germany was part of their larger disinformation strategy to undermine Germany's democratic processes. Anxiety about immigration was the fuel behind the rise of white nationalism and right-wing parties in Europe.[71]

Germany continues to be one of Putin's major targets in the Russian Information War. Russia has launched RT Deutsch, a German-language version of the Russian state-sponsored propaganda machine.[72] RT Deutsch presents the same narrative style and propaganda material that has notoriously been used by the Russian government in Kremlin disinformation campaigns.

The 2016 Brexit Campaign in the United Kingdom

When the United Kingdom (UK) announced the result of the Brexit vote was to "Leave" the European Union (EU), the world was shocked, similar to the world's reaction to the result of the subsequent US 2016 presidential election. According to polls of UK voters, "Leave voters were motivated mainly by anti-immigration sentiments." They indicated that while younger city dwellers voted to stay, older citizens living in rural areas who were less exposed to immigrants voted to leave.[73] The objective was to **dismiss** arguments highlighting the unfavorable consequences of leaving the EU, **distract** attention from concrete pros and cons by emphasizing the threat posed by newly arriving immigrants, and **distort** the economic benefits of leaving the EU.

In the six months leading up to the Brexit vote, Russian media outlets—RT and Sputnik—ran 261 stories that were anti-EU, pro-Brexit, and anti-immigration.[74, 75] Hundreds of Russian bots and trolls from the IRA were posting about Brexit on thousands of Twitter accounts.[76]

The House of Commons Digital, Culture, Media, and Sport Committee in its final report on *Disinformation and 'Fake News'* noted that "The social reach of these anti-EU articles published by the Kremlin-owned channels was 134 million potential impressions, in comparison with a total reach of just 33 million and 11 million potential impressions for all content shared from the Vote Leave website and Leave.EU website, respectively."[77] It was the same anti-immigration, pro-nationalist messaging that the Kremlin-backed Russian media used to permeate German civic discourse and impact the 2016 US election.

In 2017, the Information Commissioner's Office in the UK launched an investigation into Facebook's use of UK citizens' data and its role in the 2016 Brexit referendum and 2017 UK national elections.[78] Facebook's head of cybersecurity announced that Facebook had removed 289 pages, 75 accounts with roughly 790,000 followers, after linking this activity to Sputnik.[79] According to Facebook's findings, these pages frequently posted anti-NATO content and promoted protest movements through Facebook. In addition, Facebook "removed 107 pages, groups, and accounts that were designed to look as if they were run from Ukraine but were part of a network that originated in Russia."[80]

The 2017 French Presidential Election

Months before the final round of the French presidential election in 2017, Russian operatives launched a disinformation campaign against Emmanuel Macron's presidential bid. Two days before the presidential election, these actors released gigabytes of hacked data, including from the Macron campaign team. The incident came to be known as the "Macron Leaks." The data consisted of emails and forgeries created to denigrate Emmanuel Macron. The objective was to release large quantities of data that would **distort** Macron's record and sow **distrust** in his leadership skills. Russia's attempt to impact the outcome of the French presidential election and polarize French society, however, largely failed.

French efforts to counter the disinformation attacks were successful due to several factors:

- *Growing Sensitivity.* Previous Russian campaigns helped make the French aware of the growing threats of cyber attacks and disinformation campaigns directed toward transatlantic democracies, the degree of influence these campaigns have had on democratic civic discourse, and the extent to which they are being used to undercut the security of transatlantic partnerships and interests.

- *Timing.* France's 2017 election was a year and a half after the US election, two years after Brexit, and three years after Russian cyber attacks on German intelligence servers; this enabled France to prepare a counterresponse. As expected, the hackers released their disinformation just hours before the electoral silence period. The timing limited the spread of disinformation and the poor quality of the reporting rendered the attempt highly suspicious.

- *Structural Factors.* The French voting system posed a more challenging target:

  1. The election process is direct; therefore, interference is more obvious.

  2. Two rounds of voting enable voters to shift their decisions.

  3. The French media is dominated by mainstream and critical media sources, and therefore lacks the tabloid-style and alternative websites common in the UK and the United States.

  4. Critical thinking skills and moderate skepticism are imbedded in French culture and society.

- *Active Countermeasures.* Russian disinformation operatives did not anticipate that Macron's campaign staff would react so quickly. Because the quality of their disinformation was deemed irrelevant in their previous campaigns, the Russians assumed their same mistakes would not make any difference. For Russian trolls and hackers, quantity—not thoroughness or the quality of disinformation—was the goal.

- *Cultural Ignorance.* Disinformation was primarily in English and first spread by the American alt-right community. Russian hackers were unaware of ideological differences in French nationalism, especially pertaining to the historical significance of French-language use in media and literature, and its association with the French nationalist movement.

Several measures were taken by the French government and the Macron campaign to counter Russian attempts at election interference and disinformation attacks. The French

1. *Had learned from history.* The US 2016 election was the pivotal learning point for democracies around the world. After witnessing the impact of Russian disinformation on the US 2016 election, other democracies realized that they too were vulnerable to Russian disinformation.

2. *Had governing bodies in place to regulate.* The National Commission for the Control of the Electoral Campaign for the Presidential Election (CNCCEP) and the National Cybersecurity Agency (ANSII) were trusted governmental bodies that were designated to preserve the integrity and public confidence in electoral processes and results.[81] These agencies kept the public, the media, and political parties informed when there was a risk of cyber attacks during the campaign.

3. *Had communicated a firm resolve.* In December 2016, the minister of defense publicly announced France's new cyber command operation would consist of 2,600 cyber-warfare combatants. In addition, the minister stated that "France reserves the right to retaliate by any means it deems appropriate … through our cyber arsenal but also by conventional armed means."[82]

4. *Took technical preventative measures.* In addition to establishing the cyber command in March 2017, the French government announced that electronic voting would not be available to citizens abroad.

5. *Confused the hackers with their own game.* The Macron campaign mounted an aggressive retaliatory response to Russian phishing attempts. It used a strategy known as digital blurring and planted false information in order to confuse and distract the hackers.[83]

In conclusion, Russia has developed over the past decades a robust capability to manipulate popular perceptions. The impact of such campaigns appears to have been greatly accelerated by the recent rapid growth of social media platforms. Russia has also expanded significantly the number of countries targeted by its Digital Disinformation efforts. The French experience, however, suggests that as more countries come to anticipate such attacks, they will be able to mount more effective defenses augmented by what could potentially be even more disruptive offensive strategies.

NOTES

1. "MH17 Ukraine Plane Crash: What We Know," *BBC News*, June 19, 2019, https://www.bbc.com/news/world-europe-28357880.

2. Thom Patterson, Ray Sanchez, and AnneClaire Stapleton, "MH17 Crash Victims: Athlete, Young Brothers, Family Among Those Killed," *CNN*, July 23, 2014, http://www.cnn.com/2014/07/18/world/mourning-mh17/index.html.

3. "MH17 Ukraine Plane Crash," *BBC News*.

4. "MH17 Ukraine Plane Crash."

5. Landelijk Parket, "JIT: Flight MH17 Was Shot Down by a BUK Missile From a Farmland Near Pervomaiskyi," Openbaar Ministerie, September 28, 2016, http://adam.curry.com/art/1475112492_bD4NDhxj.html.

6. "MH17 Ukraine Plane Crash," *BBC News*.

7. "MH17 Crash: Big Buk Missile Part Found in Ukraine," *BBC News*, June

6, 2016, https://www.bbc.com/news/world-europe-36462853.

8. "MH17 Ukraine Plane Crash," *BBC News*.

9. Parket, "Flight MH17 Was Shot Down by a BUK Missile."

10. Parket.

11. Parket, animation 2.

12. Parket.

13. Cristina Maza, "Russian Propaganda? Moscow Releases Audio Blaming Ukraine for Downing of MH17 Flight That Killed Almost 300," *Newsweek*, September 17, 2018, https://www.newsweek.com/russian-propaganda-moscow-releases-audio-blaming-ukraine-downing-mh17-flight-1124371.

14. "MH17 Ukraine Plane Crash," *BBC News*.

15. "MH17 Ukraine Plane Crash."

16. Reid Standish, "Propaganda Watch: Listen to Two Russians Badly Impersonate CIA Spies to Pin MH17

on U.S," *Foreign Policy*, July 30, 2019, https://foreignpolicy.com/2015/08/12/ propaganda-watch-listen-to-two- russians-badly-impersonate-cia-spies- to-pin-mh17-on-u-s/.

17. Standish, "Russians Badly Impersonate CIA Spies."

18. Standish.

19. Standish.

20. "MH17 Ukraine Plane Crash," *BBC News*.

21. Maza, "Moscow Releases Audio Blaming Ukraine."

22. Maza.

23. Pieter van Huis, "'A Birdie Is Flying Towards You': Identifying the Separatists Linked to the Downing of MH17," Bellingcat, June 2019, 42, https://www.bellingcat.com/ wp-content/uploads/2019/06/a-birdie- is-flying-towards-you.pdf.

24. "Inside Russia's Propaganda Machine," *PBS News Hour*, July 11, 2017, https://www.youtube.com/ watch?v=xSIkkza9TVI. This list of the Five D's is inspired by Atlantic Council senior fellow Ben Nimmo's concept of "The Four D's: Dismiss, Distort, Distract, and Dismay." The expanded version drops Dismay and adds Deflect and Distrust.

25. Van Huis, "A Birdie Is Flying Towards You."

26. Van Huis.

27. Van Huis, 19.

28. Van Huis.

29. Van Huis.

30. Van Huis, 11

31. Van Huis, 12.

32. Van Huis, 11.

33. US Congress, Senate, Select Committee on Intelligence,

Russian Active Measures Campaigns and Interference in the 2016 U.S. Election, vol. 2, *Russia's Use of Social Media With Additional Views*, 116th Congr., 1st sess., 2019, 15, https:// www.intelligence.senate.gov/sites/ default/files/documents/Report_ Volume2.pdf.

34. Siva Vaidhyanathan, "The Disinformation Machine," in *Anti- Social Media: How Facebook Disconnects Us and Undermines Democracy* (Oxford: Oxford University Press, 2018), 177.

35. Vaidhyanathan, "The Disinformation Machine," 175–195.

36. Senate Select Committee on Intelligence, *Russia's Use of Social Media*, 4.

37. Senate Select Committee on Intelligence, 5.

38. Peter Stone and Greg Gordon, "Russia-Sponsored Troll Networks Targeting the U.S. May Number in the Hundreds," McClatchy DC, October 19, 2017, https://www.mcclatchydc .com/news/nation-world/world/ article179799311.html.

39. Senate Select Committee on Intelligence, *Russia's Use of Social Media*, 6.

40. Senate Select Committee on Intelligence, 6.

41. Senate Select Committee on Intelligence, 6.

42. Senate Select Committee on Intelligence, 6.

43. Senate Select Committee on Intelligence, 6.

44. Vaidhyanathan, "The Disinformation Machine," 177.

45. Vaidhyanathan, 177.

46. Richard Stengel, *Information Wars: How We Lost the Global Battle Against*

Disinformation and What We Can Do About It (New York: Grove Atlantic, 2019), 266.

47. Stengel, *Information Wars.*

48. Stengel.

49. Stengel.

50. Craig Silverman, "This Analysis Shows How Viral Fake Election News Stories Outperformed Real News on Facebook," *BuzzFeed News*, November 16, 2016, https://www.buzzfeednews .com/article/craigsilverman/viral-fake-election-news-outperformed-real-news-on-facebook.

51. Silverman, "Fake Election News Stories Outperformed Real News."

52. Vaidhyanathan, "The Disinformation Machine," 185.

53. Vaidhyanathan, 185.

54. Amanda Robb, "Anatomy of a Fake News Scandal," *Rolling Stone*, November 16, 2017, https://www .rollingstone.com/politics/politics-news/anatomy-of-a-fake-news-scandal-125877/.

55. Robb, "Anatomy of a Fake News Scandal."

56. Kurt Eichenwald (@kurteichenwald), "1. Before the year is out....the evidentiary link between Wikileaks, Russian hackers, Kremlin disinformation outlet, and Donald Trump. In 2016, I received a phone call from someone in the intelligence world telling me to keep an eye on Sputnik," Twitter, December 31, 2018, 4:21 p.m., https://twitter.com/kurteichenwald/status/1079850037088342017.

57. Eichenwald, "1. Before the year is out."

58. Lauren Gambino and David Smith, "House Benghazi Report Faults Military Response, Not Clinton, for Deaths," *Guardian*, June 28, 2016, https://www.theguardian.

com/us-news/2016/jun/28/house-benghazi-report-clinton-attack-military.

59. Chris Brown, "Putin Was 'Good' and Obama Was 'Bad': Former Russian Trolls Reveal Online Work to Create 'Fake News'," *CBC News*, March 7, 2018, https://www.cbc.ca/news/world/russia-trolls-internet-fake-news-1.4562526.

60. Vaidhyanathan, "The Disinformation Machine," 177.

61. Silverman, "Fake Election News Stories Outperformed Real News."

62. Silverman.

63. Senate Select Committee on Intelligence, *Russia's Use of Social Media*, 11.

64. Vaidhyanathan, "The Disinformation Machine," 187–188.

65. Vaidhyanathan, 180.

66. Stengel, *Information Wars*, 223.

67. Stengel.

68. Stengel, 225.

69. Stengel.

70. Stengel.

71. Stengel, 208.

72. Stengel, 228.

73. Stengel, 235.

74. House of Commons, Digital, Culture, Media and Sport Committee, *Disinformation and "Fake News": Final Report*, Eighth Report of Session, 2017–19, February 14, 2019, 70, https://publications.parliament .uk/pa/cm201719/cmselect/cmcumeds/1791/1791.pdf.

75. Stengel, *Information Wars*, 235.

76. Stengel, 235–236.

77. House of Commons, *Disinformation and "Fake News,"* 70.

78. Vaidhyanathan, "The Disinformation Machine," 180.

79. House of Commons, *Disinformation and "Fake News,"* 70.

80. House of Commons, 70.

81. Heather A. Conley and Jean-Baptiste Jeangène Vilmer, *Successfully Countering Russian Electoral Interference*, Center for Strategic and International Studies, June 21, 2018, https://www.csis.org/analysis/successfully-countering-russian-electoral-interference.

82. Conley and Vilmer, *Countering Russian Electoral Interference.*

83. Conley and Vilmer.

BLACKOUT ON THE EASTERN SEABOARD![1]

O n a typical, hot and humid Saturday evening in June, Philadelphia, Pennsylvania, experienced an unexplained five-hour blackout. The power failure occurred just before 7 p.m., emptying stores and halting subway trains. Elevators stopped and traffic lights darkened. Hospitals and nursing homes operated on generators, while restaurant-goers ate and drank by the lights of their smartphones. The setting sun provided little relief from the heat and humidity for the 72,000 customers affected by the blackout. The power began to return around 10 p.m. and was fully restored by midnight.

Two months later, a major power cascade blacked out a large portion of the eastern United States, depriving 50 million people of power—some for up to four days. The outages started in the Midwest and cascaded through sections of the northeastern United States from Washington, D.C., north to Canada. Some suspected that the Philadelphia blackout was a trial run to identify vulnerabilities in the US electric infrastructure.

The impact was economy-wide. Cellular communications were disrupted, and internet access was limited. Some areas lost water pressure, causing potential contamination of the water supply. Four million people around Detroit, Michigan, and Cleveland, Ohio, had to boil water for several days. All cargo and passenger trains traveling along the Washington–New York–Boston corridor were shut down until limited service could resume with diesel locomotives. Airplanes were grounded because passengers could not be screened. Gas stations could not pump gas, and many refineries on the East Coast ceased operations. Looting was reported in at least one city. Economic losses in the United States were estimated at as much as $10 billion. In Canada, GDP fell in August by 0.7 percent, productivity suffered a net loss of 18.9 million work hours, and shipments of manufactured goods from Ontario declined by $2.3 billion (in Canadian dollars).[2]

Studies of past outages have identified cyber attacks, overloaded systems, weather and vegetation, operator error, and computer glitches as causes of blackouts. In recent years, the threat of physical sabotage, terrorism, and cyber attacks has grown. China, Iran, North Korea, and Russia are known to have targeted US infrastructure, compromising electric utilities, dams, and the defense industrial base. The age and interconnectedness of the electricity grid have turned what once was a demonstration of efficiency into a vulnerability. What caused the Eastern Seaboard to go dark this time?

PART I. BLACKOUT ON THE EASTERN SEABOARD!

In many ways, it was a typical summer day in the eastern part of the United States. It was hot—the mercury rose above 95°F in some areas—but there were no tornadoes or other extreme weather events. It began as a slow news day, reflecting a more relaxed pace of business as many Americans took time off from work to enjoy the end of the summer. In Washington, D.C., Congress was in recess, and the president traveled to California to attend campaign events.

It was a humid day and the absence of wind made it feel unbearable for many people. Consumer and commercial air conditioners caused a surge in electricity demand. Ed Olsen, a reliability operator for the power company FirstEnergy, described the day as a typical Thursday in August.

When he arrived at work in the morning, he phoned Farzad Tehrani, the reliability coordinator in the Midcontinent Independent Transmission System Operator (MISO), which ensures the seamless distribution of power across energy producers in the central US and Canada region. During the call, they had a friendly debate about the prospects for the Cleveland Browns football team that season.

Ed was mentally focused on the coming weekend—a getaway with his family to their lakeside cabin. After work, he planned to have a quick swim at the pool before going

> An Independent Transmission System Operator (ISO) is a nonprofit organization that combines the transmission facilities of several transmission owners into a single transmission system to move energy over long distances at a single lower price than the combined charges of each utility that may be located between the buyer and seller.

home to pack. At 3:46, however, he became aware that something was terribly wrong and that the FirstEnergy electrical network was in danger of collapse—reminding him of the five-hour blackout in Philadelphia two months earlier.

The Blackout Unfolds

Earlier that morning, Ed read the turnover notes on the clipboard left from the reliability operator on the graveyard shift. The day looked typical, and the power system appeared stable. The hot temperatures meant demand for electricity to support air-conditioning was high. After the blackout, he remembered two key points from the overnight notes.

- The peak load on that day was expected to be the highest of the year at 12,165 megawatts (MW), 20 percent higher than three days earlier, but considerably below the historical peak of 13,299 MW. Five units, including two nuclear units, would be out of service, but the previous night's forecast of today's power requirements indicated adequate power.

- The Department of Homeland Security had issued a bulletin reminding operators that in late July, US intelligence agencies received reporting that several groups could attempt a physical attack during the summer involving explosions at oil-producing facilities, power plants, or nuclear plants on the east coast of the United States. Management had been nervous about the possibility of a cyber attack ever since the Slammer internet worm took down monitoring computers at FirstEnergy Corporation's Davis-Besse nuclear plant and blocked commands that operate power utilities.[3]

However, the unexpected often occurs, and power companies prepare for that. So, when a neighboring power system, Cinergy, had several transmission lines trip out of use around noon in south-central Indiana, only Cinergy—which experienced voltage and loading problems and increased generation in response—raised concerns. About the same time, Ed was becoming concerned that voltage in the FirstEnergy system was sagging, probably because of the heavy demand.

Meanwhile, Tehrani, the reliability coordinator for MISO, at 12:15 p.m. purposely turned off the automatic update feature of the State Estimator program, which assesses the current condition of the grid's operations. He told his boss that the program was not functioning properly and that he was trying to identify the problem.

Before Ed knew it, an electric power cascade had blacked out large portions of the Midwest and Northeast in the largest power blackout ever, depriving 50 million people of power for up to four days. What Ed did know was that there would be no trip to the pool tonight.

A little after 4 p.m. Eastern Standard Time, the lights went out over a large swath of the northeastern United States and parts of Canada. In a matter of seconds, large portions of Ohio, Michigan, Pennsylvania, Massachusetts, New York, Connecticut, New Jersey, Maryland, and Ontario went dark (see Figure III.1[4]). The loss of electricity

---

FIGURE III.1 ■ Extent of East Coast Blackout

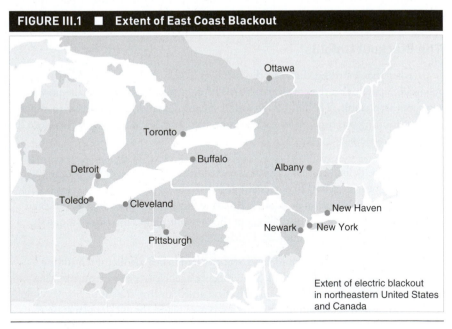

Extent of electric blackout in northeastern United States and Canada

Source: Map data from *The Boston Globe.*

not only caused the lights to go out, but also shut down airports, subways, trains, and tunnels. The loss of electric power suspended the operation of automatic doors, elevators, and entire drinking water utilities. It forced hospitals to run on limited power produced by backup generators. Cell phone towers, cash registers, and ATMs went out of commission.

In New York City, evening commuters stranded in a blackened city were forced to walk home because the city's public transportation system had ground to a halt, evoking memories of the September 11, 2001, terrorist attacks.[5] Local officials in New York City predicted that even once power was restored, it would take up to six additional hours before public transportation resumed operations. Elsewhere, the effects were keenly felt. In Cleveland, Ohio, electric pumps at the water utility shut down and deprived 1.5 million customers of drinking water; the mayor denounced price gouging by stores selling essentials such as water and batteries.[6]

Reaction and Response: "It's a Serious Situation"

While the president lunched with veterans in California, one of his senior aides informed him that a massive blackout had hit the Eastern Seaboard. With the specter of terrorism looming and millions of Americans out of power on a warm summer day, the president's hotel suite was quickly transformed into the West Coast White House Situation Room. From there, the president—with the help of the secretary of Homeland Security, White House aides, and multiple US government agencies in Washington, including the Federal Bureau of Investigation, Central Intelligence Agency, and Department of Energy—set about the task of responding to the massive blackout.

Electricity officials worked to restore power and began to sort through the information to determine the cause. The White House communications director summed up the situation: "There are a lot of different theories and we wanted to make sure that we get to the bottom of it."[7] As officials struggled to grapple with the crisis, one thing was immediately clear: the North American Energy Sector had suffered a huge blow with consequences that affected millions of Americans and Canadians.

Industry and government officials scrambled to restore service to the affected areas and identify the cause. Four-and-a-half hours after the blackout began, the White House updated the nation on what was known about the causes and consequences of the blackout. Calling the blackout a "serious situation," the president reassured the public that every effort was being made to determine what caused the blackout and that power would be restored as soon as possible. The nation turned its attention to assessing what caused the blackout and how to manage the consequences.

In New York City, the human and economic toll was large and immediate. It took 30 hours to restore power to the city.[8] During that time, transportation ground to a halt, leaving most of the people in the city in the heat and without a way home. With traffic lights out, the streets became clogged, subway trains stopped, and the three major metropolitan area airports canceled flights. Businesses closed because computers and cash registers would not operate. Cell phones became useless because cell towers stopped operating. The overall economic impact of the blackout was estimated to be between $4 billion and $6 billion for the region.[9] New York's share was more than $1 billion—or $36 million an hour—according to the New York City comptroller. More than $800 million of this was attributed to loss of productivity by closed businesses, while another $250 million was lost in perishable goods.

Maintaining security was expensive, but the city avoided the widespread looting associated with a blackout in 1977. The mayor estimated that overtime for police and other city workers totaled $10 million.[10] City officials attributed the relative calm to post-9/11 security procedures, and the plan appeared to work. Of the 850 arrests made overnight, police attributed only 250 of them directly to the blackout.[11]

Even before the lights came back on, speculation raged about the root cause and the effects of the blackout. The commentary ranged from cyber intrusion to aging infrastructure to the impact that such a widespread outage was having on public confidence. As a former Department of Energy secretary put it, "We're a superpower with a third-world electricity grid."[12] Within a day of the blackout, the House of Representatives Energy and Commerce Committee announced an investigation into the causes of the failure, and the White House announced that a task force would work to "identify the causes of the recent power outage" and "seek solutions to help prevent future outages."[13]

Challenges to Critical Infrastructure Security and Resilience in the US Electricity Subsector

Ed knew that large-scale blackouts occur—albeit infrequently—and spur incident reviews to identify the cause and to avoid a repeat event (see Figure III.2). Interconnectedness of the grid and the speed of the failure often complicate pinpointing the cause. Furthermore, elements of the grid are not time synchronized, which makes identifying the sequence of events difficult. Studies have identified overloaded systems, damage caused by weather and vegetation, operator error, and/or computer glitches as internal causes of blackouts:

- Utilities may overestimate how much reactive power capacity they have compared with demand, which could cause a sharp drop of voltage.

- Alternatively, the system might exceed safe limits without the knowledge of the operators.

- Weather is often an issue. Tornadoes during the spring and summer, along with hurricanes during the late summer and fall, commonly cause outages, as do ice and snow during the winter.

- The growth of trees in the spring and summer can result in power lines contacting trees and tripping out without the operator knowing.

- Windless days in summer pose an additional risk because extra demand makes the lines hot, causing them to expand and sag, allowing some to touch trees and other obstacles.

- The complex electric grid with short reaction times leaves little room for operator or computer error.

FIGURE III.2 ■ Select US Blackouts, 1965–2019			
Date	Incident	Number of People Affected	Cause
11/1965	Northeast Blackout	30 million	Human error
7/1977	New York City Blackout	9 million	Weather (lightning)
12/1982	West Coast Blackout	5 million	Weather (high winds)
7/1996	West Coast Blackout	2 million	High demand
8/1996	West Coast Blackout	7.5 million	High demand
6/1998	Upper Midwest Blackout	200,000	Weather (lightning)
8/2003	Northeast US and Canada Blackout	50 million	Human error/ equipment failure
9/2005	Los Angeles Blackout	2.7 million	Human error
10/2011	Northeast Blackout	3 million	Weather (snowstorm)
6/2012	Midwest and Mid-Atlantic Derecho Blackout	4.2 million	Weather (derecho)
10/2012	Hurricane Sandy Blackout	6.2 million	Weather (hurricane)
7/2019	New York City Blackout	72,000	Equipment failure

Source: Copyright 2020 Globalytica, LLC. All Rights Reserved.

In addition, there was a heightened fear of an attack by foreign adversaries on the power network. The Intelligence Community warned in early 2018 that foreign countries and terrorist groups were developing the capacity to attack segments of the US infrastructure. Prolonged denial of access to electricity, an important product on which most of the economy depends, could have a profound impact on public safety. Nuclear plants in particular have been mentioned as targets with the fear that an attack could cause a Chernobyl-style meltdown. Security experts describe the power network as vulnerable to cyber attack, a physical attack, and employee sabotage.

Many studies have pointed out the potential for compromise of energy management systems and IT infrastructure by foreign adversaries or disgruntled employees. Identified vulnerabilities include the ability to put nonessential programs on the system, loosely controlled system access and perimeter control, inconsistent patch and configuration management, and poor documentation of system security.

Foreign adversaries, such as Iran, could use a cyber attack as a hybrid weapon, sending the message, "Don't mess with me," should tensions in the Strait of Hormuz escalate. China, North Korea, and Russia could use a cyber attack to put the United States on the defensive in negotiations or as a surrogate field of conflict.

PART II. INVESTIGATION: WHAT HAPPENED?

Over the following weeks, investigators for the US-Canada Power System Outage Task Force assembled and began to analyze the evidence and interview operators. Unexpected events are common in the power industry, but blackouts do not usually happen. That is why utilities have defense-in-depth, an information-assurance concept in which multiple layers of security controls (defense) are placed throughout an IT system. The analytic challenge was to identify the unexpected event that was the root cause.

Investigators could not find signs of deliberate physical damage to power generators or lines on the day of the outage. An official in the FBI's Counterterrorism Division indicated that it had not yet found evidence that the outage was the result of terrorist or criminal activity. Nonetheless, intelligence assessments suggested there were malicious actors with the capability to disrupt the energy infrastructure with a cyber attack.

In another study, electrical engineers conducted an extended simulation of the power system on the day of the blackout and concluded that at least up until the tripping of a major transmission line at 3:05 p.m. that the system was secure enough to withstand any one of more than 800 contingencies. Modeling also suggested that loss of the Cinergy lines did not affect the blackout. Similarly, they judged that loss of the DPL Stuart-Atlanta line did not directly contribute to the blackout. In their assessment, that meant the root cause(s) of the accident happened after 3:00 p.m.

External Intrusion

An intrusion into the system by terrorists or other adversaries either directly or by using cyber techniques could not be ruled out. Earlier in the year, an internet worm crashed monitoring computers at FirstEnergy Corporation's Davis-Besse nuclear plant. The infection blocked commands that operate other power utilities. The control system was designed to operate in remote areas and over the internet to maximize functionality and interoperability with little attention to cyber security.

It did not take long before various groups claimed responsibility for the blackout:

- Several days after the attack, a major international terrorist group claimed responsibility through an Egyptian media outlet, under orders from the group's leader. The report claimed that terrorists had hit two main power plants supplying the eastern United States.

- Two weeks after the blackout, a participant in a jihadist chat room claimed that terrorist sleeper cells used the power outage to infiltrate the United States from Canada.

Meanwhile, state sponsors of terrorism, including cyberterrorism, posed a growing and alarming threat to the US critical infrastructure—particularly the Energy Sector. China posed a persistent threat to US military and critical infrastructure systems, strategically positioning capabilities to disrupt future operations.[14] North Korea, too, presented a dangerous threat, according to an internet security specialist who warned in 2018 that Pyongyang could conduct a cyber attack against US infrastructure to deter a potential military strike on its nuclear facilities.[15] Russia also had the ability to infiltrate and disrupt the US electrical distribution system—like it did in Ukraine in 2015 and 2016.[16] And in June 2019, hackers sponsored by the Iranian government targeted US government agencies and the oil and gas sectors.[17]

Computer Failure

Computer glitches particularly troubled investigators. That networks crashed at the worst possible time appeared to be more than coincidental. The failure of the alarm system at a crucial time in a way that left the operators unaware of the problem was particularly suspicious. Not knowing the system was about to fail, they took no steps to avert disaster.

The outbreak of a new virus on the internet a few days earlier also raised concerns. When the system crashed, FirstEnergy and the software provider, GE Energy, met to identify the problem. Some engineers discounted the Blaster virus because the software did not use Windows; others thought that the worm might have infected the software in a different manner. Systems analysts eventually discovered the program had been trapped in a loop when two applications had simultaneous "write access" to the data. Programmers finally identified in the million lines of coding a command that could cause the loop in a "perfect storm," which could only happen within a window of a millisecond. GE Energy engineers were skeptical because no other utility had encountered this particular problem, and they had provided customers a patch to prevent it.

Electrical engineers modeled the expected results of a reliability contingency assessment—had it been done—after the loss of the Harding-Chamberlin system. That showed that the model would have indicated some contingencies could not be covered and that the system was not in a reliable state.

A FirstEnergy system technician testified that he reported early on his shift to the control room and noticed that some remote energy management system sensors were failing. He was puzzled why no one on duty had reported that problem, so he alerted the main control room. A possible explanation is that the loss of two servers greatly slowed the computer system so screen refresh rates of 1 to 3 seconds had slowed to nearly a minute, making it frustrating for system operators to keep track of the health of the system. An IT staff member said his team was aware of the problem from automatic pages, but in the rush of events did not inform the operators of the computer problems.

Cyber investigators discovered that FirstEnergy was not running the most recent update of the software program. FirstEnergy had decided to switch to another software vendor in the near future and had not bothered to load the latest patch. At the time of the crash, GE energy technicians claimed there had never been an occurrence such as this and suggested the only solution would be a cold reboot of the system. FirstEnergy engineers rejected that as taking too long during a time of peak demand.

Weather and Vegetation

Investigators also explored if weather could have caused the blackout. On a day such as August 14, conductor temperatures can reach 212° F (100° C), and transmission lines can sag. The electric relay data showed classic signs of a tree contact short, so the investigation team visited the sites of three lines that failed. At the Hanna-Juniper outage, a worker had observed a contact with a tree. At the other sites they found tree fragments and burns that indicated there had been a different tree contact on the same day, but they could not conclude either happened on August 14. Outages were reported on those lines because of tree contact in the three preceding years. Also, FirstEnergy, in recognition of the danger of tree contact with power lines, flies over its lines twice a year to check on the condition of the right of way. The most recent flyover showed few signs of tree dangers.

Human Error and Inadequate Procedures

Experts visited the control area at FirstEnergy and voiced concerns about procedures. They noted the reliability operator was in a different room than the transmission operators. Handwritten logs were used by individuals, so there was no log of events for all to see. Briefing the next shift on conditions was haphazard at best.

Human action—as in the case of the disabling of the State Estimator (SE) automatic evaluation system—and inaction—such as failing to turn the SE back on—also lacked oversight. There were no processes to monitor an operator's action of taking down part of the system or to verify its coming back online. This lack of supervision left the system vulnerable to operator errors—both intentional or unintentional.

Specific concerns were raised about the ability of system operators to add or change software without prior authorization, and it could go undetected. In addition, procedures to update and maintain software were not defined. Some of the IT support personnel did not know how to perform diagnostic and forensic routines on these programs. Investigators also learned that FirstEnergy and other firms had inadequate ability to detect wireless intrusion and computer surveillance.

Investigators questioned Farzad Tehrani about the disabling of the SE program. He reported discovering that the Cinergy line outage did not update automatically in the SE program as many other lines do, so he had to update it by hand. He had to turn the automatic system off to figure out the problem. He claimed that he reran the program manually and got a valid solution at 1 p.m. and a contingency assessment at 1:15 p.m. When pressed as to why he had not turned the automatic update feature back on, Tehrani admitted he had been in a hurry to get to a lunch date and forgot to reactivate the automatic update feature before leaving.

Security investigators noted that uncleared personnel were occasionally allowed in sensitive areas without escort despite regulations to do so. Also, they discovered that contract personnel did not receive as stringent a level of background check as did staff.

Some analysts wondered whether nuclear power plants played a role in the black-out because several nuclear stations simultaneously lost their own power for unknown reasons at about the same time. When that happens, there is a significant danger of damaging the reactors and releasing highly radioactive materials even if the reactor is no longer critical. The lack of a national standard time complicates identifying where in the sequence the electric units fell. A sustained nuclear station outage could lead to a serious situation and is a vulnerability of nuclear plants.

Findings

The task force created to investigate the blackout made a set of forty-six sweep-ing recommendations. With a clear understanding of what had caused the blackout, government and industry officials turned their attention to developing strategies that could help to avert such large-scale blackouts in the future. What do you think caused the blackout?

APPENDIX A. THE US ENERGY SECTOR, ELECTRICITY SUBSECTOR

The US Energy Sector includes a diverse conglomeration of energy resources and assets spanning all fifty states, as well as US territories. A large number of owners and operator entities, including privately held companies and some publicly held federal, state, and local entities, comprise the sector. The vastness of the sector and the vital role it plays in everyday life make it both critical and challenging to protect.

The Energy Sector provides fuel to all the fifteen other critical infrastructure sec-tors, making them dependent on the Energy Sector to function. In fact, according to the Department of Homeland Security, "More than 80 percent of the country's energy infrastructure is owned by the private sector, supplying fuel to the transportation industry, electricity to households and businesses, and other sources of energy that are integral to growth and production across the nation."[18] Likewise, the Energy Sector is also dependent on many of these sectors. The result is a web of critical interdependen-cies (see Figure III.3).

Electricity: A High-Wire Balancing Act

Electricity is a vital commodity whose unique characteristics require a delicate and constant balance of supply and demand. Unlike other commodities, electricity must be consumed almost immediately upon generation, and it cannot easily be stored. It is generated using various fuel sources, then transmitted long distances at very high voltages, and subsequently distributed at lower voltages to customers.

From the late 1800s through the mid-1930s, the electrical grid was merely a patch-work of independently owned and operated utilities. These utilities provided genera-tion, transmission, and distribution, and they typically operated as vertically integrated monopolies within their service territory. As generation and transmission capacity grew over the subsequent decades and more nonutilities became energy producers, the grid

FIGURE III.3 ■ Web of Energy Sector Interdependencies

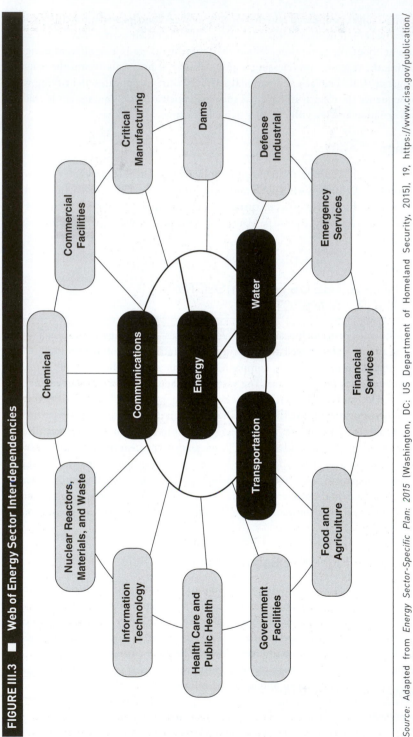

Source: Adapted from *Energy Sector-Specific Plan: 2015* (Washington, DC: US Department of Homeland Security, 2015), 19, https://www.cisa.gov/publication/nipp-ssp-energy-2015.

FIGURE III.4 ■ US Net Energy Generation by Source

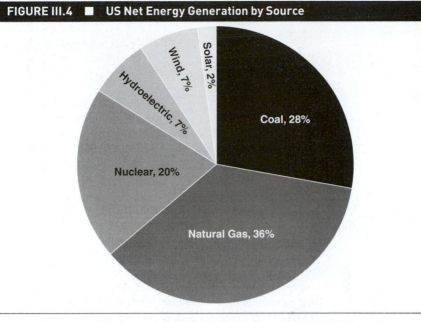

Source: Adapted from "Net Generation, United States, All Sectors, Annual," US Energy Information Administration, https://www.eia.gov/electricity/data/.

grew to incorporate many more energy assets and resources. During these early years, electricity was generated primarily by burning coal. But by the late 1970s, new technologies such as nuclear power had taken hold, and new technologies and laws ensured that alternative sources of energy, such as hydroelectric power, and renewable energy sources, such as wind and solar energy, would also be used to support the nation's growing energy needs (see Figure III.4).

At the time of the blackout, the North American electricity grid had grown to include four distinct grids, called interconnections (see Figure III.5). Generation had expanded to include a range of energy types, although coal remained the single largest source. To perform the main functions of generation, transmission, and distribution, the electricity subsector had by this time become "an integrated system of generating plants, high voltage transmission lines, local distribution facilities, [and] industrial control systems."[19] This diverse set of players had to "operate as a contemporaneous network in real time or in a synchronous manner to provide stable and reliable electricity to consumers."[20] And all participated in securing and improving the resilience—the ability to withstand natural disasters, manmade accidents, or attacks—of the US Energy Sector. This included more than 6,000 power plants with over 1,000 gigawatts of installed generation produced by coal, nuclear power plants, natural gas, hydroelectric dams, oil, and renewable sources.[21]

Regulations and Controls

Whether electricity is generated using fossil fuels (coal, petroleum, and natural gas), renewable energy (wind, solar, geothermal, solar thermal), hydroelectric power, or

FIGURE III.5   ■   The North American Power Grid

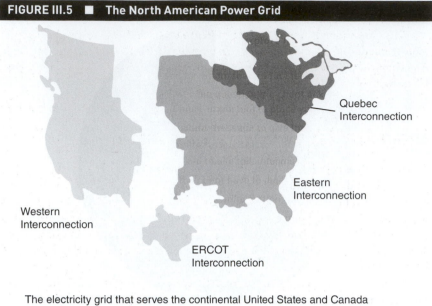

Quebec
Interconnection

Eastern
Interconnection

Western
Interconnection

ERCOT
Interconnection

The electricity grid that serves the continental United States and Canada
is actually four separate systems.

Source: Adapted from *Energy Sector-Specific Plan: An Annex to the National Infrastructure Protection Plan*
(Washington, DC: US Departments of Homeland Security and Energy, 2010), 26.

nuclear energy, several key physical, cyber, and human elements play a role in ensuring
a functioning grid. Because electricity is consumed almost instantaneously after it is
generated, operators use industrial control systems (ICS), such as supervisory control
and data acquisition (SCADA) systems to predict, monitor, and balance supply and
demand. Changes in any of the monitored activities are detected by the system, which
brings the change to the attention of the operators.[22]

These SCADA systems are essential for early detection and mitigation of a host of
potential problems that can arise on any given day that affect supply and demand. New
"smart" technologies such as sensors for monitoring loads; communication networks
to ensure timely, real-time monitoring and information sharing; and automated control devices to manage the system had begun to emerge that allow for better real-time
monitoring and control, but these technologies were still not in use in key areas.[23]

To better coordinate this delicate balancing act, many states and regions used
not-for-profit independent system operators (ISO) or regional transmission operators
(RTO) to help manage the transmission of electricity in different areas via industrial
control systems. ISOs are single-state or relatively small multiple-state entities established by federal order. RTOs perform similar or expanded services across a multistate
area and have been approved by the federal government.

Working with utility company power engineers, the ISOs and RTOs help to
monitor and balance loads and ensure that they are operating within voluntary limits. They in turn coordinate with the North American Electric Reliability Corporation (NERC), whose mission as an international, independent, self-regulatory,

not-for-profit organization is to ensure the reliability of the bulk power system (generation and high-voltage transmission).[24]

NERC was founded in 1968 by the electric utility industry to develop and promote mandatory rules and voluntary standards for the reliable operation of the North American transmission systems. The US Federal Energy Regulatory Commission, a US government organization, in turn oversees NERC.

APPENDIX B. KEY BLACKOUTS IN US HISTORY

American households lose power for more than three hours per year on average, but massive blackouts in which tens of millions of customers lose power simultaneously remain rare events.[25] Historically, the causes of massive outages have been traced to technological failures, human error, and natural causes. In the wake of past large-scale outages, industry had increased self-regulation of reliability standards, but as of mid-2019, the regulations were often voluntary and unevenly adopted across the United States.

Although there are many causes of blackouts, human error caused the two most severe outages in the northeastern United States, affecting 80 million people in the Northeast and Canada. Mistakes often prompt a cascade of events, blurring the lines between automated and manual failures.

The November 9, 1965, blackout that sent 30 million people into darkness was traced to a human error at a generation station in Ontario, Canada. A few days before the incident, a protective relay limiting the amount of power flowing through the lines was manually set too low. As electricity to this line was restricted, power flowed to other locations, causing a cascade of line overloads that ultimately caused power generation plants throughout the region to shut down automatically.[26] The blackout prompted electric utility providers in 1968 to create an electricity reliability council—now known as the North American Electric Reliability Corporation (NERC)—to develop voluntary standards for important aspects of industry operations such as equipment testing, reserve generation capacity, and reliability.

A massive blackout in 2003 was attributed to human error and a resulting equipment failure. Control room operators were unaware of critical changes to the energy flow in the electrical grid because an alarm failed to alert the operators. Transmission lines tripped as they made contact with trees, initiating a cascading failure of 508 generating units at 265 power plants across eight states and Canada.[27]

Furthermore, natural events have contributed to large-scale blackouts. The aboveground disposition of the physical aspects of the grid, particularly transformers and transmission lines, make it vulnerable to the elements and to the effects of extreme natural events.

- On July 13–14, 1977, New York City was plunged into darkness as a result of a series of four lightning strikes on transmission lines north of the city. The blackout sparked violence, looting, and arson throughout many parts of the city, and police made over 3,700 arrests across the city.[28]

Outrage over the blackout and the ensuing melee prompted the first provisions in federal legislation that enabled the US government to propose voluntary standards. The government never exercised this authority.

- In July and August 1996, extreme heat sparked two major blackouts that extended across the western United States and Canada.[29] Triple-digit temperatures caused lines to sag into inadequately trimmed trees, causing the widespread power failures. The outages prompted some members of the Western Systems Coordinating Council to agree to pay fines if they violated specific reliability standards. Otherwise, standards remained voluntary throughout the industry and violations generated no penalties.

- The mid-Atlantic derecho in June 2012 as well as Hurricane Sandy, which hit the New York City area four months later, caused major outages from Ohio to New York. Hurricane-strength winds in both storms, along with significant rainfall, damaged electric lines and other infrastructure. Hurricane Sandy occurred just a week before the national election, which created concern that the storm damage would affect voting. The damage also sparked dialogue about the effects of climate change on national security.[30]

While these types of extreme weather events have been rare in the past, statistics suggest that they are growing in frequency. Some experts, including the world's largest reinsurer, Munich Re, warned in 2012 that North America will experience an increase in the frequency and intensity of extreme weather events in the future.[31] This likelihood of extreme volatility causes a level of uncertainty that experts urge can only be mitigated by building a more resilient Energy Sector that embraces flexible responses; increased connectivity, communication, and collaboration across organizational boundaries; a willingness to challenge assumptions; and, preparing for a range of possible outcomes that stress continuity, response, and recovery.[32]

APPENDIX C. WORLDWIDE THREAT ASSESSMENT, CYBER THREATS

Excerpt of testimony from Daniel R. Coats, Director of National Intelligence, US Congress, Senate, Select Committee on Intelligence, *Worldwide Threat Assessment of the US Intelligence Community*, January 29, 2019, 5–6, https://www.dni.gov/files/ODNI/documents/2019-ATA-SFR---SSCI.pdf.

Our adversaries and strategic competitors will increasingly use cyber capabilities—including cyber espionage, attack, and influence—to seek political, economic, and military advantage over the United States and its allies and partners. China, Russia, Iran, and North Korea increasingly use cyber operations to threaten both minds and machines in an expanding number of ways—to steal information, to influence our citizens, or to disrupt critical infrastructure.

At present, China and Russia pose the greatest espionage and cyber attack threats, but we anticipate that all our adversaries and strategic competitors will increasingly build and integrate cyber espionage, attack, and influence capabilities into their efforts to influence US policies and advance their own national security interests. In the last decade, our adversaries and strategic competitors have developed and experimented with a growing capability to shape and alter the information and systems on which we rely. For years, they have conducted cyber espionage to collect intelligence and targeted our critical infrastructure to hold it at risk. They are now becoming more adept at using social media to alter how we think, behave, and decide. As we connect and integrate billions of new digital devices into our lives and business processes, adversaries and strategic competitors almost certainly will gain greater insight into and access to our protected information.

China.   China presents a persistent cyber espionage threat and a growing attack threat to our core military and critical infrastructure systems. China remains the most active strategic competitor responsible for cyber espionage against the US Government, corporations, and allies. It is improving its cyber attack capabilities and altering information online, shaping Chinese views and potentially the views of US citizens—an issue we discuss in greater detail in the Online Influence Operations and Election Interference section of this report.

- Beijing will authorize cyber espionage against key US technology sectors when doing so addresses a significant national security or economic goal not achievable through other means. We are also concerned about the potential for Chinese intelligence and security services to use Chinese information technology firms as routine and systemic espionage platforms against the United States and allies.

- China has the ability to launch cyber attacks that cause localized, temporary disruptive effects on critical infrastructure—such as disruption of a natural gas pipeline for days to weeks—in the United States.

Russia.   We assess that Russia poses a cyber-espionage, influence, and attack threat to the United States and our allies. Moscow continues to be a highly capable and effective adversary, integrating cyber espionage, attack, and influence operations to achieve its political and military objectives. Moscow is now staging cyber attack assets to allow it to disrupt or damage US civilian and military infrastructure during a crisis and poses a significant cyber influence threat—an issue discussed in the Online Influence Operations and Election Interference section of this report.

- Russian intelligence and security services will continue targeting US information systems, as well as the networks of our NATO and Five Eyes partners, for technical information, military plans, and insight into our governments' policies.

- Russia has the ability to execute cyber attacks in the United States that generate localized, temporary disruptive effects on critical infrastructure—such as disrupting an electrical distribution network for at least a few hours—similar to those demonstrated in Ukraine in 2015 and 2016. Moscow is mapping our critical infrastructure with the long-term goal of being able to cause substantial damage.

Iran. Iran continues to present a cyber-espionage and attack threat. Iran uses increasingly sophisticated cyber techniques to conduct espionage; it is also attempting to deploy cyber attack capabilities that would enable attacks against critical infrastructure in the United States and allied countries. Tehran uses social media platforms to target US and allied audiences.

- Iranian cyber actors are targeting US Government officials, government organizations, and companies to gain intelligence and position themselves for future cyber operations.

- Iran has been preparing for cyber attacks against the United States and our allies. It is capable of causing localized, temporary disruptive effects—such as disrupting a large company's corporate networks for days to weeks—similar to its data deletion attacks against dozens of Saudi governmental and private-sector networks in late 2016 and early 2017.

North Korea. North Korea poses a significant cyber threat to financial institutions, remains a cyber-espionage threat, and retains the ability to conduct disruptive cyber attacks. North Korea continues to use cyber capabilities to steal from financial institutions to generate revenue. Pyongyang's cybercrime operations include attempts to steal more than $1.1 billion from financial institutions across the world—including a successful cyber heist of an estimated $81 million from the New York Federal Reserve account of Bangladesh's central bank.

Non-State and Unattributed Actors. Foreign cyber criminals will continue to conduct for-profit, cyber-enabled theft and extortion against US networks. We anticipate that financially motivated cyber criminals very likely will expand their targets in the United States in the next few years. Their actions could increasingly disrupt US critical infrastructure in the healthcare, financial, government, and emergency service sectors, based on the patterns of activities against these sectors in the last few years.

Terrorists could obtain and disclose compromising or personally identifiable information through cyber operations, and they may use such disclosures to coerce, extort, or to inspire and enable physical attacks against their victims. Terrorist groups could cause some disruptive effects—defacing websites or executing denial-of-service attacks against poorly protected networks—with little to no warning.

The growing availability and use of publicly and commercially available cyber tools is increasing the overall volume of unattributed cyber activity around the world. The use of these tools increases the risk of misattributions and misdirected responses by both governments and the private sector.

APPENDIX D. FOREIGN CYBER ADVERSARIES: A MIXED THREAT TO US INFRASTRUCTURE

Foreign adversaries have a long history of attacking US computer systems (see Figure III.6). A computer security firm in 2016 concluded that hackers from different countries typically exhibit distinct behaviors. Chinese hackers pilfered "anything that looked

FIGURE III.6 ■ Select Foreign Cyber Attacks Against US Critical Infrastructure, 2018–2019

Date	Incident	Perpetrator
March 2019	Iranian hackers targeted thousands of people at more than 200 oil-and-gas and heavy-machinery companies across the world, stealing corporate secrets and wiping data from computers.	Iran
January 2019	The US Department of Justice announced an operation to disrupt a North Korean botnet that had been used to target companies in the media, aerospace, financial, and critical infrastructure sectors.	North Korea
October 2018	The US Department of Homeland Security announces that it has detected a growing volume of cyber activity targeting election infrastructure in the US ahead of the 2018 midterm elections.	Russia (suspected)
July 2018	Security researchers report that an Iranian hacking group had been targeting the industrial control systems of electric utility companies in the US, Europe, East Asia, and the Middle East.	Iran
July 2018	The Department of Homeland Security reveals that a campaign by Russian hackers in 2017 compromised the networks of multiple US electric utilities and put attackers in a position where they could have caused blackouts.	Russia
May 2018	Researchers reveal that a hacking group connected to Russian intelligence services had been conducting reconnaissance on the business and ICS networks of electric utilities in the United States and United Kingdom since May 2017.	Russia
April 2018	Cyber security researchers reveal that North Korean hackers targeted critical infrastructure, finance, health care, and other industries in 17 countries using malware resembling the code used in the 2014 Sony Pictures attack.	North Korea
April 2018	US and UK officials issued a joint warning that Russia was deliberately targeting western critical infrastructure by compromising home and business routers.	Russia

(Continued)

FIGURE III.6 ■ (Continued)		
Date	**Incident**	**Perpetrator**
April 2018	The UK's National Cyber Security Centre released an advisory warning that Russian state actors were targeting UK critical infrastructure by infiltrating supply chains.	Russia
March 2018	The FBI and Department of Homeland Security issued a joint technical alert to warn of Russian cyber attacks against US critical infrastructure. Targets included energy, nuclear, water, aviation, and manufacturing facilities.	Russia

Source: Adapted from "Significant Cyber Incidents," Center for Strategic and International Studies, https://www.csis.org/programs/technology-policy-program/significant-cyber-incidents.

like novel technical information." Russians penetrated systems, "mapping them and implanting hard-to-find backdoor access for potential future use." In contrast, Iranian hackers sought to do "as much damage as possible."[33]

Russia: Targeting Critical Infrastructure and Sowing Discontent

Russia's approach to cyber strategy has focused on infiltrating the critical infrastructure systems in the United States and the United Kingdom. Washington and London both issued warnings in 2018 that Moscow was trying to develop a capability to cause blackouts by accessing critical infrastructure entities through supply chains and home and business routers. Targets also included energy, nuclear, water, aviation, and manufacturing facilities.

- US officials in July 2018 revealed that a campaign by Russian intelligence in 2017 had compromised the networks of multiple US electric utilities and potentially enabled attackers to cause blackouts.

In addition, Russia has embarked on a long-term endeavor to create discord among elements of the US population through Digital Disinformation and false narratives spread mostly on social media platforms. The plan is to instill doubt about the security of election infrastructure, striking at the very heart of American democracy.

- Moscow's information operations and attempts to disrupt US election infrastructure in the run-ups to the 2016 and 2018 elections have been widely publicized, although, as a result of Digital Disinformation, separating the truth from fiction is challenging (see Case Study II).

Iran: Economic Cyber Warfare as an Asymmetric Tool

Iran's lack of conventional forms of power—economic, military, and geopolitical—has led it to develop its asymmetric tool kit to target its adversaries in the West and in the Middle East. Suffering from the burden of sanctions, Tehran has long relied on asymmetric tools such as proxies to carry out small-scale attacks against its primary enemy, Israel. Since approximately 2009, it has accelerated its cyber capabilities.[34] Iranian hackers have tended to focus on Western economic interests and its regional competitors—in particular, Saudi Arabia.

- Iran stepped up the development of its offensive cyber capabilities after being targeted by the Stuxnet virus, reportedly developed by the United States and Israel. Less than two years after the Stuxnet attack, Tehran conducted cyber attacks on US and Saudi Arabian targets.[35]

- Tehran mostly attacked major US banks between 2001 and 2013, hitting at least forty-six companies, although it also has pre-positioned malware for future attacks on energy infrastructure.[36, 37]

- In 2013, a hacker affiliated with the Iranian government tapped into the control system of a dam in New York. The hacker would have been able to operate the floodgate, had it been operating at the time, flooding nearby homes.[38]

China: Aiming at Economic and Military Secrets, More Than Critical Infrastructure

The main focus of Beijing's cyber strategy historically has been to steal corporate and government secrets to boost Chinese economic goals—including through a multiyear invasion of Western technology providers. However, Chinese efforts to target the US critical infrastructure seeking to disrupt or disable the power supply or to pre-position malware for a future attack rose in late 2018.[39] Since the beginning of 2018, Chinese cyber attacks have sought intellectual property and military plans, state secrets, personal information, and IT system access of Americans and their allies.

- Chinese government hackers and those hired by the government have concentrated on obtaining commercial, industrial, and military secrets. Most of the Chinese government's efforts are designed to steal intellectual property and trade secrets, including military plans—often targeting private-sector government contractors.

- Chinese efforts also are aimed at obtaining Personally Identifiable Information (PII) such as Social Security numbers, emails, phone numbers, addresses, or other data specific to an individual. The information stolen has included bulk data of PII from a US hotel chain, personal and IT information of a major European industrial company, and identifiable information of potential critics of Beijing.

- However, Beijing in late 2018 increased its digital attacks against US energy, financial, transportation, and health care sectors. US intelligence officials expressed concern that the breaches pre-positioned malware to disrupt operations in the future—suggesting a possible change in tactics by Beijing.[40]

North Korea: Financial Woes Lead to Cyber Theft

North Korea has targeted companies in the media, aerospace, financial, and critical infrastructure sectors. Pyongyang, however, primarily has focused its cyber efforts on financial targets to ease the burden of sanctions imposed as a result of Pyongyang's nuclear weapons program. In addition, North Korea's financially motivated attacks on the international banking sector have inspired nonstate actors, including organized crime rings, to adopt similar methods to acquire funds illegally.

- North Korean hackers targeted critical infrastructure, finance, health care, and other industries in 17 countries using malware resembling the code used in the 2014 Sony Pictures attack, which leaked employees' PII, emails, and proprietary information.

- Financially motivated cyber attacks in Vietnam, Bangladesh, Taiwan, Mexico, and Chile, among others, have been attributed to North Korea since 2015.[41] Up to $2 billion has been stolen in these cyber heists—including $81 million from Bangladesh's central bank—according to press reporting citing an unreleased UN report.[42]

- Organized crime groups and individual cyber criminals are adopting the methods used by North Korean groups to bolster their capabilities, including stealing from banks.

The Future of Cyber Warfare: Cyber Blocs?

Multinational cyber attacks have not yet become the norm, but blocs of adversaries could easily work together to conduct cyber warfare. Hacking groups affiliated with or sponsored by countries disgruntled by Western policies could launch large-scale cyber attacks, making attribution difficult. Denial and deception practices, especially if employed by multiple hackers in various locations, could further challenge investigators, hampering recovery and hindering the prevention of additional attacks.

- Foreign adversaries could cooperate in cyber warfare against the United States, the European Union, and its allies. In mid-2019, the presidents of China, Iran, and Russia met at the Shanghai Cooperation Organization summit. At the time, all three were at odds with the United States over trade and military disagreements.

Similarly, cyber criminals and "hackers for hire" could be hired or persuaded to conduct cyber attacks against critical infrastructure and other targets.

NOTES

1. Dates and locations in this case study have been altered for teaching purposes. The actual events and the cause of the outages are described in a PDF document, "Critical Thinking for Strategic Intelligence, 3e Instructors Materials," that accompanies this book and can be obtained at no cost on the CQ Press website.

2. US-Canada Power System Outage Task Force, *Final Report on the August 14, 2003 Blackout in the United States and Canada: Causes and Recommendations*, April 2004, 1, https://www.energy.gov/sites/prod/files/oeprod/DocumentsandMedia/BlackoutFinal-Web.pdf.

3. Krebs, "Hackers Did Not Cause Blackout," *Washington Post*, November 19, 2003, http://www.washingtonpost.com.

4. "Anatomy of a Blackout," *Boston Globe*, February 23, 2012.

5. "Major Power Outage Hits New York, Other Large Cities," *CNN*, August 14, 2003, http://www.cnn.com/2003/US/08/14/power.outage/.

6. "Biggest Blackout in U.S. History," *CBS News*, August 15, 2003, http://www.cbsnews.com/2100-201_162-568422.html.

7. Elisabeth Bumiller, "The Blackout of 2003: The President: Bush Doesn't Let Blackout Upset Lunch With Troops," *New York Times*, August 15, 2003, https://www.nytimes.com/2003/08/15/us/blackout-2003-president-bush-doesn-t-let-blackout-upset-lunch-with-troops.html.

8. Ken Belson and Matthew L. Wald, "'03 Blackout Is Recalled, Amid Lessons Learned," *New York Times*, August 14, 2008, https://www.nytimes.com/2008/08/14/nyregion/14blackout.html.

9. JR Minkel, "The 2003 Northeast Blackout—Five Years Later," *Scientific American*, August 13, 2008, https://www.scientificamerican.com/article/2003-blackout-five-years-later/.

10. David Teather, "Blackout Costs New York 36m an Hour," *Guardian*, August 19, 2003, http://www.guardian.co.uk/business/2003/aug/20/usnews.internationalnews.

11. William K. Rashbaum, "The Blackout: Crime: This Time Fewer Arrests as the City Stayed Dark," *New York Times*, August 18, 2003, http://www.nytimes.com/2003/08/16/nyregion/the-blackout-crime-thistime-fewer-arrests-as-the-city-stayed-dark.html.

12. Geraldine Sealy, "Fixing Power Grid Will Mean Sacrifices," *ABC News*, August 18, 2003, http://abcnews.go.com/US/story?id=90321&page=1#.UXqsqb9Z6XI.

13. "Power Returns to Most Areas Hit by Blackout," *CNN*, August 15, 2003, http://www.cnn.com/2003/US/08/15/power.outage/.

14. Jim Finkle and Christopher Bing, "China's Hacking Against U.S. on the Rise: U.S. Intelligence Official," *Reuters*, December 11, 2018, https://www.reuters.com/article/us-usa-cyber-china-idUSKBN1OA1TB.

15. Alex Hern, "North Korea Is a Bigger Cyber-Attack Threat Than Russia," *Guardian*, February 26, 2018, https://www.theguardian.com/technology/2018/feb/26/north-korea-cyber-attack-threat-russia.

16. Testimony of Daniel R. Coats, Director of National Intelligence, US Congress, Senate, Select Committee on Intelligence, *Worldwide Threat Assessment of the US Intelligence Community*, January 29, 2019, 5–6, https://www.dni.gov/files/ODNI/documents/2019-ATA-SFR---SSCI.pdf.

17. Associated Press, "Iranian Hackers Wage Cyber Campaign Amid Tensions With US," *CBN News*, June 22, 2019, https://www1.cbn.com/cbnnews/national-security/2019/june/iranian-hackers-wage-cyber-campaign-amid-tensions-with-us.

18. US Department of Homeland Security, *Energy Sector*, http://www.dhs.gov/energy-sector.

19. US Energy Information Administration, *Electric Power Industry Overview*, 2007, http://www.eia

.gov/cneaf/electricity/page/prim2/
toc.2html#netw.

20. US Energy Information Administration,
Electric Power Industry Overview.

21. US Department of Homeland Security,
Energy Sector.

22. Robert O'Harrow Jr., "Cyber Search
Engine Shodan Exposes Industrial
Control Systems to New Risks," *New
York Times*, June 3, 2012, http://www
.washingtonpost.com/investigations/
cyber-search-engineexposes-
vulnerabilities/2012/06/03/
gJQAIK9KCV_story.html.

23. Testimony of Gregory C. Wilshusen,
United States Government
Accountability Office, US Congress,
Senate, Committee on Energy and
Natural Resources, *Cybersecurity:
Challenges in Securing the Electricity
Grid*, July 17, 2012, http://www.gao
.gov/assets/600/592508.pdf.

24. North American Electric
Reliability Corporation (website),
http://www.nerc.com/page
.php?cid=1%7C7%7C11.

25. Mark Clayton, "Progress on Preventing
Blackouts," *Christian Science Monitor*,
June 18, 2007, https://www.csmonitor
.com/2007/0618/p02s01-ussc.html.

26. "1977 Great Northeast Blackout,"
Blackout History Project, George
Mason University, Fairfax,
Virginia, http://blackout.gmu.edu/
home.html.

27. Testimony of the United States
Government Accountability Office
before the US Congress, House,
Subcommittee on Oversight and
Investigations, Committee on Energy
and Commerce, *Cybersecurity:
Challenges in Securing the Modernized
Electricity Grid*, February 28, 2012,
http://www.gao.gov/assets/
590/588913.pdf.

28. "1977 New York Blackout," Blackout
History Project.

29. "1996 System Disturbances: Review
of Selected 1996 Electric System
Disturbances in North America,"
North American Electric Reliability
Council, Princeton, New Jersey,
August 2002. Retrieved from: https://
www.nerc.com/pa/rrm/ea/System%20
Disturbance%20Reports%20
DL/1996SystemDisturbance.pdf

30. Sandra I. Erwin, "Superstorm Sandy
Topples Traditional Notions of
National Security," *National Defense*,
October 31, 2012, https://archive
.fo/20130415143327/http://www
.nationaldefensemagazine.org/blog/
Lists/Posts/Post.aspx?ID=959.

31. Matt Pearce, "2012 Another
Bad Year for U.S. Disasters, and
It May Get Worse," *Los Angeles
Times*, December 24, 2012, http://
www.latimes.com/news/nation/
nationnow/la-na-nn-us-billion-
dollar-disasters20121224,0,7895195.
story.

32. Debra van Opstal, "The Resilience
Imperative," *The CIP Report*,
December 2012, https://cip.gmu.edu/
wp-content/uploads/2013/06/125_
The-CIP-Report-December-2012_
Resilience.pdf.

33. Annie Fixler and Frank Cilluffo,
*Evolving Menace: Iran's Use of
Cyber-Enabled Economic Warfare*
(Washington, DC: Foundation for the
Defense of Democracies, November
2018), https://www.fdd.org/wp-
content/uploads/2018/11/REPORT_
IranCEEW.pdf.

34. Fixler and Cilluffo, *Evolving Menace.*

35. Fixler and Cilluffo.

36. Max Kutner, "Alleged Dam Hacking
Raises Fears of Cyber Threats to
Infrastructure," *Newsweek*, March 13,
2016, https://www.newsweek.com/
cyber-attack-rye-dam-iran-441940.

37. Fixler and Cilluffo, *Evolving Menace.*

38. Kutner, "Alleged Dam Hacking."

39. Finkle and Bing, "China's Hacking Against U.S. on the Rise."

40. Finkle and Bing.

41. *APT38: Un-Usual Suspects*, FireEye, undated report, https://content.fireeye .com/apt/rpt-apt38.

42. Edith M. Lederer, "UN Report: North Korea Cyber Experts Raised Up to $2 Billion," *Associated Press*, August 5, 2019, https://www.apnews.com/ 2895639125bd49da9f215f2feb 0b58a3.

THE END OF THE ERA OF AIRCRAFT CARRIERS

Throughout history, a nation's global power has been measured in part by the size of its navy. The ability to project power across the seas is considered critical for economic viability, for national defense, and as an expression of national culture.[1] The fundamental roles of the navy include protecting its nation's interests in global commerce, responding to conflicts, supporting humanitarian efforts, providing disaster relief, and, for large global navies, projecting power. Many military experts view the navy as the most flexible of the military services. Capable of maneuvering to almost any location in the world, naval forces—and particularly aircraft carrier battle groups—have projected substantial power and influence wherever and whenever they are needed.[2]

Shipping trade routes are global assets that must remain protected. Oceans connect the nations of the world; 90 percent of global commerce and 95 percent of US imports and exports are transported on the sea. Of the world's population, 75 percent live within a few hundred miles of an ocean.[3] Without shipping, the majority of the world's population could not afford to import and export food and goods.[4]

The safe flow of goods and people is made possible by naval forces exerting their influence in waters across the globe. In 1992, the US Navy abandoned its base in Subic Bay in the Philippines following the breakdown in negotiations with the Philippine government to conclude a treaty to renew the US lease on the base. Largely because of the reduced naval presence, piracy quintupled in the next decade in the Strait of Malacca, one of the world's busiest waterways, which is located in Southeast Asia.[5] The Asian financial crisis in 1997 was a second major contributor to ongoing piracy. Vast unemployment led to increased piracy as it became a financial opportunity for poverty-stricken Malaysians and Indonesians.[6] In contrast, on the other side of the Indian Ocean off the Horn of Africa, the unprecedented cooperation of naval forces representing twenty nations has significantly reduced the level of piracy. However, the area is too large for a naval presence to prevent all piracy incidents.[7]

Naval forces are also used to preserve international stability and influence the outcome of regional conflicts. The aircraft carrier battle group functions as a navy's mechanism to project force with its ability to conduct air strikes, launch missiles, and land troops from a mobile platform—an aircraft carrier (see Figure IV.1).[8] During the war in Somalia in 2007, helicopter gunships, Special Forces teams, and cruise missiles were directed at Al-Qaeda militants from an aircraft carrier battle group.[9] In support of Operation Inherent Resolve, which began in 2014, the US-led coalition used two aircraft carriers, the USS *Carl Vinson* and the USS *Harry S. Truman*, to immediately begin launching air strikes against the Islamic State in the Levant (ISIL).[10] The French carrier *Charles de Gaulle* supported anti-ISIL operations following the November 2015 terrorist attacks in Paris.[11] Also in 2015, the USS *Theodore Roosevelt* supported US

FIGURE IV.1 ■ USS *Abraham Lincoln*

Source: US Navy photo by Mass Communication Specialist Seaman Zachary S. Welch/Released.

efforts to project power in the South China Sea to monitor China's expansion into the Spratly Islands and to underscore the importance of freedom of transit on international waters.[12]

In addition, the presence of aircraft carrier battle groups deployed around the globe enables the US Navy and its allies to complement the use of Amphibious Readiness Groups to provide humanitarian assistance and disaster-relief operations in a matter of days, if not hours.[13] Medical care and relief assistance is most critical immediately following a disaster, whether natural or man-made. The USS *George Washington*, for example, spearheaded relief efforts in the Philippines following the typhoon in 2013. It converted approximately 400,000 gallons of sea water into fresh water daily, provided rolling emergency hospital care, and delivered emergency rations to survivors.[14]

US NAVAL DOMINANCE

The United States is the dominant maritime nation with the largest navy in the world.[15] The US Navy employs a sixty-year-long strategy—to remain responsive, adaptable, and combat ready against all conflicts and challengers.[16] The navy successfully projects US diplomatic strength and military power primarily through the use of eleven active aircraft carrier battle or strike groups that demonstrate dominance, readiness, and influence across the globe.[17]

Current plans call for building ten new generation CVN-78 aircraft carriers by 2058, staggered every six years, to replace aging carriers in the current fleet. The first in this line is the USS *Gerald R. Ford*, which was to be commissioned in 2014 but the commissioning was delayed until July 22, 2017.[18, 19] The USS *Gerald R. Ford* serves as the replacement for the USS *Enterprise*, which was decommissioned in January 2013. In 2011, the US Navy projected the total cost to bring the USS *Gerald R. Ford* into service at $11.5 billion, comprising $2.9 billion in detailed design and $8.6 billion for construction and government-furnished equipment, including the nuclear reactor. The final cost has come in at approximately $14.2 billion, surpassing even the Congressional Budget Office's estimated cost of $12.9 billion based on historical patterns for building a first-in-a-class ship.[20] This is as much as Iran spends on its armed forces each year, and almost twice what it cost to build the last of the Nimitz-class carriers, the USS *George W. Bush*.[21]

The carrier strike group is considered the most superior projection of US naval power. The aircraft carrier is the centerpiece of current naval strategy. It typically supports an air wing composed of eighty aircraft and leads a battle group generally composed of 7,500 sailors, a guided missile cruiser, two guided missile destroyers, an attack submarine, and a supply ship.[22] During conflict, carriers and other surface combatants execute combat operations and support all the military services.[23] During peacetime, the carrier strike group fulfills a wide range of missions, including enhancing the ability of the US military to respond to crises, evacuating US dependents from unstable or dangerous conditions, and providing humanitarian relief.[24]

The US naval fleet is larger than the next twelve national navies combined (see Figure IV.2).[25] As of mid-2016, the US Navy comprised about 330,000 active duty personnel, 3,700 aircraft, and 289 ships.[26] Many of these Reagan-era ships will retire over the next decade without replacement due to budget constraints and the rising cost of US-built ships. The majority of the navies from other countries perform coastal or regional missions, such as patrolling national coastlines to deter smuggling and protect shipping routes. For this reason, the majority of navies worldwide operate with substantially fewer ships and personnel.[27]

Today, the US Navy is unchallenged as the blue-water superpower. A few countries are building new carriers: the UK is building two, India aspires for three, and China plans to have six or so by 2035. Japan also has plans to convert two destroyers to carry jet aircraft.[28] Some competing nations, however, are fielding anti-access/area denial technologies, such as anti-ship cruise missiles, instead of directly competing with advanced ships. The following are among the most notable second-tier contenders:

Russia. The Military Maritime Fleet of Russia is the second-largest navy in the world based on tonnage, at 845,730 tons, with over 282 warships, including one aircraft carrier.[29, 30] The Russian economy stabilized a few years after the collapse of the Soviet Union, providing the fiscal resources needed to begin modernization of Russia's naval fleet. The fleet, however, lacks technological sophistication compared to the fleets of Western navies. In 2010, Russia announced its goal to operate a modern fleet by 2020 and began building new corvettes and destroyers to protect its coastal waters.[31]

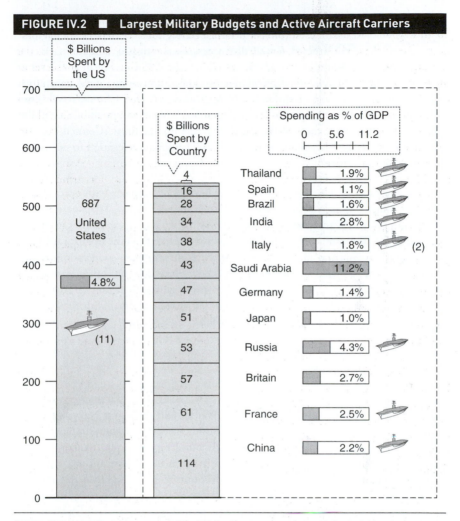

FIGURE IV.2 ■ Largest Military Budgets and Active Aircraft Carriers

Source: Nigah Ajaj, Ryan Larson, and Abby DiOrio. Pherson Associates, LLC. All rights reserved.

Contributing greatly to Russia's increase in tonnage is its production of icebreakers, making the nation a dominant force in the Arctic. As of 2016, Russia had forty ice-breakers and had begun production of eleven nuclear-powered icebreakers, scheduled to be completed by 2030.[32] The United States, in contrast, had only five functional icebreakers, one of which was about to be retired.[33]

China. China's Navy has 708,086 tons and approximately 496 ships, not including the 232 auxiliary vessels. It recently completed production of its first aircraft carrier, the *Liaoning*. In January 2016, China announced construction of a new carrier, which experts said would take at least five years to complete.[34] Although naval experts assess that China's current carrier capacity offers little utility in regionally based conflicts, the continued addition of carriers to the Chinese Navy would signal significant growth in its capabilities and its ability to project presence throughout the Asia-Pacific region.[35] The Chinese have constructed several dozen destroyers, frigates, and submarines to extend and defend their claims in the South China Sea. Their interest in and development of the Spratly Islands has been criticized by many in the international community, especially Vietnam and the Philippines.[36] In August of 2015, five Chinese naval vessels were spotted in the Bering Sea, and China announced the development of a small fleet of icebreakers for exploration of the Arctic.[37] While not an Arctic Council member, China was granted permanent observer status, which allows a delegation to sit in on all meetings but not vote.[38]

Japan. Japan has the fourth-largest navy in the world by tonnage, with over 400,000 tons, 154 ships, 346 aircraft, and over 45,000 personnel.[39] The US-Japanese security alliance after World War II restricted the growth of Japan's naval capabilities in the second half of the 20th century. Despite limitations, Japan leveraged the US-forward-based presence in East Asia and maintained a strong maritime defense cooperation strategy with the US Navy.[40] Japan's Maritime Self-Defense Force does not operate an aircraft carrier, but the navy has two helicopter destroyers capable of carrying up to fourteen antisubmarine helicopters[41] and operates four destroyers equipped with the US military's Aegis Ballistic Missile Defense system technology.[42]

United Kingdom (UK). The Royal Navy enabled Great Britain to reign as the greatest power in the world from the Napoleonic Wars through World War II. The size and strength of the nation's naval capabilities helped it expand British imperial rule and control territories on five continents.[43] The United States surpassed Britain as the premier naval power after World War II, and the Royal Navy is now the fifth-largest navy in the world with 408,750 tons. As of November 2018, it had 74 commissioned ships.[44, 45] The UK is currently building two aircraft carriers of the Queen Elizabeth class; the first is scheduled to reach initial operational capability in 2020. Due to fiscal constraints, the UK decommissioned the HMS *Ark Royal* in 2010.[46] The HMS *Queen Elizabeth* is estimated to cost $6.2 billion to build and the next in its class, the HMS *Prince of Wales*, is expected to be only one-fifth cheaper.[47]

France. The French Navy supports France's regional and international interests with 319,195 tons, more than 180 ships, 6 commandos units, 40,000 men and women, and one aircraft carrier.[48] Throughout the 19th century, the French Navy competed with Britain as a major naval power.

India. India wants to be considered a significant naval power and plans to strengthen the capabilities of its 155-warship fleet, with 317,725 tons, and expand into a blue-water navy capable of deploying outside its regional waters.[49] India still operates the INS *Vikramaditya* and the refitted Russian *Admiral Gorkov* Kiev-class carrier, and it is developing a Vikrant-class carrier,[50] replacing the fifty-year-old, 28,000-ton INS *Viratt*. It has also purchased forty-five MiG 29-K fighter jets that will operate from the two carriers.[51] These two aircraft carriers will significantly enhance India's global force projection capabilities.[52]

The Shrinking Global Naval Presence

Only half of the top ten countries with the highest total military expenditures and three other countries operate carriers with large fixed-wing aircraft, owing in large part to high shipbuilding and operating costs (see Figure IV.3).[53] Of all these countries, the US Navy has the most reliable and experienced carrier capability with advanced fixed-wing aircraft.[54]

The UK's Royal Navy was once a premier global naval power but dramatically declined post–Cold War. In 1991, 1994, and 1998, the UK drastically cut its number of warships, submarines, and personnel to save resources for an aircraft carrier, but this was unsuccessful. Defense budget cuts in 2010[55] forced it to decommission its symbolic flagship, the *Ark Royal*; the UK implemented another round of defense budget cuts in 2013.[56]

Despite its existing 341-ship-strong fleet, the US Navy fleet is also shrinking. During the Cold War, the Navy operated 600 ships.[57] Budget cuts following the end of the Cold War reduced the size of the fleet as well as funding for research, operations and maintenance, and personnel.[58] In 2015, the Congressional Budget Office released an in-depth report outlining the challenges the Navy faced in sustaining its size. The report warned that the proposed growth of surface combatants was fiscally dangerous for the next decade because the current plan asked for $4 billion more per year than the US Navy had received in decades.[59] Continuing advances in technology, however, have offset some of the negative consequences of this trend.

In May 2010, then-defense secretary Robert M. Gates asked a US Navy audience, "Do we really need 11 carrier strike groups for another 30 years when no other country

FIGURE IV.3 ■ Military Expenditures by Country, 2018 (in Billions USD)

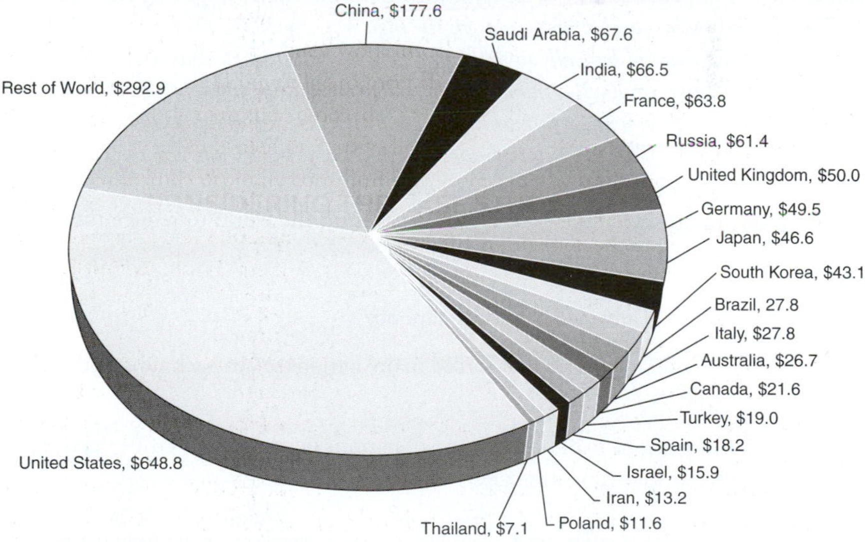

China, $177.6
Saudi Arabia, $67.6
India, $66.5
France, $63.8
Russia, $61.4
United Kingdom, $50.0
Germany, $49.5
Japan, $46.6
South Korea, $43.1
Brazil, 27.8
Italy, $27.8
Australia, $26.7
Canada, $21.6
Turkey, $19.0
Spain, $18.2
Israel, $15.9
Iran, $13.2
Poland, $11.6
Thailand, $7.1
United States, $648.8
Rest of World, $292.9

Source: Stockholm International Peace Research Institute.

has more than one? Any future plans must address these realities."[60] Gates' comments provoked an outburst both within the navy and on Capitol Hill, but US Representative Joe Sestak (D-PA) supported Gates' position. He argued that the total number of aircraft carrier strike battle groups could be reduced to eight or nine because the new generation of DVN-78 aircraft carriers is supposed to have eight times the fighting capability of the older carriers.[61] In 2015, Senator John McCain, the chair of the Senate Armed Services Committee, launched an investigation focusing on the Chief of Naval Operations to determine how to reduce future costs of constructing Ford-class aircraft carriers.[62]

Typically, the US Navy has three carriers at sea, three returning from six-month deployments, three preparing to deploy, and two in dry dock being repaired. Dry-dock periods, like midlife replacement of a nuclear core, can exceed a year. A reduction in the total number of carriers would disrupt this system, and the US Congress has legislated that the navy must retain eleven carriers in its fleet.[63]

Stark budget realities could force a change. For example, about $225 million a year is needed just to cover the typical payroll for a carrier, not counting its air wing. The annual cost of operating and maintaining a Nimitz-class carrier is $726 million; it has 6,000 people on board which is twice the size of the entire Danish Navy.[64]

ANTICIPATING A FUTURE WITH FAR FEWER AIRCRAFT CARRIERS

Imagine it is now 2030. All but four countries have mothballed their aircraft carriers, and the US fleet of aircraft carriers has been reduced by half. The movement away from large aircraft carriers was almost as dramatic as the demise of the battleship in the wake of the British sinking in 1941 of the German battleship Bismarck *and the Japanese carrier strikes on US battleships in Pearl Harbor later in the same year. Governments no longer rely on large naval fleets to support major combat operations on the high seas. By 2030, the function of aircraft carriers has been reduced basically to projecting power against small countries with limited military capabilities, conducting noncombatant evacuation operations (NEO), protecting shipping routes, and providing humanitarian aid and disaster relief.[65] What caused this dramatic sea change? This case study posits that three key drivers sparked the change and explores how the function of naval forces was transformed.*

By 2030, three key factors forced nations around the world to reduce the size of their naval fleets and eliminate aircraft carriers:

1. Technological advancements in weaponry

2. Global economic trends that forced many nations to cut back substantially on their budgets

3. A shared realization of the need for all nations to adopt more cost-effective, cooperative maritime strategies

As a result, aircraft carriers and other large surface combatants became prime candidates for budget cuts. The need to achieve national security objectives in the most cost-efficient way possible became paramount (see Figure IV.4).

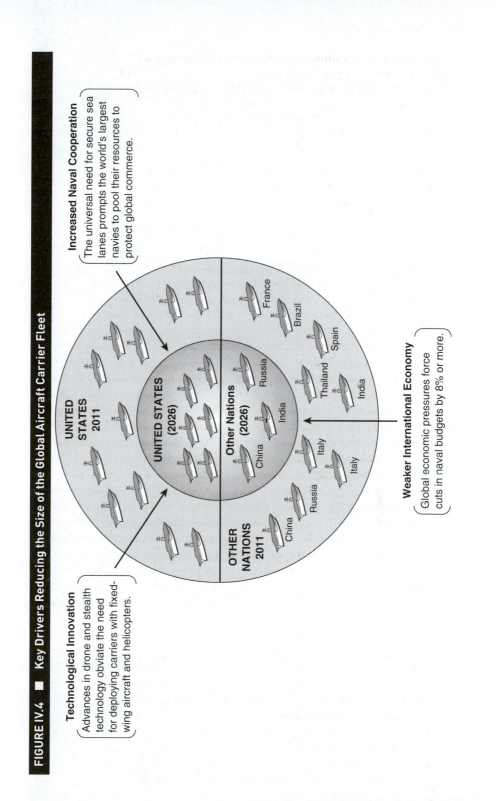

FIGURE IV.4 ■ Key Drivers Reducing the Size of the Global Aircraft Carrier Fleet

Increased Naval Cooperation
The universal need for secure sea lanes prompts the world's largest navies to pool their resources to protect global commerce.

Technological Innovation
Advances in drone and stealth technology obviate the need for deploying carriers with fixed-wing aircraft and helicopters.

Weaker International Economy
Global economic pressures force cuts in naval budgets by 8% or more.

UNITED STATES 2011

UNITED STATES (2026)

OTHER NATIONS 2011

Other Nations (2026)

France

Brazil

Spain

Thailand

India

Russia

India

China

Italy

Italy

Russia

China

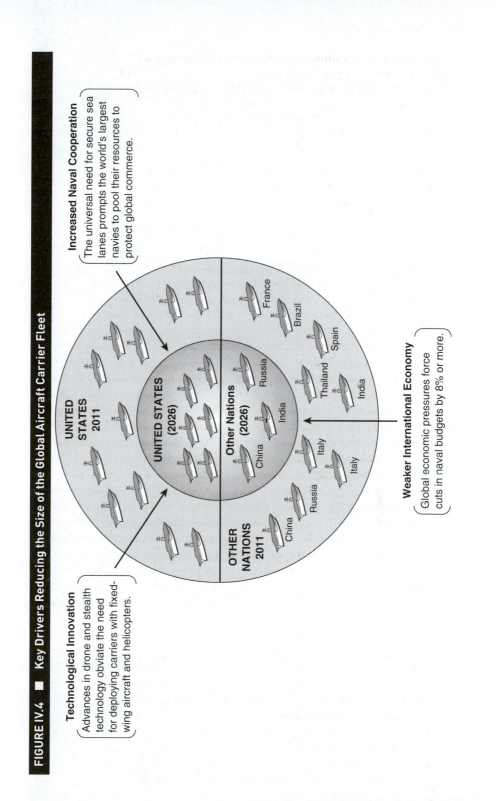

Growing Vulnerability to New Weapons Technology

In the years leading up to 2030, innovations in technology used on modern air-craft carriers and other large destroyers helped reduce the number of ships required to conduct successful naval operations. Nuclear propulsion and weapons, jet aircraft, ultrasilent diesel-electric submarines, and supercomputers strengthened the capabilities of individual ships, provided greater operational flexibility, and eventually led to a decline in the total number of ships needed to perform critical missions.[66]

Such technical advances, however, were outpaced by developments in weapons technology that put the fixed-wing carrier battle fleet at a major disadvantage in combat.[67] Weighing over 100,000 tons and carrying 4,000 personnel and up to seventy-five aircraft on board, the aircraft carrier presents a massive target for the enemy. The carrier battle group is easily detected and tracked by radar, sonar, and infrared detectors as well as by satellites providing targeting data directly to advanced anti-ship missile guidance systems and other weapons.[68]

Anti-Ship Missiles

By 2030, sophisticated anti-ship missiles became increasingly capable of disrupting strategic aircraft carrier operations and threatening the effectiveness of a carrier's defenses. The proliferation of short- to mid-range anti-ship missiles posed a serious threat to aircraft carriers. For example, Russia improved its Sizzler, a supersonic sea-skimming attack weapon that flies only thirty feet above the waves.[69] The Sizzler's maneuvering characteristics pose a challenge to carrier group defenses because of the difficulty tracking and targeting the missile during its final approach.[70] France's Exocet MM40 Block 3 extended previous versions of the Exocet missile's over-the-horizon capability to 200 kilometers. Its elaborate maneuvers can also quickly overwhelm a ship's defensive systems.[71]

China improved two of its lethal anti-carrier delivery systems, partly in response to continued US challenges to China's claims in the South China Sea. The first system, their truck-mounted DF-21 anti-ship ballistic missile called the "Carrier Killer," raised serious concerns as its warhead can move at up to ten times the speed of sound and can be launched 1,550 kilometers from its target.[72] The wide dissemination of the YJ-18 class missile became another source of concern. With initial speeds of 600 mph and a short-range Mach 3 burst capability, the YJ-18 was a game-changing development for deterrence. China hastened mass production of the missile to further deter the United States from contesting Chinese operations in the South China Sea.[73]

Of all the naval powers, China's use of these two anti-carrier missiles provided clear indications of aircraft carrier vulnerabilities. The DF-21 in particular was deemed capable of destroying a carrier; even US countermeasures would have serious difficulty intercepting multiple missiles fired simultaneously.[74] And the costs would be manageable as the Chinese can produce 1,200 DF-21 missiles for the cost of one Nimitz-class aircraft carrier.[75] Perhaps most disturbing is the presence of a 200-meter platform in the Gobi desert that is roughly the length of a carrier deck. It is thought to be a test target for the DF-21 missiles.[76]

Iranian missile capacity also increased, with mass production of Emad-class missiles, C-704K anti-ship missiles, and Fateh-100 ballistic missiles retrofitted with infrared targeting sensors.[77] In February 2015, after Iran demonstrated it could destroy a mock Nimitz-class US aircraft carrier, spending on these missiles was heavily increased.[78] Iran was further emboldened when its firing of an Emad-class missile near the USS *Truman* in the Strait of Hormuz in October 2015 was not met with reciprocating fire.[79]

Another factor compounding the danger posed by anti-ship missiles is that they can be launched from a variety of platforms, including surface ships, submarines, fixed-wing aircraft, helicopters, and coastal batteries. This was first demonstrated during the Falkland Islands War in 1982, when an Argentine light-strike fighter configured to carry the Exocet missile disabled and sank a Royal Navy destroyer. The successful Exocet attack alerted navies worldwide to the tangible threat of anti-ship missiles.[80]

The increasing ranges of the Sizzler, the Chinese DF-21, the Exocet, and other anti-ship missiles made navy carrier fleets increasingly vulnerable and increasingly pushed them to operate farther and farther from their targets, minimizing the impact of their embarked air wings.

As technology continued to advance, the threat increased, as shown in Figure IV.5. For example, Iran and Pakistan over the past decade have been able to launch missiles as far as 180 and 200 kilometers, respectively, and the Chinese have been capable of launching missiles from ships with almost the same range as the United States. According to a study by a Washington think tank, in future wars a carrier would have to remain over 1,000 nautical miles (1,850 kilometers) away from the coastline of a capable adversary country.[81]

Supercavitating Torpedoes

Improvements in self-propulsion technology for torpedoes made them even more dangerous. A supercavitating torpedo can immobilize an aircraft carrier on detonation. In the past, water friction and turbulence prevented torpedoes from achieving speeds of greater than 35 knots and frequently damaged the torpedo or caused it to veer off course. By generating a cushion of air between the torpedo and the surrounding water, the process of cavitation has increased a torpedo's speed to 200 knots, making it a much greater threat to large surface combatants.[82]

Drone Aircraft

The need for aerial force projection with large battle wings was called into question with the rapid development of drone technology. Many argued that drone technology had made fixed-wing aircraft carriers an artifact of the past. As unmanned drones increasingly demonstrated their success in combat, the military's commitment to carrier-launched manned fighter aircraft weakened, raising questions about viability and the cost of carrier-based aircraft. The US Congressional Budget Office reported in 2030 that the Pentagon went ahead with its 2011 plan to purchase more than 700 medium- and large-sized drones at a cost of nearly $40 billion over the next ten years.[83]

FIGURE IV.5 ■ Ship-to-Surface and Anti-Ship Missile Ranges		
Ship-to-Surface Missiles		
Country	**Missile**	**Range (km)**
China	DF-21 (CSS-5)	1770–2150
USA/UK	Tomahawk	1250–2500
USA	ArcLight (DARPA) *	3700
* DARPA development project for the farthest reaching naval ship launched missile		
Anti-Ship Missiles		
Country	**Missile**	**Range (km)**
Pakistan	Qader	200
Iran	CSS-N-8/Saccade	180

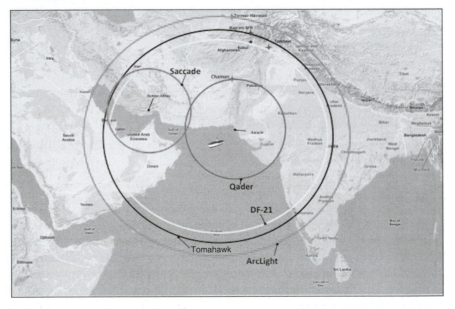

In 2015, the US Navy established a goal of acquiring over seventy Fire Scout and over forty Global Hawk drones, both of which can taxi and take off autonomously.[84]

Prior to 2011, naval doctrine stated that a carrier was only as effective as its air wing's ability to conduct air strikes.[85] Fixed-wing and rotary-wing aircraft historically made up an air wing. However, in every year since 2010, the US Air Force trained substantially more drone "pilots" than new fighter and bomber pilots, and drone aircraft were increasingly tasked to conduct missions previously assigned to carrier-based aircraft.[86] The introduction of the F-35 Joint Strike Fighter, for example, has made it easier to accomplish the air force's mission from other sea-based platforms.[87]

Drone technology is offering the opportunity to the US Navy to revolutionize the traditional carrier air wing by having dedicated refueling drones; returning dedicated intelligence, surveillance, and reconnaissance (ISR) aircraft to the carrier; and increasing the carrier strike range at a cost significantly lower than the F-35. The navy accommodated this change, in part, by developing drone aircraft that launch from aircraft carriers. Deployed in 2014, the thirty-eight-foot-long X-47B was the first drone capable of taking off from and landing on an aircraft carrier.[88] Each new version was smaller in size and supported a longer operational range, making it less necessary to have mobile sea-based launch platforms.

The navy, however, cancelled the X47B program in 2016. The primary mission of the navy's new drone, the MQ-25 Stingray, will be to refuel jet airplanes with pilots. This decision prodded Eric Sayers, a former consultant to the US Indo-Pacific Command to say, "This is as short-sighted a move as I have seen Washington make on defense strategy decisions."[89]

Drones made a comeback by 2030. Many now are the size of hummingbirds, equipped with sensors and micro cameras and easily deployable without any requirement for land- or carrier-based landing strips. Underscoring this trend, drones as small as dragonflies are expected to become operational by 2030 or sooner.[90] Such improvements in drone technology have significantly increased the vulnerability and eroded the combat value of large aircraft carriers and their supporting fleets.

Succumbing to Growing Budgetary Pressures

The lengthy global financial crisis and economic recession that began in 2008 and the 2020 COVID-19 pandemic forced major cuts in defense budgets and funding for naval operations across the globe. Prior to 2010, acquisition of new surface combatants represented a large portion of annual procurement funding for most navies, but when faced with necessary defense cuts, navy ships were most affected.

The UK's *Strategic Defence and Security Review 2010* proposed to cut defense spending by 8 percent, and Parliament approved. Given the severity of the budget cuts, the Royal Navy had little choice but to decommission its flagship aircraft carrier, the *Ark Royal*.[91] In 2000 the Royal Navy had thirty-two principal surface combat ships. This number fell to twenty-three in 2010 and by 2016 was reduced to just fourteen.[92] In 2016, the fleet included only six Type 45 destroyers, which play a critical role in defending aircraft carriers. Several weapons systems were also scaled back in order to increase the budget for unmanned aircraft and more sophisticated communications systems.[93] At question is whether sufficient funds can be found to support the production of two new Queen Elizabeth–class carriers.

The Royal Navy's budget proved insufficient to cover projected expenditures for the next ten years, and actual cuts were as high as 15 percent for several more years. By 2020, manpower levels were below 30,000 personnel and several thousand more personnel were cut by 2030.

Beginning in 2012, growing budget deficits left the United States with little choice but to follow the UK's lead and impose substantial cuts to the Department of Defense (DOD) budget.[94] In 2010, the United States was spending more in total military expenditures than the next nine highest spenders plus the only other countries that also operate aircraft carriers—Brazil, Spain, and Thailand (see Figure III.2).[95] This could not be sustained.

The congressional budget sequester of 2013 was a system shock to the entire US military, and particularly the US Navy. Defense spending was reduced from $553 billion to $518 billion, and the Navy significantly stalled many of its programs. The budget only grew to some $520 billion in the next several years, requiring further freezing of funding for the entire defense infrastructure and threatening the continuation of the program to construct more Ford-class carriers.[96]

For most developed countries, military spending was less than or about 2 percent of the country's gross domestic product (GDP). In contrast, the United States in 2015 spent $623 billion of its total federal budget on defense. This amounted to 3.4 percent of the total US GDP of some $16 trillion.[97]

Further budget cuts in subsequent years decreased the US defense budget by over $50 billion annually—a decrease on average of almost 10 percent a year. In the decade prior to 2030, the budgetary pressures required a series of major cuts to naval forces that helped produce about $500 billion in savings for DOD.[98] Most of the cuts were taken from weapons programs, military service budgets, and retirement health benefits.[99]

The US defense budget grew substantially under the Trump administration, but major cuts needed to offset COVID-19 expenditures were mandated by the administration that came to power in 2021. The US Navy was forced to reduce substantially the number of its surface naval vessels, including aircraft carriers and destroyers. The decommissioning of five aircraft carriers beginning in 2025 saved over $50 billion. The Navy delayed production of the *John F. Kennedy* CVN-79 carrier and cancelled production of two other Ford-class carriers, resulting in additional savings of some $25 billion in operations and maintenance costs as well as construction costs.[100] The navy saved another $50 billion by redistributing procurement funds for twenty-two planned DDG-51 destroyers.[101]

The Move to More Cooperative Strategies

The United States increasingly emphasized maritime security as a primary naval function, citing, in part, the growing trend toward globalization.[102] In recognition of this trend, the United States sought to embed itself in a broad set of cooperative maritime agreements with other naval powers. In our future scenario, growing technological and economic challenges spurred the United States to broker cooperative arrangements with India, Japan, Russia, and China.[103]

The United States had a solid base to work from in promulgating this new policy. Although the world relied heavily on the US Navy to protect the busiest and most dangerous shipping routes, eleven of the thirteen largest navies in 2011 were American allies. Recognizing the efficiencies that could be garnered by sharing the burden, the United States promoted a policy of collaboration and convinced both Russia and China, who faced similar technological and budgetary challenges, to enter into cooperative relationships as well.

By 2030, the policy of cooperative engagement generated a new set of global maritime agreements that decreased the burden on the US Navy. The new US maritime strategy promoted a policy of protecting the common interests of all nations willing to defend prosperity and peace worldwide.[104] As a result, the primary mission of the US Navy evolved from operating as a combat-oriented power presence to working collaboratively with other nations to protect vital sea lanes and provide humanitarian relief in the event of man-made and natural disasters.

The resolute support of the United States also spurred the growth of the International Maritime Organization (IMO). The IMO became a streamlined global naval coalition made up of member nations cooperating to protect and secure high-risk sea lines of communication (SLOCs) from piracy and terrorism. A growing number of nations signed on to the IMO's cooperative charter. IMO members concluded several multilateral and bilateral maritime agreements that designated various member navies to ensure safe transit of coastlines and high-risk areas. The role of less expensive and more agile or amphibious helicopter carriers was enhanced, particularly in supporting humanitarian operations.

The Strait of Malacca and the Gulf of Aden received particular attention. Both zones represent high-risk areas for piracy, and both have witnessed a surge in radical Islamist activity. In addition, both regions are major SLOCs for oil transportation and are, therefore, high-value targets for maritime pirates who reside close to shore.[105]

A key diplomatic breakthrough was the transfer of primary responsibility to China, Japan, and India to protect maritime commerce in the high-volume Strait of Malacca, located between Malaysia and Singapore. In 2025, China agreed to accept responsibility for securing the eastern sector of the SLOC because 80 percent of its oil traversed the strait.[106] India likewise agreed to secure the Indian Ocean and the western portion of the Malacca Strait. Japan volunteered the services of one of its 18,000-ton helicopter-carrying destroyers that can operate up to eleven helicopters from its flight deck.[107]

Prior to the strengthening of the IMO, piracy in the Gulf of Aden and the Bight of Benin had cost the world economy between $10 billion and $15 billion per year.[108] Recognizing the need to stifle this threat to global security and economic health, the navies of the United States, Russia, India, the UK, France, and a dozen smaller states entered into a cooperative—and increasingly successful—arrangement to jointly patrol the waters off the Somali and Nigerian coasts.[109]

THE WORLD OF 2030: FEWER RESOURCES AND NEW PRIORITIES

In our future scenario, technological advances, budgetary pressures, and the move to more collaborative naval security arrangements spurred larger navies—including the United States, Russia, the UK, and France—to reduce substantially the number of active surface ships by 2030. The number of large aircraft carriers worldwide plummeted from twenty in 2011 to less than a dozen in 2030. In 2011, only nine of twenty-eight NATO members were in compliance with NATO's requirement that they spend at least 2 percent of their country's GDP base on defense. By 2030, over two-thirds of NATO's member states were in compliance.[110] A key factor contributing to this shift was popular perception that money spent on defense would be directed primarily to promote global commerce and to ensure the safety of the seas.

The decrease in combat-oriented operations and missions due to a shift in maritime strategy also enabled the US Navy and other navies to focus more attention on providing humanitarian assistance. With an increase in both the number and severity of natural disasters and pandemics worldwide, the navies of the world came under growing pressure to coordinate their relief activities. Growing civil unrest also increased the demand for overseas evacuations of civilian noncombatants and nonessential military personnel. Navies remained uniquely capable of executing NEOs, and many of the newly negotiated maritime cooperation agreements included burden-sharing formulas to optimize the effectiveness and efficiency of such operations.

Now it is time to turn the clock back to the present day. Do today's budgetary challenges and emerging technologies argue for a fundamental relook at global naval strategy? Is the fixed-wing aircraft carrier battle group about to meet the same fate as the battleship did in the wake of the sinking of the *Bismarck* and the attack on Pearl Harbor? If so, what key factors should drive current naval strategic planning? What would be the implications of these major shifts for military planners in 2030?

NOTES

1. Jeremy Black, "A Post-Imperial Power? Britain and the Royal Navy," *Orbis: A Journal of World Affairs* 49, no. 2 (2005): 13.

2. Daniel Goure, *Enabling the Carrier Strike Group* (Arlington, VA: Lexington Institute, April 2011), http://www.lexingtoninstitute.org/library/resources/documents/Defense/Enabling_The_Carrier_Strike_Group.pdf.

3. James Conway, Gary Roughead, and Thad W. Allen, *A Cooperative Strategy for 21st Century Seapower*, US Navy, October 2007, http://www.navy.mil/maritime/Maritimestrategy.pdf.

4. US Department of the Navy, *Naval Doctrine Publication*, March 28, 1994, http://www.dtic.mil/doctrine/jel/service_pubs/ndp1.pdf.

5. Robert D. Kaplan, "America's Elegant Decline," *The Atlantic,* November 2007, http://www.theatlantic.com/magazine/archive/2007/11/america-8217-s-elegant-decline/6344/.

6. Catherine Zara Raymond, "Piracy and Armed Robbery in the Malacca Strait: A Problem Solved?" *Naval War College Review* 62, no. 3 (2009), http://www.usnwc.edu/getattachment/7835607e-388c-4e70-baf1-b00e9fb443f1/Piracy-and-Armed-Robbery-in-the-Malacca-Strait--A-.

7. Lauren Ploch et al., *Piracy off the Horn of Africa*, Congressional Research Service, April 19, 2010, http://fpc.state.gov/documents/organization/142669.pdf.

8. Goure, *Enabling the Carrier Strike Group.*

9. Julie Cohn, *Terrorism Havens: Somalia*, Council on Foreign Relations, June 2010, http://www.cfr.org/somalia/terrorism-havens-somalia/p9366.

10. US Department of the Navy, "Harry S. Truman CSG Launches First OIR Missions," December 29, 2015, http://www.navy.mil/submit/display.asp?story_id=92573.

11. Hendrick Simoes, "US, French Carriers Begin Combined Airstrikes Against ISIS," Military.com, February 25, 2015, http://www.military.com/daily-news/2015/02/25/us-french-carriers-begin-combined-airstrikes-against-isis.html?ESRC=topstories.RSS.

12. Yeganeh Torbati, "Pentagon Chief Visits U.S. Carrier in Disputed South China Sea, Blames Beijing for Tension," *Reuters*, November 5, 2015, http://www.reuters.com/article/us-southchinasea-usa-carter-idUSKCN0ST35J20151105.

13. This case study focuses on the viability of aircraft carriers that carry large or advanced fixed-wing aircraft. Amphibious or helicopter carriers are excluded from this study but also play a vital role in naval maritime operations, especially those operations requiring ground forces to assist in humanitarian assistance and other tasks. They are smaller but perform many of the same missions; some are equipped with vertical short takeoff and landing (V/STOL) aircraft.

14. US Department of the Navy, *The Aircraft Carrier: More Than a Warship*, November 2013, http://navylive.dodlive.mil/2013/11/14/the-aircraft-carrier-more-than-a-warship/.

15. Walter Pincus, "Challenging the Navy's Numbers," *Washington Post,* December 30, 2011, http://www.washingtonpost.com/world/national-security/challenging-the-navys-numbers/2011/12/29/gIQANfTSPP_story.html.

16. US Department of the Navy, *Naval Doctrine Publication*.

17. The US Navy usually maintains ten active aircraft carriers, with an eleventh carrier in extended shipyard availability status to perform tasks such as nuclear fuel/core replacement in midlife. See Daniel Whiteneck et al., *The Navy at a Tipping Point: Maritime Dominance at Stake?* CNA Annotated Briefing, CNA Analysis & Solutions—Advanced Technology and Systems Analysis Division, March 2010, http://www.cna.org/sites/default/files/research/The%20Navy%20at%20a%20Tipping%20Point%20D0022262.A3.pdf.

18. Ronald O'Rourke, *Navy Ford (CVN-78) Class Aircraft Carrier Program: Background and Issues for Congress*, Congressional Research Service, December 17, 2015, https://www.fas.org/sgp/crs/weapons/RS20643.pdf and Zachary Cohen, "US Navy's $13B Aircraft Carrier Can't Fight," *CNN Politics*, July 25, 2016, https://www.google.com/?gws_rd=ssl#q=Zachary+Cohen,+US+Navys+%2413B+Aircraft+Carrier+Cant+Fight,+CNN.

19. Corey Todd Jones, "President Trump Commissions USS *Gerald R. Ford* (CVN 78)," *Navy News Service*, July 22, 2017, https://www.navy.mil/submit/display.asp?story_id=101579.

20. Jones, "President Trump Commissions USS *Gerald R. Ford*."

21. "Aircraft Carriers Are Big, Expensive, Vulnerable—and Popular," *The Economist*, November 14, 2019, https://www.economist.com/briefing/2019/11/14/aircraft-carriers-are-big-expensive-vulnerable-and-popular.

22. Jones, "President Trump Commissions USS *Gerald R. Ford*."

23. Rowan Scarborough, "New Navy Budgets May Sink Plans for Carriers: Fight Is on to Save Flattop Fleet," *Washington Times,* January 16, 2012, http://www.washingtontimes.com/news/2012/jan/15/new-navy-budgets-may-sink-plans-for-carriers.

24. Goure, *Enabling the Carrier Strike Group*.

25. Carol R. Schuster and Richard J. Herley, *Surface Combatants: Navy Faces Challenges Sustaining Its Current Program*, report to congressional committees, US General Accounting Office, National Security and International Affairs Division, http://www.fas.org/man/gao/ns97057.pdf.

26. US Department of the Navy, "Navy Personnel," June 24, 2016, http://www

.navy.mil/navydata/nav_legacy
.asp?id=146.

27. US Department of the Navy, "Status of the Navy," December 7, 2011, http://www.navy.mil/navydata/navy_legacy_hr.asp?id=146.

28. "Aircraft Carriers Are Big, Expensive, Vulnerable—and Popular," *The Economist.*

29. Kyle Mizokami, "The Five Most-Powerful Navies on the Planet," *The National Interest*, June 6, 2014, http://www.nationalinterest.org/feature/the-five-most-powerful-navies-the-planet-10610?page=3.

30. "Is the Russian Navy Bigger Than US's?" milflug.com, https://migflug.com/jetflights/russian-navy-bigger-than-uss/.

31. Seth Cropsey, *Ebb Tide* (Washington, DC: Hudson Institute, September 1, 2010), http://www.hudson.org/research/7235-ebb-tide.

32. The White House, "Fact Sheet: President Obama Announces New Investments to Enhance Safety and Security in the Changing Arctic," September 1, 2015, https://www.whitehouse.gov/the-press-office/2015/09/01/fact-sheet-president-obama-announces-new-investments-enhance-safety-and.

33. The White House, "Fact Sheet: President Obama Announces New Investments."

34. "Details of China's New Aircraft Carrier Revealed," *The Maritime Executive,* January 3, 2016, http://www.maritime-executive.com/article/details-of-chinas-new-aircraft-carrier-revealed.

35. US Department of Defense, Missile Defense Agency, *Aegis Ballistic Missile Defense*, March 31, 2016, http://www.mda.mil/system/aegis_bmd.html.

36. Rupert Wingfield-Hayes, "Flying Close to Beijing's New South China Sea Islands," *BBC News*, December 14, 2015, http://www.bbc.com/news/magazine-35031313.

37. Colin Clark, "As Chinese Ships Cruise Arctic for First Time, Will U.S. Build New Icebreakers?" *Breaking Defense*, September 3, 2015, http://breakingdefense.com/2015/09/as-chinese-ships-cruise-arctic-for-first-time-will-u-s-build-new-icebreakers/.

38. Franz-Stefan Gady, "Russia and China in the Arctic: Is the US Facing an Icebreaker Gap?" September 7, 2015, http://thediplomat.com/2015/09/russia-and-china-in-the-arctic-is-the-us-facing-an-icebreaker-gap/.

39. *World Air Forces: 2015*, Flight Global Insight, 2015, https://d1fmezig7cekam.cloudfront.net/VPP/Global/Flight/Airline%20Business/AB%20home/Edit/WorldAirForces2015.pdf.

40. "India Will Have Two Aircraft Carrier Strike Forces by Around 2015," *Times of India*, January 20, 2011, http://articles.timesofindia.indiatimes.com/2011-01-20/india/28359441_1_aircraft-carrier-cbgs-refit.

41. Prashanth Parameswaran, "Japan Launches New Helicopter Destroyer," *The Diplomat*, August 29, 2015, http://thediplomat.com/2015/08/japan-launches-new-helicopter-destroyer/.

42. Tim Fish, "Japan Rises to the Challenge of Cuts and New Threats," *HIS Jane's*, April 4, 2009, http://www.janes.com/products/janes/defence-security-report.aspx?ID=1065927179.

43. Frederik Van Lokeren, "Russia's Naval Modernization: Analysis," *The Geopolitical and Conflict Report*, March 21, 2012, http://gcreport.com/index.php/analysis/163-russias-naval-modernization.

44. "List of Active Royal Navy Ships," September 2019, https://en.wikipedia

.org/*wiki*/List_of_active_Royal_Navy_ships.

45. Mizokami, "The Five Most-Powerful Navies on the Planet."

46. Royal Navy, HMS *Queen Elizabeth*, http://www.royalnavy.mod.uk/ our-organisation/the-fighting-arms/ surface-fleet/aircraft-carriers/hms-queen-elizabeth.

47. "Aircraft Carriers Are Big, Expensive, Vulnerable—and Popular," *The Economist*.

48. Royal Navy, HMS *Queen Elizabeth*.

49. French Navy, "Strengths," July 18, 2011, http://www.defense.gouv.fr/ english/navy/forces.

50. S. Anandan and K. A. Martin, "Navy Floats Out First Indigenous Aircraft Carrier," *Hindu*, December 30, 2011, http://www.thehindu.com/news/ national/article2758985.ece.

51. David Scott, "India's Drive for a Blue Water Navy," *Journal of Military and Strategic Studies* 10, no. 2 (2007–2008), http://jmss.org/jmss/index.php/jmss/ article/viewFile/90/100.

52. Scott, "India's Drive for a Blue Water Navy."

53. Sam Perlo-Freeman et al., *Trends in World Military Expenditure, 2015* (Stockholm, Sweden: Stockholm International Peace Research Institute, April 2016), http://books.sipri.org/ files/FS/SIPRIFS1604.pdf.

54. Ronald O'Rourke, *China Naval Modernization: Implications for U.S. Navy Capabilities—Background and Issues for Congress*, Congressional Research Service, October 20, 2011, http://www.fas.org/sgp/crs/row/ RL33153.pdf.

55. Thomas Harding and James Kirkup, "Navy to Reduce to Smallest Size Ever to Save Carriers," *Telegraph*, October 7, 2010, http://www.telegraph.co.uk/

news/uknews/defence/8049674/Navy-to-reduce-to-smallest-size-ever-to-save-carriers.html.

56. Bryan McGrath, *NATO at Sea: Trends in Allied Naval Power*, American Enterprise Institute, September 18, 2013, https://www.aei.org/publication/ nato-at-sea-trends-in-allied-naval-power/.

57. Black, "A Post-Imperial Power? Britain and the Royal Navy."

58. Robert D. Kaplan, "The Navy's New Flat-Earth Strategy," *The Atlantic,* October 24, 2007, http:// www.theatlantic.com/magazine/ archive/2007/10/the-navy-8217-s-new-flat-earth-strategy/6417/.

59. Congressional Budget Office, *An Analysis of the Navy's Fiscal Year 2016 Shipbuilding Plan*, October 2015, https://www.cbo.gov/ publication/50926.

60. Schuster and Herley, "Surface Combatants: Navy Faces Challenges Sustaining Its Current Program."

61. Pincus, "Challenging the Navy's Numbers."

62. Kris Osborn, "Navy Launches New Aircraft Carrier Study to Find Cost Savings," Military.com, March 30, 2015, http://www.military.com/ daily-news/2015/03/20/navy-launches-new-aircraft-carrier-study-to-find-cost-savings.html.

63. Osborn, "Navy Launches New Aircraft Carrier Study to Find Cost Savings."

64. "Aircraft Carriers are Big, Expensive, Vulnerable—and Popular," *The Economist*.

65. Scarborough, "New Navy Budgets May Sink Plans for Carriers."

66. Kaplan, "America's Elegant Decline."

67. Henry J. Hendrix and J. Noel Williams, *Twilight of the $UPERfluous*

Carrier, US Naval Institute, May 2011, http://www.usni.org/magazines/proceedings/2011-05/twilight-uperfluous-carrier.

68. Scarborough, "New Navy Budgets May Sink Plans for Carriers."

69. O'Rourke, "China Naval Modernization."

70. Tony Capaccio, "Navy Lacks Plan to Defend Against 'Sizzler' Missile," Bloomberg.com, March 23, 2007, http://www.bloomberg.com/apps/news?pid=newsarchive&sid=a5LkaU0wj714.

71. Capaccio, "Navy Lacks Plan to Defend Against 'Sizzler' Missile."

72. O'Rourke, "China Naval Modernization."

73. Michael Pilger, *China's New YJ-18 Antiship Cruise Missile: Capabilities and Implications for U.S. Forces in the Western Pacific*, US-China Economic and Security Review Commission, October 28, 2015, http://origin.www.uscc.gov/sites/default/files/Research/China%E2%80%99s%20New%20YJ-18%20Antiship%20Cruise%20Missile.pdf.

74. RAND Corporation, *Research Brief: Chinese Threats to US Surface Ships*, 2015, http://www.rand.org/pubs/research_briefs/RB9858z4.html.

75. Charles Clover, "China Parades 'Carrier-Killer' Missile Through Beijing," *Financial Times Beijing*, September 3, 2015, http://www.ft.com/cms/s/0/b94d907a-507a-11e5-b029-b9d50a74fd14.html#axzz4CuEaitBB.

76. "Aircraft Carriers are Big, Expensive, Vulnerable—and Popular," *The Economist*.

77. Voice of America, "Security Council Asked to Investigate Iran Missile Test," October 24, 2015, http://editorials.voa.gov/content/security-council-asked-to-investigate-iran-missile-test/3020671.html.

78. Associated Press, "Iran's Revolutionary Guard Attacks Mock US Aircraft Carrier in Naval Drills," *Guardian*, February 25, 2015, http://www.theguardian.com/world/2015/feb/25/iran-revolutionary-guard-attacks-mock-us-aircraft-carrier.

79. Amanda Macias and Reuters, "The White House Has Delayed Imposing New Financial Sanctions on Iran as Tensions Mount Between the 2 Nations," *Business Insider*, December 31, 2015, http://www.businessinsider.com/tensions-iran-us?pundits_only=0&get_all_comments=1&no_reply_filter=1.

80. MBDA Missile Systems, "EXOCET," June 2011, http://www.mbda-systems.com/mediagallery/files/EXOCET-family_background.pdf.

81. "Aircraft Carriers are Big, Expensive, Vulnerable—and Popular," *The Economist*.

82. James S. Corum, "Argentine Airpower in the Falklands War: An Operational View," *Air & Space Power Journal*, August 20, 2002, http://www.airpower.au.af.mil/airchronicles/apj/apj02/fal02/corum.html.

83. "Missile Technology: Peril on the Sea," *The Economist*, June 10, 2010, http://www.economist.com/node/16295552.

84. Government Accountability Office, *Defense Acquisitions Report*, March 2015, http://www.gao.gov/products/GAO-15-342SP.

85. Government Accountability Office, *Defense Acquisitions Report*.

86. Goure, *Enabling the Carrier Strike Group*.

87. Elisabeth Bumiller and Thom Shanker, "Microdrones, Some as Small as Bugs, Are Poised to Alter War," *New York Times*, June 19, 2011, http://

www.nytimes.com/2011/06/20/
world/20drones.html?_r=1.

88. Scarborough, "New Navy Budgets May Sink Plans for Carriers."

89. "Aircraft Carriers are Big, Expensive, Vulnerable—and Popular," *The Economist.*

90. Bumiller and Shanker, "Microdrones."

91. "The Changing Shapes of Air Power," *New York Times,* June 19, 2011, http://www.nytimes.com/interactive/2011/06/19/world/drone-graphic.html.

92. "Warships' Faltering Engines Leave Navy All at Sea," *Financial Times Weekend*, January 30–31, 2016, 4.

93. "Defence Review: Cameron Unveils Armed Forces Cuts," *BBC News*, October 19, 2011, http://www.bbc.co.uk/news/uk-politics-11570593.

94. Royal Naval Staff Policy Team, *Strategic Defence and Security Review 2010: Royal Navy Internal Communications Supporting Question and Answer Pack*, October 2010, http://www.rfa-association.org/cms/attachments/309_RN%20SDSR%20IC%20QsAs%20Pack%20_Final_%20v9.pdf.

95. Andrew Tilton, *The Outlook for the US Economy*, white paper, Goldman Sachs, October 2011, http://www2.goldmansachs.com/gsam/docs/fundsgeneral/general_education/economic_and_market_perspectives/wp_economic_outlook.pdf.

96. Amy Belasco, *Defense Spending and the Budget Control Act Limits*, Congressional Research Service, July 22, 2015, https://www.fas.org/sgp/crs/natsec/R44039.pdf.

97. Office of Management and Budget, *Federal Budget of the United States Government*, 2015, https://www.whitehouse.gov/sites/default/files/omb/budget/fy2015/assets/budget.pdf.

98. "Defence Spending in Eastern Europe: Scars, Scares and Scarcity," *The Economist,* May 12, 2011, http://www.economist.com/node/18682793.

99. Stephen Losey, "Extended Pay Freeze, Layoffs Likely," *Federal Times,* November 28, 2011, http://www.federaltimes.com/article/20111128/BENEFITS01/111280301/1001.

100. Tony Capaccio. "Navy Releases Worst-Case Cost for Next-Generation Warship," *Washington Post,* January 2, 2012, http://www.washingtonpost.com/business/economy/navys-worst-case-cost-overrun-tops-1billion-for-aircraft-carrier-gerald-ford/2011/12/29/gIQAbbmoUP_story.html.

101. Capaccio. "Worst-Case Cost for Next-Generation Warship."

102. Benjamin H. Friedman and Christopher Preble, *A Plan to Cut Military Spending*, CATO Institute, November 2010, http://www.downsizinggovernment.org/defense/cut_military_spending.

103. Conway, Roughead, and Allen, *A Cooperative Strategy for 21st Century Seapower.*

104. Robert Farley, "The False Decline of the US Navy," *American Prospect,* October 23, 2011, http://prospect.org/article/false-decline-us-navy.

105. James Kurth, "The New Maritime Strategy: Confronting Peer Competitors, Rogue States, and Transnational Insurgents," *Orbis: A Journal of World Affairs* 51, no. 4 (2007), http://www.fpri.org/orbis/5104/kurth.newmaritimestrategy.pdf.

106. Kurth, "The New Maritime Strategy."

107. Jason J. Blazevick, "Defensive Realism in the Indian Ocean: Oil, Sea Lanes and the Security Dilemma," *World Security Institute* 5, no. 3 (2009), http://www.chinasecurity.us/pdfs/JasonBlazevic.pdf.

108. James Dunnigan, "Japanese Aircraft Carriers Back in Business," *Strategy Page*, April 15, 2009, http://www .strategypage.com/dls/articles/ Japanese-Aircraft-Carriers-Back-In-Business-4-5-2009 .asp.

109. Ploch et al., *Piracy Off the Horn of Africa*.

110. Africa Economic Development Institute, *Africa Economic Institute: Pirates of Somalia*, March 2, 2009, http://africaecon.org/index.php/ exclusives/read_exclusive/1/1.

PUZZLING FOOD
POISONINGS IN GERMANY

Germany faced an outbreak of the *Escherichia coli* (*E. coli*) virus in the summer of 2011 that was more toxic, virulent, and widespread than most previous outbreaks experienced throughout the world.[1] Public health officials were perplexed and concerned. They did not know the cause of the outbreak but were under growing pressure to advise the public on how to avoid becoming ill.

E. coli is a type of bacteria often found in animal and human intestines that can contaminate human food and water sources (see Figure V.1). According to Martin Wiedmann, a professor of food science at Cornell University, "There are vast differences between *E. coli*—some that cause no diseases and then types that cause severe infections. Some serotypes cause urinary tract infection and some cause diarrhea." He went on to mention, however, that most do not cause the severe type of reaction observed in Germany.[2]

Healthy adults generally recover from *E. coli* infection within a week, but children and the elderly have a higher risk of organ failure, typically of the kidneys. The risk factors and virulence of the infection vary with the strain, and some infections are more deadly and resistant to antimicrobials than others.[3] One concern is that the

---

FIGURE V.1 ■ **The *E. coli* Bacteria**

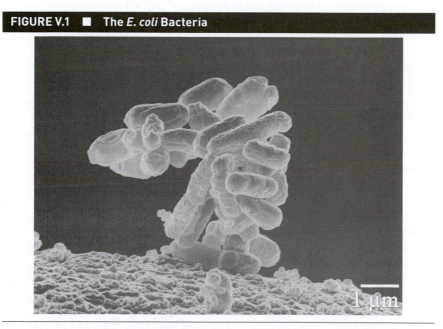

Source: Photo by Eric Erbe, digital colorization by Christopher Pooley, both of the US Department of Agriculture, Agricultural Research Service. [Public domain]/Wikimedia Commons.

widespread use of antibiotics has contributed to the evolution of new and increasingly antibiotic-resistant strains of bacteria. This can result in bacterial infections that are far more dangerous to the general population.

DISTURBING EARLY REPORTS

Many families in Germany were disturbed to hear reports in late May 2011 that an *E. coli* outbreak had killed 16 people and caused between 276 and 700 people to become seriously ill. Even more alarming were stories that 85 of the individuals who had become sick were at risk of renal failure.[4] According to press sources, the bacteria were most likely to be found in cucumbers, but it was unknown whether the cucumbers in question came from Spain or Germany or were contaminated while in transit to Germany. Some speculated that the infected cucumbers originated in Denmark or the Netherlands. Others warned that shoppers should be wary of other raw vegetables, such as lettuce and tomatoes.[5]

Concern rose as the reported number of confirmed cases reached 1,150 on May 31. Two of the infected individuals were in the United States, and the American press noted the possibility of the outbreak spreading there. The reports prompted the US Food and Drug Administration (FDA) to flag Spanish produce for risk of infection because Spain was most often cited as the likely source of the tainted goods. At that time, however, the FDA did not express major concern because only small amounts of Spanish produce are exported to the United States.

Europeans had much more reason to be alarmed. In Germany, the typical number of cases of sickness stemming from the *E. coli* virus is about 60 per year, but people were learning that over 1,000 cases had been reported and the number was mounting every day. Even more disturbing were reports of unusually high rates of complications and deaths from what increasingly appeared to be a rare and particularly virulent strain of the bacteria.[6]

By June 1, the number of cases in Germany had increased to 1,500, with a fatality rate of 5 percent.[7] On the same day, a press report from Hamburg stated that Spanish produce was to blame. German officials said the type of produce that was the source of the infection was unknown, however, so they advised people to avoid all fresh produce as a precaution until the source could be identified.[8] Consumers in Germany responded by avoiding many forms of produce, including cucumbers, lettuce, and tomatoes.

The problem was that no one knew which food was infected and how it came to be infected. For example, the food source could have been infected in a production facility where it was washed or sorted. Equipment that processed the food could have also processed something else that contained *E. coli*, spreading the bacteria from one food source to another. Other possibilities were that the food was infected by wildlife fecal material in a farmer's field or the bacteria were transmitted through a water source. If a farmer used surface water from a field to water crops, the food source could have been contaminated by birds or other wildlife.[9]

More and more people all over Europe were becoming sick. The highest incidence of cases was in northern Germany, but the World Health Organization (WHO) reported in June 2011 that Austria, Denmark, France, Netherlands, Norway, Spain,

Sweden, Switzerland, and the United Kingdom had also notified the organization of cases in their countries (see Figure V.2).[10] In all cases except two, the individuals had recently visited northern Germany or, in one case, had contact with a visitor from northern Germany. Such press reporting spurred a major drop in purchases of German produce, and German farmers estimated losses at about $7 million per day.[11]

On June 2, the number of confirmed cases rose to 1,614, with 18 deaths, mostly in Germany.[12] British press sources reported that the strain found in the current outbreak in Germany had never before been seen in humans. Instead of affecting primarily the sick, elderly, and young, it was affecting individuals of all ages. The article implied that the virus was particularly toxic and virulent.[13] The Beijing Genomics Institute in Shenzhen (BGI-Shenzhen), China's flagship genome center, reported on June 2 that at the request of German doctors it had sequenced the genome in a record-setting three days.[14] Its preliminary analysis showed that the "current infection is caused by an entirely new super-toxic *E. coli* strain" that was highly infectious and had never been

FIGURE V.2 ■ *E. coli* Cases in Europe

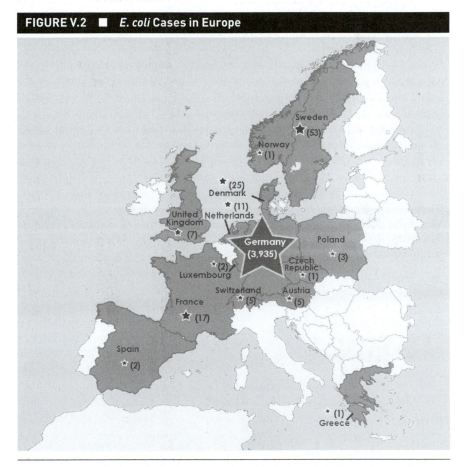

Source: Adapted from World Health Organization, "EHEC Outbreak: Increase in Cases in Germany," June 2, 2011, http://www.who.int/csr/don/2011_06_02/en/index.html.

involved in any previous outbreaks in Europe. BGI-Shenzhen, which was collaborating closely with the University Medical Center Hamburg-Eppendorf in Germany, added that the new strain carried several antibiotic-resistant genes that made antibiotic treatment extremely difficult.

The World Health Organization and BGI-Shenzhen described the strain found in Germany as similar to a strain found in the Congo that was known to cause severe abdominal pain and diarrhea. Infected patients in the Congo had also experienced haemolytic uraemic syndrome (HUS), which affects the blood and kidneys and can be fatal. Treatment involved the use of antibiotics along with possible kidney dialysis.[15]

In subsequent days, salad vegetables from northern Germany were mentioned as the most likely cause, but the exact source of infected produce could still not be confirmed.[16] Evidence was mounting, however, that the source was bean sprouts.[17] Some argued this made sense because far more women were affected than men, and women are more likely to eat bean sprouts than men. Moreover, bean sprouts usually are eaten raw, which would increase a person's vulnerability to infection.[18]

ECONOMIC COSTS AND ALLEGED MISMANAGEMENT

Across Europe, Germany received criticism for its poor handling of the health crisis. The outbreak was causing hundreds of millions of euros in losses for farmers (see Figure V.3).[19] The European Union (EU) offered €210 million to compensate the farmers, but the farmers estimated their loss at €417 million as of June 8, with the end of the crisis still not in sight. They demanded that the government provide compensation for the full amount of losses.[20]

Spanish farmers were particularly incensed and threatened to sue. Farmers there reported financial losses of €200 million per week, the large amount reflecting the

FIGURE V.3 ■ Economic Impact of Food Poisoning in Europe	
Farmers Losses per Week (as of June 8, 2011)	**Million Euros**
Spain	200
Italy	100
Netherlands	50
Germany	30
France	30
Belgium	6
Denmark	.75
Lithuania	.15

Source: European Farmers' Union Copa & Cogeca.

economic impact of initial suggestions that Spanish cucumbers were the probable source of infection. German tests later established the cucumbers were not in fact the source of the outbreak, but the damage to Spain's economy was already done.

German officials were also criticized for involving too many agencies in the investigation and for providing information that was not scientifically confirmed. Skeptics noted that no scientific evidence had been found linking the Spanish cucumbers to the health crisis, nor had any evidence been uncovered that pointed conclusively to German bean sprouts.[21] The premature release of information regarding the potential source of the infection had increased fears and harmed businesses needlessly.

On June 8, German Health Minister Daniel Bahr declared that the worst of the outbreak appeared to be over: "I cannot sound the all clear, but after analyzing

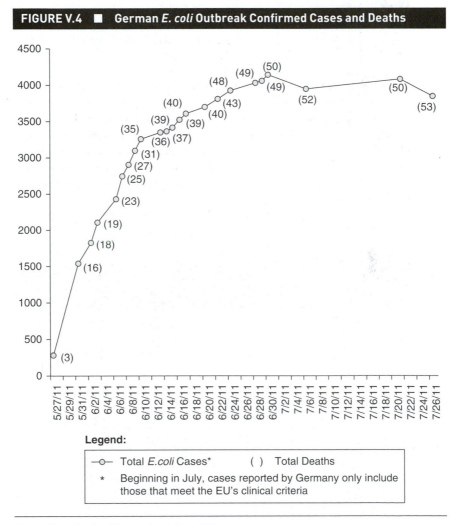

FIGURE V.4 ■ German *E. coli* Outbreak Confirmed Cases and Deaths

Legend:

—○— Total *E.coli* Cases*   ( )   Total Deaths

*   Beginning in July, cases reported by Germany only include those that meet the EU's clinical criteria

Source: Alysa Gander, Pherson Associates, LLC.

the latest data we have reasonable cause for hope. The worst of the illness is behind us."[22] While some new cases were expected, German officials believed the outbreak had peaked at some 2,400 confirmed cases. Hundreds of the patients reported kidney complications, and 24 people had died from consuming the infected produce. German officials suspected that the most likely source was a bean sprout farm in northern Germany.

Two weeks later, officials announced that forensic tests identified two factors that contributed to the particular toxicity and virulence of the strain. At this point 2,684 cases had been recorded, including 810 that involved kidney failure (25 percent of reported cases) and 39 that led to death. In addition, at least 100 individuals who experienced kidney failure did not fully recover. Officials noted that they would need kidney transplants or would have to undergo dialysis for the rest of their lives.[23]

German officials did not formally declare the outbreak over until July 26, 2011. By this point, 53 people had died in Europe and North America, and 3,843 cases of infection had been confirmed by WHO, including 855 who developed the rare, life-threatening complication HUS (see Figure V.4).[24] Outbreaks had occurred in two different locations—a large one centered in northern Germany and a smaller cluster focused around the French city of Bordeaux. The strain of *E. coli* identified in the outbreaks was STEC O104:H4.[25]

In late July, the Robert Koch Institute, Germany's national disease control agency, announced that it would shut down its monitoring center but intensify surveillance in case of any resurgence. The European Food Safety Authority (EFSA) announced that, based on an analysis of information from the French and German outbreaks, "the most common likely link was a lot of fenugreek seeds used to grow sprouts imported from Egypt by a German importer."[26]

MAKING SENSE OF THE SITUATION

Most strains of *E. coli* live in both animals and humans. At first, the outbreak was assumed to have originated in animals, but later evidence suggested that the strain was human specific. A study of *E. coli* outbreaks in the United States between 1982 and 2002 showed that 20 to 30 percent of the food poisoning outbreaks were linked to contaminated vegetables, especially alfalfa sprouts, lettuce, spinach, parsley, and cantaloupes.[27, 28]

In early June, Flemming Scheutz, head of the WHO Collaborating Centre for Reference and Research on Escherichia and Klebsiella in Copenhagen, Denmark, said, "This strain has never been found in any animal, so it is possible that it could have come straight from the environment into humans."[29] Several other experts interviewed during the crisis suggested that it could have originated from humans and then was later transmitted to bean sprouts.

In September 2011, German officials announced plans to improve how such outbreaks would be managed in the future.[30] For example, instead of allowing institutions to take up to eighteen days to report cases suggesting an outbreak to the authorities, a new goal was set to reduce this time to only three days. Physicians were encouraged to perform only minimal testing before reporting cases and to increase the amount of information available to federal authorities tasked with determining the pattern of an outbreak.[31]

The German government also established a clear chain of responsibility linking the various levels of regulatory agencies. Officials hoped this would address problems that emerged regarding confusion over which agencies were responsible for various tasks and an overall lack of communication. In contrast, administrative officers at hospitals and physicians were applauded for communicating remarkably well during the crisis and showing great creativity in dealing with the outbreak.[32]

Between 2009 and 2019, 16 cases of Hemolytic Uremic Syndrome (HUS) have been identified, in people, including children, who have been to the Hurghada region of Egypt. Standard procedure now is to follow up each individual case. Often it is difficult, however, to learn the specific source of the STEC infection in Egypt. The most common ways people get infected is by eating contaminated food or water, coming in contact with another infected person, or contact with animal feces.[33]

NOTES

1. European Centre for Disease Control and Prevention, "Escherichia coli (E. coli)," http://ecdc.europa.eu/en/healthtopics/escherichia_coli/Pages/index.aspx.

2. Meredith Melnick, "Q&A: A Food-Safety Expert Explains Germany's E. coli Outbreak," *Time Heartland*, June 1, 2011, http://healthland.time.com/2011/06/01/qa-a-food-safety-expert-explains-germanys-e-coli-outbreak.

3. European Centre for Disease Control and Prevention, "Escherichia coli (E. coli)."

4. "How Serious Is Germany's E. coli Outbreak?" CNN.com, June 2, 2011, http://www.cnn.com/2011/WORLD/europe/05/31/germany.e.coli.qanda/.

5. "How Serious Is Germany's E. coli Outbreak?" CNN.com.

6. JoNel Aleccia, "Two in U.S. Infected in German E. coli Outbreak," MSNBC.com, May 31, 2011, http://www.msnbc.msn.com/id/43227702/ns/health-infectious_diseases/t/two-us-infected-german-e-coli-outbreak/#.TsNOo3GRI7A.

7. "In Germany 365 New Cases of Virulent E. coli Food Poisoning: Breaking News," *Sky Valley Chronicle, Washington State News,* June 1, 2011, http://www.skyvalleychronicle.com/BREAKING-NEWS/IN-GERMANY-365-NEW-CASES-OF-VIRULENT-E-COLI-FOOD-POISONING-677122.

8. "In Germany 365 New Cases of Virulent E. coli," *Sky Valley Chronicle, Washington State News.*

9. Melnick, "Q&A: A Food-Safety Expert Explains Germany's E. coli Outbreak."

10. World Health Organization, "EHEC Outbreak: Increase in Cases in Germany," June 2, 2011, http://www.who.int/csr/don/2011_06_02/en/index.html.

11. Alan Cowell and William Neuman, "Virulent E. coli Strain Hits Germany and Puzzles Officials," *New York*

Times, June 1, 2011, http://www
.nytimes.com/2011/06/02/world/
europe/02ecoli.html?pagewanted=all.

12. Stephen Adams, "German E. coli
Outbreak: Q&A," *Telegraph,* June 2,
2011, http://www.telegraph
.co.uk/news/health/news/8553303/
German-E.coli-outbreak-QandA.html.

13. Adams, "German E. coli Outbreak:
Q&A."

14. "Chinese, German Researchers
Identify Sequence of Deadly E. coli,"
English News, June 3, 2011, http://
www.chinadaily.com.cn/china/2011-
06/03/content_12637639.htm.

15. Adams, "German E. Coli Outbreak:
Q&A."

16. Adams.

17. Gina Kolata, "Unusual Traits Blended
in German E. coli Strain," *New York
Times,* June 22, 2011, http://www
.nytimes.com/2011/06/23/health/
research/23ecoli.html.

18. Kolata, "Unusual Traits Blended in
German *E. coli* Strain."

19. "E. coli: Germany Says Worst of Illness
Is Over," *BBC News*, June 8, 2011,
http://www.bbc.co.uk/news/world-
europe-13691087.

20. "E. coli: Germany Says Worst of Illness
Is Over," *BBC News.*

21. "E. coli: Germany Says Worst of Illness
Is Over."

22. "E. coli: Germany Says Worst of Illness
Is Over."

23. Kolata, "Unusual Traits Blended in
German *E. coli* Strain."

24. David Milliken, "Germany Declares
End to E. coli Outbreak," *Reuters*, July
26, 2011, http://www.reuters.com/

article/2011/07/26/us-germany-ecoli-
idUSTRE76P42B20110726.

25. Gretchen Vogel, "*E. coli* Outbreak
Blamed on Egyptian Fenugreek
Seeds," *Science,* July 5, 2011, http://
www.sciencemag.org/news/2011/07/
egyptian-fenugreek-seeds-blamed-
deadly-e-coli-outbreak-european-
authorities-issue.

26. Vogel, "*E. coli* Outbreak Blamed on
Egyptian Fenugreek Seeds."

27. Suengwook Seo and Karl R. Matthews,
"Influence of the Plant Defense
Response to Escherichia Coli O157:H7
Cell Surface Structures on Survival
of That Enteric Pathogen on Plant
Surfaces," *Applied and Environmental
Microbiology*, August 15, 2012, http://
aem.asm.org/content/78/16/5882.

28. "Pathogenic E. Coli Binds to Fresh
Vegetables," *ScienceDaily*, April 15,
2014, http://www.sciencedaily.com/
releases/2014/04/140415203813.htm.

29. Marian Turner, "German *E. coli*
Outbreak Caused by Previously
Unknown Strain," *Nature:
International Weekly Journal of
Science,* June 2, 2011, http://www
.nature.com/news/2011/110602/full/
news.2011.345.html.

30. Marian Turner, "Germany Learns From
E. coli Outbreak," *Nature News,* http://
www.nature.com/news/2011/110912/
full/news.2011.530.html.

31. Turner, "Germany Learns From *E. coli*
Outbreak."

32. Turner.

33. "English E. Coli Cases Linked to
Travel to Egypt," *Food Safety News*,
July 17, 2019, http://www
.foodsafetynews.com/2019/07/english-
e-coli-cases-linked-to-travel-to-egypt/.

VI

THE CASE OF IRAQ'S ALUMINUM TUBES

In 2002, the United States Intelligence Community (IC) published a National Intelligence Estimate (NIE) asserting that Iraq was continuing to develop nuclear weapons. Moreover, it judged that the aluminum tubes that Iraq was procuring from China were destined for a gas centrifuge assembly that would produce highly enriched uranium for nuclear weapons.

In the years following the Iraq War, which concluded in 2011 when the United States withdrew its combat troops, intelligence analysts and experts ultimately attributed the analytic failures documented in the NIE report to a lack of methodological rigor. Various postmortems concluded that the analytic judgments in the estimate were based on faulty assumptions, lacked evidentiary underpinning, omitted evidence that was inconsistent with their key finding, and did not give proper attention to the possibility of adding a null hypothesis that Iraq no longer had a weapons of mass destruction (WMD) program. Furthermore, consideration should have been given to the possibility that there was no connection between the purchase of the aluminum tubes and Saddam Hussein's interests in rebuilding Iraq's WMD program.

THE NATIONAL INTELLIGENCE ESTIMATE

In October 2002, the US Congress asked the US Intelligence Community (IC) to produce an NIE on the status of Iraq's weapons of mass destruction program. Drawn largely from a Central Intelligence Agency (CIA) intelligence assessment, the NIE concluded that Iraq was reconstituting its nuclear program—a judgment that rested largely on the analysis of a large order of aluminum tubes that Iraq had purchased from an Australian subsidiary of a Chinese manufacturer. Analysts believed the aluminum tubes would be used as a key component in a gas centrifuge, a highly effective device used to enrich uranium. Many argued that Iraq's procurement of the aluminum tubes demonstrated that Iraq would soon have nuclear weapons capability, bolstering the case that Iraq's WMD programs posed a sufficient threat to justify US military intervention.

Many analysts assumed that Saddam Hussein would continue to develop WMD programs despite the limitations placed on Iraq by the United Nations Security Council. In the aftermath of the Gulf War, the IC determined that it had underestimated the extent of Saddam Hussein's WMD programs. This mistake was attributed in part to the lack of intelligence reporting regarding Iraq's prewar WMD capabilities. It contributed decisively to the hardening of assumptions in 2002 concerning Saddam's desire to maintain WMD programs and his history of deception efforts.[1]

As the controversy swirled around the status of Iraq's WMD programs and the threat they posed to US national security, US president George W. Bush and senior advisers asked the IC to write an NIE and release an unclassified version of the estimate to the public. Prior to publishing the NIE, IC analysts would have benefitted from addressing more thoroughly the following questions: How confident are we in this assessment? Is there any chance the key judgments could be wrong? Are we certain that our underlying assumptions are well-founded and that the most critical evidence provides a solid foundation for this intelligence assessment?

THE EVIDENTIARY TRAIL

Following Iraq's retreat from Kuwait at the end of the Gulf War, the United Nations (UN) Security Council passed Resolution 687 on April 3, 1991. The resolution mandated that Iraq was not authorized to develop, acquire, or manufacture nuclear weapons or any nuclear weapons material. Iraq was required to disclose all locations, amounts, and types of any nuclear material it had in its possession to the International Atomic Energy Agency (IAEA) for supervised destruction. The strict sanctions denied requests to import a wide range of material, prohibiting Iraq, for example, from importing material for conventional military use, such as ground-to-ground rockets.[2] In addition, the resolution established the United Nations Special Commission (UNSCOM) to assist IAEA with the removal of nuclear weapons and to oversee the inspection and elimination of Iraq's chemical and biological weapons.[3]

From 1991 to December 1998, thousands of inspections conducted by UNSCOM and IAEA documented evidence of previously unknown Iraqi programs for developing biological, chemical, and nuclear weapons. IAEA inspections discovered an Iraqi nuclear weapons program that employed thousands of nuclear scientists and researchers.[4] These discoveries revealed an extensive weapons program previously unknown to the IC, particularly the CIA. They also unveiled the extent of Iraq's efforts to deny information to the UN and the United States prior to the Gulf War.

Efforts to locate and destroy Iraq's WMD capabilities were not fully realized as mandated by UN resolutions. Iraq's resistance to inspections intensified throughout 1998, leading directly to Operation Desert Fox. Over four days in December 1998, US military air raids struck Iraqi military and security targets that were believed to house remaining known WMD facilities and infrastructure.[5] The US military considered Operation Desert Fox a success. Strikes hit 85 percent of intended targets and 74 percent were "highly effective."[6] IAEA's final report submitted to the UN Security Council detailed nuclear inspection activities through December 1998 and concluded that

> Extensive verification activities in Iraq, since May 1991, have yielded a technically coherent picture of Iraq's clandestine nuclear programme. These verification activities have revealed no indication that Iraq possesses nuclear weapons or any meaningful amounts of weapon-usable nuclear material, or that Iraq has retained any practical capability (facilities or hardware) for the production of such material.[7]

FIGURE VI.1 ■ **Aluminum Tubes Suspected of Being Used for Uranium Enrichment**

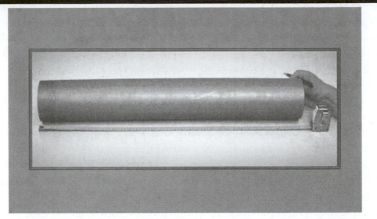

Source: US State Department. Slide 31 of Colin Powell's UN Security Council Iraq disarmament presentation (February 5, 2003), alleged aluminum tube for uranium enrichment.

In late 2000 and early 2001, the CIA was alerted that Iraq had commissioned a company in China to manufacture 60,000 7075-T6 aluminum tubes without UN authorization (see Figure VI.1). No evidence was found that Iraq was pursuing other supplementary purchases necessary for uranium enrichment other than the tubes. The CIA closely monitored the progress of the order through production. In July 2001, officials seized a shipment of 3,000 tubes in Jordan.

Analysts assumed Iraq's procurement of the aluminum tubes was covert in nature; the CIA was alerted by Australian intelligence almost immediately following the discovery of Iraq's order through an intermediary party.[8] The security practices surrounding the acquisition, however, were significantly different than those taken by Iraq to acquire nuclear weapons material prior to the Gulf War.[9] The process Iraq followed in 2002 for purchasing the tubes was more similar to how Iraq purchased conventional weapons—using multiple procurement agents, receiving quotes from multiple manufacturers, and accessing public forums to seek information about potential suppliers.

Analysis of the high-strength 7075-T6 aluminum tubes with an outer diameter of 81mm and an inner diameter of 74.4mm led intelligence experts to believe that the tubes were intended to be a component in a cascade-type uranium-enrichment centrifuge similar to designs Iraq had developed in the 1980s. Here are two key findings that led analysts to their conclusions:

- The inner tube diameter was similar to the dimensions of a tube used as a rotor in a Zippe-type gas centrifuge.[10]

- The length and wall-thickness dimensions of the seized tubes were similar to the size of the rotors found in a Beams-type gas centrifuge Iraq had developed in the 1980s.

The inner and outer dimensions, however, were the exact same dimensions of tubes Iraq acquired in the 1980s as motor casings for short-range rockets as part of its Nasser-rocket program.

Iraq was prohibited from importing the tubes because the outer diameters exceeded 75mm. The UN had previously sanctioned aluminum tubes with similar dimensions and specifications as controlled material in 1991's Resolution 687.[11] Tubes with diameters exceeding 75mm were considered to be a potential key component in nuclear applications (see Figure VI.2).

The seized tubes were anodized. The anodization process would protect the tube from harsh environments and usually was used to avoid corrosion—a standard military practice to protect weapons being stored outdoors. Analysts questioned why Iraq would increase the cost of production by anodizing the tubes. Some analysts concluded that the coating would help protect them en route to Iraq. Other experts argued that this was not the case; they noted the anodized coating could potentially produce a negative reaction with the uranium gas within a centrifuge.[12]

IC analysts were also concerned that the aluminum tubes were manufactured with tolerances that exceeded requirements for non-nuclear applications. Tolerances establish how precise the machining dimensions must be during the manufacturing process.[13] Analysis of Iraq's procurement history showed a progression of Iraqi scientists' requests seeking increasingly tighter levels of tolerance for the tubes.[14] The Department of Energy (DoE) argued the practice could be evidence that inexperienced Iraqi scientists were over-specifying tolerances, attempting to reverse-engineer weapons.[15] In

FIGURE VI.2 ■ Nuclear Centrifuge Cascade With Aluminum Tubes

Source: US Department of Energy. Overhead view of rows of centrifuge units at the Gas Centrifuge Enrichment Plant in Piketon, Ohio.

addition, during the 1980s, Iraqi scientists frequently over-specified the tolerances of various weapons materials in an attempt to improve operational efficiency.[16]

CIA analysts concluded that because Iraq had procured 60,000 aluminum tubes, the tubes were intended for a cascade-type centrifuge. The inefficiency of this type of design led the CIA to estimate that Iraq would need at least 25,000 operating centrifuges to realistically produce sufficient uranium for one nuclear weapon.[17] An alternative explanation for such a large order was that corroded rocket casings had ruined most of Iraq's arsenal of 81mm rockets and they needed to be replaced.

Drafting the National Intelligence Estimate

In 2002, Congress requested a report evaluating the state of Iraq's continuing WMD programs. Approaching the drafting of the NIE, analysts had little credible evidence to indicate that Iraq's nuclear program had restarted; however, Saddam Hussein's attempt to purchase aluminum tubes, that were ultimately seized in Jordan in 2001, aroused suspicion and required further analysis.

Most IC analysts believed that Saddam Hussein was committed to a robust WMD program. He had pursued and executed WMD programs from the 1980s to before the Gulf War. During the Iran-Iraq war in 1988, Saddam directed what later became known as the Halabja poison gas attack, which killed 5,000 and injured over 10,000 Kurdish people.[18]

Saddam Hussein's policies and behavior appeared to analysts as unchanging, and they could think of no reason why he would want to cease and desist.[19] Despite the destruction of known WMD material and facilities from 1991 to 1998, Iraq maintained the capability to rebuild facilities and restart its programs. Because of unaccounted material and documents and incomplete inspections prior to Operation Desert Fox, the possibility existed that he had more of a base to work from in reconstituting his programs.[20] Saddam Hussein had concealed Iraq's WMD programs successfully prior to the Gulf War, and analysts believed Iraq was capable of obtaining the technical expertise needed to restart its weapons programs despite rigorous UN sanctions.[21]

Analysts believed that Iraq had the financial resources required to pursue a costly clandestine program. In May 2002, the US Government Accounting Office (GAO) reported that from 1997 to 2001, Iraq received $6.6 billion in illicit revenue from oil smuggling and humanitarian-goods sellers who had paid surcharges and kickbacks on sales to the Hussein regime either directly or indirectly (see Figure VI.3). Of that

---

FIGURE VI.3 ■ UN Security Council Oil for Food Program

The UN Security Council's Oil-for-Food Program was chartered in 1996 to provide humanitarian relief to Iraq after strict sanctions were imposed in 1990. The program allowed income from the sale of a predetermined quantity of oil to be used to finance the purchase of humanitarian goods. The UN system required that all revenue garnered from the export of oil be maintained in an escrow account, that remained out of Saddam Hussein's control. The payment structure, however, did not anticipate Saddam's use of kickbacks to get around these controls.

Source: Copyright 2020. Pherson Associates, LLC. All rights reserved.

total, the GAO study estimated that in 2001 alone, Iraq earned $1.5 billion in illicit oil sales funneled through Syria, Jordan, Turkey, and the Persian Gulf and another $700 million from surcharges and contract kickbacks.[22] A subsequent report published in 2003 calculated total illicit revenue as approaching $9 billion.[23]

The relatively advanced and heavily concealed nuclear program discovered at the end of the first Gulf War was judged possible only because of a robust and successful program of deception orchestrated by Saddam Hussein.[24] During UN inspections, suspicions of Saddam Hussein's deceptive plans were amplified by Iraq's resistance to disclose its weapons capabilities prior to 1991. From the beginning of inspections in 1991 until 1995, Saddam Hussein denied the existence of any biological weapons. By falsifying and forging documents as well as misrepresenting facilities, Iraq concealed its biological warfare program from UNSCOM.[25]

Analysts explained away the absence of evidence of WMD programs on the grounds that Iraq was continuing its efforts to conceal its weapons programs to evade discovery. Saddam Hussein's continuous denial of information led analysts to suspect they were aware of only a fraction of Iraq's WMD efforts, and that Iraq was demonstrating sophisticated efforts to disguise its program from inspectors and intelligence collectors.[26] Despite an extended campaign by UN inspectors to dismantle Iraq's WMD programs during the 1990s, analysts believed Saddam Hussein had covertly worked to reinvigorate a nuclear program while inspectors were still in Iraq. Furthermore, after the inspectors withdrew from Iraq in 1998, analysts argued that Saddam Hussein's attempts to reconstitute the program could have gone into high gear. A chief UN inspector stated "the absence of evidence means, of course, that one cannot have confidence that there do not remain weapons of mass destruction."[27]

MAKING THE INTELLIGENCE CALL

Intelligence Community analysts and agencies were not of one mind in assessing the significance of the aluminum tubes procurement seized in Jordan.

- The CIA believed that Iraq's efforts to procure high-strength aluminum tubes were of significant concern. In early 2002, the CIA concluded that the aluminum tubes were well suited as a rotor in a Beams-type centrifuge with some modifications to the thickness of the tubes' walls and smoothing of the interior of the cylinder (see Figure VI.4). The official report to Congress assessed that "all intelligence experts agree that Iraq is seeking nuclear weapons and that these tubes could be used in a centrifuge enrichment program."[28]

- The Defense Intelligence Agency (DIA) and the National Ground Intelligence Center (NGIC) agreed with CIA. NGIC, specializing in ground forces, concluded that the aluminum tubes did not meet specifications for use in rockets, and argued that the tube specifications made it a poor technical choice as a rocket body.[29]

FIGURE VI.4 ■ Composition of a Beams-Type Nuclear Centrifuge

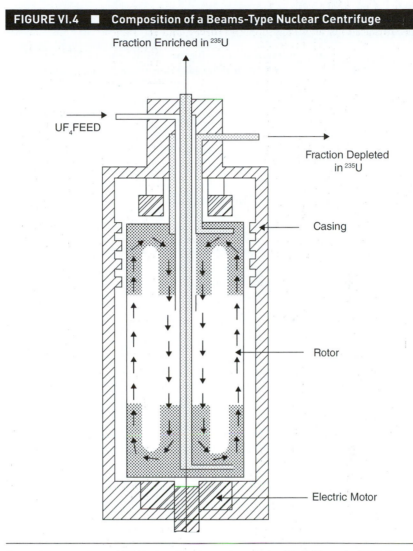

Source: Image courtesy of US Nuclear Regulatory Commission (NRC). From the "NRC Fact Sheet," April 25, 2007.

- The Department of Energy (DoE), which is responsible for US centrifuge enrichment development, challenged the conclusion that the technical specifications only supported a nuclear-use theory. DoE analysts disagreed that the dimensions of the tubes exceeded the requirements for rocket applications, arguing instead that the tubes were more suitable for conventional military use, such as artillery ground-to-ground rockets.[30] DoE's findings regarding the composition and dimensions of the tubes consistently matched aluminum tubes used as casings for 81-mm rockets during Iraq's 1990s rocket program.[31] Furthermore, a 1996 report from IAEA claimed that Iraq's Nasser-81 rockets used aluminum tubes with the exact same specifications, and Iraq's supply was declining.[32]

- The State Department's Bureau of Intelligence and Research (INR) agreed with DoE's analysis.[33] INR analysts believed that a conventional rocket program was a more plausible explanation for the procurement.

Preceding the submission of the NIE to Congress, the White House developed a media strategy in early September 2002. News interviews given by key White House officials, including vice president Dick Cheney, secretary of state Colin Powell, and national security council adviser Condoleezza Rice aired within hours of each other. Each strategically presented details of the confiscated aluminum tubes as evidence that Iraq was pursuing nuclear weapons. Days later, president George W. Bush petitioned the United Nations, saying,

> We know that Saddam Hussein pursued weapons of mass murder even when inspectors were in his country. Are we to assume that he stopped when they left? The history, the logic, and the facts lead to one conclusion: Saddam Hussein's regime is a grave and gathering danger.[34]

Congress received the NIE in October 2002. The key findings of the NIE stated that while "Saddam does not yet have nuclear weapons or sufficient material to make any, he remains intent on acquiring them."[35] The key judgments in the estimate were described as being provided with "High Levels of Confidence."[36] They included the following assessments:

- Iraq is continuing to expand its WMD programs without UN authorization.

- The National Intelligence Council (NIC) lacks awareness and evidence of significant portions of Iraq's WMD programs.

- Because of the lack of evidence, the NIC believes that only a portion of Iraq's WMD efforts are known to the IC due to Saddam Hussein's continued denial and deception efforts.[37]

NOTES

1. Commission on the Intelligence Capabilities of the United States Regarding Weapons of Mass Destruction, *Report to the President of the United States*, March 31, 2005, 10.

2. *Report on the U.S. Intelligence Community's Prewar Intelligence Assessments on Iraq*, US Congress, Senate, Select Committee on Intelligence, 108th Congr., 1st sess., July 7, 2004, 20–21, http://web.mit.edu/simsong/www/iraqreport2-textunder.pdf.

3. United Nations Security Council, Resolution 687, 1991, http://www.un.org/Depts/unmovic/documents/687.pdf.

4. Sharon A. Squassoni, *Iraq: U.N. Inspections for Weapons of Mass Destruction*, Congressional Research Service, March 13, 2003, https://www.everycrsreport.com/files/20030313_RL31671_31906345b53943f15fb-f5329e79af43b3e60e790.pdf.

5. Bryan Wright, "Iraq WMD Timeline: How the Mystery Unraveled," *National Public Radio*, November 15, 2005, http://www.npr.org/templates/story/story.php?storyId=4996218.

6. Charles D. Ferguson, "Lessons of Desert Fox," *Boston Globe*, February 14, 2006, http://www.boston.com/news/globe/editorial_opinion/oped/articles/2006/02/14/lessons_of_desert_fox/.

7. Mohamed el Baradei, *Report of the Director General of the IAEA in Connection With the Panel on Disarmament and Current and Future Ongoing Monitoring and Verification Issues*, February 9, 1999, http://www.iaea.org/OurWork/SV/Invo/reports/s_1999_127.pdf.

8. *Intelligence on Iraq's Weapons of Mass Destruction*, Parliament of the Commonwealth of Australia, Parliamentary Joint Committee on ASIO, ASIS and DSD, December 2003, http://www.aph.gov.au/Parliamentary_Business/Committees/House_of_Representatives_Committees?url=pjcaad/wmd/report.htm#fullreport.

9. David Albright, *Iraq's Aluminum Tubes: Separating Fact From Fiction*, Institute for Science and International Security, December 5, 2003, http://www.isis-online.org/publications/iraq/IraqAluminumTubes12-5-03.pdf.

10. *Prewar Intelligence Assessments on Iraq*, Senate Select Committee on Intelligence, 20–21, 96.

11. United Nations Security Council, Resolution 687.

12. David Barstow, William J. Broad, and Jeff Gerth, "The Nuclear Card: The Aluminum Tube Story—A Special Report; How the White House Embraced Disputed Arms Intelligence," *New York Times*, October 3, 2004, http://www.nytimes.com/2004/10/03/international/middleeast/03tube.html.

13. Albright, *Iraq's Aluminum Tubes*, 16.

14. Albright.

15. *Intelligence Capabilities of the United States Regarding Weapons of Mass Destruction*, Report to the President of the United States.

16. El Baradei, *Report of the Director General of the IAEA*.

17. Albright, *Iraq's Aluminum Tubes*.

18. "1988: Thousands Die in Halabja Gas Attack," *BBC News*, March 16, 1988, http://news.bbc.co.uk/onthisday/hi/dates/stories/march/16/newsid_4304000/4304853.stm.

19. Robert Jervis, "Reports, Politics, and Intelligence Failures: The Case of Iraq," *The Journal of Strategic Studies* 29, no. 1 (February 2006): 23, https://warwick.ac.uk/fac/soc/pais/people/aldrich/vigilant/fjss_lr_3-52.pdf.

20. Joseph Cirincione et al., *WMD in Iraq: Evidence and Implications*, Carnegie Endowment for International Peace, January 2004, http://www.carnegieendowment.org/files/Iraq3FullText.pdf.

21. *Intelligence Capabilities of the United States Regarding Weapons of Mass Destruction*, Report to the President of the United States.

22. *Weapons of Mass Destruction: U.N. Confronts Significant Challenges in Implementing Sanctions Against Iraq*, United States General Accounting Office, National Security and International Affairs Division, May 2002, http://www.gao.gov/new.items/d02625.pdf.

23. Kenneth Katzman, *Iraq: Oil-For-Food Program, International Sanctions, and Illicit Trade*, Congressional Research Service, April 16, 2003, https://fas.org/sgp/crs/mideast/RL30472.pdf.

24. *Intelligence Capabilities of the United States Regarding Weapons of Mass Destruction*, Report to the President of the United States.

25. *Intelligence on Iraq's Weapons of Mass Destruction*, Parliament of the Commonwealth of Australia.

26. *Iraq's Weapons of Mass Destruction Programs*, National Intelligence Estimate, Central Intelligence Agency, October 2002, http://www.gwu.edu/~nsarchiv/NSAEBB/NSAEBB129/nie_first%20release.pdf.

27. Squassoni, *Iraq: U.N. Inspections for Weapons of Mass Destruction*, 11.

28. *Unclassified Report to Congress on the Acquisition of Technology Relating to Weapons of Mass Destruction and Advanced Conventional Munitions: 1 January Through 30 June 2002*, Central Intelligence Agency, June 2002, https://www.cia.gov/library/reports/archived-reports-1/jan_jun2002.html#4.

29. Jervis, "Reports, Politics, and Intelligence Failures: The Case of Iraq."

30. Albright, *Iraq's Aluminum Tubes*.

31. *Prewar Intelligence Assessments on Iraq*, Senate Select Committee on Intelligence.

32. *Prewar Intelligence Assessments on Iraq*, 91.

33. Douglas Jehl, "The Reach of War: Intelligence; Tiny Agency's Iraq Analysis Is Better Than Big Rivals," *New York Times*, July 19, 2004, http://www.nytimes.com/2004/07/19/world/reach-war-intelligence-tiny-agency-s-iraq-analysis-better-than-big-rivals.html?pagewanted=all&src=pm.

34. George W. Bush, "President's Remarks at the United Nations General Assembly," New York, September 12, 2002, http://georgewbush-whitehouse.archives.gov/news/releases/2002/09/20020912-1.html.

35. *Iraq's Weapons of Mass Destruction Programs*, National Intelligence Estimate.

36. *Iraq's Weapons of Mass Destruction Programs*.

37. *Iraq's Weapons of Mass Destruction Programs*.

GLOSSARY OF TERMS

ABCs of sharing information: A mnemonic to remind analysts that the four best practices for sharing information are to *ask* the other person for more information, *brief* the other person on the facts, *continue* cooperative communication, and *document* the facts. (88)

Abduction: A third kind of logical reasoning, in addition to deduction and induction, that generates the guesses or hypotheses whose consequences can be derived by deduction or evaluated by induction; abductive reasoning starts with a set of facts, based on which the analyst develops a hypothesis that, if true, would provide the best explanation for those facts. (174, 199)

Access: The ability to view a document or scene directly or to speak with or listen to another person; a criterion used jointly with expertise in assessing the competence of an observer in providing testimonial evidence. (127, 135)

Active voice: A verb's relationship to the nouns in the sentence when the actor or subject performs the action. (276)

Ad hominem argument: A logical fallacy that focuses on characteristics of the person making a claim rather than the claim itself. (188)

Ad populum argument: A logical fallacy when popular behavior or opinion is used to argue a point rather than factual evidence. (188)

Affinity diagrams: The organization of data or information into logical groups. (32)

AIMS: A mnemonic used to remind analysts of the need to identify the *audience*, *intelligence or policy issue*, *message*, and *storyline* when drafting a paper. (22, 50, 188)

Analysis: The method of breaking an entity into its component parts. (3, 28, 59, 111)

Analysis of Competing Hypotheses (ACH): The process of generating multiple hypotheses and then discarding hypotheses for which there is inconsistent data, leaving only those that cannot be refuted as most viable. (199, 202)

Analysis by Contrasting Narratives: A technique for analyzing complex problems by identifying the narratives associated with entities involved in the problem. (98)

Analyst's Roadmap: The five stages of best practices for producing a quality analytic product. (1, 47, 170, 269, inside back cover)

Analytic Spectrum: The four categories and analytic thinking skills related to lines of argumentation: descriptive, explanatory, evaluative, and estimative. (19, 48, 61, 73, 175, 250)

Analytic Standards: The foundational assessment criteria fused to conduct a regular program of review of analytic products. (38, 39, 208, 247)

Anticipatory intelligence: The ability to sense, anticipate, and warn of emerging conditions, trends, threats, and opportunities that may require a rapid shift in national security posture, priorities, or emphasis. (65)

Appeal to authority: A logical fallacy in which the opinion of a recognized expert is automatically seen as valid. (188)

Argument Mapping: A visual technique for evaluating an argument by separating claims and evidence to make it easier to think about complex issues and share the reasoning behind conclusions. (183, 200, 201, 211, 214)

Artificial Intelligence: The theory and development of computer systems able to perform tasks that normally require human intelligence, such as visual perception, speech recognition, decision making, and translation between languages. (28, 95, 102, 329)

Assumption: Something that is taken for granted or is accepted as true or as certain to happen. (163, 171)

Authenticity: When an object or a thing is exactly what it appears or is claimed to be. (132)

Bottom line up front (BLUF): Stating the most important analytic judgment at the beginning of an article and following it with supporting data and argumentation. (274, 284)

Circleboarding™: A simple version of Starbursting that focuses on exploring the answers to the journalist's classic questions—Who, What, How, When, Where, and Why—and which adds one more question: So What. (21)

Circular argument (or tautology): A logical fallacy that uses the claim or conclusion as part of the support for the argument. (187)

Circumstantial evidence: Evidence based on conclusions that rest on observations as well as some assumptions that the analyst has made. (120)

Client Checklist: A technique that helps analysts tailor a product to the needs of the principal client or customer sets to ensure that the product addresses their specific concerns and requirements. (12)

Cluster Brainstorming: A silent brainstorming technique that allows participants to alternate between divergent and convergent thinking, thereby generating new ideas. (65, 107, 266)

Cognitive bias: Mental error caused by the brain's simplified information-processing strategies. (68, 236)

Cognitive psychology: A branch of psychology concerned with mental processes (as perception, thinking, learning, and memory), especially with respect to the internal events occurring between sensory stimulation and the overt expression of behavior. (25, 61)

Collaboration enablers: Four critical enablers of effective collaboration: (1) engaged leadership, (2) the presence of collaboration cells, (3) consistent policies, and (4) a supportive technical and administrative infrastructure—described in the study on collaboration prepared by the US Office of the Director of National Intelligence (ODNI). (87)

Collaboration imperatives: The six imperatives required for developing a robust collaborative environment: (1) mission criticality, (2) mutual dependence, (3) mutual trust, (4) incentives, (5) access and agility, and (6) a common understanding—as described in the study on collaboration prepared by the US Office of the Director of National Intelligence (ODNI). (83)

Collaboration principles: A doctrine consisting of three core principles: (1) responsibility to provide, (2) empowerment to participate, and (3) a user-driven environment—described in the study on collaboration prepared by the US Office of the Director of National Intelligence (ODNI). (85)

Competence: A factor used jointly with credibility in assessing testimonial evidence that involves the observer having both access to the activity and expertise to interpret what it means. (134)

Competencies: The skills, abilities, behaviors, and other characteristics that professionals need to meet the challenges in their current and future work. (5, 35)

Complexity Manager: A structured technique that helps analysts and decision makers understand and anticipate changes in complex systems by systematically evaluating all the interactions of the key variables. (97)

Computational Thinking: A set of problem-solving methods that involve expressing problems and their solutions in ways that a computer could execute. (59)

Concept Map: A graphical technique for visualizing the relationships between concepts that is often used for organizing and representing knowledge. (30)

Concept Paper: A document that lays out your product's key questions, clients, research plan, sources and methods, line of argument, needed resources, and time line. It serves as a contract between you, your boss, and your collaborators. (49, 51, 55, 114, 188)

Context: The environment in which you are working. (10, 12, 25, 56, 62, 214)

Coup Vulnerability Methodology: An expert-driven, empirically based analytic methodology that assesses the level of political-military tensions in a country and thereby the potential for a military coup. (102)

CREATE model: A mnemonic used as a guiding framework for presenting analysis in the digital era that focuses on the **C**onsumer, **R**elevance, **E**nable the decision, **A**ccess, **T**ime, and **E**lements. (235, 283)

Creativity: The ability to transcend traditional ideas, rules, patterns, relationships, or the like, and to create meaningful new ideas, forms, methods, and interpretations. (192, 231)

Credibility: The quality of being believed or accepted as true, real, or honest. (5, 133, 150, 229, 230, 249)

Critical thinking: The adaptation of the processes and values of scientific inquiry to the special circumstances of Strategic Intelligence. (inside front cover, xxvii, 25, 56, 172)

Cross-Impact Matrix: A structured technique that identifies a list of variables relevant to a particular analytic project and assesses how they influence each other. (33, 82, 97)

Cultural perspective: A criteria used for assessing the credibility of testimonial evidence that focuses on the extent to which an observer's cultural and intellectual heritage and exposure to the world will influence how that observer reports what he or she observed. (121, 133, 135)

Cyber Source Attribution: The process of identifying the source of a cyber attack launched over computer networks against specific targets, for the purposes of disruption, infiltration or destruction. (136)

Data visualization: The process of interpreting data in visual terms or putting it into visible form with the use of graphics. (257)

Deception: The effort to influence the perceptions, decisions, and actions of another to the advantage of the deceiver. (137, 288)

Deception Detection: A technique consisting of a set of checklists analysts use to assess whether sources, informants, opponents, or competitors are attempting to mislead the client or hide important information. (199, 200, 214, 288)

Decomposition: To separate something into its constituent parts or into simpler elements. (30, 59)

Deductive reasoning: A logical process in which a general conclusion is drawn based on specific and complete evidence (or premises). If the evidence is true, the conclusion must be true. (172)

Delphi Method: A structured technique for obtaining ideas, judgments, or forecasts from a dispersed panel of experts involving several rounds of questioning and reassessment; it is often done anonymously. (82, 83)

Descriptive Analysis and research: Reports or summaries of what is known about situations, people, places, and objects. (62, 176)

Design Thinking: An iterative process that seeks to understand the user, challenge assumptions, and redefine problems in an effort to identify alternative strategies and solutions that might not be immediately apparent. (59)

Diagnostic data: Data that help distinguish, characterize, or identify a particular activity or object or that provide a precise indication of what is being observed. (63)

Diagnostic reasoning: The application of hypothesis testing to the evaluation of a new development, the assessment of a new item of information, or the reliability of a source. (199, 202)

Digital Disinformation: The use of the internet and social media platforms to manipulate popular perceptions for partisan political or social purposes. (105, 120, 139, 151, 208, 215, 236)

Distraction (or red herring): A logical fallacy that cites irrelevant points to distract attention from the issue being argued. (188)

Dual Process theory: A theory that posits two systems of thinking: System 1, which is intuitive, fast, efficient, and often unconscious, and System 2, which is analytic, slow, deliberate, and conscious. (66)

Empathy: The ability to see the world through others' eyes. (8, 59)

Empirical analysis: Analysis that uses statistics and data-based computer models to apply quantitative techniques to known data and that is capable of being verified or disproved by observation or experiments. (67, 100)

Estimative Analysis: Analysis that looks to the future, asking what might happen next and proactively anticipating courses of action that decision makers may take in response to potential stimuli. (48, 64, 180)

Evaluative Analysis and research: Analysis that examines the significance of a problem or topic of interest as it relates to a client's interests, using logic to interpret and make judgments about various meanings behind the data. (63, 179)

Expertise: The ability of an observer to understand fully what he or she has observed; used jointly with access in assessing the competence of an observer in providing testimonial evidence. (2, 27, 66, 135, 172)

Explanatory Analysis and research: Analysis that probes the reason or cause of a situation, getting at why it has happened or is developing in the way portrayed by valid sources. (63, 177)

False analogy: A logical fallacy that occurs if an argument is supported with evidence that is not essentially similar. (187)

False dichotomy: A logical fallacy that occurs when a set of opposing forces or possibilities is reduced to only two options, misrepresenting the complexity of the situation. (187)

Foresight Techniques/analysis: Systematic methods of identifying alternative trajectories by developing plausible stories based on critical uncertainties to inform and illuminate decisions, plans, and actions. (21, 31, 64, 107, 211, 267)

Gantt Chart: A type of process map that uses a matrix to chart the progression of a multi-faceted process over a specific time period. (32)

Geospatial Thinking: The use spatial reasoning to match data to frames that involve the location, extent, distribution, pattern, association, interaction, or change of data within a geospatial sphere or space. (59, 95)

Getting Started Checklist: A technique that helps analysts develop a strategy for crafting a paper or launching a new project that focuses on how to obtain the best information, tap the best expertise, and incorporate the right techniques in the most efficient way possible. (49)

Hasty generalization: A logical fallacy that uses a general claim based on insufficient or unrepresentative evidence. (187)

Heuristics: Experience-based techniques that can generate a quick solution that is not guaranteed to be optimal. (68, 69)

High Impact/Low Probability Analysis: A structured technique that sensitizes analysts and decision makers to the possibility that a low-probability event might actually happen and stimulates thinking on how best to deal with the potential dangers or exploit the possible opportunities that could result. (34, 44)

Historical analogy: The comparison of current events to what has happened in the past, either in one's personal experience or in history. (33, 198)

Hypothesis: A potential explanation or conclusion that is to be tested by collecting and presenting evidence. It is a declarative statement that has not been established as true; an educated guess based on observation that needs to be supported or refuted by more observation or through experimentation. (191)

Hypothesis Generation: The process of identifying a comprehensive and preferably mutually exclusive set of hypotheses to explain a given phenomenon. (198)

Inadequate sampling: A logical fallacy that occurs when the subset used as a measure to draw a conclusion is too small. (187)

Indicators Generation, Validation, and Evaluation: A structured technique used to seek early warning of a future event that is often paired with scenarios to identify which of the scenarios is developing. A good indicator is validated by the five characteristics and evaluated for its diagnosticity. (211)

Inductive reasoning: A logical process in which a generalized conclusion or claim is proposed that contains more information than the observations or experience on which it is based; the claim is outside the known facts and is possibly or probably true, but it could be false. (172, 188)

Influence Diagrams: A technique to illustrate hierarchical or other power relationships among individuals or organizations. (32)

Intuitive traps: Common errors and mental mistakes analysts make when evaluating evidence, describing cause and effect, estimating probabilities, and evaluating intelligence reporting. (68, 70)

Inverted Triangle model: A method for organizing an analyst's thoughts and information in a logical progression that begins with the most important concept, thought, or idea and concludes with the least important. (274, 275)

Issue Redefinition: A structured technique for experimenting with different ways to define an issue. (1, 34)

Joint Escalation: A process where two disputants agree to refer a disagreement to a higher authority to seek resolution of the issue and provide their superiors with the same description of the problem. (90)

Key Assumptions Check: A systematic effort to make explicit and question the working assumptions that guide an analyst's interpretation of evidence and reasoning about a particular problem. (21, 76, 82, 107, 152, 163, 221, 266)

Machine Learning: The scientific study of algorithms, and statistical models that computer systems use to perform a specific task without using explicit instructions, relying on patterns and inference instead. (95, 105)

Matrix: A rectangular arrangement of elements into rows and columns used to organize, collate, and compare information from a variety of sources. (97, 115, 194, 249)

Miles' Law: The phrase "Where you stand depends on where you sit," which was coined by Rufus E. Miles Jr., a former federal administrator and senior fellow at the Woodrow Wilson School, Princeton University. (41)

Mindfulness: The quality or state of being conscious or aware of something; being able to distinguish one's personal observations from observation of the external world. (4)

Mind Mapping: A graphical technique for visualizing connections between several ideas or pieces of information often used in note taking, brainstorming, problem solving, and project planning. (21, 30) .

Mindsets: A mental model formed from beliefs, assumptions, concepts, and information retrieved from memory that guides perception and the processing of new information. (6, 41, 62, 67, 214)

Missing evidence: Evidence that one would expect if a hypothesis were to be proven but that has not been found yet. (121)

Multiple Hypothesis Generation: A technique for generating a wide array of hypotheses by breaking the established hypothesis into its component parts, generating and ranking the permutations that are created, and selecting those that are most deserving of attention. (20, 199, 210, 266)

Multiple Scenarios Generation: A systematic method for brainstorming multiple explanations of how a situation may develop when considerable uncertainty and several underlying key drivers are present. (30, 44, 97, 183, 194)

Mutual Understanding: A process where two sides meet with a facilitator and each side explains the other side's position in a manner that leads the other side to believe its position has been appropriately represented. (90)

Near Misses: When an analyst or the organization either gets it wrong, but no one noticed, or almost gets it wrong, but the error was not critical to the analysis at the time. (223)

Negative evidence: Evidence that can be used to disprove a hypothesis. (120)

Network Analysis: The process that strives to make sense of the data represented by a network chart by grouping associations and identifying patterns in and among those groups. (32, 97, 128)

Non sequitur: A logical fallacy that asserts a relationship between a conclusion and a premise where none exists. The conclusion does not follow the premise. (187)

Objectivity: One of three factors used to assess the credibility of testimonial evidence that focuses on whether observers attend to the evidence of their senses and do not let their motivations or expectations determine what they believe. (135, 206)

Observational sensitivity: One of three factors used to assess the credibility of testimonial evidence that focuses on the accuracy of the observation based on the conditions of observation and the physical condition of the observer at the time of observation. (135)

Opportunities Incubator™: A decision support technique for identifying actions that can facilitate the emergence of positive scenarios and thwart or mitigate less desirable outcomes. (65)

Outside-In Thinking: A technique to identify the broad range of global political, economic, military, environmental, technological, social, and other forces that are outside an analyst's area of expertise but may profoundly shape an issue. (19, 34, 82, 118)

Passive voice: A sentence structure in which the actor is absent or is the object of the action specified by the verb. (276)

Persuasion: An effort to evoke a change in someone's attitude or behavior; in analysis, persuasion is the writer's or speaker's ability to convince readers or an audience to believe what he or she is saying and to trust the writer's or speaker's skill in accurately portraying events, context, and potential. (230)

Political Instability Risk Assessment model: A technique for describing the critical dimensions of the political instability process needed to assess a government's vulnerability to civil unrest, conspiracy, insurgency, turmoil, and peaceful political change. (100)

Post hoc, ergo propter hoc: A logical fallacy that claims if one event preceded another, the first event must have caused the subsequent event to occur. (188)

Premortem Analysis: A reframing technique that reduces the risk of surprise if a prediction or an analytic judgment proves unfounded by evaluating how it could go wrong and making necessary corrections before delivering the analysis. (153, 197, 214, 220, 266, 288)

Process Map: A visual technique for diagramming a complex process by distinguishing how work is actually done from how it should be done as well as what functions a system should perform from how the system is built to perform those functions. (32)

Quadrant Crunching™: A structured brainstorming technique that uses key assumptions and their opposites as a starting point for systematically generating a large number of alternative outcomes. (20, 65, 97, 266)

Quadrant Hypothesis Generation: A technique that arrays the two key driving forces on a 2×2 matrix to generate four mutually exclusive hypotheses. (198)

Qualitative analysis: The analysis of nonnumeric data, such as words, pictures, or objects, to describe a trend, event, or object or to deliver a judgment. (66)

Quantitative analysis: The analysis of numerical data, usually with the assistance of computers, to test hypotheses and construct statistical models to explain what has been observed. (66, 249)

Quasi-quantitative analysis: The use of computer-based models that attempt to deal with the unknown or unknowable by incorporating expert estimates into their algorithms. (67, 102)

Question Method: A technique for organizing a paper that addresses a key client's concerns in priority order. (22, 60)

Red Hat Analysis: A structured technique for predicting the behavior of other people or groups by trying to replicate how they think by putting one's self "in their shoes." (9, 18, 155, 288)

Reliability: The extent to which an experiment, test, or measuring procedure yields the same results on repeated trials or a source accurately represents what he or she has observed consistently over a period of time. (127, 134)

Satisficing: Drawing conclusions based on the first data that is available and selecting the first explanation that seems to work. (118, 191, 233)

Scope Note: A short note at the beginning of a paper that frames the topic, setting the stage for efficient reading. (272)

Sensemaking: The simultaneous automatic process by which the brain fits data into a frame or mental model and fits a frame around that data. (4, 26)

Simple Hypotheses Generation: A structured brainstorming technique that employs sticky notes to identify key forces and factors, arrays them into affinity groups, and labels each group. (198)

Situational logic: Considering all the known facts and underlying forces at work at a particular time and place and postulating several plausible alternative explanations consistent with what is known. (197)

Slippery slope: A logical fallacy that relates the first and last steps in a causal chain when the intervening steps have not occurred. (188)

Source Summary Statement: The author's evaluation of the credibility of the sources and analytic judgments contained in the product. (124, 125, 229, 247, 249)

Starbursting: A form of brainstorming that focuses on generating questions rather than answers, focusing on the journalist's classic Five Ws and an H: Who, What, How, When, Where, and Why. (21)

STEMPLES+: A mnemonic that represents **S**ocial, **T**echnological, **E**conomic, **M**ilitary, **P**olitical, **L**egal, **E**nvironmental, and **S**ecurity factors plus additional potential factors such as demographic, psychological, religious, and cultural that should be considered when trying to identify key drivers in an evolving situation. (30)

Structured Analytic Techniques (SATs): Techniques that employ a step-by-step approach that externalizes the analyst's thinking in a manner that makes it readily apparent to others, thereby enabling it to be reviewed, discussed, and critiqued piece by piece or one step at a time. (4, 28, 30, 64, 67, 77, 90, 97, 108, 152, 161, 198, 210, 219, 266)

Structured Self-Critique: A systematic procedure used to identify weaknesses in the analysis by reviewing an analytic product against a series of checklists. (108, 197, 220, 266, 288)

Synthesis: Building knowledge by combining and comparing separate elements or components to form a coherent whole, looking at the relationships among the parts, and assessing the totality of the system. (170, 194)

System 1 thinking: An intuitive and often unconscious thought process that is fast and efficient and draws upon available knowledge, past experiences, and long-established mental models. (66, 193)

System 2 thinking: A slow and purposeful process that involves deliberate conscious reasoning and critical thinking skills. (66, 193)

Tangible evidence: Objects open to direct inspection—including original documents, pictures, or physical objects—by persons who intend to use them in drawing a conclusion. (104, 118, 132)

Target analysis: A subset of intelligence analysis that uses network analysis techniques and specialized tools to discover the identities and vulnerabilities of key intelligence objectives. (63)

Tautology (or circular argument): A logical fallacy that uses the claim or conclusion as part of the support for the argument. (187)

Terms of Reference (TOR): A formal document based on an established template that captures all the pertinent issues that will be addressed in an article; usually signed by the author, his or her supervisor, and other key stakeholders. (52)

Testimonial evidence: Reports of a development, conversation, or event by another person that is not open to direct observation by the analyst. (120, 134)

Topic sentences: Creating an outline by writing down the likely topic sentences that will be used to begin each paragraph to ensure that all the main points are captured, and the line of argument flows smoothly. (229, 273)

Toulmin model: A six-part model of argument—consisting of a claim, data, warrant, backing, modality, and rebuttal—that was introduced by British philosopher Stephen Toulmin in his book *The Uses of Argument*, published by Cambridge University Press in 1958. (175)

Traditional analysis: Analysis that relies on expert judgment, case studies, and personal experience to evaluate known data qualitatively. (66, 67, 186)

Venn diagram: A visual technique for displaying relationships among classes through overlapping circles; the overlaps indicate elements of separate groups that have something in common. (32, 183, 263)

Veracity: One of three factors used to assess the credibility of testimonial evidence that focuses on the truthfulness and genuineness of the observer in reporting what the observer believes he or she has observed. (124, 135)

Visualization: The formation of mental visual images; the act or process of interpreting in visual terms or putting it into visual form. (32, 104, 202, 207, 236, 256)

Warning analysis: Applying all-source information, expert insights, and specialized tradecraft to help policy officials prevent or limit damage from external threats; *tactical warning* seeks to detect and deter specific threats to avoid surprise and block or blunt damage, while *strategic warning* addresses perceived dangers in broader terms to inform policymaker decisions on general security preparedness. (65, 98, 188, 212, 292)

Warrant: The warrant in the Toulmin model is the assumption on which the claim and the evidence depend; it is the link between the data and the claim. (175)

What If? Analysis: A technique that posits an event has occurred with the potential for a major positive or negative impact and then explains how it came about. (20, 211)

Whiteboarding: A process usually involving drawing on a whiteboard to obtain peer reactions when conceptualizing a paper, constructing a line of argument, or seeking coordination on a Concept Paper, Terms of Reference, or draft paper. (47)

LIST OF NAMES

Last Name	First Name	Title	Page
Madsen	Peter	Professor of Business	223
Marcus	Gary	Professor of Psychology	110
McGuire	William J.	Social Psychologist	231
Medina	Carmen	Central Intelligence Agency Deputy Director for Intelligence	10, 11, 206
Miles Jr.	Rufus E.	Bureau of the Budget Manager	41
Mingus	Charles	American Jazz Bassist and Composer	231
Munger	Charlie	Investor, Businessman, Philanthropist	28
Neuman	W. Lawrence	Professor of Sociology	75
Noonoo	Stephen	Editor, Consultant	59
Palin	Michael	English Comedian	169
Peirce	Charles Sanders	Logician, Philosopher	174
Perlis	Alan J.	Computer Scientist and First Recipient of the Turing Award	281
Pherson	Randolph H.	National Intelligence Officer for Latin America	135, 164, 207
Pillar	Paul	National Intelligence Officer for the Middle East	206, 209
Popper	Karl	Philosopher of Science	199
Roam	Dan	Author and Consultant	256
Rumsfeld	Donald	US Secretary of Defense	115
Schmidt	Eric	Software Engineer and CEO	110
Schum	David	Professor of Law	118, 132, 134, 135
Schwartz	Peter	Management Consultant, Futurologist	65, 196
Soroush	Abdulkarim	Islamic Philosopher	17
Stares	Paul	Director of Center for Preventive Action, Council on Foreign Relations	197
Tinsley	Catherine H.	Professor of Management	223
Toulmin	Stephen	Philosopher, Educator	175
Tufte	Edward	Professor, Statistician, Graphics Designer	266
Vigen	Tyler	Author, *Spurious Correlations*	109
Weiss	Charles	Professor, Georgetown University	241
Whitehead	Alfred North	Mathematician, Philosopher	186
Williams	Joseph M.	Professor of English Language and Literature	116
Yacoubian	Mona	Senior Advisor on the Middle East, United States Institute of Peace	197

RECOMMENDED READINGS

PHERSON PUBLICATIONS

Structured Analytic Techniques for Intelligence Analysis, 3rd ed. Randolph H. Pherson and Richards J. Heuer Jr. Washington, DC: CQ Press/SAGE, 2021.

Critical Thinking for Strategic Intelligence, 3rd ed. Katherine Hibbs Pherson and Randolph H. Pherson. Washington, DC: CQ Press/SAGE, 2021.

Cases in Intelligence Analysis: Structured Analytic Techniques in Action, 2nd ed. Sarah Miller Beebe and Randolph H. Pherson. Washington, DC: CQ Press/SAGE, 2015.

How to Get the Right Diagnosis: 16 Tips for Navigating the Medical System. Randolph H. Pherson. Coral Gables, FL: Mango Publishing, 2020.

Intelligence Communication in the Digital Era: Transforming Security, Defence and Business. Rubén Arcos and Randolph H. Pherson, eds. London: Palgrave Macmillan, 2015.

Handbook of Analytic Tools and Techniques, 5th ed. Randolph H. Pherson. Tysons, VA: Pherson Associates, 2019.

Analyst's Guide to Indicators. Randolph H. Pherson and John Pyrik. Tysons, VA: Pherson Associates, 2018.

Analytic Briefing Guide. Randolph H. Pherson, Walter Voskian, and Roy A. Sullivan Jr. Reston, VA: Pherson Associates, 2017.

Analytic Production Guide. Walter Voskian and Randolph H. Pherson. Reston, VA: Pherson Associates, 2016.

Analytic Writing Guide. Louis M. Kaiser and Randolph H. Pherson. Reston, VA: Pherson Associates, 2014.

Psychology of Intelligence Analysis. Richards J. Heuer Jr. Reston, VA: Pherson Associates, 2007.

Rethinking Intelligence: Richards J. Heuer, Jr.'s Life of Public Service. Richards J. Heuer Jr., edited by Randolph H. Pherson. Tysons, VA: Pherson Associates, 2018.

To order any of the above publications, go to https://shop.globalytica.com/collections/ publications

PART I. HOW DO I GET STARTED?

Ariely, Dan. *Predictably Irrational: The Hidden Forces That Shape Our Decisions.* New York: HarperCollins, 2008.

_____. *The Upside of Irrationality. The Unexpected Benefits of Defying Logic*. New York: HarperCollins, 2010.

Browne, M. Neil, and Stuart M. Keeley. *Asking the Right Questions: A Guide to Critical Thinking*, global ed. Upper Saddle River, NJ: Pearson Education, 2015.

Cohen, Allan R., and David L. Bradford. *Influence Without Authority*, 3rd ed. Hoboken, NJ: John Wiley, 2017.

Covey, Stephen M. R. *The Speed of Trust: The One Thing That Changes Everything*, updated ed. New York: Simon & Schuster, 2018.

Duhigg, Charles. *The Power of Habit: Why We Do What We Do in Life and Business*. New York: Random House, 2012.

Dweck, Carol S. *Mindset: The New Psychology of Success*, updated ed. New York: Random House, 2016.

Dyer, Jeffrey H., Hal Gregersen, and Clayton M. Christensen. *The Innovator's DNA: Mastering the Five Skills of Disruptive Innovators*. Brighton, MA: Harvard Business, 2011.

Gawande, Atul. *The Checklist Manifesto: How to Get Things Right*. New York: Metropolitan Books, 2009.

Gigerenzer, Gerd. *Gut Feelings: The Intelligence of the Unconscious*. London: Penguin, 2007.

Gladwell, Malcolm. *Blink: The Power of Thinking Without Thinking*. New York: Little, Brown, 2005.

_____. *Outliers: The Story of Success*. New York: Little, Brown, 2008.

_____. *Talking to Strangers: What We Should Know About the People We Don't Know*. New York: Little, Brown, 2019.

_____. *The Tipping Point: How Little Things Can Make a Big Difference*. New York: Little, Brown, 2000.

Gregersen, Hal. *Questions Are the Answer: A Breakthrough Approach to Your Most Vexing Questions at Work and in Life*. New York: HarperCollins, 2018.

Groopman, Jerome. *How Doctors Think*. Boston: Houghton Mifflin, 2007.

Harrison, Guy P. *Why You Should Question Everything*. New York: Prometheus Books, 2013.

Heath, Chip, and Dan Heath. *Decisive: How to Make Better Choices in Life and Work*. New York: Crown Business, 2013.

Johnson, Steven. *Where Good Ideas Come From: The Natural History of Innovation*. New York: Riverhead Books, 2010.

Kahneman, Daniel. *Thinking, Fast and Slow*. New York: Farrar, Strauss and Giroux, 2011.

Kent, Sherman. *Strategic Intelligence for American World Policy*. Princeton, NJ: Princeton Legacy Library, 2016. First published in 1966.

Kirby, Gary R., and Jeffrey R. Goodpaster. *Thinking*, 4th ed. Upper Saddle River, NJ: Pearson Education, 2007.

Klein, Gary. *The Power of Intuition: How to Use Your Gut Feelings to Make Better Decisions at Work*. New York: Currency, 2004.

_____. *Seeing What Others Don't: The Remarkable Ways We Gain Insights*. New York: Public Affairs, 2013.

_____. *Sources of Power: How People Make Decisions*, 20th anniversary ed. Cambridge: MIT Press, 2017.

_____. *Streetlights and Shadows: Searching for the Keys to Adaptive Decision Making*. Cambridge: MIT Press, 2009.

Moore, David T. *Critical Thinking and Intelligence Analysis*. Washington, DC: National Defense Intelligence College, 2009.

Mudd, Philip. *The HEAD Game: High-Efficiency Analytic Decision Making and the Art of Solving Complex Problems Quickly*. New York: Liveright Publishing, 2015.

Pease, Bruce. *Leading Intelligence Analysis: Lessons From the CIA's Analytic Front Lines*. Washington, DC: CQ Press/SAGE, 2020.

Pink, Daniel H. *A Whole New Mind: Why Right-Brainers Will Rule the Future*. New York: Riverhead Books, 2006.

Quarmby, Neil. *Intelligence in Regulation*. Annandale, New South Wales, AU: Federation Press, 2018.

Sapolsky, Robert M. *Behave: The Biology of Humans at Our Best and Worst*. New York: Penguin, 2017.

Taleb, Nassim Nicholas. *The Black Swan: The Impact of the Highly Improbable*. New York: Random House, 2007.

Vandepeer, Charles. *Asking Good Questions: A Practical Guide*. Golden Grove Village, South Australia: Freshwater Publishing, 2017.

PART II. WHERE IS THE INFORMATION I NEED?

Arcos, Rubén, and William J. Lahneman, eds. *The Art of Intelligence: Simulations, Exercises, and Games*. Lanham, MD: Rowman & Littlefield, 2014.

Bazzell, Michael. *Open Source Intelligence Techniques*, 7th ed. Middleton, DE: IntelTechniques.com, 2019.

Booth, Wayne C., Gregory G. Colomb, Joseph M. Williams, Joseph Bizup, and William T. Fitzgerald. *The Craft of Research*, 4th ed. Chicago: University of Chicago Press, 2016.

Clark, Robert M. *Intelligence Analysis: A Target-Centric Approach*, 6th ed. Washington, DC: CQ Press/SAGE, 2019.

_____. *Intelligence Collection*. Washington, DC: CQ Press/SAGE, 2014.

_____. *The Technical Collection of Intelligence*. Washington, DC: CQ Press/SAGE, 2010.

Creswell, John W., and J. David Creswell. *Research Design: Qualitative, Quantitative, and Mixed Methods Approaches*, 5th ed. Thousand Oaks, CA: SAGE, 2018.

Denning, Peter J., and Matti Tedre. *Computational Thinking*. Cambridge: MIT Press, 2019.

Domingos, Pedro. *The Master Algorithm: How the Quest for the Ultimate Learning Machine Will Remake Our World*. New York: Basic Books, 2015.

Duke, Annie. *Thinking in Bets: Making Smart Decisions When You Don't Have All the Facts*. New York: Portfolio, 2018.

Elgersma, Erik. *The Strategic Analysis Cycle Handbook*. London: LID Publishing, 2017.

_____. *The Strategic Analysis Cycle Toolbook*. London: LID Publishing, 2017.

Ellenberg, Jordan. *How Not to Be Wrong: The Power of Mathematical Thinking*. New York: Penguin, 2014.

Grabo, Cynthia M. *Anticipating Surprises: Analysis for Strategic Warning*. Lanham, MD: University Press of America, 2004.

_____, and Jan Goldman. *Handbook of Warning Intelligence: Assessing the Threat to National Security*. Lanham, MD: Scarecrow Press, 2010.

Hackman, Richard J. *Collaborative Intelligence: Using Teams to Solve Hard Problems*. San Francisco: Berrett-Koehler, 2011.

Hawkins, Jeff. *On Intelligence*. New York: Times Books, 2004.

Lowenthal, Mark M., and Robert M. Clark. *The 5 Disciplines of Intelligence Collection*. Washington, DC: CQ Press/SAGE, 2015.

Merry, Sally Engle, Kevin E. Davis, and Benedict Kingsbury, eds. *The Quiet Power of Indicators: Measuring Governance, Corruption, and Rule of Law*. New York: Cambridge University Press, 2015.

Michalko, Michael. *Thinkertoys*, 2nd ed. Berkeley: Ten Speed Press, 2006.

Neuman, W. Lawrence. *Social Research Methods: Qualitative and Quantitative Approaches*, 8th ed. Upper Saddle River, NJ: Pearson Education, 2020. Kindle.

Root-Bernstein, Robert, and Michele Root-Bernstein. *Sparks of Genius: The 13 Thinking Tools of the World's Most Creative People*. Boston: Houghton Mifflin, 1999.

Schum, David A. *The Evidential Foundations of Probabilistic Reasoning*. Evanston, IL: Northwestern University Press, 2001.

Schwartz, Peter. *The Art of the Long View*. New York: Doubleday, 1996.

Singer, P. W., and Emerson T. Brooking. *LikeWar: The Weaponization of Social Media*. New York: Houghton Mifflin Harcourt, 2018.

Stengel, Richard. *Information Wars: How We Lost the Global Battle Against Disinformation and What We Can Do About It*. New York: Atlantic Monthly Press, 2019.

Stringer, Ernest T. *Action Research*, 4th ed. Thousand Oaks, CA: SAGE, 2014.

Surowiecki, James. *The Wisdom of Crowds: Why the Many Are Smarter Than the Few and How Collective Wisdom Shapes Business, Economies, Societies, and Nations*. New York: Random House, 2004.

Tetlock, Philip E. *Expert Political Judgment*. Princeton, NJ: Princeton University Press, 2005.

_____, and Dan Gardner. *Superforecasting: The Art and Science of Prediction*. New York: Broadway Books, 2015.

Weinberg, Gabriel, and Lauren McCann. *Super Thinking: The Big Book of Mental Models*. New York: Penguin, 2019.

PART III. WHAT IS MY ARGUMENT?

Cooper Ramo, Joshua. *The Age of the Unthinkable: Why the New World Disorder Constantly Surprises Us and What We Can Do About It*. New York: Little, Brown, 2009.

Fingar, Thomas. *Reducing Uncertainty: Intelligence Analysis and National Security*. Stanford, CA: Stanford University Press, 2011.

George, Roger Z., and James B. Bruce. *Analyzing Intelligence: Origins, Obstacles, and Innovations*, 2nd ed. Washington, DC: Georgetown University Press, 2014.

Govier, Trudy. *A Practical Study of Argument*, 7th ed. Boston: Wadsworth, 2014.

Jervis, Robert. *Why Intelligence Fails*. Ithaca, NY: Cornell University Press, 2010.

Mayberry, Katherine J. *Everyday Arguments: A Guide to Writing and Reading Effective Arguments*, 3rd ed. Boston: Houghton Mifflin, 2009.

Williams, Joseph M., and Gregory G. Colomb. *The Craft of Argument,* 3rd ed. New York: Pearson Longman, 2007.

PART IV. HOW DO I CONVEY MY MESSAGE EFFECTIVELY?

Berinato, Scott. *Good Charts: The HBR Guide to Making Smarter, More Persuasive Data Visualizations*. Boston: Harvard Business Review Press, 2016.

Campbell, Joseph. *The Hero With a Thousand Faces*, 3rd ed. Novato, CA: New World Library, 2008.

Cialdini, Robert B. *Influence: The Psychology of Persuasion*, rev. ed. New York: William Morrow, 1995.

Gallo, Carmine. *Five Stars: The Communication Secrets to Get From Good to Great*. New York: St. Martin's, 2018.

Heath, Chip, and Dan Heath. *Made to Stick: Why Some Ideas Survive and Others Die*. New York: Random House, 2007.

Knaflic, Cole Nussbaumer. *Storytelling With Data: A Data Visualization Guide for Business Professionals*. Hoboken, NJ: John Wiley, 2015.

Koegel, Timothy J. *The Exceptional Presenter: A Proven Formula to Open Up and Own the Room*, expanded ed. Austin, TX: Greenleaf Book Group, 2007.

Pinker, Steven. *The Sense of Style: The Thinking Person's Guide to Writing in the 21st Century*. New York: Penguin, 2014.

Roam, Dan. *The Back of the Napkin: Solving Problems and Selling Ideas With Pictures*. London: Penguin, 2009.

Strunk, William, Jr., and E. B. White. *The Elements of Style*, 50th anniversary ed. New York: Pearson Education, 2009.

Williams, Joseph M., and Joseph Bizup. *Style: Lessons in Clarity and Grace*, 12th ed. New York: Pearson, 2017.

Wong, Dona M. *The* Wall Street Journal *Guide to Information Graphics*. New York: W. W. Norton, 2010.

Yau, Nathan. *Data Points: Visualization That Means Something*. Indianapolis, IN: John Wiley, 2013.

Zinsser, William. *On Writing Well*, 30th anniversary ed. New York: HarperCollins, 2012.

CASE STUDIES

National Security

"The Best of 2019." *Foreign Affairs*, December 20, 2019.

Betts, Richard K. *Enemies of Intelligence: Knowledge and Power in American National Security.* New York: Columbia University Press, 2007.

Brugioni, Dino A. *Eyeball to Eyeball: The Inside Story of the Cuban Missile Crisis.* New York: Random House, 1990.

Janis, Irving L. *Victims of Groupthink: A Psychological Study of Foreign Policy Decisions and Fiascos.* New York: Houghton Mifflin, 1972.

Lowenthal, Mark M. *Intelligence: From Secrets to Policy*, 8th ed. Washington, DC: CQ Press, 2019.

Pillar, Paul. *Intelligence and U.S. Foreign Policy: Iraq, 9/11, and Misguided Reform.* New York: Columbia University Press, 2011.

Rose, Gideon, and Jonathan Tepperman, eds. *The Clash of Ideas: The Ideological Battles That Made the Modern World—and Will Shape the Future.* New York: Foreign Affairs, 2012.

Rovner, Joshua. *Fixing the Facts: National Security and the Politics of Intelligence.* Ithaca, NY: Cornell University Press, 2011.

Stober, Dan, and Ian Hoffman. *A Convenient Spy: Wen Ho Lee and the Politics of Nuclear Espionage.* New York: Simon & Schuster, 2001.

Walton, Timothy. *Challenges in Intelligence Analysis: Lessons From 1300 BCE to the Present.* New York: Cambridge University Press, 2010.

Public Safety

Karabell, Zachary. *The Leading Indicators: A Short History of the Numbers That Rule Our World.* New York: Simon & Schuster, 2014.

McDowell, Don. *Strategic Intelligence,* rev. ed. Lanham, MD: Scarecrow Press, 2009.

Moose, Charles A., and Charles Fleming. *Three Weeks in October: The Manhunt for the Serial Sniper.* New York: Penguin, 2003.

Morgenson, Gretchen, and Joshua Rosner. *Reckless Endangerment: How Outsized Ambition, Greed, and Corruption Led to Economic Armageddon.* New York: Times Books, 2011.

Osbourne, Deborah. *Out of Bounds: Innovation and Change in Law Enforcement Intelligence.* Washington, DC: Joint Military Intelligence College, 2006.

Ratcliffe, Jerry H. *Strategic Thinking in Criminal Intelligence*, 2nd ed. Annandale, New South Wales, AU: Federation Press, 2009.

Steiner, James E. *Homeland Security Intelligence.* Thousand Oaks, CA: CQ Press/SAGE, 2015.

US GOVERNMENT PUBLICATIONS

Commission on the Intelligence Capabilities of the United States Regarding Weapons of Mass Destruction. *Report to the President of the United States.* March 31, 2005. https://www.gpo.gov/fdsys/pkg/GPO-WMD/pdf/GPO-WMD.pdf.

Directorate of Intelligence. *Style Manual and Writers Guide for Intelligence Publications.* 8th ed. Washington DC: Central Intelligence Agency, 2011.

House of Commons, Digital, Culture, Media and Sport Committee. *Disinformation and "Fake News": Final Report.* Eighth Report of Session 2017–19, 2019. https://publications.parliament.uk/pa/cm201719/cmselect/cmcumeds/1791/1791.pdf.

Johnston, Rob. *Analytic Culture in the U.S. Intelligence Community.* Washington, DC: Center for the Study of Intelligence, Central Intelligence Agency, 2005. https://www.cia.gov/library/center-for-the-study-of-intelligence/csi-publications/books-and-monographs/sherman-kent-and-the-board-of-national-estimates-collected-essays/6words.html.

Kent, Sherman. "Words of Estimative Probability." *Studies in Intelligence.* Fall 1964. https://www.cia.gov/library/center-for-the-study-of-intelligence/csi-publications/books-and-monographs/sherman-kent-and-the-board-of-national-estimates-collected-essays/6words.html.

National Academies of Sciences, Engineering, and Medicine. *A Decadal Survey of the Social and Behavioral Sciences: A Research Agenda for Advancing Intelligence Analysis.* Washington, DC: National Academies Press, 2019. https://doi.org/10.17226/25335.

National Research Council. *Intelligence Analysis: Behavioral and Social Scientific Foundations.* Washington, DC: National Academies Press, 2011. https://doi.org/10.17226/13062.

9/11 Commission. *Final Report of the National Commission on Terrorist Attacks Upon the United States.* New York: W. W. Norton, 2005. govinfo.library.unt.edu/911/report/index.htm.

Office of the Director of National Intelligence (ODNI). "Intelligence Community Directive 203: Analytic Standards." January 2, 2015. https://www.dni.gov/files/documents/ICD/ICD%20203%20Analytic%20Standards.pdf.

———. "Intelligence Community Directive 206: Sourcing Requirements for Disseminated Analytic Products." January 22, 2015. https://www.dni.gov/files/documents/ICD/ICD%20206.pdf.

———. "Intelligence Community Directive 208: Writing for Maximum Utility." December 17, 2008. https://www.dni.gov/files/documents/ICD/icd_208.pdf.

Select Committee on Intelligence, United States Senate. *Report of the Select Committee on Intelligence, United States Senate, on Russian Active Measures, Campaigns and Interference in the 2016 US Election: Russian Efforts Against Election Infrastructure, With Additional Views.* October 9, 2019. https://www.intelligence.senate.gov/sites/dep;fault/files/documents/Report_Volume2.pdf.

US Department of Justice. *The Mueller Report: The Final Report of the Special Counsel Into Donald Trump, Russia, and Collusion.* April 18, 2019. https://www.justice.gov/storage/report.pdf.

INDEX

Note: Page references indicating figures are marked as (fig.).